OTTO

NOTORIOUS

History's Villains and Why They Matter

Hi Denise
Thank you

WELBECK

First published in 2025 by Headline Welbeck Non-Fiction
An imprint of Headline Publishing Group Limited

1

Cataloguing in Publication Data is available from the British Library

Hardback ISBN 978 1 0354 2031 5
Trade Paperback ISBN 978 1 0354 2032 2

Typeset in 12/16pt Sabon MT Pro by Six Red Marbles UK, Thetford, Norfolk

Printed and bound in Great Britain by Clays Ltd, Elcograf S.p.A.

MIX
Paper | Supporting responsible forestry
FSC® C104740

Headline's policy is to use papers that are natural, renewable and recyclable products and made from wood grown in well-managed forests and other controlled sources. The logging and manufacturing processes are expected to conform to the environmental regulations of the country of origin.

Headline Publishing Group Limited
An Hachette UK Company
Carmelite House
50 Victoria Embankment
London EC4Y 0DZ

The authorised representative in the EEA is Hachette Ireland, 8 Castlecourt Centre, Dublin 15, D15 XTP3, Ireland (email: info@hbgi.ie)

www.headline.co.uk
www.hachette.co.uk

For my sister, Pippa Fairbanks

CONTENTS

CHAPTER ONE

SCAPEGOATS

Hunting Witches

Mr Harrison was missing.

The 70-year-old steward, a well-respected man in the Gloucestershire town of Chipping Campden, had last been seen striding down Church Lane in the late afternoon, on his way to collect rents from local villages.

It was now nine o'clock, Thursday 16 August 1660. Dusk had fallen, darkness was encroaching and he had yet to return home.

William Harrison was very much a creature of habit and this was not his 'usual custom'. And so it was that Mrs Harrison sent their servant, John Perry, out into the night to look for his master – only for him to disappear as well.

* * *

The sun rose at 5 a.m. the following morning but already Edward Harrison, William's adult son, was marching purposefully towards the village of Charingworth.

On the outskirts of the small settlement, he came across the family servant John, who told him that he had got lost in dense fog during the night and had taken refuge – in a hedge. Perry had already visited Charingworth and learned from locals that Mr Harrison had been there the previous day, before heading on to nearby Ebrington. The two men set out together and met a man called Daniel who told them that he too had seen Mr Harrison but knew nothing more.

It was harvest time so most locals had been up since dawn working in the fields. With nobody else around, Edward and John decided to head back to town in the hope that William had returned ahead of them, but on the way they encountered a woman who told them that while leesing* in a nearby field she had found some items of clothing. They returned to the spot and retrieved a bloodied cravat, a hat which had been hacked with a knife and a battered comb†, all of which belonged to Mr Harrison.

Clearly something terrible had happened and as news of the unsettling discovery spread, the 'hue and cry'‡ was raised and the people of Chipping Campden abandoned the harvest and spread out across the countryside in search of a body.

As they went, Mrs Harrison started to eye the servant, John Perry, with growing suspicion and by the following morning, he was standing in the dock.

Perry's testimony – set out 16 years later in an account penned by a local nobleman and justice of the peace called Sir Thomas Overbury – went like this: Just after 9 p.m., while starting to look for Mr Harrison, John had met an associate, William Reed, who agreed to help him. The two men then set off towards Charingworth but John, who was afraid of the dark, soon lost his nerve and suggested that they return to the town and fetch a horse. Given the urgency of the task, this might sound a bit ridiculous, but in late seventeenth-century England, nyctophobia (fear of the night) was a very common affliction in the countryside. Belief in the 'Realm of Darkness' was real and people genuinely thought that witches, goblins, elves and fairies lived in the woods beyond their homes and came out at night. So, John Perry's concerns make perfect sense in the context of his time.

Fear can be contagious and that perhaps was why Reed then abandoned Perry at 'Mr Harrison's Court gate'. Having lost his wingman,

* Essentially harvesting for her family's own provision – an ancient custom reserved for the poorest in rural society.

† Probably a carved 'nit comb', a common item in Puritan England. In the age before mass production and plastics these were expensive items made from tortoiseshell or a single piece of carved bone.

‡ The ancient system of raising an alarm through shouts and clanging.

Perry loitered in the street until another man called Pearce came along and he was able to convince him to accompany him on his mission. The two walked 'one bow's shot'[1] into the fields behind the church before thinking better of it and returning to the gates of the big house once more. There they parted and Perry retired to the henroost where he bedded down, 'slept not' and only arose when the parish clock struck 12.

Once again this seems like a peculiar thing to do, but during the late seventeenth century many people indulged in 'biphasic sleep' which saw the night-time divided into two halves with a waking break in the middle – in which chores were done and sex was had. Perry's curious crepuscular routine bothered the magistrate far less than the fact that having woken up, Perry set off to look for his master again – without an apparent care in the world. For, as the justice of the peace pointed out, if he had been afraid of the dark at 9 p.m., then what had changed in the ensuing three hours? Perry explained that while it had indeed been pitch black at nine, the moon was shining brightly by midnight, so he felt safer about venturing forth.

Records for the phases of the moon on 16–17 August 1660 show that it was indeed at 85 per cent strength, so he was telling the truth.

As Perry retraced Mr Harrison's steps, a 'great mist arose' and, disorientated by it, he hid in a hedge and slept until dawn before going on to Charingworth where he enquired after Harrison at the house of Edward Plaisterer. Edward told him that he had paid William £23 (£3,805 in 2025 money) but that Harrison had not stayed to chat. From there Perry went to the home of William Curtis, who said Harrison had called and left empty-handed. And shortly after that he encountered William Harrison's son Edward on the road.

Curtis, Plaisterer, Pearce and Reed all confirmed Perry's account but the magistrate, who was clearly armed with an investigative mind worthy of that great fictional TV detective Lieutenant Columbo, had 'just one thing' bothering him. Twice that long night, John Perry had returned to the Banqueting House – and yet on neither occasion had he bothered to check whether William had come home. How did he know he wasn't there?

Perry explained that he had seen a light through Mr Harrison's window which 'never used to be there so late when he was at home' and this indicated that Harrison wasn't in.

Now it must be said that there is something a bit odd about Perry's account and all that dithering, napping and the walking around in circles has led many of those who have written about the 'Campden Wonder' to question his motives. The Victorian Scottish writer Andrew Lang[2] went as far as to suggest that it demonstrated that he was 'conspicuously crazy' and that his evidence sounded 'like a tale told by an idiot'. But that seems unfair. Given that his master had seemingly disappeared into thin air, in the notoriously dangerous back lanes of Gloucestershire and that the young man admitted he was afraid of the dark, none of Perry's behaviour seems that unreasonable.

The magistrate, however, was unimpressed and ordered he be held pending further enquiries. Perry was carted off to a cellar beneath a local inn and then transferred to the town lock-up. The building no longer exists, so we don't know if it was wooden or a purpose-built conical stone structure like others, still standing, locally – but without doubt it would have been windowless, cramped and dark. In 1660 a suspect could be held without charge for as long as was deemed necessary and when the door was slammed behind him, Perry would have had no idea when he would next see the light of day.

Which might explain what happened next.

Solitary confinement can have a significant detrimental impact on mental health. Recent studies in the US have found that prisoners held in solitary are six times more likely to commit suicide and often experience significant long-term mental health challenges as a result. These events were taking place in the latter half of the seventeenth century and as such there is no contemporary psychiatric report on the state of Perry's health – but human beings are human beings and given his subsequent behaviour it is not a stretch to suggest that this anxious young man might have had some sort of breakdown.

Unfortunately, when weighing the facts of this case we are obliged to rely on just one primary source. That account comes courtesy of local landowner and justice of the peace, Sir Thomas Overbury – who may (or may not) have been the presiding magistrate in the case. Overbury wrote his version in 1676, some 16 years after the events took place, and if he was the magistrate, for reasons we shall see, he may have had good reason to spin the facts.

All history is but a cold crime scene in which there are victims, suspects, clues, eyewitnesses and red herrings. As with any great 'whodunnit' there are motives to be found, alibis to be established and nobody present at the time of events should be above suspicion – or have their word entirely trusted. As we re-examine the details of this peculiar case and indeed all the other case files that follow in this book, we shall meet many more 'unreliable narrators', with skin in the game. We shall find too that some of history's most notorious figures have been stitched up and that sometimes the good guys are actually the baddies – while many a societally appointed historical villain is in fact the victim.

Our task is to sift the available evidence, to assess the innocence or otherwise of the accused and, like any great cop, to rely on experience and instinct too. And our journey starts with one of the most intriguing unsolved cases in English legal history, for the simple reason that it demonstrates all of the above.

Overbury called his version of events a 'True and Perfect Account', but all witness testimony is suspect and truth is always subjective. Indeed, the very title should probably ring alarm bells and lead us to ask what motive he had for writing something so definitively titled. That said, as our only witness on the ground, we are also obliged to rely on his testimony too – for the simple reason that there is no other – and reading between the lines, Overbury does hint at Perry's increasingly fragile state.

Having initially claimed that he did not know what had happened to Mr Harrison, after a few days in the lock-up, Perry radically altered his story. He now said, perhaps under duress, or maybe because he was starting to mentally deteriorate, that his master had been killed by a tinker, before changing his mind and saying that he had been murdered by persons unknown and thrown in the 'bean-rick'*.

* A storage barn for beans.

A search was made, but no body was found.

Ever wilder statements followed until Perry insisted that if he was released from the lock-up he'd tell all. On Friday 24 August, he once again stood in the dock. In his new version of events, he said that ever since he had started working for Mr Harrison, his older brother Richard, and widowed mother Joan, had pestered him as to ways in which they could rob his boss.

John testified that while out looking for his master on that fateful night, he had bumped into Richard, who had determined there and then to do the deed. Shortly thereafter having pointed them in the right direction, John then came across Richard and his mother, standing over the elderly man, who was shouting, 'Ah, rogues, will you kill me?'

Only for Richard to do just that.

The Perrys then dragged the body to the 'sink', a large pond nearby and threw Harrison's body in. Joan handed John the comb, hat and collar which he hacked with a knife and planted in a thick furze bush. The rest of his testimony matched the account he had already given and the magistrate immediately ordered that Joan and Richard Perry be arrested.

The pond and the fish pools were drained. The ruins of Campden House, burned down in the not-so-distant civil war, were searched too but no body was found, and meanwhile Joan and Richard Perry set about denying everything. Richard accepted that he had met his brother in the street on the evening of Harrison's disappearance but that was all and he called John a 'villain to accuse them wrongfully'.[3]

In a rural town like Chipping Campden, which then had a population of about 1,600 people, the suggestion that Harrison had been murdered by his servant's family caused a sensation and now all eyes followed the Perrys everywhere they went. As the family were marched from the magistrate back to the lock-up that Saturday afternoon, a ball of ribbon fell from Richard Perry's pocket and when it was recovered, John, who had been walking ahead, identified it as the murder weapon that had been used to strangle Mr Harrison.

The next day, having been marched to the church, in the hope perhaps that the local vicar Reverend Bartholomew would extract a confession from them, they passed Richard's family home. Seeing him outside, his two youngest children rushed to greet him and, in the hullabaloo, they suffered nosebleeds which were 'looked upon as ominous'[4] by those standing nearby. Children can get nosebleeds all the time of course, but in that profoundly superstitious century, even the most mundane things could become 'a sign' and this otherwise innocuous event soon became deeply problematic for the suspects, for the simple reason that local gossip had it that old Mrs Perry was a witch.

Though fear of witches was as old as the hills, in the seventeenth century, Britain was suffering a prolonged bout of hysteria about 'sorcerers' which stemmed back to the reign of King James VI of Scotland (later James I of England). Much of that derived from the character of the man himself and judging from his peculiar behaviour, many modern historians have concluded that the King was suffering from a complex, perhaps hereditary, mental health condition that had been exacerbated by the traumatic execution of his mother, Mary Queen of Scots, at Fotheringhay Castle in Northamptonshire in February 1587. Two years later, the King lost the other great love of his life when his favourite, Esme Stewart, the First Duke of Lennox, was sent into exile by Scottish nobles on account of rumours about the two men's relationship. The 23-year-old James was then betrothed to the 14-year-old Anne of Denmark – and the union was to have all sorts of fatal consequences, partly on account of the weather and partly due to the King's innate paranoia.

James's bride's first attempt to cross the North Sea to Scotland in the autumn of 1589 nearly ended in disaster when an enormous storm broke and her flotilla was obliged to take shelter in Norway. Hearing the news, James gallantly determined to go and fetch her himself, only to get caught in the same tempest and end up in the same Norwegian port and it was only in November of that year that the couple were finally united in Copenhagen. All through the winter, the storm raged on and it was not until the spring of 1590 that the couple managed to make safe passage back to Scotland.

This unusual weather event was a huge deal at the time and later inspired William Shakespeare to write both *The Tempest* and the opening scene of *Macbeth* – but its greater impact came on the psychosis of the King. For as James and Anne made their peripatetic way home, he came to believe that all their trials and tribulations at sea had been caused . . . by witches. James VI was not alone in this. Back in Copenhagen, the authorities had already arrested a woman called Ane Koldings and under torture had extracted a confession from her in which she had claimed full responsibility for the bad weather. In July 1590 she was burned alive at the stake alongside 12 other women accomplices and soon after that, James became convinced that there was in fact a Europe-wide pandemic of witchcraft and that the problem was particularly acute in Scotland.

In the ensuing hysteria, 70 women were rounded up in North Berwick and Edinburgh and promptly executed and soon a campaign of mass, unhinged, state-sanctioned killing was under way. Over the ensuing century, an estimated 2,500 (mostly) women were arrested and executed on trumped-up charges of sorcery in Scotland alone. Considering the country then had a population of less than a million, this was a staggering figure and all of it was given the royal seal of approval – by the paranoid king. King James came to regard himself as the leading expert on the subject and in 1597 published a book, *Daemonologie*, which in a series of dialogues set out how best to deal with witches. Following the death of his first cousin once removed, childless Elizabeth I, in 1603, James VI of Scotland became James I of England too and soon his book was rocketing up the seventeenth-century equivalent of the Amazon chart south of the border.

The witch-hunts continued into the reign of Charles I who became king in 1625.

The seventeenth century was a time of deep political and religious turmoil in Britain and as bad events spawned even greater hell, witches made for perfect scapegoats. All of the troubles of the world, whether they be storms in the North Sea, crop failures, wars or disappearing stewards could not be explained rationally – but they could be put down to their sorcery. And the mass hysteria only got worse as some very wicked people indeed started to portray themselves as the heroes of the hour.

Matthew Hopkins, who from 1644 styled himself the Witchfinder General and who flogged his book *The Discovery of Witches* on the back of his depraved activities, was one such villain. Aged 24, Hopkins claimed to have overheard two women discussing an encounter with Satan in Manningtree in Essex and henceforth he and his accomplice, John Stearne, began terrorising the women of East Anglia. Their terrible modus operandi went like this: having decided that someone was a witch, the men would kidnap her, strip her naked and torture her until she confessed all.

The term 'Witchfinder General' was Hopkins' own invention and he was operating without any actual legitimacy, but his influence was such that few dared to question him. Those who did only risked invoking his ire and in his book, Hopkins addressed the subject of his 'expertise' directly:

Query 3: From Whence proceeded his skill? Was it from his profound learning or from much reading of learned authors concerning that subject?

Answer: From Neither of both, but from experience which though it be meanly esteemed of, yet the surest safest way to judge by.

Or in other words, Mr Hopkins was – like so many modern trolls – a graduate of 'the university of life'.

Hopkins' depraved career ended with his death on 12 August 1647, when he was aged just 27. But across its course he had executed 19 women, murdered at least four more and carried out acts of sexual violence against scores of others under the guise of 'investigation'.

Though the most infamous witch-hunter of the era, Hopkins activities too were in fact but the tip of the iceberg. During the seventeenth century, at least 500 innocent people were executed in England alone on charges of sorcery, with 85 per cent of them women. Village healers and midwives were a particular prey. Widows, eccentrics, and those with physical disabilities or mental health conditions were prime targets too. Neighbours or family members who fell out would often accuse each other of being witches and if a crime was committed and no other suspect could be found, it was usually the local 'hag' who got the blame.

The last three people executed for witchcraft in England were hanged in Devon in July 1682, but north of the border the terror lasted another 40 years. The final victim, Janet Horne, who was executed in Dornoch, Scotland in 1722, was probably suffering from dementia. Janet's daughter had been born with undeveloped feet and locals whispered that at night she turned her daughter into a pony and rode her about in the hills. Mother and daughter were put on trial – and found guilty. The daughter managed to escape but her bewildered old mother was tarred and feathered and paraded through the streets in a barrel. Having warmed her hands at the pyre that had been built for her, the local people pushed her into the flames.

In this frenzied climate of superstition, mere 'signs' and unexplained events were enough to condemn you – and that undoubtedly was why the people of Chipping Campden came to believe that old Joan Perry was a witch and that she was responsible for Mr Harrison's disappearance.

Confirmation bias then took hold as the townsfolk began making 'sense' out of all manner of incidents that had involved the Perry family during the previous months, and soon all manner of stories were tumbling forth. A year before his disappearance, William Harrison and family had been at a 'lecture' one market day, when someone had broken a window at the Banqueting Hall and made off with 'seven score pounds' (£23,219 in 2025). John Perry now revealed that his brother was the thief and that he had buried the money in his garden, promising to divide it among the family. Once again, a search was ordered and once again nothing was found.

Another even more bizarre event which had occurred just a few short months before Mr Harrison's disappearance was also now recalled. On the Eve of May Day, just four days before the Restoration of Charles II, the almshouses beside St James's had rung to the screams of a man. As locals gathered to see what was going on, John Perry appeared clutching a pitchfork and claimed that he had fought off two men, dressed in white, who were armed with swords. Now the servant changed his story and said that this was all a ruse to create an alibi for the subsequent robbing of Mr Harrison. Which didn't actually make any sense as he had earlier claimed that the attack on Harrison had been spontaneous – but nobody seemed to notice.

In September 1660 the Assizes (court sessions) were held in Gloucester and in the absence of a body* the judge, Sir Christopher Turnor, refused to try the Perrys for the murder of Mr Harrison in 1660. Instead, they were charged with the burglary at the Banqueting House in 1659 and, likely acting on advice, the family pleaded guilty.

On the face of it this was a smart move because under the terms of the Act of Indemnity and Oblivion, passed the previous month, anyone who had committed a crime during the period of Cromwell's Protectorate was given an automatic pardon. However, by admitting guilt on the one charge, it was now assumed that they had committed the murder too. Trapped in a nightmarish catch-22, the family were ordered to be held in Gloucester Castle, until such time as Harrison reappeared or his body was found.

Imprisoned in the Norman fortress, John's mental health appears to have deteriorated even further and he began insisting that his mother and brother were trying to poison him, which was why he 'durst neither eat nor drink with them'. Nowadays we know that an irrational fear of being poisoned is a classic symptom of schizophrenia with paranoia, but in 1660 – when neither term existed – nobody knew that and some people at least may have believed him.

On 3 March 1661, the family landed in front of the Assizes once more. This time all three pleaded not guilty, but up before judge Sir Robert Hyde, a cousin of the Chancellor of the Exchequer, their fate was sealed. Hyde, 65, had risen suddenly and belatedly to the top of the legal system – for no other reason than that he hadn't done much under Cromwell – and was thus deemed to be loyal to the Crown.

As pompous as he was incompetent, Hyde was completely out of his depth in the case and as one former Lord High Chancellor of Great Britain, Frederic Maugham, put it in 1958, he 'was not worthy of the position'

* Habeas corpus – aka 'show us the body' – was enshrined in Magna Carta (article 39) in 1215. However, it was not until 1679 – some 19 years after these events – that a parliamentary act properly set out the law.

entrusted to him. Late to influence, Hyde blundered forward and having ignored the absence of a body and John's temporary insanity plea he took the word of local gossip instead. In 1661, hearsay was still admissible as evidence in English murder trials and juries were allowed to return verdicts based on 'private knowledge'.[5] That meant they could be influenced by rumours of witchcraft and when the guilty verdict was passed, Hyde sentenced the entire family to death.

Some days later, the mother and her two sons were marched to a spot called 'No Man's Land', just outside Chipping Campden. On a triangular patch of land at Fish Hill, which is nowadays a designated picnic area, the authorities set about the dreadful task of execution. Joan was hanged first – in the hope that the spell she had cast on her sons might be broken with her death – but as the old widow swung, no miracle was forthcoming. Richard was next, pleading with his brother to tell the truth and protesting his innocence to his final breath.

John came last and as he stood at the scaffold he made one final, cryptic statement. Insisting he 'knew nothing of his master's death, nor what (had) become of him,' he suggested that those present 'might hereafter possibly hear'.[6]

Moments later, he was swinging from a rope.

Richard and Joan were buried beneath the gallows while John was 'hung in chains' – left to rot on public display, as carrion birds pecked his flesh to the bones.

And as if all that was not gruesome enough, one final macabre twist was to follow.

Sir Anthony à Wood, a dedicated collector of contemporary miscellany, who purchased a copy of Overbury's *The Campden Wonder* in the 1670s, wrote a tantalising footnote at the end of his pamphlet which takes up events. According to Wood, three days after the execution, a mysterious 'gentlewoman pretending to understand witches' rode up to the scaffold and ordered that Joan's grave be dug up. At the time it was thought that a dead witch's corpse held healing powers and the horsewoman probably wanted access to the body to that end. But when the earth was drawn back, her steed took fright and reared up, smashing the rider's head against the iron casing containing John's body – before throwing her lifeless body into the grave.

You'll be unsurprised to learn that henceforth, local people preferred to steer clear of Fish Hill. Some believe that the area is haunted and one local historian, Jill Wilson, claims to have been 'reliably informed that even today no one is prepared to take a tractor there to plough after dark'.[7]

But back in that spring of 1661, with the Perrys now gone, the townsfolk must have felt immense relief. After all, the wicked witch and her murderous accomplices had been dispatched. Order had been restored, justice delivered and the respectable merchants of Chipping Campden could now go about their business, while the little children slept soundly in their beds.

And that feeling no doubt persisted – right up to the moment, about 18 months later – when Mr Harrison walked back into town.

* * *

Chipping Campden today looks much as it did in 1660. This is the picture-perfect rural England that you see on old biscuit tins and 'good old days' social media posts, and though the narrow, golden limestone streets of the town may be dotted with fancy coffee shops and SUVs, you could be forgiven for thinking that you had walked into the pastel illustrations of a 1950s Ladybird book.

The row of almshouses, the church of St James's and even the gates to the ruins of the great house remain largely as they were in the seventeenth century, and you can glimpse the old Banqueting House, which now belongs to the Landmark Trust, from the graveyard behind the church. The track William Harrison set out on that August day some 360 years ago is now the B4035.

And if you prompt and nudge, then the local people are still happy to talk about the mysterious events that took place here in 1660.

The volunteers in the historical society, housed in the Old Police Station, have their various fascinating insights and theories; so too does the helpful guy in the bookshop and after a few pints in the Eight Bells you can barely move for people willing to hold forth on the subject of the so-called Campden Wonder. Some believe the story as told by Thomas Overbury, others blame or half-blame the Perrys still and almost everyone continues to speculate about what really happened to Mr Harrison during his prolonged absence from the town.

Given this ongoing contemporary fascination, one can only imagine what the seventeenth-century Campdenians made of it all. For starters, Harrison's immediate return must have caused seismic cognitive dissonance, as those involved in the trial and execution of the Perrys struggled to make sense of it all. Anthony à Wood's addendum to the Overbury pamphlet claims that when the news reached the self-regarding judge, Sir Robert Hyde, he took extreme exception to the messenger:

'For bringing him false news and commanded the jailer commit him to prison.'

Questions aplenty must have been asked or whispered behind the old steward's back and perhaps at the bidding of Thomas Overbury, Mr Harrison wrote his own extraordinary account of his disappearance – which went like this:

That evening of 16 August 1660, having collected the £23 from Edward Plaisterer, William was making his way home when, at the narrow furze break by Ebrington (where his clothes were later found) he met a horseman forcing his way through the gap. Fearing he would be knocked over, William bumped the animal on its nose with his walking stick, only for the whole encounter to descend into a seventeenth-century furze break* incident. For, taking exception to the attack on his horse, the rider struck the old man with a rapier and as he did, two other men appeared out of nowhere and joined in the attack. One of them passed a sword through William's thigh and the three men then handcuffed him, threw a cloak over him, lifted him on to the back of a horse and galloped off into the night.

Quite what they wanted with a septuagenarian steward was unclear, but having sped across the country with their prisoner clinging on for

* Road rage.

dear life, they bedded him down in an isolated house, where 'a little girl' fed him broth and brandy. By mid-afternoon on the Sunday, having stuffed William's pockets with money, for reasons which, once again, are a little bit opaque, the motley group arrived in Deal in Kent. Why they had carried their wounded prisoner 198 miles to the South East of England instead of taking him to the port of Bristol, which is just 60 miles away, is not explained.

In Deal, instead of stealing the £23 (£3,805) or taking back the money which they had put in his pockets, they sold William to a man called 'Wrenshaw' for £7 (£1,158). Harrison was then put on board a ship which sailed towards the Atlantic. But after six weeks at sea the captain came and told him, 'And the rest who were in the same condition' (for yes, there were others) that they were under attack by three 'Turkish ships' brimming with pirates. Rather nobly, given that they had all been kidnapped and were about to be sold on in America, William and his fellow prisoners offered to 'fight in defence of the ship', but the unscrupulous Captain Wrenshaw cut a deal with the Turks and Harrison and the others were handed over. Some weeks later, their galley arrived at port in the Western Mediterranean and the Englishmen were marched two days to a prison. There, a group of 'officers' started enquiring after their CVs. One prisoner said he was a surgeon, another a weaver and William claimed skill in 'physic'.[8]

Harrison now became the 'property' of an 87-year-old Turkish physician, who lived near Smyrna (Izmir) on the western coast of modern-day Turkey.

Smyrna was a thriving commercial hub, attracting merchants from all over the world and since 1592 had been a base for the British-backed Levant Company – which, like its better-known equivalent in South Asia, 'The East India Company', was establishing itself as a commercial force in the Ottoman Empire. Harrison makes no mention of any of the above in his account, nor does he do much to describe his surroundings, but he does sketch a thin portrait of his 'owner'. The old anonymous physician claimed that he had once been to the British Isles and added, somewhat incongruously, that he'd visited the small market town of

'Crowland, in Lincolnshire, which he preferred before all other places in England'.[9]

By Harrison's account, the two men struck up an uneasy bromance and the older man even gifted William a silver bowl from which he derived a nickname for his servant: 'Boll'. It wasn't all days of wine and roses, however, and on one occasion, after Harrison had been out collecting 'cotton wool', the master became angry and drew a small dagger, only for William to cry out to Jesus – whose divine intervention stayed the older man's hand.

Quite why Christ had waited so long and not intervened when William was attacked with a sword, or kidnapped, or carried across England, or captured by pirates or sold into slavery is not expanded upon.

After a year, the old physician told 'Boll' he was dying and advised him to make a run for it. The master died a few days later and William fled to a nearby port where he met two Prussian sailors, on a ship bound for Lisbon, who stowed him away in exchange for the silver bowl. When they arrived in Portugal, he hung about the docks until he met a man from 'Wisbech in Lincolnshire' (which is in fact in Cambridgeshire) who, feeling sorry for him, procured his passage back to Dover. From there he went to London and having been 'furnished with necessaries', by parties unknown, made his way to Chipping Campden.

This version of events, published alongside Thomas Overbury's account in 1676, was probably written contemporaneously to events and was likely some sort of witness statement. Certainly, the story quickly became well known and, in that summer of 1662, the tale of the Campden Wonder went viral in Restoration England. Broadside ballads and pamphlets, the TikTok and Twitter/X of the day, delivered a highly emboldened version of events and two extant examples, both in Sir Anthony à Wood's collection, were rediscovered on the shelves of the Bodleian Library in Oxford in 1945.

The ballad was penned within weeks of Harrison's return and has a foreword which seeks to make sense of it all within the context of witchcraft. While accepting that the steward is still alive, Joan and her sons still get the blame for his disappearance:

It appears the Widow Perry was a witch, and after her sons had robbed him, and cast him into a Stone Pit, she by her witchcraft, conveyed him upon a rock in the sea near Turkey, where he remained four days and nights, till a Turkish Ship coming by took him and sold him into Turkey, where he remained for a season.[10]

The second publication, dated 1662, and published by Charles Tyus at the 'three Bibles on London Bridge' also turns the tale into an anti-witchcraft religious tirade. Once again 'Widow Perry' gets censured, for it was she who 'by her wicked conjuration' managed to transport Mr Harrison, Star Trek-like, to Turkey 'where he remained the space of four days bare headed, his hat being left near Campden'.

Both texts make a big deal out of how Mr Harrison's 'love and pity' for young John Perry was rewarded with betrayal and the pamphlet trots out Exodus 22 verse 18 which instructs that *'thou shalt not suffer a witch to live'*. That line, courtesy of the King James Bible (1611), was the go-to justification for the persecution of 'witches' at the time, despite it being a probable mistranslation.*

The Campden Wonder went on to become one of England's most celebrated 'Unsolved Mysteries' and for the next 300 years, many an academic, historian and author set out to solve the riddle. In 1959, the Oxford historian and academic Sir George Clark helpfully compiled the best known of them into a slim tome entitled *The Campden Wonder* and here's a flavour of what lies inside.

Writing in 1860, a lawyer called John Paget (1860) blamed John Perry's deteriorating mental health for events, suggesting that he was suffering from a 'remarkable form of mental disease which induces the sufferer to charge himself and others with imaginary crimes'. Paget hardly bothered with the disappearance of Harrison and instead concentrated on why Perry had given a false confession. The Scottish historian Andrew Lang, who found a copy of Overbury's account and

* The Hebrew word in Exodus is *mekhashepha* which translates as 'mystic mutterings' or 'herb-cutters'; its deliberate misinterpretation was later used as proof that God had given the green light to kill women.

published his own hot take on events in 1904, took a slightly different angle and suggested that 'the Perrys were probably not of the best repute' and many of the other writers, journalists and lawyers who follow in the pages of Clark's collection make much the same assumptions.

All of these writers were not only men, but came from a certain social class, and while they tend towards broad sympathy for the Perrys, inevitably class and intellectual prejudice invariably come into play. Some take a legal angle, others pore over tiny details in the Overbury account but few really consider either why the Perrys were scapegoated in the first place or why William Harrison was believed at the time. If he was.

Prior to disappearing from Chipping Campden, William had been local landowner Lady Juliana Noel's man on the ground and some texts in Clark's compilation suggest he was reinstated as steward, a post which in the interim had been managed by his 'unpopular' son Edward. In fact, there is no evidence that Edward ran the estate in his father's absence and while William may have briefly taken up the reins, by 1665 a man called John Goodwin was receiving rents on behalf of the Noel family and he was out of the job.

By then William would have been in his early seventies and could theoretically have been retired. But this is at odds with the surviving records and he seems, for example, to have remained, like Sir Thomas Overbury, a governor of the local grammar school; so it's equally possible that he may have lost the trust of his employer and been let go.

If Lady Noel had read Harrison's account, she would have had every reason to question his credibility. For while it is peppered with incidental details – like the small girl who brings him brandy and broth or the silver bowl or the people he keeps encountering who mention random towns in England – it is singularly lacking in more substantive ingredients and most of all, a little thing called 'the ring of truth'. Apart from the ship's captain – Wrenshaw – nobody is named. If William really had been on a slave ship for over a month, alongside a surgeon and a bread-cloth weaver, you might have thought for example that he would have learned their identities too. There is no description of the Turkish climate or the exotic places he visited, nor does he name the two ships that brought him home or the identities of their captains.

So why did anyone buy it? Well, to understand that we must explore the other great paranoia that plagued England at the time – the fear of being kidnapped by Barbary pirates – and in 1660 that terror was every bit as real as that of witches. Although, unlike the prevailing wiccaphobia it was at least rooted in some reason.

For across the region, from the late sixteenth century onwards, thousands of people had been captured by Barbary (from Berber) Corsairs and sold into slavery. While the Corsairs operated out of makeshift ports and city states along the Maghreb (modern-day Morocco, Algeria, Tunisia and Libya), elaborate stories about their crimes meant that they were feared far beyond the region.

As far back as Crusader times, 400 years earlier, the perceived 'Muslim hordes' had been seen as barbarians at the gates of Europe. Plays, including William Shakespeare's *Othello* (1604) and the anonymously written *Lust's Dominion* (1600) portrayed Moorish men as predatory, lascivious, wicked, violent killers. Despite England doing trade with the Ottoman Empire throughout the seventeenth century, even respectable traders were circumspect. The parish records for Chipping Campden show that in the 1620s, when Harrison was still a young man, two 'Turks', most probably cloth merchants, briefly visited the town and were swiftly given 4d (about £4 in 2025 money) to move on.

But come the 1660s the generalised terror of all things 'Turkish' felt more real than ever because it genuinely seemed as if that the threat was at the doorstep.

One of the earliest Corsairs was Aruj Barbarossa (in Turkish: Oruç Reis), who in the late fifteenth century, alongside his three brothers, attacked Christian ships and looted the Spanish coastline. Barbarossa's nickname might have derived from the Italian words for 'Red Beard' or perhaps from his Barbary (aka 'barbarian') associations. Either way, he achieved wealth and fame and again, like the contemporary English pirate Sir Francis Drake, garnered renown and glory among his followers for fighting off the encroaching Spanish Empire – while imbuing fear and loathing in everyone else. By 1516, his power was such that he and his brothers had established their own Sultanate and Oruç Reis became the ruler of Algiers.

In the following century, like their Christian counterparts, these Muslim privateers diversified into slavery. In 2004, Robert Davis, of the University of Ohio, caused a stir when his book *Christian Slaves, Muslim Masters: White Slavery in the Mediterranean, the Barbary Coast and Italy 1500–1800* claimed that between 1 million and 1.25 million people had ended up in bondage as a result. Davis's figures are highly controversial and based on estimates extrapolated from scant available data. Either way and despite even his highest estimates being way below the numbers traded by white Europeans, the miserable Barbary slave trade was real and as much a fact as the transatlantic one. So – much like modern terrorism – while the fear factor in England was exaggerated well beyond the bounds of the actual risk involved, it nevertheless felt real and many English men and women would lie in bed at night fearing that they would be a victim of an atrocity.

While the Corsairs originally focused largely on the Mediterranean, their raiding parties eventually carried off prisoners from as far away as Iceland. Most male captives were set to work doing hard labour but, and just as described by Harrison, the more educated among them became 'servants' in rich people's homes.

The British Isles and Ireland at first went relatively unscathed, but by the early seventeenth century that had changed. In 1625, Mount's Bay in Cornwall was raided and 60 men, women and children were kidnapped and sold into slavery. Over the next two decades the attacks became ever more audacious. In 1627, the island of Lundy in the Bristol Channel was occupied by the Salé Rovers, a group of pirates from the 'Republic of Salé', a Barbary enclave in modern-day Morocco. Led by a former Dutch sea captain, Jan Janszoon, who had converted to Islam after being captured by Corsairs, the Rovers raised a green Moorish ensign over the island and for the next five years, picturesque Lundy – now owned by the National Trust – became an Islamic State.

It was from that base, in 1631, that Corsairs attacked the village of Baltimore, a Protestant enclave in Catholic Ireland, before carting off 108 English settlers. This attack was organised with help from one of

Janszoon's prisoners, a fisherman from Dungarvan called John Hackett who had directed the pirates to Baltimore as revenge against the English colonisation of Ireland. He was later captured and tried at the Assizes in Cork before being executed. The Salé Rovers on Lundy were routed in the 1630s but they simply set up shop elsewhere and the attacks continued. In 1645, even as the English Civil War was raging inland, a raid on Penzance in Cornwall saw 240 people captured and by the 1650s many fishermen feared putting out to sea.

Those who escaped came home with astonishing stories.

Writing in his diary on 8 February 1660, just a few months before Harrison disappeared, Samuel Pepys recounted meeting a sea captain called Mootham and his friend, Mr Dawes, who regaled him with tales of their captivity in Algiers:

'I went to the Fleece Tavern to drink; and there we spent till four o'clock, telling stories of Algiers, and the manner of the life of slaves there! And truly Captn. Mootham and Mr. Dawes (who have been both slaves there) did make me fully acquainted with their condition there: as, how they eat nothing but bread and water.'

Such prisoners commanded high sums and the 'redemption business' in which intermediaries would negotiate the release of hostages from the Barbary pirates was itself a thriving industry, much as it is today in places like Colombia, Afghanistan and Haiti.

Seeking to upend the business model, in 1655 the Lord Protector Oliver Cromwell sent Admiral Robert Blake with a fleet of 15 ships, on a mission to the Mediterranean to extract compensation from the Christian 'Knights of Malta' who were also engaged in the practice and to teach everyone in the region a valuable lesson. Faced with this fleet of modern warships, most of the Corsairs and Knights quickly capitulated and only the Dey of Tunis refused to cough up. The ensuing sea battle ended in a decisive victory for Cromwell's men and put an end to the threat in the short term, while establishing the English Navy as a regional power. But the piracy and kidnapping never completely went away and everyone in England in 1660 knew about Blake and the Barbary pirates.

Congregations across the country were weekly encouraged to donate money for the ransom and relief of English slaves and in that context, William Harrison's otherwise unlikely story may have seemed credible – at least to the credulous.

If Harrison did make the story up, he would have had plenty of sources to plagiarise.

Piracy was a common trope in literature at the time. In *Hamlet* (1601), the Danish Prince is bound for England when he is captured and ransomed. The Spanish writer Miguel de Cervantes, himself taken prisoner by Turkish pirates in 1580, used his experiences as source material for *Don Quixote*, written in 1605 and which was translated into English in 1612. The allegorical nature of Harrison's story also bears all the hallmarks of 'Young Beichan', one of the best-known ballads of the era which relates how the title character:

Sailed East, and he sailed West,
Until he came to famed Turkee,
Where he was taken and put in prison,
Till of his life he was wear-ee![11]

In the story, a young maiden brings him food and drink and having been sold into slavery, he ends up with a master whose hand is stayed by divine intervention when he attacks the hero. The ballad was popular in the eighteenth and nineteenth century but the source material is far older, so while William Harrison's account is not entirely unbelievable it should perhaps be afforded roughly the same credibility as those who plagiarise stories about being abducted by UFOs.

While we may never know what really happened to William Harrison, we can speculate as to his motive for disappearing in the first place and as in any cold case, the time of the 'crime' is key.

When William Harrison vanished that August in 1660, England was experiencing a period of unparalleled social upheaval. Three months earlier, on 25 May, King Charles II had returned from exile in the Netherlands and was restored to the throne four days later, on his thirtieth birthday. The decade of Republicanism, known somewhat euphemistically in

England as the Interregnum,* which had been preceded by another decade of civil wars, may technically have ended – but the terrible wounds of it all still festered.

Immediate post-Restoration England was an unsettled place to say the least and many were waiting to see what would happen next. For those who had in turns fought for and then served the Protectorate, it was a time of considerable uncertainty.

Chipping Campden, positioned on a junction between the roads that linked the Royalist cities of Oxford and Worcester and the Roundhead bases at Warwick and Coventry, had seen it all. During the civil wars, marauding soldiers, from both sides, had regularly plundered anything that was not bolted down. And despite, ostensibly, being a Cavalier (Royalist) stronghold, the town had actually suffered most during the five months in the winter and spring of 1645 when the notorious Royalist commander, Colonel Henry Bard, had garrisoned his men in the great manor house. The Jacobean building, completed by Lady Juliana's father, the wealthy silk mercer Sir Baptist Hicks just 30 years earlier, at a cost of £29,000, was an architectural wonder, but having 'committed many outrages to the inhabitants', Bard burned the main house to the ground before laying waste to the crops in the surrounding countryside to stop them falling into Cromwell's hands. Despite their supposed loyalty to the Royalist cause, this would have enraged locals, not least the steward, William Harrison, who would have been obliged to stand by and watch as the grand building that was in his care descended into a pile of ashes.

The 11 years of Puritan rule that followed the death of Charles I on 30 January 1649 may have brought further deprivations, but at least some degree of stability had returned. Life for most people largely went on as it had before, and with peace restored it was in many ways better than the decades that had led up to it.

History – as the hoary cliché goes – is written by the winners and so we have tended to see the English Puritans as joyless Christmas-cancelling, theatre-closing miseries. The liquidation of Charles I's assets which saw

* When 'normal' government is suspended between the reigns of monarchs.

his art collection sold off and the perceived assault on church shrines has not helped the cause of Puritan PR, and many among us continue to view the Interregnum as a time of iconoclasm and gloom. But the truth is a little more nuanced. While Christmas, and indeed all festivals, were technically banned, for example, the law had in fact been passed under the reign of Charles I, and in an age before policemen, proved almost impossible to enforce. Likewise, while theatres were also closed, the Republic in fact witnessed a flowering of early English opera and secular art and Oliver Cromwell was most certainly not the philistine that Stuart (and later royal) propagandists would have us believe. Indeed, he is even thought to have appeared in a cameo as the Roman God 'Jove' in a pastoral entertainment staged in 1657, written by the poet Andrew Marvell.

It's also worth noting that much of the whitewashing and iconoclasm that we blame on the Interregnum was actually done much earlier in the sixteenth and fifteenth centuries and in some cases by eighteenth-century Protestant and Methodist enthusiasts. We blame it all on Cromwell and the Puritans because the Victorians did and because it is one of those satisfying neat 'good stories' that nations like to tell themselves.

That is not to say that the Lord Protector was not guilty of other crimes of course. Cromwell was the perpetrator of many egregious acts and committed mass slaughter following the invasion of Ireland between 1649 and 1653 for which he is still, rightly, abhorred. That conquest bore witness to a series of war crimes, including the massacre of soldiers – and hundreds of civilians – at Drogheda and Wexford in 1649. The forging of a Protestant English-led reign of prolonged tyranny on the island would see an estimated one fifth of the population die as a result of violence, famine and disease, shaping and colouring Irish history across the next 400 years.

As such, Cromwell is rightly seen as one of England's most infamous tyrants in the country. But the same was not the case back across the Irish Sea where some sections of society positively flourished under the Protectorate. For those 'onside' with the project and who wanted to build a New Jerusalem and a more egalitarian society, this was in fact a golden age. There was, for example, a high degree of religious freedom for anyone who was not a Catholic, and nonconformist sects and certain minorities thrived. From 1656, albeit in an informal agreement, Jews who had ostensibly been expelled from England in the thirteenth century were allowed to practise their faith once more. And for Presbyterians, Baptists and Quakers, the Protectorate provided a period of welcome tolerance that saw their movements prosper.

That all ended abruptly with the Restoration and many people who had backed the Cromwells were now up to their necks in trouble.

On paper, the Indemnity and Oblivion Act, passed on 25 August 1660, gave amnesty to all those who had been part of the Protectorate but that excluded the 104 individuals deemed guilty of the 'regicide' of Charles I. The treatment of these renegades was unforgiving to say the least and even those who had already died did not escape punishment. Oliver Cromwell and 23 other deceased accomplices were dug up and then 'executed' before having their heads cut off and placed on spikes on public display.

In that summer and autumn of 1660, London bore witness to scenes of abject horror as once respected men were publicly hanged, drawn and quartered (of which more later).

The blind poet John Milton, who in 1667 would write his Restoration era masterpiece *Paradise Lost*, was nearly one of the victims. From before Charles I's execution in 1549, Milton had written extensively in support of the regicide and in favour of the republic. He was even appointed Secretary for Foreign Tongues under Cromwell's administration, making him responsible for the dissemination of the nation's correspondence in Latin overseas. And even as the Protectorate crumbled in the wake of Cromwell's death, he wrote in support of it. The Restoration spelled disaster for him both financially, as he had invested his savings in now worthless government bonds, and personally, since his life was now in danger. So, following Charles II's coronation, he very sensibly went into hiding.

An arrest warrant was issued on 16 June 1660, and he only re-emerged once the Indemnity and Oblivion Act was passed on 25 August, but even that didn't save him and he was immediately imprisoned in the Tower of London. That autumn his books and letters were publicly burned, and this once venerated figure was only saved from execution through the intervention of the poet, Andrew Marvell, who was now a Member of Parliament.

As happens after any counter-revolution or time of political change, a lot of far less principled weathervaners* had noted in prevailing winds and swapped sides. Samuel Pepys who, as a 15-year-old St Paul's scholar had played truant to witness the beheading of Charles I and who had henceforth been an avid republican, was one of many who switched. On the death of Cromwell in 1658, Pepys suddenly became a staunch monarchist, and both accompanied the new king on his return from exile and ended up being invited to Charles II's coronation.

In short, while the new regime came preaching reconciliation, not everyone was convinced and this is one compelling reason as to why William Harrison may have fled.

One reason may have been that Harrison and his family had Presbyterian tendencies. When the Banqueting House was robbed that summer afternoon in 1659, they were, according to Sir Thomas Overbury, at 'a lecture', essentially a Baptist service, and there are other subtle clues in the story too. 'Smyrna', the city to which Harrison claimed to have been taken after his 'kidnapping', was famous for its textile industry, and given that Chipping Campden was also a centre of the wool industry in the seventeenth century it might have influenced his choice of destination. But Smyrna was also home to one of the 'original seven churches', central to St John's Book of Revelation in the New Testament, which, in turn, was itself critical to the Baptist outlook on the world.

Smyrna in the 1660s was a hotbed of radical millenarist† thinking and home to the Rabbi and False Messiah, Sabbatai Zevi, who exerted a huge influence on Baptists who believed that the social and political upheaval of the time heralded the coming Apocalypse. People establishing an alibi don't just pluck random places out of thin air.

The return of the Stuart dynasty was bad news for Baptists – who now had to go back undercover. The good guys were now the bad guys,

* A weathervaner is a commentator or influencer who bends with the times.

† Millenarianism: belief in a future millennium following the Second Coming of Christ.

at least in the eyes of the state, and William was firmly on the wrong side of history. But he may have been on the wrong side of the law too. Prior to the destruction of the Manor House by Royalist forces, Harrison is thought to have carried off some of its more valuable belongings and stashed them away. There is nothing to suggest that they were returned to Lady Juliana Noel subsequently and it is possible that the supposedly loyal retainer feared that any audit might expose his deed.

William – like many people who follow in this book – was not only a victim but a perpetrator too. And his return might well have led to a further tragedy.

A scribbled note at the bottom of the Oxford antiquary Anthony à Wood's copy of Overbury's text reads:

'After Harrison's return John was taken down and buried and Harrison's wife (being a snotty and covetous presbyterian) hung herself in her own house – why the reader is to judge.'

So, judge we must.

Did Harrison, like Milton, think that it might be a good idea to disappear? Did he perhaps stage that robbery on the Banqueting House which saw £140 taken and then use it along with the £7 in stolen rent to hide away until the aftermath of the Restoration had passed?

Did he go to Crowland or Wisbech – those places he so randomly mentioned in his credibility-defying alibi? Two towns, just 18 miles apart, and both less than a day's walk east of the Rutland estates of Lady Juliana Hicks.

Did his sensational return pull the wool from Mrs Harrison's eyes? Did she now see her husband in a completely different light? Did she start to question everything that had happened? And perhaps everything that had happened in their long marriage before that? Did her tears of joy at this apparent miracle turn to wretched despair and suspicion? Did his terrible confession cause this pious Baptist woman to appreciate that her own actions had sent the guiltless Perry family to the gallows and in that realisation, did she take her own life?

We don't know. And we will never know.

All we can say with any certainty, is that on a spring day in March

1661, the Perry family were marched to a hill outside Chipping Campden and hanged for a crime that they had not committed.

Sacrificial victims to the collective cognitive dissonance of a town that could not comprehend why one of its most important citizens had seemingly vanished into thin air.

* * *

Western civilisation's most enduring scapegoat is undoubtedly Lucifer, and as he looms so large in our collective consciousness, it comes as a surprise to find that he is something of a latecomer to both theology and our human story. The Old Testament contains just nine references to *Ha-Satan,* meaning God's 'accuser' or 'advocate' and in that early Jewish scripture he is less a red-horned devil and more God's 'advocate'.

He first appears in the first Book of Chronicles, written around the sixth century BCE, which tells the story of the Jewish people from the Garden of Eden to the Edict of Cyrus and the Restoration of the Temple at Jerusalem. The Two Books of Samuel cover many of the same events and in particular the reign of David and his son Solomon, but there is one significant discrepancy between the two accounts.

Both Samuel (1 & 2) and Chronicles feature the story of a census carried out by King David which incites God to one of his routine massacres of the people of the Earth. But while in Samuel 2 it is made clear that this is God punishing David for not carrying out the count in accordance with his instructions in 1 Chronicles 21, the census is blamed squarely on someone (or something) called *Ha-Satan,* the Hebrew word for 'adversary':

'Now Ha-Satan stood up against Israel and moved David to number Israel.'

We naturally need to tread carefully where the historicity of the Old Testament is concerned, and there's a fairly big question mark as to whether King David even existed, but this does sound very much like a politician blaming an unpopular policy on something or someone who sits beyond his control. And any one of us can recognise that.

The writing of the Chronicles coincided with Judaism coming into close contact with another much bigger faith. In 598 BCE, the people of

Judah were invaded by the Chaldeans (aka proto-Babylonians) and 10,000 people were carried off in an event known as 'The Babylonian Captivity'. In Babylon, the Jews encountered Zoroastrianism, the first great monotheistic religion, and subsequently Judaism would never be the same again.

Zoroastrianism was said to be based on the ideas of the Iranian prophet Zarathustra, who was claimed to have lived some 7,000 years previously. Zoroastrians viewed the world quite differently to the Jews, believing that the twin heavenly brothers, the God Creator Ahura Mazda and his evil sibling, the spirit Ahriman, were engaged in a perpetual battle between good and evil. Until then the notion of 'good and evil' had been largely alien to the Jewish people and they latched on to this compelling idea and incorporated it into their faith. It was not the only thing they borrowed from the Babylonians.

Zoroastrianism promulgated the notion of universalism – the belief that there was one perfect God who rules over everything and that those who turn to him will find salvation.

The faith also believed that Ahura Mazda was aided in his work by the 'Yazatas' – a group of semi-divine beings who could move between heaven and earth and operate in the human world on his behalf. Both ideas were subsumed into Judaism and the idea of God having messengers was turned into the notion of 'angels' while adherents to the faith started to see 'good and evil' at every turn.

In 539 BCE, the first Achaemenid King, Cyrus the Great, issued an edict allowing the Jews to return home to rebuild the Temple of David. The Jews took Zoroastrian ideas with them and while the period of Babylonian Captivity had been traumatic, it was also transformative. Those new ways of looking at the world would go on to shape Christianity, Islam, Baha'ism and a thousand spin-off faiths including Scientology and Mormonism, and indeed it continues to inform modern secular thinking – some 2,500 years later. Most critically of all, the idea of Satanic forces and good and evil had now entered the bloodstream of Abrahamic monotheism and henceforth the world and the people in it was viewed in terms of light and shade.

With the promulgation of Christianity from the first century CE onwards, Lucifer went from having a walk-on part in scripture (an omnimalevolent Satan still does not exist in Judaism) to playing a starring role in the narrative. The ultimate go-to bad guy finally went mainstream when in 313 CE, Emperor Constantine I converted to Christianity.

The polytheistic Romans, whose religion was heavily influenced by that of Ancient Greece, saw the world differently to Christians. They believed that their 12 major gods were the creators and guardians of Rome and unlike Christianity there was no overarching 'moral code' governing it all. The notion of 'moral dualism' and the battle between 'benevolence and malevolence' just wasn't important until Christianity's inroads changed everything. By the end of the early fourth century CE, the Jewish-Christian-Zoroastrian notion of a world defined by a constant struggle between good and evil was firmly ensconced in European civilisation.

The consequences of this cannot be understated and it is thanks to the Romans embracing Christianity that the notion of 'good and evil' still informs western global politics, our laws, our justice system, our collective morality and even, as this book sets out to prove, the way we interpret history.

Subsequent to the rise of Christianity, theologians went looking for Satan retrospectively. The Revelation of St John, the last book of the New Testament, twice refers to him as a serpent, so inevitably from quite early on, writers including first-century Justin Martyr and the fourth-century Saint Augustine turned the talking snake in the Garden of Eden into Satan. Henceforth he was blamed (along with that conniving woman Eve) for the Fall of Man and all the subsequent bad stuff that human beings do.

Satan, like all the best bad guys in history and literature, was also far more interesting than the perfect hero of the narrative.

In 1667, four years after William Harrison's miraculous reappearance on the streets of Chipping Campden, the republican poet John Milton penned *Paradise Lost* and handed Satan the starring role. In Milton's retelling and in ideas forged out of the rise and fall of Cromwellian England, Satan became easily the most fascinating character in the story.

In Milton's version of events, the Dark Prince's greatest flaw is pride, but like all the best baddies he is also a radical thinker and a complex villain who makes for a sympathetic anti-hero. Unlike God, Satan is self-aware, charismatic, flawed and thus very human indeed, and this Miltonesque Satan is the one that persists most in our popular culture and imagination as a result. The fallen angel, banished to a land of chaos, where he plots and schemes against the Creator out of a sense of betrayal.

The Serpent-Satan is a critical thinker too. Because he is, after all, the first figure to dare to question the ultimate power of God's authority and challenge his hegemony. But undoubtedly it makes him history's first fall guy too, because his suffering and his ignominy demonstrates the price that is paid by those who rise to notoriety.

Throughout history, societies have sought out scapegoats upon whom all the troubles of the world can be blamed. Switch on your TV, scroll down your social media, turn on your radio and you will find them soon enough. They come at us as 'fighting-age men on boats' who claim to be fleeing wars but who are really coming to fleece the taxpayer and steal our jobs and women. They are the minorities you are encouraged to fear and loathe, whether they be black, South Asian, Chinese, Palestinian, Jewish, Muslim, gay, poor or Mexican. These are the monsters who will displace you, kill you, brainwash your children or enslave us all with their wicked ideology. They are the mendacious, feckless underclass, the commie trade unionists, the wokerati, the illuminati, the transgender monsters and of course, the poor. Depending on your perspective they are either the 'eco warriors' or the 'environmental terrorists'. They are the left, the right, they are centrist dads and all the cracks in between.

And if we can just defeat these latter-day witches and demons, then all will be well.

Many philosophers have sought to understand scapegoating and its place in society. For some, it is an inherent paradox, since the bullies pursuing the scapegoats tend, wrongly, to believe themselves to be the victims and fail to appreciate that the very subjects of their loathing and villainisation are in fact the real injured party. Which of course is precisely what happened in Chipping Campden.

The French philosopher René Girard (1923–2015) popularised the notion of the 'Scapegoat Mechanism', the idea that all societies, by their nature, need a metaphysical relief valve that can be activated at times of conflict or plague or civil unrest. Inevitably – and as history has shown repeatedly – that usually means pinning all the blame for the crisis on one group or, in rarer cases, a single individual. Scapegoats give a community something to unite against without creating another crisis and that means that the scapegoat must come from a marginalised, weaker group of people that nobody else will stand up for.

Fear of a common enemy is a powerful societal glue which binds communities together, drives resolve and forges identity as the real or imagined common threat is eliminated. And more and more today we once again see leaders and autocrats rise on the promise of slaying the beast and, in doing so, selling the myth that everyone who gets on board will live happily ever after.

Some of the 'notorious' people in this book served just that purpose and none more so than the Perry family.

In 1661, in the midst of great uncertainty and fear, the scapegoat mechanism sprang into action and the townspeople heaped their collective fears on to three innocent people.

Joan Perry – whose only crime was to have been old and widowed.

John Perry – whose fragile mental health saw him drag his family to oblivion.

And Richard Perry – the young father whose children raced to hug him, only for their delicate noses to seal his fate.

Notoriety, you see, can happen for all manner of reasons.

And – as the Perry family discovered to their cost – they are not always rational.

CHAPTER TWO

THE TRAITORS

Why Turncoats Matter

Shortly after the Japanese attack on Pearl Harbor on 20 December 1941, a 30-year-old immigrant with a curious Scouse-German accent presented himself at a recruiting office hoping to join the US Navy.

'Name?' barked the naval officer sitting at the desk.

'Hitler!' shot back the potential recruit.

'Good to see you Mr Hitler and my name is Rudolf Hess.'

The young man was telling the truth. And it was more than just an unfortunate coincidence because William Patrick Hitler was in fact Adolf Hitler's nephew via his half-brother Alois. Born in Toxteth, Liverpool in 1911, William's father had abandoned the child and his mother in 1914 – claiming that he was going off to make a fortune as a gambler before marrying bigamously and siring a second child in Germany.* However, Alois had stayed in touch and in 1929 William had moved to Berlin where, aged 18, he hoped to cash in on his uncle's rising fortunes. In 1939, he would give a revealing interview to *Look* magazine[1] about what happened next:

'We had cakes and whipped cream, Hitler's favourite dessert. I was struck by his intensity, his feminine gestures . . . (and the) . . . dandruff on his coat.'

Uncle Adolf found the boy a job at the Reichskreditbank only for the

* Heinz Hitler was a committed Nazi who was tortured to death in a Soviet PoW camp in 1942.

hapless William to get sacked for harassing women, before becoming a car salesman. While a popular British song would later propagate the myth that Adolf Hitler was monorchidic,* what was certainly true was that in the early 1930s the German dictator had a very troublesome 'Willy' indeed. William's mounting frustration at his failed career prospects culminated in a spectacularly ill-judged threat to expose 'family secrets' if Adolf didn't step up and make some calls. That resulted in his uncle doing his signature shouting-and-flailing-his-arms-about thing, so William swiftly pegged it back to England in 1938, where he wrote an article entitled 'Why I Hate My Uncle.' That piece caught the eye of the US newspaper tycoon Randolph Hearst, who paid him to go on an American lecture tour, only for William to get stranded stateside when war broke out in 1939.

That first attempt in 1941 to enlist failed, and it was only in 1944, having written to President Roosevelt, that he was allowed to sign on as a naval corpsman. He left the armed forces in 1947 and changed his name, first to Hiller and then to Stuart-Houston before dying in 1987.

Some lives leave such a terrible stain on history that they render their surnames obsolete. Search 'Hitler' in the German phone directory and you get '0' returns and while there are 2,000 people with that name in Peru, much the same happens anywhere else. Belonging as it does to modern history's worst mass murderer, Hitler's name lives on only in infamy and he is not alone in that.

Joseph Stalin, Charles Ponzi, Vidkun Quisling and Judas Iscariot have all left enduring eponymic marks on the lexicon and indeed, to be compared to Judas is, in the words of Bob Dylan, who suffered that fate in Manchester in May 1966, to be called the name of the 'most hated man in history'. Dylan's crime that night was to have broken faith with his folk fans by 'going electric' which, as he told *Rolling Stone* magazine in 2012, is not exactly 'equitable to betraying our Lord and offering him up to be crucified'.[2]

Although perhaps for his fans it was – because treachery, like beauty, lies in the eye of the beholder. Almost all of history's most infamous villains would have seen themselves as the hero of their own narrative.

* Only availed of one testicle.

Just as Guy (nicknamed Guido) Fawkes, the most famous of the 13 conspirators who tried to kill King James I by blowing up Parliament in 1605, thought he was on the right side of history – so Judas Iscariot, if he existed, probably believed he was the good guy too.

The historicity of Jesus Christ is a veritable minefield, and debate rages as to whether he even existed at all, but suffice to say that a good number of secular scholars of early Christian history consider that Jesus Christ was probably a real person – one of the dozen or so 'Messiahs' heading up religious cults in Judea around the first century CE. Many of them agree too, that one of his followers, perhaps called Judas Iscariot, probably betrayed him to the authorities. But annoyingly, for someone so hugely important in terms of culture and history in the Judaeo-Christian world, the paper trail to prove any of the above is very scant indeed. The only reliable sources for Christ's existence are a near contemporary account by the Jewish-Roman historian Flavius Josephus in *c.*95 CE (60 years after Jesus's presumed death) and a later reference by the senator-historian Tacitus in about 116 CE. The rest is speculation, although as messianic cults, even today, tend to strongly resemble each other, we can certainly fit Jesus's group into that broader framework and make assumptions based on his and his followers' behaviour.

Most cults have a strong charismatic leader who demands absolute loyalty from their followers and full commitment from them. The bigger ones tend to clash with the authorities too and that causes friction and dissent within the group, leading followers to switch sides or otherwise betray the largest target for anyone looking to undermine a cult: the leader. As a result, almost every cult in history, from Christianity to Mormonism to Thatcherism, has had its Judas.

While establishing the historicity of Jesus is hard enough, Judas is an almost impossible nut to crack as he barely gets a mention outside of the four gospels. St Paul, founder of Christianity, who died in *c.*64 CE makes no reference to him by name at all and matters are made more complicated because 'Judas' (which is a Greek form of the Hebrew Judah) was a common name in Judea at the time. Even within Jesus's immediate circle there was another Apostle called Judas and one of Jesus's brothers also bore the name.

Some have speculated that Judas Iscariot (meaning 'from Kerioth') may have been Jesus's accountant because the Gospel of John tells us he oversaw the disciples' kitty, and in chapter 12 adds that he had been siphoning off funds:

'He was a thief; as keeper of the money bag, he used to help himself to what was put into it.'[3]

But as this detail comes at a point where Judas has just attacked Jesus for wasting expensive oil on his feet, rather than giving it to the poor, John himself might have been engaging in a bit of spin. Whatever his role and whether real or made up, what is beyond any doubt is that for someone who merits just 23 mentions in the New Testament, Judas Iscariot has gone down as one of history's worst people.

In *Inferno*, written by Italian poet Dante Alighieri in the early part of the fourteenth century as part one of his *Divine Comedy*, the author reserves the ninth circle of hell for traitors, for it is:

'The deepest and the darkest place, the farthest from the heaven that girds all.'

Those who dwell there are trapped in a sea of frozen brine, shed from the six eyes of the three-headed Lucifer, who weeps frenziedly, like some defective Tiny Tears horror doll. As he bawls, he munches on the three worst villains of history and they are all traitors: Marcus Brutus, betrayer of his friend Julius Caesar, his fellow plotter Gaius Cassius Longinus and Judas who gets pride of salivating place in the monstrous central cakehole. Dante, as you can probably sense from the above, had a bit of a thing about turncoats.

Like one of those amateur genealogists on Facebook who claim descent from the 'Anglo-Saxons', Dante believed, on fairly scant evidence, that his ancestors were 'Ancient Romans' and blamed Brutus and Longinus for the downfall of the Empire and thus his antecedents' and his own misfortunes. The Northern Italy of his day was a fragmented mess of warring city states, split between the Holy Roman Empire supporting the Ghibellines and the Guelphs who backed the Pope. Dante fought for the latter and subsequently found himself on the winning side – but revolutions always eat their children and when the Guelphs split, the poet was obliged to flee into exile in Rome. The 'Black Guelphs' of Florence viewed him as a traitor, but he thought them the real apostates and as both sides threw brickbats at each other, it informed all those circles of hell. Judas took pride of place because Dante believed that by betraying the Messiah, the traitor had shaken God's perfect order and was thus responsible for all the misery that followed – including his own. But in doing so, the author was tapping into something far deeper. For Dante knew, as we all do, that beyond the struggle between imagined good and perceived evil lies the even greater battle – between trust and treachery.

Multiple studies across the last 50 years have shown that trust is, as any agony aunt or uncle can tell you, the most important thing in human relationships. It informs not only how we see our partners but also how we assess our friendships and this is unsurprising, because the need for loyalty has been hard-wired into us from the time of our nomadic ancestors who had to rely on each other for their very survival.

Distrust is not the opposite of trust – it is its enemy and as anyone who has ever been betrayed will tell you, once it is lost, it is almost impossible to regain. Culturally speaking, Judas is more than the mere agent of Jesus's betrayal. He has come to represent the apotheosis of our worst and most primitive fears.

Not everyone has had it in for Judas. The first and second century Christian Gnostics (meaning truth) – who argued that the world had been created by an inferior deity, distinct from the God of Scripture – made the case for him, and the Gospel of Judas, rediscovered in Egypt in the 1970s, portrayed Judas as Christ's great friend and enabler. In popular culture, Tim Rice and Andrew Lloyd-Webber did the same with their 1970 musical *Jesus Christ Superstar*, which turns Iscariot into arguably the most enigmatic character in the story; an individualist who tries to speak reason to power.

The Rice-and-Webber Judas, like the Satan of *Paradise Lost*, is a rationalist whose very treachery is a catalyst of change. Without him there would have been no trial, no crucifixion, no resurrection and, therefore, no Christianity. It is a point that most Christian theologians for a long time deliberately obfuscated, instead using Judas's betrayal as an excuse to persecute, dehumanise and murder the Jews.

From the eleventh century onwards, Judas was depicted in art and literature as the embodiment of perfidy and was representative of the worst racist tropes associated with 'Jewishness': crooked, unreliable, scheming, money-grabbing, ugly, thieving, individualistic and treacherous. This depiction became a big part in Jews becoming a condemned people blamed for all the woes of the world – but even as they were, the role of the traitor, Judas, remained distinct. For while the scapegoat is either a figment of the collective imagination (Satan) or an innocent victim (John Perry, the Jews), the traitor is the sum of all our worst nightmares for the simple reason that they come from within and among us.

The genuine threat that treachery can pose to group homogeneity was long ago turned on its head by rulers and autocrats seeking to use it for their own ends, and for centuries Judas's example was used as a means of crushing dissent. In England, for over 800 years, treason was viewed as the most heinous crime of all and even 'imagining' bad things happening to the monarch was enough to get men hanged, drawn and quartered.*

The first noble to suffer that fate was Dafydd ap Gruffydd, the last true Prince of Wales, who in September 1283 was sentenced to death for high treason against King Edward I (aka Longshanks). Having conquered and quashed the people of Wales that year, Longshanks wanted to make an example of his prisoner and sought out the most egregious penalty possible.

Gruffydd was no traitor. Quite the opposite in fact, as he was fighting for his nation's independence – but mere truth did not wash with Longshanks. On 3 October, Dafydd ap Gruffydd was dragged by horses through Shrewsbury, half hanged by a rope and then disembowelled, beheaded and chopped up into four pieces. His head was then carried across England to London Bridge where it was stuck unceremoniously on a spike.

This abhorrent method of execution was used intermittently in the

* Women were burned at the stake and from 1790 executed by hanging.

decades that followed and with Edward III's Treason Act (1351) it became the standard penalty for the offence. Guy Fawkes's co-conspirators were all killed this way, and he would have been too had he not cheated the system by jumping off the gallows and breaking his neck. Following the Restoration in 1660, nine of the ten men found guilty of regicide were hanged, drawn and quartered too. The last person to suffer the penalty in public was David Tyrie, a clerk at the Portsmouth Naval Office, who was executed on 24 August 1784 for engaging in correspondence with the French. On the day, a crowd of 100,000 gathered on Southsea Common and the man from the *Hampshire Chronicle*[4] reported what happened next:

'After hanging exactly twenty-two minutes, he was lowered upon the sledge . . . his head was severed from his body, his heart taken out and burnt, his privates cut off, and his body quartered. He was then put in a coffin and buried among the pebbles by the sea-side; but no sooner had the officers retired, but the sailors dug up the coffin, took out the body, and cut it in a thousand pieces, every one carrying away a piece of his body to shew their messmates.'

Death was not the end of it. Traitors also had their lands and possessions forfeited and it was not until the 1870 Forfeiture Act that hanging, drawing and quartering was formally abolished alongside those lost rights of inheritance.

Even so, well into the twentieth century, high treason remained the ultimate crime and was a capital offence until 1998, when under the terms of the European Convention on Human Rights (ECHR), the UK finally committed to its abolition. Until very recent times, traitors were still being executed. In December 1945, Nazi collaborator John Amery, whom we shall meet again in Chapter Ten, was found guilty of collaborating with Hitler and hanged at Wandsworth prison. A year later, the propagandist William 'Lord Haw Haw' Joyce became the last person to be hanged in Britain for the crime although an additional five people were also executed under the Treason Act (1940) which was aimed at spies and saboteurs.

World War I, by contrast, saw just one execution for high treason – and that was of the once celebrated diplomat Sir Roger Casement.

Unlike Judas, Fawkes or Joyce, Casement's name elicits a different response depending on where you are in the world. In parts of Northern Ireland and particularly in Antrim, even today, it can still provoke a not entirely welcome response. To the south, in Dublin and the Republic of Ireland, he is remembered as one of 'The Sixteen' martyrs who, during the Easter Uprising of 1916, were executed for trying to gain independence and is a hero.

On a trip to the Tower of London, while researching this book, a Scottish beefeater was enthralled when I explained what I was doing and said: 'Ah yes, Roger Casement – now there is a story,' before pulling out a large black book which showed where all the inmates in the Tower's history had been kept.

But say his name elsewhere and you can get an altogether different response.

When I told acquaintances that I was writing about Sir Roger, while a couple nodded in appreciation, many greeted the news with eyes gazing skyward and the same question repeated over and over:

'Who was he again?'

* * *

Just before 5 p.m. on Monday 22 February 1965, a group of Irish diplomats and British civil servants gathered beneath arc lamps in the small cemetery at Pentonville prison in North London and, as snow tumbled down on their thick winter coats, looked on as six prison guards began to dig into the ground.

The yard contained the unmarked graves of 120 men executed there between 1900 and 1961 and among their number were some very infamous figures indeed including quack homeopath 'Dr' Hawley Harvey Crippen, hanged for murdering his wife Cora in 1910, and the necrophiliac serial killer John Christie, executed in 1953. But the exhumation party had not come for Christie or Crippen but for the body of Sir Roger Casement, CMG – diplomat, explorer, human rights advocate – hanged on 3 August 1916, for high treason.

Progress was slow. London's frozen soil was reluctant to give up its bones and after an hour, the guards had managed to remove just two feet of clay. At 7.30 p.m. a solitary skeletal thumb was spotted and then, piece by piece, the dead man's remains were drawn to the surface until at around 10.20 p.m. it was agreed that the gruesome work was done. One of the Irish diplomats noted that the prison guards were visibly moved by their task and that mood continued into the following day when Sir Roger's remains were carried with 'great reverence' to a waiting hearse. The Irish Embassy delegation sought to give the Englishmen extra gratuities for their efforts but were refused on account of it being 'contrary to regulations'[5] – although a subsequent gift of Waterford crystal was received by the prison guards.

Distrust of the British and legitimate concerns that in a cemetery made up of 120 unmarked graves it wasn't unfeasible to suppose that the wrong body had been raised, saw rumours run rife in Ireland and the whispering continued for decades. As recently as 1998, the Sinn Fein newspaper, *An Phoblacht,* was suggesting that the coffin had been filled with rocks. But papers found in the UK National Archives in 2003,[6] tell another story. Correspondence from 1969 between British civil servants shows beyond doubt that the body, dug up four years previously, was Casement's, because prison records from 1916 revealed that he had been thrown naked into the grave. The British were reluctant to divulge that, even in 1969, because it looked very much like an act of deliberate desecration. Which it undoubtedly was.

Casement's relics were flown to Dublin and lay in state at the former prison, Arbour Hill, where in 1916, 14 of his fellow Irish Republican comrades had been taken to be buried after their own executions. This was the culmination of 40 years of efforts by the Irish State to bring him home and it was no coincidence that it had come in the immediate wake of Sir Winston Churchill's death in January 1965. As a member of Herbert Asquith's pre-World War I Liberal government, Churchill had expressed enthusiasm for Irish Home Rule,* hoping it would satiate the Irish people's desire for autonomy while keeping them within the United Kingdom.

* Home Rule was the move to secure autonomy for Ireland not independence.

However, as Ireland had marched towards full independence, he had taken it very personally indeed and in the face of this perceived betrayal had, between 1919 and 1921, supported the deployment of the ruthless paramilitary Black and Tans on the island who then carried out a series of atrocities.

The scars left by Ireland's struggle for independence ran deep on both sides of the Irish Sea across the twentieth century and all the while Roger Casement's legacy lingered like the ghost at Banquo's feast. In September 1953, at a lunch with Irish Taoiseach, Éamon de Valera, the Irish premier once again raised the possibility of repatriating Casement and an ageing Winston Churchill fobbed him off with an excuse about the laws on treason being 'specific and binding'. Sir Winston had made that up over his soup because nowhere in the statutes on treason did it say anything about not being able to dig up a body.

On 1 March 1965, four weeks after Churchill's funeral, thousands of Dubliners looked on as Casement's coffin took its final journey to the Glasnevin cemetery on the outskirts of the capital. There, the 82-year-old Éamon de Valera, now president of Ireland, heaped praise on him and acknowledged that it wasn't just Ireland that owed Casement a debt:

'His name would be honoured, not merely here, but by oppressed peoples everywhere, even if he had done nothing for the freedom of our own country.'

The Glasnevin funeral was an ending, but not the one Casement had wanted. Languishing in Pentonville in the last weeks of his life, he had written of his wish to be buried at Murlough Point, Antrim – close to Magherintemple, the house which was just about the only place he ever called home. London had refused, so a small delegation had gone north, removed a sod of turf from Murlough and placed it on his tomb. It was the epilogue to a life as brimming with symbolism as any that ever sprang from the island of Ireland.

In order to understand his ending and indeed why all of this mattered so much we first need to go back to the beginning.

Roger David Casement was born on 1 September 1864 in Sandycove, Dún Laoghaire, then known as Kingstown, in County Dublin. The town would later achieve literary fame as the setting for its role in the opening chapter of James Joyce's masterpiece, *Ulysses* (1922) a novel which itself makes a passing reference to Casement. The fourth of the four surviving children of Captain Roger Casement Senior and his wife, Anne (née Jephson), his paternal family were descendants of the Protestant Ascendancy, the group of predominantly Anglican colonists who, from the seventeenth century onwards, took advantage of the conquest of Catholic Ireland and confiscation of land by Cromwell and later William of Orange, to secure political and economic supremacy over the island. Roger Senior's father, Hugh, owned a Dublin-based shipping business and it made enough money to send his son on 'a grand tour of Europe' and then, in 1840, buy him a commission as a Cornet (2nd lieutenant) in the 3rd Light Dragoons. Buying your way into the Dragoons didn't come cheap, and Casement's cornetcy set Hugh back a whopping £840 (£71,250 in 2025 money) – although the money was essentially a 'deposit' for good behaviour and could be redeemed by being sold on. Roger Senior served in India in the usual round of acquisitive imperial wars until, in 1848 and foreshadowing the events in his son's life, he did something quite extraordinary. Selling his commission for a cut-price £350 (£34,688) Casement left South Asia and travelled to Hungary to fight in the war of independence against Austria.

That seismic year of 1848 had seen revolutions across Europe but the one in Hungary would outlast them all. Rising resentment of the imperial big brother had caused the Diet (parliament) in Budapest, under the leadership of lawyer and journalist Lajos Kossuth, to revolt against Vienna and its boy Archduke Franz Joseph, then just 17. With the charismatic Kossuth viewed in the West much as Volodymyr Zelenskyy was following Putin's invasion of Ukraine in 2022, the heroic struggle soon became an international cause célèbre and it drew Casement's romantically inclined father in.

By his account, Roger Senior, then 29, was no mere bystander either. In later years he would regale his family with the story of how he had dashed across Europe on horseback to the very dining table of Lord Palmerston at Number 10 Downing Street to secure British help in aiding supplies to the rebels. The epic tale made a huge impression on Roger but it's doubtful that Casement Senior ever met Kossuth, let alone rode a horse – Paul Revere-like – across the continent. In a sense that didn't matter as much as the impact that the story had on his son. Three decades later, Roger Junior would write that the (probably fictional) action demonstrated that his father had:

'An Irishman's innate sympathy with the oppressed and an enmity towards the oppressor.'[7]

The revolution lasted until 1849 when Russian Tsar Nicholas I intervened and sent 300,000 men into Hungary to impose martial law. Kossuth fled via England to America where he hoped to garner support, but his mission ended in failure, and he was obliged to return to London. Though feted as a major celebrity, the shifting sands of politics and his long life saw him fade into relative obscurity, although when he died in Italy in 1894, he remained a broadly admired figure.

Protestant Roger and Catholic Anne met in Paris shortly after Kossuth's retreat into exile and, following a whirlwind romance, made more thrilling still by the elicit nature of their respective sectarian inheritances, married. Their daughter, Nina, was born in 1856 and Charles (1861), Thomas (1863) and finally Roger (1864) followed. Money was tight because in 1848 Hugh Casement had lost everything and emigrated to Australia. The young family led a nomadic life in England, France and Ireland forever running short on funds until tragedy struck in 1873 when Anne died in childbirth. The loss sent Roger Senior into a spin. He dumped his children with his brother John at the family home of Magherintemple, took up spiritualism and moved to the town of Ballymena 27 miles away, where he died four years later in the town's only pub, the Adair Arms.

The children, now orphans, were separated, and Roger was sent off to board at the Ballymena Church of Ireland School. Holidays were spent with his mother's sister Aunt Grace and her husband Edward Bannister in Liverpool, or back at Magherintemple in Ballycastle. 'Roddie' was something of a star among the Casements and Bannisters on both sides of the Irish Sea. With a trace of an Irish accent, he was tall, handsome, softly spoken, intelligent, poetic, thoughtful and very much an aesthete. Roddie was interested in nature, poetry, people, history and roaming about and as Ballycastle sits across the bay from Rathlin Island, Roger would sometimes hire a boat across the strait to the island and explore that wild and extraordinary place. Rathlin was also the site of an infamous incident when in 1575 some 600 people taking refuge there and consisting largely of older men, women and children along with a cohort of 200 Scottish troops had been murdered in cold blood by the pirate, Sir Francis Drake and his co-malefactors – the mercenary, John Norreys and the remorseless English coloniser Walter Devereux, the 1st Earl of Essex.

Though the atrocity remains little known beyond Northern Ireland, largely because Drake in particular is still, quite bizarrely, viewed as a 'hero' in England, Roger was well versed in events and over time developed a fascination for the rest of the Irish history and culture that he had never been taught in school.

He was a voracious reader too and his favourite childhood book was *The Last of the Mohicans,*[8] James Fenimore Cooper's novel of 1826 about a vanishing group of indigenous people in the North American colonial wars. By coincidence the book would later be a favourite of that other part-Irish dreamer and revolutionary Ernesto 'Che' Guevara.

Those who knew him, even in his teenage years, were struck by his innate sensitivity, compassion and very un-Victorian, wobbly upper lip. The author and adventurer, Fred Puleston,[9] who knew Casement in Africa in the 1880s, wrote that:

'Casement's disposition and make up was the gentlest imaginable. He was always sweet-tempered, ready to help, condemning cruelty and injustice in any form. Indeed, he was so emotional, tender and sympathetic that when his fox terrier (Spindle) got at cross purposes with a wild hog and had his stomach ripped open (he) was unable to control his feelings and wept like a girl.'

In the introduction to a book of his poems, published in 1918, Casement's cousin Gertrude Parry concurred:

'Even as a little boy he turned with horror and revulsion from cruelty of every description: he would tenderly nurse a wounded bird to life and stop to pity an overloaded horse.'[10]

Gertrude also observed that *'there was a curious remoteness to him sometimes'* and that he often retreated into an internal world and that may in part have been that throughout his teenage years and on into later life, Roger Casement harboured the secret that he was gay. To be homosexual anywhere in the late nineteenth century was tough and examples abounded of what happened if you got caught. Oscar Wilde, the most famous Irishman of the time, born just ten years before Roger, was a case in point. In the space of just a few weeks in the spring of 1895, Wilde went from being the most celebrated author of his day to being a social pariah; prisoner number C.3.3., condemned to two years of hard labour at Pentonville and later Reading Gaol for the crime of falling in love with a man.

On release, Wilde went into exile in Paris (France had legalised homosexual acts in 1791) where he died satisfyingly unrepentant in 1900, aged 46, but his example served to show the fate that befell those gay men who were found out.

Three years later, in 1903, while spending time socialising in Funchal and Las Palmas in Portugal on his way to Africa, news reached Casement of another victim of the homophobic witch-hunts of the time.

The senior military officer, General Sir Hector Macdonald, KCB, DSO had had a distinguished military career and was widely regarded as a hero of the Mahdist and Boer Wars, before being posted to Sri Lanka (then called Ceylon) as Commander in Chief of British forces in 1902. There the brusque Macdonald soon made himself unpopular with the island's imperial governor and members of the British colonial community and when rumours of his sexual relationships with men spread, he fled back to London where he was told that unless he returned to Ceylon and cleared his name, his reputation would never recover. Macdonald didn't board a ship to the colonies but instead travelled to Paris, where, having booked a room at the Hotel Regina, he shot himself in the head.

'Pitiably sad,' Casement wrote in his diary at the time, *'the most distressing case this, surely, of its kind and one that may awaken the national mind to saner methods of curing a terrible disease than by criminal legislation.'*[11]

Casement too would one day have his homosexuality fatally turned against him, but all of that was to come and back in 1880, aged 15 and having just left school, the concern was mostly about what he would do next with his life. Someone decided that young Roger should go into the family shipping trade and Uncle John and Edward Bannister found him a job as a clerk at the Elder Dempster Shipping Company in Liverpool, where Roger took an instant dislike to both his boss, Alfred Jones, and the grind of office drudgery. Following an act of insubordination, over a refusal to deliver office post for the hated Jones, it was decided that a life at sea might suit the boy better and so in 1883, aged 18, Casement became purser on the SS *Bonny*, which sailed between the UK and West Africa.

This otherwise insignificant appointment would go on to alter the course of millions of lives, spawn the template for the modern NGO and topple a king from his private African fiefdom.

* * *

In June 1890, a Polish-Ukrainian ship's captain, Józef Korzeniowski, travelling up the Congo river to take charge of a river steamer, the *Florida*, was temporarily waylaid at the port of Matadi. Suffering miserably in the heat and increasingly unnerved by the brutality he was witnessing all about him, his spirits were briefly lifted by an encounter with an Irish employee of the 'Congo International Association':

'Made the acquaintance of Mr Roger Casement which I should consider as a great pleasure under any circumstances and now it becomes a positive piece of luck. Thinks, speaks well, most intelligent and very sympathetic.'

The two men shared lodgings and over the next two weeks made short trips to arrange porters for Korzeniowski on his onward trip to Kinshasa. On 20 June 1890, Korzeniowski wrote that he 'parted with Casement in a very friendly manner'.

The Polish-Ukrainian sailor had literary ambitions and was working on his first novel, *Almayer's Folly*, which was published in 1895. But his feverish onward journey would inform his most famous work, *Heart of Darkness*, which appeared under his pen name 'Joseph Conrad' in April 1899. Over the next 26 years, the two men would meet again, and

Conrad's reminiscences would reflect the changing fortunes of his friend's path. Thirteen years after that first meeting, in 1903, and with Casement's fame rising, Conrad boasted of the association to the Scottish explorer RB Cunninghame Graham:

'I can assure you that he has a limpid personality. I've seen him start off into an unspeakable wilderness swinging a crook handled stick for all weapons, with two Bulldogs . . . at his heels and Luanda boy, carrying a bundle for all company. A few months afterwards, it so happened that I saw him come out again, a little leaner, a little browner, with his stick, dogs, and Luanda boy and quietly serene as though he had been for a stroll in a park.'

A great and entertaining story but most certainly untrue – for having spent those initial two weeks together the men did not meet again until six years later, in 1898, at the London dinner of the Johnson Society.[12] The idea that they spent months together in the Congo was the novelist Conrad's invention.[13]

At the time of their first meeting, Casement had recently left the employ of the Elder Dempster Shipping Company and was working for the American adventurer, journalist, soldier and colonist Henry Morton Stanley. Stanley had become famous after going looking for David Livingstone in modern-day Tanzania in 1872, supposedly greeting him with the famous words 'Dr Livingstone, I presume', but nothing you or I learned in school or childhood picture books was true and in fact Stanley made the line up years later just as he did the details of his life.

In fact, Henry Morton Stanley was not even called 'Henry Morton Stanley', and though he claimed to be the adopted son of a New Orleans businessman, he was in fact a Welsh-born stowaway called John Rowlands who had left Britain in 1859, aged 18. In search of fame and fortune he had borrowed someone else's name and played fast and loose with his own biographical details. That is not unusual among history's most famous 'heroes' and it certainly worked in Stanley's case because 'Wizard-of-Oz-like' he eventually became the man he had always imagined himself to be. From 1879, Stanley worked in an ostensibly philanthropic capacity as an envoy of King Leopold II of Belgium who had recently established the grandly named International Association for the Exploration and Civilization of Central Africa (the IACC).

In fact, the organisation was a front for what amounted to a mass criminal enterprise.

Belgium was a new country, which had only been established under the then-monarch's father King Leopold I in 1831 and, like any start-up nepo-baby, Leopold II was hungry to be recognised in his own right. Contemporary accounts don't do him any favours. His first cousin, Queen Victoria, thought him 'very odd', whose habit of 'saying disagreeable things to people' made him as 'unfit, idle and unpromising an heir apparent as was ever known'.[14]

A singularly ungainly man, who was forever tripping over his ceremonial sword, nature had also gifted him with an extravagantly long nose which made him a source of global diplomatic mockery.

'It is such a nose,' wrote the British Prime Minister Benjamin Disraeli, 'as a young prince has in a fairy tale, who has been banned by a malignant fairy.'[15]

On becoming king in 1865, it quickly became apparent that the scale of his proboscis was matched only by that of his imperial ambition. Dreaming of an empire to rival that of the neighbouring Netherlands, this very dull and dangerous man set about looking for blank spots on the world map to make his own. There were just two problems. Firstly, everything worth annexing had gone already and secondly, Belgium didn't have much claim on what was left. Leopold solved the problem in one fell swoop by making the colonial equivalent of a star signing. Henry Morton Stanley, very much the man of the moment, was hired to head up and promote his noble cause of saving the people of the Congo from their 'savagery' and it catapulted Leopold into the premier league of imperialist land grabbers.

In 1876, the Belgian king set up the IACC with the mission to explore Central Africa and 'civilise' its inhabitants. In a cunning move, he made the association Europe-wide, giving the impression that it genuinely was not about Belgian ambition. Unfortunately, that led to competing interests so in 1879 Leopold pared it back, bought out the competition and renamed it the International Association of Congo. At the 1884 Berlin Conference, convened by Bismarck to sort out the claims on Africa by the major powers, the Belgian monarch set himself apart by making a convincing case that his intentions in Central Africa were entirely altruistic and pledged that Belgium would end slavery, cannibalism and tribal wars. The USA and Germany backed him and in 1885, the Congo Free State was established. Unlike the empires of Britain, France and other imperial powers, the 'Congo' was Leopold's alone, making him de facto head of the largest private estate in Africa.

From 1884, Casement was employed as a surveyor and worked on the Sanford Expedition which ran under the umbrella of the International African Association. After a brief stint as a lay preacher and missionary followed by a rather unfortunate and very off-brand spot of elephant hunting, Casement took a different role working on the construction of a grand railway project which it was hoped would bypass the unnavigable lower Congo delta and make exploitation of the interior easier. However, when the cost of the project spiralled and the Belgian government directly intervened to fund it, Casement's conscience was pricked and, as he later put it, he suddenly realised he was 'on the high road to becoming a regular Imperialist jingo'.[16]

The talented and personable Casement was already on the British Colonial Office radar and in 1892, aged 28, they hired him to work for the British government in the 'Oil Rivers Protectorate' in modern-day Nigeria.

As he started his new job, events in Congo began to take a very dark turn indeed, for though Leopold was continuing the pretence of posing as a great philanthropist, in truth he was chiefly interested in making money and things were really not going well on that front. The Belgian king's primary source of income came from the ivory trade, but that murderous business was unpredictable at best, and he was starting to get into some serious debt before salvation arrived from a most unlikely source.

In October 1887, a Scottish-born vet and part-time inventor called John Dunlop, then living in Downpatrick in Northern Ireland, was tinkering with ways to improve his son's tricycle when he came up with the idea for a new type of pneumatic tyre. Soon he had perfected the model and applied for a patent and things quickly took off from there. Inflatable rubber tyres had in fact been developed some 40 years earlier in France in 1846, but the success of Dunlop's innovation, arriving in tandem with the development of the cycle chain, gave birth to the 'safety bicycle' which sparked a global 'bike boom'. By 1896, the USA alone was producing a million cycles a year and soon the demand for rubber had skyrocketed.

But there was a not inconsiderable problem with this new and burgeoning trade because rubber trees take from seven to ten years to grow to maturity and soon demand was massively outstripping supply. All was not lost, however, because natural rubber, in the form of vines, grew in abundance in Central Africa and – as Henry Morton Stanley had found while traversing the region – it was quite literally dripping off the trees. Leopold II had unwittingly hit the jackpot and was now in fact sitting on a fortune. Soon and with the help of his brutal colonial army, the Force Publique, he was ruthlessly exploiting his assets. Harvesting the rubber was not easy, however, as it involved lathering the raw latex on to the gatherer's arms, chest and legs before peeling it off on arrival at a depot. This was excruciatingly painful and labour-intensive work, and more to the point it was very badly paid, and as a result there was not exactly a queue of volunteers willing to rip their skin and chest hair off for the trinkets and brass wire on offer as payment.

'The native doesn't like making rubber. He must be compelled to do it,' a Force Publique officer, Louis Chaltin, wrote in his diary in 1892.[17]

So, to force the people of the region to harvest the rubber sap for free, a violent system of attrition was developed. Villages were raided, women and children were kidnapped, and the chief of the district was told that they would only be sold back when the quota was delivered and 'the rubber tax' paid. An orgy of violence ensued as the 'tax' was levied and while the Belgian government did not officially condone it, in practice hostage-taking, mutilation, rape and murder became almost mundane. A five-volume set of instructions for colonisers, called the *Manuel du Voyageur et du Résident du Congo* even instructed Belgian settlers on how to conduct their hostage-taking, and the diaries of Belgian colonists are littered with tales of appalling atrocities. The account of Louis Leclercq, an officer in the Force Publique, from June 1895 is typical:

'*A man from Baumaneh, running through the forest shouting for his lost wife and child, came too close to our camp and received a bullet from one of our sentries. They brought us his head. Never have I seen such an expression of despair and fear . . . we burned the village.*'[18]

Those who did not submit had their hands, noses and ears cut off or were murdered 'pour encourager les autres'. The purported 'civilising' mission to bring Christian light to the 'heart of darkness' had descended into an abomination of murder and amputation to feed the West's insatiable desire for pneumatic bicycle tyres.

But King Leopold II was growing fabulously rich, so that must have been a comfort to him. His private state in fact received half of everything made by the rubber barons who were themselves raking in a 700 per cent profit on every kilo of rubber harvested. In *King Leopold's Ghost*, the definitive book on the atrocity, the author Adam Hochschild estimates that by 1900, Leopold's personal wealth was somewhere in the region of 220 million Belgian francs (about £1.57 billion in 2025 money) making him the richest man in the world in his era and likely the richest monarch in world history up to that point.

The first attempts to raise the alarm came from two African American adventurers.

In 1890, George Washington Williams, a former soldier in the Unionist army turned Baptist minister who was also the first black congressman in Ohio, arrived in the Congo Free State via Brussels, where he had been afforded a brief audience with the Belgian king. Leopold had impressed him with his usual rot about his civilising mission, but in Africa, Williams saw the reality and was moved to write an open letter to Leopold which was published in July 1890. The Belgian monarch did not take kindly to some uppity black American pastor lecturing him on his fiefdom, and his imperial minions immediately sought to discredit Williams – a pattern that would continue for the next 20 years. George fell ill in England on his way home to

America the following year and died of TB in Blackpool before his work could be done, but he had taken the first important step in revealing the truth.

The following year, a 25-year-old Virginia-born preacher, William Sheppard, arrived in the Congo with the mission of establishing a Presbyterian church in the region. As William was also black and the Presbyterian church was racist, he was technically consigned to a secondary role under his white friend and fellow preacher, Samuel Lapsley, but Sheppard was very much the man in charge. Conditioned by white American society's view of African people, Sheppard had been expecting to encounter an 'inferior' race but was swiftly disabused of the idea. The Kuba of the interior had a rich and ancient culture that refused to bend to the proselytising efforts of two American missionaries and, while Lapsley struggled with their refusal to convert, Sheppard merrily gave up and started studying the local culture instead. Far from being 'savage' this was *'the finest looking race I had seen in Africa, dignified, graceful, courageous, honest, with an open smiling countenance (and) really hospitable.'*[19]

Following Lapsley's death, Sheppard became the first foreigner to reach the ancient Kuba capital at Ifuca and met the Kuba King Kot a-Mbweeky II who, having initially ordered his beheading, changed his mind and befriended him instead. Unfortunately, Sheppard had unwittingly opened the interior to the West and the Belgians soon moved into the breach and started exploiting the rubber. In 1899, when fighting broke out around the Kasai River, Sheppard was sent by his church to investigate and stumbled across a camp run by Zappo Zap warriors, who proudly revealed the fate for those who would not pay the 'rubber tax'. Sheppard saw a pile of dismembered hands, removed as proof for the Belgian authorities that those who had not paid up had been killed.

Utterly appalled by what he had seen, he began writing exposés for the Presbyterian press.

At about the same time, Edmund Morel, an Anglo-French shipping clerk, stumbled across evidence of another kind. Morel, then in his mid-twenties, was an employee of the Elder Dempster shipping line, the same company that Roger Casement had worked for as a teenager. Morel was bilingual so when the Liverpool-based firm needed someone to supervise the operations of a subsidiary in Antwerp, they sent him to Belgium where he soon met Leopold II's private army of colonial executives.

Morel quickly appreciated that the statistics he was meticulously recording for Elder Dempster did not match those being published by the Congo Free State in Belgium. Someone was cooking the books and siphoning off a considerable margin for themselves and, suspecting fraud, he raised this and other concerns with the 'Secretary of State' for the King's colony only to be shouted at for his perceived 'indiscretion'. Morel had also stumbled on to something else, and something far more disconcerting. A considerable discrepancy existed between shipments that sailed back and forth between Boma in the Congo Free State and the Belgian port. Cargo ships arriving at Antwerp were brimming with goods including vast consignments of ivory and rubber – but the only items going the other way were weapons, ammunition, mercenaries and luxury goods for the Belgian colonists. There was, in short, no market among the indigenous peoples and that could only mean one thing.

The Belgian king's highly productive colony was running off the broken backs of slavery.

Morel turned whistleblower and Elder Dempster's attempts to promote, buy and then bully him into silence failed. By 1901, he was a campaigning journalist bent on revealing the truth of Belgian atrocities. Through his efforts, and aided and abetted by Sheppard's, a global outcry ensued and by early 1903 Morel's campaign was being debated in the House of Commons. A motion was passed in May that year condemning Belgian activities, and the Foreign Office dispatched their consul at the port of Boma in the Congo Free State to go and investigate. His name was Roger Casement.

The pecking order in the British diplomatic service in the nineteenth century was based, like everything else, on wealth, influence and social hierarchy. As late as 1891, diplomatic attachés were expected to have a private income of £6,400 (£677,000 in 2025) to supplement their £400 (£42,000) a year salary, meaning that the service was staffed in large part by extremely posh and highly incompetent toffs. Casement was a rare example of someone rising on merit and had proved his mettle, in 1895, when he had been sent as British consul to Lorenzo Marques on Delagoa Bay, a Portuguese protectorate in East Africa. The port was linked to Pretoria by rail, and he had gathered intelligence there in the lead up to the Second Boer War. The role provided excellent training for this subsequent mission in the Belgian Free State.

In June 1903, Casement travelled into the interior and began gathering testimony and over the next few months, while fretting constantly in his diaries over the health of his dog, John, he unravelled what was going on in what would become a landmark human rights report. Casement knew the region well, from his travels a decade earlier, and noticed immediately that significant depopulation had taken place. At the town of Ikoko he noted 'perhaps 600 people – once 4,000 or 5,000' and observed 'the country a desert, no natives left'. Stories of atrocities poured forth from those he met; tales of villagers being brutalised and tied up and worse. On 6 September he met a boy called Epondo who told him that his hand had been cut off by a Congolese auxiliary.

At first, the Belgians feigned concern and even offered their assistance in investigating the matter, but simultaneously they began a media counter-offensive and the CFS even commissioned a book by an 'anonymous' Belgian called *The Truth About the Civilisation in Congoland*. It argued that all the good intentions of kindly King Leopold II had been deliberately distorted by the mendacious British and it was all backed up with some artfully selected quotes from great men like, well, Sir Henry Morton Stanley.

Casement finished his investigation in the autumn of 1903 and his White Paper was presented to the Houses of Parliament in February 1904. Taking the form of a travelogue and written in a detailed and measured tone, Roger sought to explain the depopulation of the region, provide balance and give voice to the people who had been brutalised:

My informant . . . said he saw the prisoners being taken away to Irebu under guard of six black soldiers and tied up with native rope so tightly that they were calling aloud with pain . . . Upon their release, two of these men died . . . and two more . . . died soon after their return.[20]

Casement's testimony was compelling but rested largely on statements from local African people, so the Belgian authorities moved to dismiss it all as hearsay promulgated by 'savages.' The story of Epondo, which made up a little over two pages of the 60-page report, was of particular interest, as Casement had personally reported the guard to the Belgian colonial authorities. They gathered their own counter-testimony which suggested that the boy had in fact lost his hand after being bitten by a boar. The criticism risked undermining the credibility of the whole report and Casement had considerable trouble pushing back against it. As the months passed, the Foreign Office itself appeared increasingly keen for the whole issue to go away and as the Belgian government had now launched its own Commission of Inquiry, the British felt that it was a case of 'job done'.

Fearing the scale of the atrocity was going to be whitewashed, Casement teamed up with Edmund Morel, who had just launched the Congo Reform Association (CRA), to campaign against the Belgian king's regime. The CRA went on to set the blueprint for the modern non-governmental organisation (NGO). Morel, Casement and colleagues lobbied MPs and ministers, garnered celebrity endorsements, including Joseph Conrad, Mark Twain and Sir Arthur Conan Doyle, and made full use of the mass media available at the time.

Critical to their efforts was the evidence provided by Alice Seeley-Harris, a missionary, English teacher and pioneering early photojournalist, who had taken pictures of victims of Belgian brutality on her box Brownie camera. Those photos not only revealed the shocking extent of crimes against local African people but also humanised the victims and had a profound effect when published in Morel's book, *King Leopold's Rule in Africa*, which appeared in 1904.

In addition to garnering support from famous people and keeping the issue alive in the press, Morel was a brilliant and charismatic public speaker and a natural campaigner, who delighted in annoying powerful people. That made him a lot of enemies, and by dint of his association with him, it made Casement enemies too. In July 1904, the Foreign Office offered Roger a post as a consul in Lisbon, Portugal, which was then one of the best diplomatic gigs going, in the hope that it would shut him up. Flattered into taking up the position, Casemene found the post unrewarding and, pleading ill health, soon quit and returned to England where he started campaigning alongside Morel again.

Leopold was not going to give in without a fight and began using every means available to discredit Casement and Morel. In 1905, the appropriately named Henry Wellington Wack, a tame US lawyer kept on King Leopold's payroll to write flattering apologia about him, published a book titled *The Story of the Congo Free State*, which heaped praise on the King. The vast, sycophantic, telephone directory of a tome – running to some 472 pages – reserved particular ire for the English, whom Wack accused of hypocrisy:

'(Particularly when) the interests of the pseudo-humanitarians and those of the traders happen to coincide. On such occasions, fortunately somewhat rare, the spectacle of cant and Commerce in alliance is enough to bring a smile to the face of a sphinx.'[21]

Beyond the pompous rhetoric, Wack had an actual trick up his sleeve and trotted out evidence which suggested that Edmund Morel was corrupt. Wack showed that he had paid an Italian man called Antonio Benedetti to write a fake atrocity report to serve his ends. Benedetti was in fact an agent provocateur, employed by the Belgians, who had deliberately approached Morel and Casement with the intent of discrediting them. Casement had been distrustful of his motives from the start and wrote to Morel saying: 'I am awfully suspicious of him; he looks like a rascal.'[22] But Morel had already drawn up the contract and when Benedetti signed it, he immediately leaked it to the Belgian newspaper *Independence Belge*, which published the story in December 1904. The 'evidence' became central to Wack's thesis, which appeared the following year.

But it was not enough to save Leopold's private fiefdom.

The combination of Casement's report, Morel's campaigning, Sheppard's writing, Seeley-Harris's photographs, celebrity backing and the Belgian government's own report, which vindicated them all, saw the tide shift. In 1905, Mark Twain (a huge fan of Morel) reignited the cause with his satirical pamphlet 'King Leopold's Soliloquy', which ridiculed the King. The Belgian monarchy countered with its own 'satirical' publication, *An Answer to Mark Twain,* which purported to be written by Morel and the Congo Reform Association and juxtaposed 'damning testimony' alongside lovely pictures showing the 'reality' of life in the African state; all happy, smiling villagers and booming plantations. The publication also dragged up the Epondo case. As satire goes it was about as amusing as a box of porridge oats.

The endgame played out and, in 1908, Leopold was obliged, by his own government, to relinquish control over his vast African estate. Brussels then took over the administration of the Congo instead.

The following year, Sheppard would be accused of libel by a Congo-based Belgian rubber firm and when he won the case, was celebrated as a hero in his homeland. The *Boston Herald* gushed: 'He has not only stood before kings, but he has also stood up to them. In pursuit of his mission of serving his race . . . this son of a slave . . . has dared to withstand all of the power of Leopold.'[23] He died, aged 62, in Kentucky in 1927.

Morel went on to become a peace campaigner and in August 1917 was imprisoned by the British state for 'sending anti-war literature to a neutral country'. Had he lived 150 years earlier, it would have seen him hanged, drawn and quartered but instead he got six months hard labour at Pentonville. Morel held all the major powers equally responsible for World War I and did not believe that Germany alone should accept blame for events. In 1922, as the Labour candidate for Dundee, he went on to sensationally defeat the incumbent (National) Liberal MP, Winston Churchill, whom he thoroughly despised. Two years later, following attempts to nominate him for the Nobel Peace Prize, Morel died suddenly of a heart attack aged 51.

In the wake of his report and the success of the campaign against the Congo Free State authorities, Casement's star was in the stratosphere. Aged 40, he was easily Britain's most famous diplomat but having challenged Belgian imperialism, he was now wrestling with the matter of where his own loyalties lay. Back in June 1904, while resting and recuperating at Magherintemple, and just prior to his mission to Portugal,

Casement had helped organise the first Feis na nGleann a few miles along the coast from Ballycastle. Ostensibly a celebration of the cultural heritage of Ireland, and largely inspired by the Welsh Eisteddfod, beneath the bunting and beyond the Irish dancing, something radical occurred. This first Feis was a meeting of spirits for the many diverse and sometimes competing groups pushing Ireland towards Home Rule and/or independence, and Casement met figures including Rose Young, Francis Bigger, Ada MacNeill, Bulmer Hobson (later of the Irish Republican Brotherhood) and Eoin MacNeill who would become Chief of Staff of the Irish Volunteers (later the IRA). Casement's involvement and his subsequent radicalisation would lead inexorably to his martyrdom – or treachery depending on how you wish to view it.

While Casement's conversion to the cause did not come overnight, it was hardly surprising that this romantically inclined and very thoughtful man, who had fought so hard for the rights of others, should now turn his thoughts to Ireland. After all, the parallels were there. The majority Catholic population of Ireland, which in the late nineteenth century made up 90 per cent of its people, had long been rendered a subordinate, powerless underclass. The Irish penal laws, introduced from 1695 onwards in the wake of William and Marys' subjugation of Ireland, had seen generations of Irish Catholic people suffer iniquities.

For almost 150 years, Catholics were banned from owning weapons, or speaking Gaelic, or studying medicine or law, or entering a profession. The 'Popery Act of 1703' prohibited them from passing on their land to their eldest sons, meaning that property had to be split up or sold and as a result, 90 per cent of the people of Ireland collectively owned less than 10 per cent of the land. It was not until 1829 and through the campaigning efforts of the 'Liberator' Daniel O'Connell that the Catholic Emancipation Act changed all the above, although as the Catholic Irish population had now become a socio-economic underclass, most of them still had no rights to vote* let alone money to put food on the table.

* The Representation of the People's Act 1918 would see Ireland's franchise more than double overnight from 700,000 to two million. It was the last time a united Ireland voted in a British general election.

In other words, for hundreds of years the forces of British colonialism, in the shape of the Crown and the Protestant Ascendancy, had exploited Ireland, stolen the best land, fenced off plantations, set the people against themselves, rendered the Catholic majority a disenfranchised underclass, intimidated and bullied the people into compliance and looked on as most of the population had descended into poverty and starvation. During the Irish famine, which lasted from 1845 to 1852, just ten years before Casement was born, at least a million people died. Blight and failed harvests had seen the potato crop, on which a third of the entire population depended for sustenance, wiped out. And the callous disregard among England's ruling classes for the crisis that followed only exacerbated the situation, while giving succour to the cause of Irish Home Rule.

Just as the Congo delta had been depopulated by the egregious excesses of Leopold's rule, so Ireland had borne witness to massive population decline. In addition to the disease and the starvation, another two million Irish people fled the island for America, Canada, Britain and Australia, meaning that between 1841 and 1851, the population of Ireland dropped by 25 per cent.

That is not to say that by 1905 the Irish people, edging irrevocably towards Home Rule, were suffering anything like the terrible excesses of brutality witnessed under King Leopold – but the history was there and the wholly justified grievance with it. It was recent and raw, and the righteous sense of injustice and enmity lingered – as it still does.

Roger Casement was a man of many paradoxes. A Protestant Dubliner who was often mistaken for being an Englishman. A lover of animals who went on elephant hunts. A stubborn and opinionated firebrand who was riddled with self-doubt. A man happiest alone but who also adored the company of others. A stickler for rules who was capable of extreme recklessness. And, perhaps most strikingly of all, a dedicated servant of the British Empire who became an Irish Republican revolutionary. And it was in this last contradiction and his final act that he found the meaning and the roots that had eluded him all his life.

In 1905, in the wake of his report, Casement was awarded a CMG by King Edward VII in his birthday honours list. Roger gave 'illness' as his excuse for non-attendance at Buckingham Palace, but in reality, he had agonised over whether to accept it at all and could not bring himself to go. To have rejected the award would have hindered his career progress because even today, it would be a brave and reckless civil servant who snubbed the overtures of the King.

A decade later, in 1915, when he publicly divested himself of the CMG and sent it to the Foreign Office, officials noted that the medal had never been removed from its case.

* * *

In 1906, Casement was offered the job of consul in Santos, Brazil and accepted the role. On arrival he found that his predecessor had bled the finances dry, that the consular offices were in a state of considerable disrepair and that record keeping had gone out of the window, and he immediately set about putting things back in order while firing off letters to his superiors – as was his habit.

Ever in search of a cause, he found it in the queue of distressed British seamen who queued daily at the consulate. Failing to secure Foreign Office help, Casement essentially set up the Edwardian equivalent of a GoFundMe campaign and went cap in hand round the wealthier British residences in the area seeking donations. His excessive zeal and endless memos made him as many enemies as friends, but he was an asset and he was famous, and he was thus promoted rapidly.

Come 1908, he was the new Consul General in Rio de Janeiro – placing him one rank below the British ambassador to Brazil.

In his new capacity, he wrote a series of reports for the UK Board of Trade while making notes about conditions for indigenous people in the country whose culture and environment was already being impacted by 'progress'. Recurring bouts of illness saw him spend time in Barbados recuperating, before he returned to Rio where he befriended a host of foreign delegations and formed a bond with Baron von Nordenflycht, his German counterpart.

Now at the top of the diplomatic food chain, Casement was becoming reckless with his opinions. Relations between Germany and Britain were already in an increasingly perilous state of affairs in 1908, with both countries engaged in a naval arms race and mutual rattling of sabres, but despite that, Casement began to confide in the baron about his growing dislike of the British government and his belief in the cause of Irish freedom. It was an extraordinary lack of judgement which led Nordenflycht to realise that Casement was a potential intelligence asset.

Something curious can happen in the psyche of career expats. The distance and the hankering for a rarely visited home can lead many to romanticise and idolise the old country to the point of fiction. Living in some detachment in Brazil, Casement increasingly viewed Ireland and her people in ever more idealised terms and so, bored and listless in Rio and increasingly annoyed with his Anglocentric superiors, his dedication to the cause of Irish Home Rule hardened. Taking a £50 (£5,000 in 2025 money) share in the nationalist Irish daily *Sinn Fein* he began to write furiously and anonymously for it.

Casement had been a member of the Irish League since 1904 and under the pseudonym 'Seán Bhean Bhocht' he now wrote a series of articles for nationalist publications, while simultaneously working as a British civil servant.

Roger was ever more frustrated at the lack of progress in the cause and in letters to his cousin, Gertrude Bannister, he railed against the hibernophobia of 'Anglo-Saxon' politicians in Westminster.[24] His deputy, Ernest Hambloch, would later recall him 'marching up and down the room with ungainly strides (mouthing off) a torrent of violent abuse not only of the English but of everything British'.[25] The anger was real, and a man once noted for his calm demeanour was becoming demonstrably radicalised by the cause. He started referring to England with the pejorative 'Sasana' (Saxons) and in his diary called it a 'beastly hole'.[26]

Casement also began to actively promote Irish interests in Brazil, as distinct from those of the British Isles, and in official correspondence complained that as Irish trade figures were included in the overall 'British' figure, it was impossible to work out how productive the Irish economy was. Roger was now walking two perilous tightropes at once, for not only was this most outwardly English of diplomats supporting the Irish Republican cause, but simultaneously he was taking ever greater risks in his private life. Casement was keeping two sets of private journals in parallel, which would later be dubbed the 'white' and 'black' diaries. In the former he kept observations, details of meetings with friends and colleagues and accounts. In the latter he kept notes on his internal world, and there are extensive notes on what he had witnessed among the indigenous Indian people: '*Clear marks of flogging – one small boy, a child, quite recent red weals unhealed and many other small boys show marks of flogging.*'[27] They also included numerous, often random, sexual encounters, which by 1910 and 1911 were becoming both more explicit and more abundant in nature.

'*Thursday 28 July 1910: Splendid testemunhos – soft as silk & big & full of life – no bush to speak of. Good wine needs no bush. Carlos Augusto Costa – 189 Rua dos Ferreiros, Funchal 7/6 Very fine one – big, long, thick. Wants awfully and likes very much. Joao – Big £1,12. 6. Internacional Hotel. Bella Vista.*'[28]

Reading these accounts in his published diaries feels like an intrusion. After all, they were not written for publication but for his own pleasure. There is no getting away from the fact that they are deeply problematic too, for while it is tempting to make excuses on his behalf, quite bluntly many of those encounters with local youths feel reminiscent of any modern middle-aged sex tourist taking advantage of economically disadvantaged people. Nothing is entirely straightforward in the saga that is 'Roger Casement' and one episode is particularly problematic for those wishing to burnish his halo.

Key among the events cited by his detractors was his attempt to 'adopt' two local boys called 'Omarino' and 'Ricudo' from Peru in the summer of 1911. The two young men were in their late teens and while there is no suggestion of physical abuse, his removal of them to London, where he paraded them about before sending them, dressed in feathers, to be painted by the celebrated artist William Rothenstein, aroused understandable discomfort. Casement later regretted his behaviour and the two young men, who seem to have enjoyed their adventure, were sent home. But his interest in teenage boys was well documented and unfortunately, this misjudgement was no one-off as such stories had peppered his career.

During that first Brazilian posting in Santos in 1906, he took in a young Irish stowaway and henceforth declared that he was his 'valet'. While staying with English friends in Rio, the valet was given a fold-up bed in the servant's quarters and the perceived insult threw Casement into a gigantic fury which ended with him insisting that they share a room. His hosts and great friends, the Keevils, took things at face value and believed that Casement was simply making a stand on the grounds that he refused to abide by class conventions. But frankly that seems somewhat naive.

It is hard and perhaps foolish to judge the actions of a man at a distance of over 100 years. Casement inhabited a world in which his sexuality was a crime, and as a straight man living in the twenty-first century, I have never suffered such prohibitions or fear, so it is hard to imagine what was going through his head.

What can be said is that while Casement was undoubtedly engaging in sexual exploitation in using rent boys, he didn't really have much of a choice barring self-imposed celibacy.

The notion that a British vice consul in Rio could be openly gay, even in a country that had legalised homosexuality in 1831, was anathema in 1910. What was he meant to do? Spend his life in a torment to placate the perverse and hypocritical moral landscape of his time? There is anyway some suggestion that a few of these encounters were much more than purely sexual in nature. On a trip to Buenos Aires, he had an intense encounter with a youth called 'Ramon' with whom he was afforded the rare luxury of living life openly. When they were separated and he returned to Ireland on leave, the couple exchanged letters and were clearly besotted with each other.

On a visit to Belfast, he met a bank clerk called Joseph Millar Gordon to whom he gifted a motorcycle, and the two men seem to have had an intense connection as well.

But throughout his adult life, Casement was most likely in, albeit unrequited, love with one man above all others: Herbert Ward, his best friend and companion whom he had met when the two men worked for Stanley, surveying and building the African International Association railway. Ward went on to write books about his adventures and through that work met Edmund Morel whom he later introduced to Roger. In the early years of their friendship, Ward thought highly of his friend and wrote once that:

'No man who walks the earth at this moment is more absolutely good and honest.'[29]

Some have speculated that they may have been romantically involved and while Herbert later settled down and married, for Casement, Herbert was clearly 'the one'. An extraordinarily intense, albeit cropped, photo of these two very handsome men can be found online and in the Irish state archives and the reader is invited to judge the image for themselves.

In 1909, news began filtering into the consulate in Rio of a fresh human rights atrocity playing out in a disputed area of the Amazon basin, between Peru and Brazil, known as Putumayo. The interests of big rubber were at play once again but this time a British registered firm, the Anglo-Peruvian Amazon Rubber Co (PAC) and its Barbadian employees were being blamed for the abuses.

The first accounts came from a campaigning local journalist, Benjamin Saldaña Rocca, and were later backed up by testimony from an American engineer called Walter Hardenburg, who had travelled through the region between 1907 and 1908. Hardenburg had witnessed terrible deeds and believed the company and its suppliers were effectively enslaving the indigenous peoples in service of rubber harvesting. In a distinct echo of events in the Congo Free State, people were being assaulted, bullied, maimed, raped and murdered to enforce quotas. An article on PAC abuses by Hardenburg was published in the *Truth* magazine in London in 1909 and quickly gained international traction.

Casement travelled to Putumayo, ostensibly to investigate abuses by Barbadian immigrant workers who were citizens of the British Empire and thus under his jurisdiction. In the process he exposed the criminal enterprise of the gangster rubber baron Julio Cesar Arana.

Casement's two reports, written in 1910 and 1911, were, if anything, even more sensational and ground-breaking than his work in Central Africa. Bristling with indignation at the state of affairs and using distinctly undiplomatic language which branded the PAC operation 'revolting' and 'unspeakable', he wove together hard evidence of atrocities with the first-hand testimony of dozens of indigenous people, many of whom bore the scars of their beatings. He interrogated the Barbadians he met too. Casement referred to Arana and his co-conspirators as 'villains' and in between the clarity, the integrity and the closely documented accounts, his anger veritably fizzes off the pages.

Arana's employees included a psychopathic enforcer called Armando Normand who was known to starve his workers to death as a punishment and was accused of multiple abuses against men, women and children, which included routinely whipping those who failed to meet quotas. Another man, Andres O'Donnell, was accused of crimes that amounted to ethnic cleansing and in late 1911, having fled to Barbados, Casement would try to have him arrested and extradited to Britain. One of the symptoms of Casement's growing nationalist sympathies was that he had lost all perspective where Irish people were concerned and believed that his fellow kinsmen were all imbued with a sort of innate good. Mixed-race O'Donnell's actions rocked that naive certainty.

Casement's two reports on the atrocities sparked outrage in Britain and the government acted against PAC while putting pressure on the authorities in South America to do something. The Foreign Secretary, Sir Edward Grey, moved effectively and in 1913 PAC was liquidated. Arana never faced charges and went on to be a senator in Peru, but satisfyingly he lost everything in 1939 and died penniless and forgotten in the 1950s.

Casement was now at the peak of his global repute and Sir Edward Grey pushed for him to be rewarded for his work. In the 1911 Coronation honours list, he was given a knighthood and appreciating that the title 'Sir' would open necessary doors and perhaps genuinely flattered, he gratefully accepted. His letter of acceptance opened with the line: 'I find it very hard to choose the words in which to make acknowledgement of the honour done to me' before going on to express how 'graciously pleased' he was. This like so much else would soon be used against him.

Casement was now being honoured by the very establishment he had come to hate and it was all the more extraordinary because he had secretly been a member of Sinn Fein for the last six years and was actively agitating, albeit surreptitiously, in the fight for Irish independence – a cause which posed an existential threat to the very empire itself.

After all, central to opposition to Irish Independence among Unionists, Conservatives and even Liberals like Winston Churchill was the belief that if Ireland achieved freedom from London, then everything else would come tumbling down too. If the United Kingdom was to let Ireland go its own way, then how could the British argue that the people of India, Africa or elsewhere should not also be given independence?

Casement was then the nation's most famous diplomat. Feted in Washington, Paris and the rest of the world, he was the very apogee of 'global Britain' and in fact represented all the best things that it liked to believe it stood for. Now, as he knelt in submission before the King and received his knighthood, this former disciple of imperial prepotency was becoming the empire's Judas.

* * *

In early January 1915, five months after the start of World War I, Irish PoWs at a camp in Limburg an der Lahn in the west of Germany were surprised to find themselves being addressed by an umbrella-wielding, striking-looking 'Englishman' in a pinstripe suit. The tall and imposing figure identified himself as Sir Roger Casement and claimed to be the 'Irish ambassador to Germany' (no such role officially existed). He then went on to explain that he was there, on behalf of the Irish Republican Brotherhood, to recruit an 'Irish Brigade' which would be used to fight a war of independence against the British overlords.

Most of the prisoners in the camp had never heard of him and were more than a little unimpressed by his call to arms. Some booed, others started chanting the name of John Redmond, the moderate nationalist politician, who had managed to push the pre-war Liberal government to grant Home Rule for Ireland in September 1914 and others still started laughing mockingly in an attempt to drown out his words.

'How much are the Germans paying you?' someone shouted and soon a chorus had joined in and were asking the question after everything he said until, having realised that the mob was against him, Casement sought to leave. But departing the camp was easier said than done, for as he stepped off the stage and passed through the men, they started to push and jostle him to the extent where he had to bat them off with his umbrella before getting rescued by a group of German guards.

Quite how Casement had ended up in Germany, actively seeking to recruit men of the British Armed Forces to fight for Irish liberation is a tale unto itself.

Having resigned from the Foreign Office in 1913, Casement had immediately begun to pour all his efforts into the cause. To that end he had joined the Provisional Committee of the Irish Volunteers, a paramilitary forerunner of the IRA which had been organised in response to the formation of the Ulster Volunteers, a Protestant-backed pro-union outfit founded by the politician Edward Carson to oppose Home Rule. Having toured Northern Ireland – where he appeared on public platforms espousing the case for independence – he switched his attention to the US where he used his celebrity and reputation to raise money for the cause.

Appreciating that the 'Carsonites' were busy stockpiling arms in anticipation of the coming clash between unionists and republicans, Casement also helped organise shipments of weapons into the island.

There is a definite sense of a shift in his character and in his writing at this point. The long years abroad, dreaming about an idealised Ireland and a romanticised people, had undoubtedly instilled a militant spirit within him and – like so many revolutionary dreamers before and since – he was clearly losing perspective and perhaps all reason with it. Casement, like nationalists throughout time, now saw the world in purely binary terms in which all the British people were baddies and all the non-unionist Irish were either victims or heroes. It was deluded to say the least because Casement himself was a product of the Protestant Ascendancy and indeed was often mistaken for an Englishman.

His ill-judged visit to the PoW camp demonstrated that all rational perspective had been lost because, after all, those Irish soldiers he was seeking to recruit were volunteers. They had, to a man, willingly signed up to fight for Britain and were not about to have their heads turned by someone in a suit who was in league with the enemy. Reports of German atrocities as well as the singularly harsh conditions they had endured in captivity had not exactly softened most of them up for recruitment either and out of the thousands of prisoners held at Limburg, initially just 52 joined Casement's Brigade.

Roger had arrived in Germany three months earlier in the company of his latest valet and bodyguard, an impoverished, Norwegian-born US immigrant called Adler Christensen whom he had met in August 1914 while visiting Clan na Gael leader John Devoy and a German diplomat, Count Johann Bernstorff in New York. Though married, a fact which he seems to have kept from his boss, Christensen was soon having a relationship with Casement, who was obviously infatuated with his lover. On their way to Germany, Christensen, taking advantage of the fact of their intimacy, took it upon himself to contact Mansfeldt Findlay, head of the British diplomatic mission to Oslo, to whom he revealed that he was having 'unnatural relations' with Casement.

Secret affidavits gathered by British Special Branch[30] in 1916 would later reveal that on three occasions in Norway, hotel staff had caught Casement in bed with Christensen who was subsequently told that if he were able to get Roger 'knocked on the head' and bring him to the British delegation, he would be amply rewarded. Sir Edward Grey, who just five years previously had secured Casement's knighthood, even drew up a promissory note offering Christensen £5,000 (£429,000 in 2025 money) if he betrayed his boss.

Biographers disagree over what exactly Christensen was up to and to whether Casement had in fact hatched the entire plot from the beginning himself, or simply wheedled it out of his valet. What we do know is that the former diplomat got his hands on the promissory note relatively quickly and began using it against the British as proof of their skulduggery. On 28 March 1915, the *New York Times* reported that:

'Sir Roger Casement, who has been making sensational anti-English statements in Berlin since the war began, recently asserted that his valet had been bribed by the British Minister to procure his murder. The valet, Adler Christensen, in a long interview in the Hamburger Fremdenblatt, *likewise told of several interviews he had with Mr Findlay in which he said he was bribed to procure the death of the former Irish nationalist leader.'*

The report quoted Findlay's letter in full, and misinformation flew back and forth as each side blamed the other. Casement was now distrustful of his lover and wrote in his diary:

'I am not sure of Adler. His air and manner have greatly changed since he came back – or rather since he went away. He confesses that he now "admires Findlay! Findlay is a man."'[31]

Looking back some 110 years later, Christensen seems to have been a man who was utterly devoid of a moral compass and while there is no evidence that he ever took a penny to turn Judas and betray his lover, that was probably more down to incompetence than loyalty to Roger.

On 1 February 1915, Casement wrote a long letter to Sir Edward Grey in which he tried to divest himself of his honours. Pointing out that he had already surrendered his pension, he lambasted the British government for its part in the Findlay affair and then signed off in characteristically diplomatic style:

'I am sir, your most obedient humble servant.'

Grey did not reply.

By year's end, Casement was in failing health and losing what faith he had had in the depleted ranks of the 30 men who were now left in his 'Irish Brigade'. In fact rather than drawing in republican heroes, his pathetic band had attracted some of the worst men in the camp, many of whom simply wanted a ticket home and failing that, a means to secure 'back pay' and improved rations. Some began to fear that by colluding with the Germans, they were now committing high treason and faced possible execution and while Casement sought to placate their fears, telling them that they were 'Irish' and not beholden to British court martials, it is doubtful whether even he believed that.

Casement also got involved in the periphery of a plan known as 'The Hindu German Conspiracy' which aimed to foment rebellion in British-controlled South Asia. That involvement suggests to some academics that Casement's mission was more anti-imperialist than anti-British in nature, but his written words somewhat contradict that.

In letters home and articles for pro-republican publications and the German English-language propaganda sheet *The Continental Times*, he railed ever more frenziedly against England which he was now calling the 'Tyrant of the Earth' and the 'World Enslaver'. Ill or not, Casement continued to write at the same extraordinary pace as he had done his entire adult life – an average of about 3,000 words a day – making him certainly the most prolific Irish Republican writer of the time. Never adept at learning foreign languages, let alone Irish Gaelic, which he tried and failed to master repeatedly, he struggled to pick up any German and mostly communicated with his local allies and contacts in broken French or English.

As 1915 turned to 1916, the Germans appeared to lose all but passing interest in Casement and his small band of volunteers, and funding for weapons and training was virtually cut off at the very moment when it was needed most.

For in Ireland, come the spring of 1916, the military council of the Irish Republican Brotherhood were actively plotting the overthrow of British rule. The plan was to take advantage of the nationwide holiday on Easter Monday, 24 April 1916, and to that end, the rebels needed guns and troops. Casement turned to Berlin and lobbied hard but the Germans were unwilling to get behind the uprising, believing that it was doomed to failure. Having initially promised officers, troops and 200,000 rifles, they eventually reduced the offer to 20,000 guns and no men at all.

With the die cast, Roger Casement decided that he had no other option but to head home.

On 4 April 1916, he and six others climbed into SM U20, a submarine that had capacity for just four passengers in addition to its 35-strong crew, and set off across the North Sea. The sub subsequently broke down and the little band were obliged to transfer to SM U-19, which was even more cramped. A sick man already, the voyage, in the desperate conditions of a submerged diesel boat, only made Casement's health problems worse. Now calculating that without sufficient German support, the uprising was indeed doomed to fail, he planned to get ahead of the shipment of weapons that was travelling under cover of a captured British cargo ship, the *Aud*, and warn the leaders off the rebellion, before a bloodbath ensued.

British intelligence had got wind of the *Aud* and tracked it the whole way. On 20 April it was intercepted by HMS *Bluebell* and having been directed to Cork harbour was scuttled by its crew on 22 April. A day earlier, a very sickly Roger Casement and his band of unmerry men had disembarked from their submarine and clambered into a collapsible boat – which promptly collapsed. The swim to the shore in the icy Atlantic waters did for him and realising that he was too ill to make the onward journey, he sent one of his disciples, an Irish American called John McGoey, to raise the alarm and to stop the rebellion. McGoey never reached Dublin, for having calculated that the game was up he fled for the hills instead.

Casement was arrested shortly thereafter, while resting in a nearby Celtic ring fort. He claimed, unconvincingly, to be an English author out for a stroll, but his famous face had gone ahead of him and when weapons were found nearby, he was taken into custody. At the station the prisoner was quickly identified as the once celebrated diplomat turned German collaborator, Sir Roger Casement.

It was now Good Friday, 21 April 1916, and his terrible martyrdom was about to run its course.

* * *

Casement had been moved to London and was being interrogated by Basil Thomson, head of the CID and Captain Reginald Hall of British intelligence when news broke, on Easter Monday, that the uprising had begun.

That afternoon at a lively emergency session of Parliament, the newly elected populist Independent MP Noel Pemberton Billing, who just a month earlier had won his seat in a wartime by-election, railed against the Judas Casement and asked PM Herbert Asquith to inform the house 'when this traitor will be shot?'[32] to rousing cheers from both sides of the house.

The Easter Uprising failed and, in its aftermath, Casement was transferred from Brixton to the Tower of London, where for the next two weeks he was held in solitary confinement. We have already seen the impact that such imprisonment can have on an inmate and his mental health deteriorated rapidly. In his cell, a house in the outer walls of the Tower, he was guarded by a Welsh corporal called 'King' who in the 1970s would reveal to a biographer[33] that Casement tried to kill himself. Roger had hidden a phial of poison in his hair, but for the cyanide to work, he had to introduce it straight into his bloodstream and when his attempt failed, he tried to kill himself by swallowing the rusty bent nails with which he had cut open his skin instead.

That attempt also failed.

On 13 May 1916, the 14 leaders of the uprising were executed by firing squad at Kilmainham Gaol in Dublin. Their bodies were then taken to Arbour Hill and unceremoniously buried. And the effect of it all seems to have energised Casement who almost immediately started to bounce back. Two days after the 14 were executed in Dublin, a preliminary hearing was held in London and it resulted in his transfer to Brixton prison hospital where his spirits and conditions started to lift. As he sat in his cell, his allies and friends rallied too and his ever-loyal cousin, Gertrude Bannister, led the charge. Approaching famous figures, including George Bernard Shaw, Arthur Conan Doyle and Alice Stopford Green, she and they began campaigning for clemency.

The sensational case of Rex v Sir Roger Casement – Britain's most famous diplomat turned Irish traitor – quickly gained worldwide attention and across the pond became a veritable cause célèbre. America had yet to enter the war on Britain's side and the powerful media tycoon, William Randolph Hearst, who 20 years later would organise young

William Hitler's tour of the USA, came in behind Casement's cause. Back in Britain nobody played a more prominent role than the Irish playwright George Bernard Shaw, who, while professing that he was 'no Casementite', helped set out the supporting evidence for the defence. Shaw argued, convincingly, that Roger simply could not receive a fair trial in an English court in the current circumstances as the entire apparatus of the state and the press were fundamentally biased against him.

The case opened on Monday 26 June 1916 at the Royal Courts of Justice in the Strand, and it was the hottest ticket in town. Casement's supporters, including the former British ambassador to Brazil, Sir William Haggard, and Grace Duggan, fiancée of Lord Curzon, the recently departed Viceroy of India, struggled to get a seat as the legal theatre played out in the blistering atmosphere of a heatwave.

The former diplomat was charged with high treason 'by adhering to the King's enemies elsewhere than in the King's realm – to wit in the Empire of Germany – contrary to the Treason Act, 1351.' Six counts of betrayal were listed, five of which related to his visits to prison camps to recruit PoWs and the last for engaging on a 'warlike and hostile expedition'.

Leading the prosecution case for the Crown was Sir Frederick (F.E.) Smith, KC, MP, then the Attorney General and, coincidentally both Winston Churchill's best friend and a fulsome Ulster Unionist who – as would be pointed out during the trial – had himself helped ship armaments to the paramilitary Ulster Volunteers.

No English barrister would step up to defend Casement, so his team was headed by Dublin-born Alexander Sullivan KC. Taking George Bernard Shaw's lead, Sullivan argued that the wording of the 1351 Treason Act only applied to crimes committed on British soil and that as he had been in Germany, Casement could not be tried fairly under its terms. Much was made of the absence of commas in the ancient act – as it had been written in Norman French which did not use them – and as such the line which translated as: 'Adherent to the King's enemies in his realm giving them aid and comfort in the realm and elsewhere' could be read in two different ways.

Sullivan also made a big deal out of the hypocrisy at play, not least regarding Smith himself arming the Ulster Volunteers. Smith went in hard. Highlighting Casement's character flaws and his willingness to accept a knighthood from the King just two years before turning Judas-like against the state, he described the treachery as: 'as malignant in quality as it was sudden in origin'.

This was turning into far more than just a trial of a former diplomat who had tried to recruit some PoWs. To the British establishment, through his deeds and betrayal, Casement had come to epitomise the very soul of the errant Emerald isle itself. Here was the manifestation of the wilful child, Ireland, who despite years of brutalisation at the hands of the patriarch, was daring to turn its back on the abusive family home and forge a place for itself in the world. Perhaps appreciating his own growing symbolism, on 27 April it was announced that Casement wished to make a statement to the court. The news was met with a rush from all quarters, as members of the public jostled with court reporters to get back into the courtroom after lunch.

The man from the *Daily Mail* described what happened next:

'When the Clerk of Arraigns called the name of the prisoner, Sir Roger stood up with a sheaf of papers shaking in his hands. His face was pale with the pallor of old ivory. His debonair attitude, his feather-lightness had suddenly vanished and here was a man shaking all over and holding on to the dock rail to steady himself.'[34]

Casement pulled himself together and gave an electric performance which railed against the injustice of using an archaic 565-year-old law against him:

'Today a man may forswear God . . . without fear or penalty . . . all earlier statutes having gone the way of Nero's edicts against the Christians; but that constitutional phantom "the King" can still dig up from the dungeons and torture-chambers of the Dark Ages a law that takes a man's life and limb for an exercise of conscience.

'The law that I am charged under has no parentage in love and claims the allegiance of today on the ignorance and blindness of the past. I am being tried, in truth, not by my peers of the live present, but

by the fears of the dead past; not by the civilization of the twentieth century, but by the brutality of the fourteenth; not even by a statute framed in the language of the land that tries me, but emitted in the language of an enemy land.

'Edward III was king, not only of the realm of England, but also of the realm of France, and he was not king of Ireland. Yet his dead hand to-day may pull the noose around the Irishman's neck.'

It was an extraordinary speech which laid bare the hypocrisy of the law, the humbug of British imperialism, the cant of the establishment and the inherent fallacy that a man could be sentenced to death for treachery, purely by dint of where he had been born and what he believed. Roger Casement was patently no Judas. It was the British state that viewed him as such because it chose – on the back of a 600-year-old law – to deem his loyalty to his real homeland, Ireland, as treachery.

The jury retired on 29 April and took less than an hour to reach a verdict. The defendant was found guilty, sentenced to death and removed to Pentonville to await execution. The following day, in an act of very British pettiness, he was formally stripped of the knighthood he himself had previously attempted to return.

Casement was the first person to suffer degradation of the honour since Francis Mitchell in 1621.

Casement's legal team appealed his sentence and on 17 July, Sullivan reiterated his arguments. The appeals judges deliberated over whether two spaces in the parchment were 'equivalent to commas' before concluding that they were – and the sentence was upheld.

Arthur Conan Doyle made one final attempt to save his friend's life and organised a petition which was signed by many of those famous people who had crossed Casement's path down the years. The campaign gained traction on both sides of the Atlantic and many rallied to help the condemned man. The brutal manner in which the Easter Rebellion had been crushed and the execution of its ringleaders had received international condemnation, not least in the USA Irish diaspora, and Casement's considerable fame went before him which gave considerable succour to his cause.

However, even as Conan Doyle fought the famous diplomat's corner, copies of the prisoner's private 'black diaries' were being surreptitiously distributed ahead of him.

The diary extracts were proof, in the British authorities' minds, of Casement's 'sexual and moral degeneracy' and the circulation of extracts was a deliberate act of state-sponsored homophobia designed to blacken his reputation. This evidence appalled some of those who saw it and turned them from the cause.

Ever since, there has been an ongoing debate as to the authenticity of those diaries and whether they were in fact fakes knocked up at MI7's forgeries department. It's a bitter debate – infused in no small part by suspicion and a very nasty dose of rank homophobia with some Casement supporters, even now, refusing to accept that this great Irish hero was gay. Suffice to say that a broad consensus of historians and academics now accept that Casement wrote the diaries. And while there are some minor discrepancies between white and black accounts, it seems inconceivable that a forger would have been able to go to such extraordinary lengths, and in such a very short space of time, to fabricate such a detailed and believable account of his sexual and non-sexual encounters across 1903, 1910 and 1911. We are talking thousands of words, detailing hundreds of encounters and days and appointments. It simply would not have been feasible. And more to the point, Roger Casement was very obviously gay.

In a discussion on the *Bad Gay* podcast in May 2020, one of the hosts, Huw Lemmey, put it thus:

'If they are forgeries, I think the forger was gay . . . the references to thrusting . . . this is a pornographic mindset . . . he also uses gay Congo slang so if they were forgeries they did an extremely good job.'[35]

During the trial, F.E. Smith and Sullivan discussed jointly whether the diaries might be used in court to argue that Casement was 'guilty but insane' thus saving him from the executioner's rope. Sullivan was told that he could inspect the originals, but Casement did not wish to pursue that line of defence – which strongly suggests he knew the diaries were both genuine and his own. After all, if they had been forged, he would have sought to weaponise them against the Crown as he had done over the promissory note in Norway in 1915.

In his fate, the sickly Casement had already calculated that he would be a martyr and appears to have been reconciled with it. Perhaps he was from the start. As he left the U-boat for Ireland that Good Friday morning in April, the captain, Raimund Weisbach had asked him if he needed anything else and he had replied: 'Only my shroud.'

Others were not and even the Irish Judas had his Judases too. When Arthur Conan Doyle approached Joseph Conrad and Herbert Ward and asked them to lend their names to the petition, they both refused. Conrad had already turned decisively against Casement. The war was personal to him, as it was for so many, and he had been in Poland – then a part of the Austro-Hungarian Empire when it began. His elder son, Borys, aged just 17, was serving at the front and was fighting at the Battle of the Somme, which had begun just three weeks before Casement's trial started. Conrad's fears for his boy's safety were in his own words: 'a continual wound and distraction'.[36]

Herbert Ward's refusal to step up and help cut even more deeply. Ward had actually turned against Roger from the start of World War I and as it played out, his annoyance with his old friend turned to hate. Ward was 51 in 1914, too old to sign up for active service but wanting to 'do his bit' had volunteered to serve at the front as a lieutenant in the Number 3 Ambulance committee instead. Displaying extraordinary courage, he was mentioned in dispatches and awarded the Croix de Guerre, before getting seriously injured during a bombardment in 1915 and invalided home.

His wounds would contribute to his premature death in the Spanish influenza epidemic in 1919 but three years previously, in January 1916, while Casement was failing to recruit PoWs in Germany, a little part of Ward had already died. For it was that month that he received news that his eldest son Charles had been killed at Neuve Chapelle while serving at the front. Later that year he and his wife, the remarkable sculptor Sarita Sanford, changed their youngest son's name by deed poll from 'Roger' to 'Rodney'.

Those who remained loyal to Casement suffered too. In late July, his cousin Gertrude Bannister, the Senior Mistress at St Anne's School for girls in Caversham, England, was told that the governors had decided to dismiss her on the grounds that her name 'had become public'.

Back home at Magherintemple there was considerable disquiet too, not least because Roddie's cousins were serving as officers in the Royal Navy.

As he waited around to die, Casement began to pen a series of farewell letters to old acquaintances and loved ones – or at least those who were still talking to him. His mind had turned to his fate and to dreams of the Antrim coast and to his cousin Elizabeth Bannister he wrote:

'Don't let my body lie here – get me back to the green hill by Murlough – by the McGarry's [sic] house looking down on the Moyle – that's where I'd like to be now and that's where I'd like to lie.'[37]

Execution was marked for 3 August 1916 and timed to be reported the following day – on the second anniversary of the outbreak of war – for maximum propaganda effect. This traitor's terrible example would be contrasted against those of the hundreds of thousands of men who had willingly and heroically given their lives in defence of the British Empire.

Casement awoke early that final morning and having finally been received into the Catholic Church under the terms of *articulo mortis**, took his first and last Holy Communion before being escorted to the scaffold by the executioner John Ellis. His last recorded words were: 'Lord have mercy upon my soul.'

At six minutes past nine, the Pentonville prison bell rang, signalling that the prisoner was dead and the crowd that had gathered outside its walls drifted quietly away.

A deliberately invasive and unnecessary autopsy followed before his body was thrown naked into that Pentonville grave and covered in quicklime.

---

* Casement claimed his Catholic mother had him secretly baptised on a childhood trip to North Wales. The Catholic Church in fact only accepted him because he was about to die.

English pettiness continued in the wake of his death. Plain Roger Casement now became the first entry in the history of *Who's Who* not to make it into the biographical sequel *Who Was Who*.

* * *

In republican circles, the death of this remarkable man was swiftly forged into the realms of myth. That caused problems of its own because Roger Casement was as flawed as he was heroic – not least because this Protestant, gay, former diplomat did not conform to the usual stereotypes of an Irish rebel. His mythologisers were particularly disconcerted by his sexuality.

In 1936, an American author called William J. Maloney published a book called *The Forged Casement Diaries*, which essentially claimed that the British government had blackened his name and it inspired W. B. Yeats to write a famous poem called 'The Ghost of Roger Casement', which was published the following year:

'Draw round, beloved and bitter men
Draw round and raise a shout;
The ghost of Roger Casement
Is beating at the door.'
~ W. B. Yeats

The poem accused the British propagandist, Alfred Noyes, of promulgating the 'fake diaries' and to confuse matters further, Noyes himself then wrote a letter to Irish newspapers suggesting he had indeed been conned into perpetrating disinformation.

In 1957, Noyes turned completely on his former employers at the Home Office and even published a book called *The Accusing Ghost*, which argued that the diaries were indeed forgeries. That argument rumbles on and it's tempting to surmise that the refusal by many in the republican community, over many decades, to accept the diaries were his and insist instead that they must be British forgeries has as much to do with that 'embarrassing truth' as it does with understandable mistrust of the British establishment. Even today, more than a century after his death, Casement continues to be denied his true sexual identity and the conspiracy theory rumbles on in academic circles and the comments sections of online book reviews.

In the years that followed his reinterment, Casement's reputation and legend rose and fell with the tides of Irish history and the 'troubles' which from 1969 onwards cast a further dark shadow over Anglo-Irish relations once more. His name, once so celebrated or berated depending on your point of view, drifted from broader public perception in Britain, whose establishment for the most part continued to view neighbouring Ireland as a naughty and sometimes dangerous wayward child rather than a friend and sovereign equal.

And Roger, nomadic for so much of his life, continues to be denied that last resting place he craved too.

Setting aside the many misjudgements of his life, some truths are a given. Roger Casement was a brave, brilliant, forward-thinking man whose human rights work set the template for NGOs and Irish foreign policy across the century and a quarter that followed. This handsome, debonair, gay icon was also the quintessential romantic revolutionary. A writer of poetry and an idealist who dreamed of a better future for the dispossessed people of the world.

Though famous both in life and death, his name does not resonate today as much as other figures in the struggle for Irish freedom and the reason perhaps is that there is something about him that remains forever just out of reach.

* * *

The role of the traitor is to serve as a warning to the rest of society. Through their heinous betrayal of the rest of us they define the overarching mores and shared values of the broader society and the time in which they lived, and that is why the likes of Vidkun Quisling and William Joyce (Lord Haw Haw) live on in infamy.

But life and history are not fairy tales and as in the case of Roger Casement, loyalty is a complicated business. Sometimes the societal 'bad guy' is the good guy and it is contemporary society or the establishment itself that is the antagonist.

Having been caught distributing leaflets at their university in Munich in February 1943, Sophie Scholl, a member of the anti-Nazi White Rose movement, was tried, alongside her brother Hans and their friend Christoph Probst, for treason. Their crime – which amounted to an attempt to warn their fellow students against the evil, extremism and state-sanctioned killing that had been normalised in Nazi Germany – resulted in their executions by guillotine four days later. Their names lived on only in infamy as traitors and terrorists who had dared to work against the Fatherland, but in 1945 and following the defeat of the Nazi regime, the narrative was corrected and Sophie and her fellow activists became the real heroes of the story.

But it gets even more complicated because the waters of true patriotism are forever muddied – and some, whom we might reasonably dub 'treacherous', might believe that they were doing the right thing.

Philippe Pétain, the one-time hero of Verdun, who in the 1920s and 1930s was viewed as one of France's greatest military heroes, is now broadly remembered as a villain for making peace with the Nazis after the fall of Paris in 1940. Pétain did so, he claimed, because he thought that he was doing his duty and saving France from the worse fate of total occupation. His erstwhile friend and protégé Charles de Gaulle as well as those who fought to save France from occupation disagreed and with the liberation of France in 1944, Pétain was arrested, put on trial and sentenced to death as a traitor. Though that was later commuted to solitary confinement – for life – when Pétain died in 1951, he did so in disgrace and his name lives on in ignominy among all but his defenders on the nationalist far right of French politics.

Then there is the case of the Foreign Office diplomat 'Kim' Philby who was awarded an OBE for his wartime intelligence work in 1946 and at the peak of his career, was very nearly promoted to the very top of MI6. It was only in 1963 that it was revealed that across the previous 20 years he had been a double agent who had betrayed countless agents and colleagues to the KGB. Having fled to Moscow he was then celebrated as a hero and given a whole breast-full of medals by the USSR including the 'Order of Lenin' for his loyalty and work.

The Russians, and indeed many British communists, saw Philby as a hero and the Soviets put his face on stamps and celebrated him as such. In fact, under the autocratic reign of Vladimir Putin, the rogue agent is once again being celebrated by the modern Russian Federation and a road near the Kremlin was named after him as recently as 2018, while the intelligence agency (FSB) honours him and his work with a full biography on their website.

Many of history's most celebrated heroes could equally be seen as turncoats too and depending on your point of view, George Washington, the first president of the United States, is just such an example. Washington, after all, spent much of his early life as a loyal citizen of the British Crown and was even the commander of the Virginia Regiment before leading 'the colonists' to revolt. Conversely, Benedict Arnold, still viewed in the USA as one of the nation's worst traitors, could just as well be deemed a 'patriot' on the other side of the Atlantic, for having been born a British subject, he served in the colonial army and in siding with England against the rebels was only returning to the fold.

People become traitors for any number of reasons. Some do so for glory, others out of revenge or ideology or for want of cash and others still simply because they enjoy the game. But Roger Casement, like so many other freedom fighters in history, was undeserving of the epithet – because after all he wasn't really a traitor at all.

So while Britain has artfully sought to forget him, in the Republic of Ireland, he is celebrated still, albeit up to a point.

There are obvious tributes like Casement Park, the Gaelic football stadium named after him, as well as that statue on the Dublin coast and his grave at the Glasnevin cemetery. But even so and much like Judas in the celebrated Da Vinci fresco of *The Last Supper*, it can also feel that even in Ireland, his face is cast in shadow. The stadium and the monument both sit on the edges of the capital and though his grave lies near the entrance to the famous cemetery, in truth it occupies an underwhelming patch of grass by the tarmac, where the hearses turn around.

It might all just be coincidence of course, but when you go looking for him, it can feel as if this English-accented, career diplomat, Protestant son of Ulster has never been fully invited in. It's striking, for example, that his image is absent from the very places you might most expect to find him, so while Bono and Yeats feature prominently in the National Portrait Gallery in Dublin, there is no sign of the revolutionary martyr.

In Northern Ireland, the trail goes colder still and that is far less surprising. At the northern coastal town of Ballycastle in Antrim, where he spent so much of his youth, I found almost no hint of him at all – until I drove out of town to the family home at Magherintemple. The Casements still live at the great house and I was warmly welcomed in and given a tour by his kinsman Patrick, who was only too happy to discuss his relative's life and legacy and remind me that Roger should really be far better remembered for his human rights work than he is.

And – as I left – it was Patrick who kindly pointed me in the direction of Roger Casement's ghost.

With the sun dipping that afternoon, I drove away from Ballycastle and up towards Murlough Point, the place where Roger had wanted to be buried. The weather was dependably unruly and there was a sense among my family, who were along for the ride, that everyone else would rather be in the pub.

Turning off the narrow lane we bumped along a still smaller track until a large, rudimentary wooden cross loomed at the cliff edge. This was the spot that Casement had dreamed of in those last weeks of his life – and as we clambered out of the hire car and into the elements, the four of us were stunned into silence.

The wind was coming in hard off the sea and white waves were breaking fiercely on the coastline beneath us. Sinister black clouds swirled above our heads as the last rays of light cast down on Rathlin Island looming across the bay. Here was Ireland in all its raw, sensational, savage beauty – the very manifestation, in fact, of everything any poet or dreamer might imagine this place to be.

My 17-year-old daughter was now clinging to the cross in a brilliant yellow raincoat that stood out starkly against the brooding sky. With her long red hair blowing in the gale and her blue eyes alight and burning with life, she was drinking it all in.

She turned and yelled across the wind: 'Dad! Dad! Who was he again?'

And in that moment – I think I understood.

CHAPTER THREE

PEASANTS

Who Really Fears the Mob?

It was the morning of 21 December 1989 and the *Conducator* (ruler) of the Socialist Republic of Romania, Nicolae Ceausescu, had just stepped out on to the balcony of the Central Committee building in Bucharest to a rapturous welcome.

Beneath him, in Palace Square, a 'spontaneous' 100,000-strong crowd were cheering his name and waving red banners and portraits of him and his wife, Elena, and as he surveyed the vast spectacle, the Conducator could not possibly have foreseen what was about to happen next.

The great leader thanked his 'comrades' and started to deliver one of his trademark, mind-numbingly boring speeches until, about eight minutes in, a curious scream erupted from the back of the crowd and a single word started to echo about the square:

'TI-MI-SO-ARA! TI-MI-SO-ARA! TI-MI-SO-ARA!'

Aghast at the peasants' insolence, the taken aback Conducator tapped his microphone and tried to speak once again but as he did, the noise turned to a roar and soon his bodyguard, the aptly named Florian Rat, had appeared behind him in a pork pie hat and was shouting:

'They are entering the building!'

Seconds later the live state broadcast was cut.

Confused studio technicians were not sure what was happening and voices on the surviving audio suggest that they thought an earthquake may have caused the disturbance. Eventually they managed to re-establish the link and when it resumed, an enraged Ceausescu was now shouting: 'Sit down and keep calm!' while his wife stood beside him, screaming angrily at the crowd.

'Return to the square, comrades!' the Conducator added dolefully – but by now nobody was listening, because in a panic, the state militia had detonated tear gas canisters and chaos had descended on the square.

'Down with the murderers!' the people were now shouting, 'Romania awake!'

The TV audio then picked up Elena's voice as she told her husband:

'Talk to them; promise them something.'

And so, he did just that. Looking for all the world like a bewildered child chasing a bolting stallion with a half-nibbled carrot, Nicolae started making promises. There would be a 'pension rise', a 'family allowance rise' and a 2,000 lei upgrade in state pay (*c.*£2.50 in 2025 money) he said; but it was all to no avail and soon the great leader and his entourage had left the balcony and disappeared inside.

By day's end, dozens were dead and hundreds more wounded on the streets, but believing themselves invincible, the Ceausescus opted to ride it out in their heavily guarded headquarters. It was to prove to be a fatal error of judgement.

The next morning, a soldier on an armoured vehicle in the streets beyond the dictator's stronghold symbolically removed the magazine from his machine gun and waved it at the crowd. Across Bucharest the cry went up: 'The army is on our side!' and the Ceausescus now had no option but to flee.

At 11.25 a.m. a helicopter appeared above the Central Committee building and as it touched down, the dictator and his entourage ran to greet it. Ceausescu spoke with his pilot, Lieutenant-Colonel Vasile Malutan, who told him that he could not possibly carry so many people but was ordered to make it happen anyway and shortly after that, the French aircraft limped into the grey sky. Space was so tight on board that the mechanic had to sit in the dictator's lap.[1] Above the noise of the rotors and the engines, Malutan was ordered to fly to Snagov, a small town some 60 kilometres northeast of Bucharest, where the self-styled 'Genius of the Carpathians' owned a villa which had been 'liberated' from the Romanian royal family.

On the brief journey north, the Ceausescus had time to reflect on how it had all gone so wrong.

Throughout the course of 1989, the rusting gates of the Iron Curtain had been creaking back and as Soviet leader Mikhail Gorbachev's rapprochement with the West had blossomed, there had been a wider push for reform beyond the USSR. Protests in Poland, which started in 1988, had caused the first dominoes to tumble and subsequently the Berlin Wall had fallen too. As the Romanian dictator's helicopter staggered through Romanian airspace, the Velvet Revolution continued apace in nearby Czechoslovakia and neighbouring Hungary was changing too.

But while the Ceausescus' current woes were linked to this wider Eastern and Central European pattern, they only really had themselves to blame.

Under the Conducator, Romania had not been just another Soviet satellite state. Though a signatory to the Warsaw Pact in 1955, during the 1960s the country had witnessed a period of 'de-Stalinisation' which had seen it cut its own unique groove. This had led to some surprising outcomes and following the Soviet invasion of Czechoslovakia in 1968, Ceausescu had even gone as far as to stand on that same balcony in Palace Square and condemn the USSR. That move resulted in some considerable global acclaim and under his leadership Romania went on to make overtures to the West even as it cosied up to China, North Korea and Moscow.

Henceforth, the Conducator had walked the perilous tightrope between the competing sides in the Cold War. Ceausescu was the first communist dictator to host a US president, the first to recognise West German sovereignty, the first world leader to offer condolences to Cuba after the execution of Che Guevara in Bolivia in 1968, the first to join the International Monetary Fund in 1972 and the only one to compare himself favourably with Vlad the Impaler – whom we shall meet later. Alone among the Eastern Bloc nations, Romania participated in the 1984 Los Angeles Olympics and Ceausescu was the only communist dictator to ever get knighted by Queen Elizabeth II.

In turn, the West deliberately courted Romania in the belief that he was a weak chink in the Iron Curtain and purported to believe that the 'enlightened' autocrat was someone they could do business with. In fact, nothing could have been further from the truth because since a state visit to North Korea, Ceausescu had effectively become Europe's Kim Il Sung.

On that trip to Pyongyang, in 1971, the Ceausescus had witnessed the DPRK's 'Juche' policy first-hand and were impressed. Juche's guiding principles highlighted the importance of nationalism, isolationism and fiscal and political autonomy, but the bit that the Conducator had really liked was how it was all propped up by a massive personality cult. Subsequent to their return home, the Ceausescus plagiarised the lot and Juche became the template for the dear leader's July Theses, announced in the summer of 1971, which plunged the country headlong into a full-blown cultural revolution.

Shortly thereafter, Bucharest's lively, cosmopolitan nightlife disappeared – soon to be followed by anything joyous or clever. Books that offended the sensibilities of the regime were banned, art was suppressed and Romania's rich theatre culture was all but eradicated as companies were obliged to put 'representatives of the workers'[2] on their boards and ensure that they produced Soviet realist operas and plays. The incurious and unsophisticated Ceausescus were particularly suspicious of writers, and anyone who owned a typewriter was obliged to apply for a licence. Even purchasing paper could land you in hot water – assuming you could find it – and anyone seeking to take some deep breaths and relax in the face of it all was out of luck too – because just for good measure, Elena and Nicolae banned yoga as well.

At the same time, millions of dollars were pumped into the Ceausescu cult of personality and a heavily doctored image of the leader was posted in schools and offices across the land. Nicolae's *omagiu* (birthday homage) held in January became a major national event that by the 1980s had officially replaced Christmas.

The July Theses was not only cultural but economic as well, and through a policy of *Systemisation* it sought to modernise and homogenise Romania.

In the early 1970s, a third of the adult population still worked in agriculture in a vast patchwork of mainly subsistence smallholdings which had changed little across the last 1,000 years. These peasant farmers represented a vision of Romania which was at odds with the dictator's enormous self-regard, and so Nicolae decreed that the country would make a progressive leap forward, whether the peasants liked it or not. Churches, synagogues and historic buildings that stood in the way of his vision were demolished, villages erased off the map and country folk were moved to shoddily built Soviet apartment blocks on the outskirts of the cities.

Romania, which had never wanted for fresh fruit and vegetables, was soon suffering food shortages and collective hunger pangs.

Not everyone in the regime was convinced by the July Theses and early on, some dared to voice concern including Ion Iliescu, former head of propaganda and Minister for Youth – who had once been a close ally of the Ceausescus. For having the audacity to voice an opinion he was pushed to the sidelines of the regime.

As the 1970s gave way to the 1980s, Romania's woes worsened considerably, not least because the hundreds of millions of US dollars that had previously been used to paper over the cracks in the Ceausescus' incompetence and mismanagement disappeared overnight. In the previous decade, as the bad boy of the Warsaw Pact, Romania had been handed billions in loans by international banks and the Shah of Iran, who had sold the regime dirt-cheap oil. But when he was ousted by the Ayatollah and fled to Egypt in February 1979, everything turned to rahat* in Bucharest. By 1982, Romania had foreign debt amounting to $13 billion ($42 billion in 2025 money) obliging Ceausescu to take a line of credit from the IMF on the condition that he reined in spending. Romanians went on to suffer a prolonged bout of desperate austerity and beyond the capital, food, fuel, electricity, medicine and just about everything else either disappeared off the shelves or was severely rationed. Public services were stripped to the bone and by 1982 the average Romanian family's standard of living had fallen by 40 per cent.

* Romanian word for 'shit'.

The misery was compounded by the twin curses of rampant inflation, which saw basic commodities skyrocket in price, and the AIDS pandemic which hit Romania harder than anywhere else in Europe. Government denial made matters worse and cash-strapped hospitals were obliged to recycle syringes as they struggled to deal with the crisis. About 70 per cent of those who contracted HIV/AIDS were children, who by now were just about the only thing the country had in abundance as contraception and abortion (along with divorce) were illegal.

The terrible Petri dish of grinding poverty, HIV/AIDS and the attendant baby boom saw cases of child abandonment hit unprecedented levels, and by 1989 there were at least 100,000[3] children living in orphanages (known as 'the slaughterhouses of souls') in a country with a population of just 22 million.

Throughout it all, the hapless Ceausescu behaved as if Romanians were living in a socialist paradise and insisted that everything was peachy. Obliged, by circumstances, to introduce rationing, the Conducator insisted that it had nothing to do with shortages and was instead part of a national health drive. In a positively Orwellian turn of events, the starving people were actually told that 'Romanians eat too much' and Nicolae took to delivering a series of lectures on state TV about the benefits of dieting. Everyone with a brain knew that the 'Rational Eating Programme' was cover for the terrible food shortages blighting the country[4], but nobody dared whisper that truth outside their homes.

All the while, the preposterous and costly vanity project known as the 'House of the People' continued to be built. This gigantic building, covering 365,000 square metres and employing a team of 700 architects, came to be symbolize all that was wrong with Romania. Built to incorporate an enormous balcony and a gigantic boulevard, this would be the stage on which the Conducator planned to bore not thousands but potentially millions to death as vast crowds waved his picture and chanted his name.

Grotesque, ugly and ill-conceived, it would have been funny if people had not been starving in its shadow.

Despite himself suffering from diabetes, Nicolae Ceausescu did not go on a diet and he and his family continued to live in luxury as they filled their Swiss bank account with cash. At their 80-room Primaverii (Spring) Palace in Bucharest, with its opulent rooms and gold-plated bathrooms, the leader, his wife and three children liked nothing more than to settle down in their private cinema and watch their favourite film, *The Great Gatsby* (1974), starring Robert Redford and Mia Farrow without an apparent paradox in the world.

As they sat munching crisps and sipping beers on the sofa in front of the giant screen, in the rest of Romania, entertainment began to disappear bit by bit. Regional radio went first and then in 1985, the hugely popular second TV channel TVR2, Televiziunea Română 2, disappeared too. With the remaining channel reduced to just a few hours and then a few minutes a day, programming now consisted largely of the diabetic president telling his starving people that they were fat and, frankly, it was no replacement for J.R. Ewing.

Romanian people, you see, had developed a love affair with Western television shows and in addition to *Dallas* had a particular fondness for the British drama series *The Onedin Line* which they had been able to watch throughout the early 1980s. Suddenly deprived of their weekly dose of Larry Hagman and Jessica Benton, those who were able to began tuning into the CIA-backed Radio Free Europe or pointing their TV aerials in the direction of Hungary or Bulgaria instead and in the process, they opened the doors to another world.

The change in listening and viewing habits particularly resonated with the sizeable population of bourgeois ethno-Hungarians in Transylvania who had already been considerably riled by state policies of cultural homogenisation. From the early 1980s onwards, the university town of Timisoara, near the Hungarian border, had been a veritable hotbed of activism and a dissident priest called Laszlo Tokes had made a name for himself as a critic of the regime. His activities drew the attention of the Securitate, and that story was then picked up by Hungarian TV, which beamed it back into Romania.

In October 1989, locals in Timisoara blocked an attempt by officials to evict Tokes and very quickly this 'ethno-Hungarian' protest became the focus for wider, regional discontent. In response to protests on Sunday 17 December, the local militia drove their armoured vehicles aggressively into the centre of the city and began firing over the heads of protesters. Grainy video footage of the incident appeared to show a group of schoolchildren caught up in what looked like an atrocity and when Romanian news channels failed to report the event, rumours about the scale of the killing began to burn out of control across the country.

A small number of people may have been killed and many scores had most certainly been beaten up or arrested, but the actual numbers were hugely inflated and unfortunately for the Conducator it was those unreliable figures that the global media latched on to. When the hugely respected French AFP news service broadcast footage of 19 bodies and mistakenly reported that this was a fraction of the 4,630 who had died in the violence and when Radio Free Europe latched on to the report and broadcast it back into Romania – a full-scale uprising became inevitable.

It later transpired that the 19 corpses had been deliberately dug up from a mass paupers' grave for the benefit of the cameras. The children in the square had not been hurt either. The lack of good, reliable on the ground sources had distorted matters – and in fact the dictator's efforts to totally control the news had backfired on him. Scrambling to cover events, foreign journalists had made mistakes and Ceausescu's enemies had benefitted as a result.

As the couple fled for Snagov, the cacophony of disinformation only got louder and spread wider. Within hours of their helicopter taking off, wild rumours were abounding of Securitate snipers, perched on high buildings, firing randomly into the streets. In response, the military – which was now firmly on the side of the people – started to hand out weapons to members of the public and a series of tragic accidents followed as untrained citizens began shooting Kalashnikovs at moving shadows.

The Ceausescus, meanwhile, had run out of options. Having reached their villa in Snagov they tried calling for help from the compound telephones, only for the numbers to ring out. The couple had suddenly run out of friends and lackeys and even their once loyal pilot Malutan wanted nothing to do with them. Determined to ditch them at the first opportunity, his heart sank when Elena and Nicolae ordered him to fly on to Pitesti with their two bodyguards. An uncomfortable journey ensued until Malutan said that they were short of fuel and was ordered to land.

On the ground, the rest of the party hijacked two cars and drove off towards a nearby model village leaving the relieved pilot behind.

The deluded couple were convinced that they would receive a warm welcome from the local workers, as they had done once before – but instead they were met with a barrage of stones and were forced to flee to a nearby military base where they were promptly arrested.

All those millions of Swiss francs could not save them now and the communist Dracula and his bride were about to meet their end.

On 24 December, Buckingham Palace – which just ten years earlier had played host to the couple on a state visit – announced that Her Majesty the Queen had revoked the dictator's knighthood and a day later, a trial was convened in front of ten military judges in the town of Târgovişte. The Ceausescus were charged on five counts, found guilty of all and sentenced to death. As they were marched to the place of execution, the leader began humming the 'Internationale' until his irritated wife told him:

'Stop it, Nicu. Look, they are going to shoot us like dogs.'[5]

Moments later, the 'Geniuses of the Carpathians' lay dead in a pool of blood. In four days, they had gone from being the most powerful people in Romania to common criminals.

The executions had one remarkable and immediate result. As news of their deaths spread that 25 December afternoon, people across Romania went out and bought trees, decorations, alcohol and food and by nightfall almost the whole country was celebrating Christmas for the first time in decades.

The new regime was led by members of the old including Ion Iliescu, the once close ally of Nicolae and Elena who had turned against them. In the weeks, months and years that followed, Romania started to change – albeit slowly. In 1990 the country held its first free elections which saw Iliescu sweep to power. He went on to be president of Romania for the next decade – in a term of office that was beset by allegations, scandals and controversy.

Good things happened too. *Dallas* and *The Onedin Line* made their way back on to the TV. Contraception and abortion were legalised and following a referendum in 1991, a new constitution was adopted too.

By their very nature, popular revolutions invariably spawn impossible expectations and as in so many other post-Cold War European nations, the brief dawn of hope was soon eclipsed by cynicism, disappointment and corruption. The old communist guard, though now divested of their Lenin busts and red flags, were soon trying to roll back on the promises of a brighter future while the wealthy oligarchs and gangsters they had enabled, moved in and grew richer.

Romania's onward path was slow and painful, and hand in hand with moderate democratic progress came more economic woes, more political instability and more misery for the poorest in society. The country ascended to the EU and joined the euro in 2007 and for some it all heralded opportunity. Startups flourished and the early noughties were a good time for investors and the automotive industry in particular. Eventually, the country rose to become the seventh largest economy in the eurozone and the educated urban middle class became indistinct from those in neighbouring EU countries in clothing and manner. That same bourgeoisie went on to demand and enjoy economic and political reforms and for university-educated people and the middle classes, life was better and despite economic and political setbacks continues to forge forward.

But beyond the thriving metropoles, life for millions of ordinary Romanians has gone on much as it did before. Even as late as 2025, a third of the adult working population are still employed in the agricultural sector and a staggering 98 per cent of Romanian farms are smallholdings, operating on less than ten hectares of land. These modern-day peasant farmers earn, on average, about one third of the salary of other EU farmers and remain one of the most deprived labour forces in Europe.

The distance between the haves and have nots is as great as it ever was, with the only difference being that there are many more 'haves' than there used to be. Inevitably that has left Romania exposed to the egregious threats of foreign meddling and populist politics and all the disinformation, misery and manipulation which that disease can bring. Nostalgia is one hell of a drug and in recent years some politicians have even encouraged the people to hanker after the 'good old days' when Nicolae and Elena ate cake and watched Robert Redford films in their private cinemas – while orphan children starved in the frozen streets.

* * *

The fall of the Ceausescus is a story filled with an array of extraordinary characters, but none are more fascinating than the crowd.

Whether demonstrating in Timisoara, storming the Central Committee building or hounding the dictator to his end, the 'people' are very much the main protagonists in events and when Elena urges her husband to 'promise them something, talk to them' it is almost as if she is urging him to speak to a single entity.

Crowds are fascinating and all of us at some time in our lives will have experienced the transformative sensation that comes with being in one. If you have ever attended a concert, a sporting event or even a political demonstration, you will know how it feels to be part of the mass and how, in the process, we pool our own individuality as we become a cog in a greater whole.

The experience can be liberating and exhilarating and more to the point it can occasionally bring change, which is why, across the centuries, nothing has put the fear of God into ruling elites quite like the presence of a mob.

In the wake of the popular revolutions and uprisings that broke out in Europe in the mid-nineteenth century, many authors turned their attention to the nature of the human herd and its unique collective psychology. In 1841, a Scottish journalist called Charles Mackay wrote an influential book called *Extraordinary Popular Delusions and the Madness of Crowds*, but undoubtedly the most enduring text on the subject came in 1895 courtesy of a French polymath called Gustave Le Bon in his classic work *The Crowd: A Study of the Popular Mind*.

Le Bon was fascinated by the impact of the group on the individual and how people metamorphosise collectively when they become part of a mass. For Le Bon, presence within a collective engenders a sense of anonymity and that can lead to a loss of personal responsibility too.

'An individual in a crowd is a grain of sand amid other grains of sand which the wind stirs up at will.'[6]

By Le Bon's thesis, as crowds dilute both a private sense of liability and integrity, that can make them dangerous and unpredictable. Those amorphised within them and caught up in the moment can lose rationality and even become prone to manipulation and out of character behaviour. This is why otherwise peaceful individuals might suddenly turn violent during, for example, an anti-globalisation protest or a riot whipped up by right-wing rabble-rousers, and start kicking in the windows of the local McDonald's or setting fire to hostels housing asylum seekers.

Crowds, by their nature, don't think critically and can easily be swayed by a charismatic leader. In a crowd we can all risk losing our judgement and rationality which is why so many rioters who end up in the dock will say that they didn't know what came over them, while their defense counsels insist that it was all very out of character. Drawing on examples from recent history and anticipating the rise of the twentieth-century's despots and tyrants, Le Bon wrote that 'the masses have never thirsted after truth. Whoever can supply them with illusions is easily their master' and 'whoever attempts to destroy their illusions, is always their victim'.[7]

'Crowds have a great tendency towards hero worship,' he added, noting that the most effective mobs are usually aroused by symbols, colour, spectacle, flags, repetition, emotion, and are also driven by a sense of anger and injustice and, most of all, simple ideas. Unwittingly, his book was to become a sort of 'how to' guide for Nazis and cigarette marketeers alike. All the worst and most effective elements of Le Bon's theses are present in those pre-war mass rallies at Nuremberg and in advertising aimed at encouraging people to smoke. They are there too in the online world of influencers, TikTok trends, populist political parties and crypto-currency echo chambers.

While most crowds are usually peaceful, no two are ever the same and any mass gathering – and particularly one that has been fomented in anger – always has the risk that it will turn ugly.

Following the death of Mark Duggan, a black British man who was shot by police on the streets of London on 4 August 2011, just such a touchpaper was lit and the tinderbox went up. In the days that followed, righteous anger metamorphosed into widespread civil disobedience that seemed to have little to do with Duggan's death and as matters spiralled, the usual order of things was shaken. The rioting, which began in Tottenham, quickly spread to other boroughs and between 6 and 11 August, violence and fear stalked the streets of London.

In my own neighbourhood in South East London, cars and shops were set alight and masked figures and fear roamed the streets in a febrile and volatile atmosphere which shook all the usual certainties of the community.

As police struggled to contain the situation, London's Mayor, Boris Johnson, holidaying in Canada, reluctantly boarded a plane and came home only to be heckled by angry residents in Clapham who wanted to know where the hell he had been and how it had all been allowed to happen. Johnson told them he understood their anger and with the heckling continuing, took a brush and performatively swept the streets.

Meanwhile, the disturbances had spread to other cities and across that week an estimated 2,815 properties were looted, firebombed or damaged. The riots claimed five lives and saw hundreds of police officers and members of the public injured. By the end of August, an estimated £100 million worth of damage had been done and more than 3,000 people had been arrested.

What was striking, at least for one anonymous journalist at the *Daily Mail*, was that 'respectable' people had been caught up in the madness too. In the wake of the unrest, all sorts of individuals ended up in the dock and the tabloid breathlessly reported that 'a grammar school girl', a 'ballet dancer' and an 'organic chef' had all been involved – 'in moments of madness'.

Justice was soon being dished out – and it was only in hindsight that efforts were made to understand what had really gone on. Ten years after the riots, Vernel Dolor, sentenced to two years for his part in the violence, offered his reasoning for taking to the streets in August 2011 to the BBC:

'People's livelihoods were affected and people's shops were damaged and I fully understand that. And whatever part I played in that I fully accept responsibility for it. But I urge people to see the other side of the coin (too). Behind the riots, there was a community that was strained and frustrated. Frustrated by the very people that are supposed to be helping them. So, it was like we had to enact some sort of violence for things to be heard.'[8]

And in those words, Vernel could have been echoing the sentiments of England's rural peasantry – in 1381.

* * *

Throughout history many an elite has faced its 'Ceausescu Moment'. The point when *the crowd* metamorphoses into *the mob,* when the cheers turn to jeers and when the pliant peasants decide that they have had enough. And although no TV cameras were there to capture it, in June 1381 the ruling Plantagenet elite of England very nearly suffered that fate.

In the early months of that year, an excommunicated priest called John Ball began touring the county of Kent, preaching a gospel of civil disobedience. For 20 years or more, Ball had been less a thorn, more an axe, in the side of the church establishment and was well known for calling out their humbug through social media-like maxims including the famous couplet:

'When Adam delved and Eve span, who then was the gentleman?'

Ball's sermons had made him a hero among the working classes and an enemy of the ruling elite. The rebel cleric had particularly incited the ire of the Archbishop of Canterbury, Simon Sudbury, within whose diocese he conducted most of his sedition. Sudbury had repeatedly tried and failed to silence him and though Ball had been excommunicated in the 1360s and technically wasn't allowed to preach, even that didn't stop him.

Come the late winter of 1380, Sudbury was one of the most important people in England and was now not only its most senior cleric but also its newly appointed Lord Chancellor. These should have been his salad days, but John Ball's tiresome insistence on preaching the actual teachings of Jesus Christ was spoiling the prelate's fun and so he decided to move against him.

In the spring of 1381, Ball was arrested and thrown into Maidstone jail, where he festered in a dark, windowless, black hole on a site now occupied by the Century Sports nightclub. It seemed to be game over for Ball, but just as Ceausescu would discover to his cost 600 years later, rebel priests make formidable enemies and this game of ecclesiastical *whack a mole* was only just warming up.

The important role played by churchmen is just one of the parallels between the Romanian revolution and the great uprising of 1381; another is the lack of reliable, on the ground, eyewitness testimony.

Romanians in 1989 could at least turn their aerials towards Hungary or Bulgaria but even today, anyone wishing to understand the fourteenth-century peasants' revolution in England has just four major sources to fall back on.

They are:

- *The Anonimalle Chronicle*, written by an anonymous, well-connected scribe at the Abbey of St Mary in York, who may have witnessed some of the events.
- An account by Thomas Walsingham, a Benedictine monk, whose contempt for the rabble and admiration for some among the ruling elite is conspicuous in its bias.
- A chronicle by Jean Froissart, a French court historian. Less partisan than the other two he demonstrated a good understanding of the factors that led to the revolt.
- The chronicler Henry Knighton – who while, like the others, denounced the peasants, was unique in not condemning the rebels as wicked and accepted that they gathered with good reason.

Much has been done in recent years to uncover other sources, including most notably legal records, but these four chronicles remain the meat and three veg of the history of the 1381 revolt. Some of it remains positively spellbinding and Froissart's account of John Ball's sermon delivered to the peasant army encamped on Blackheath in South East London in June 1381 is particularly dumbfounding stuff:

'Things cannot go on well in England, nor ever will until everything shall be in common, when there shall be neither vassal nor lord, and all distinctions levelled . . . How ill they have used us . . . They have wines . . . and if we drink, it must be water. They have handsome seats and manors, when we must brave the wind and rain in our labours in the field; but it is from our labour they have the wherewith to support their pomp . . . Let us go to the king, who is young, and remonstrate with him on our servitude, telling him we must have it otherwise, or that we shall find a remedy for it ourselves.'[9]

We don't expect this sort of revolutionary language in late fourteenth-century England and that, perhaps, is down to our many inherent prejudices about our peasant ancestors.

In 1381, the word 'peasant' had yet to enter the vocabulary and rural people were referred to as 'rustici' or 'villeins'. That second word which originally meant 'bound to the soil' is highly illustrative, as its evolution in meaning from 'peasant' to 'person of uncouth manners' to 'criminal' really tells you everything you need to know about the contempt in which the ruling classes have long held of those beneath them in the social hierarchy.

In a sense, 'villein' was the precursor to modern societal terms of scorn like 'chav', 'hoodie' or 'road man' and it demonstrates too how rural folk of that era continue to have a terrible PR problem well into our own. In large part that is because they left no paper trail. In an age when just 5 per cent of the population could read or write, the majority of people gifted posterity with no letters, diaries or journals and that impacts considerably on our view of them. And there's another problem too. For much of history and well into the nineteenth and twentieth centuries, the majority of historians were either establishment lackeys, out and out propagandists or simply not interested in the mass of ordinary people who were thus forged into extras, or comedy sidekicks in the 'real story' of our 'fabulous' kings and queens.

That has done our opinion of the majority of our ancestors no favours at all, not least because the ordinary people in the fourteenth century were by no means all dim-witted Baldrick types dwelling in mud huts and roasting turnips.

So before we go any further, let's take a brief moment to liberate them from the stereotype.

Agricultural society in the Middle Ages was complex and tiered and to generalise about 'everybody' is always a bit of a mistake, but in general and as court and legal records show, our Plantagenet era rural ancestors were well versed in their rudimentary civil rights, perfectly prepared to stick up for themselves and were natural experts in injustice – as it was served to them daily.

They were not averse to the menace of misinformation too and in 1377 a 'Great Rumour' took hold in South Eastern and Western England which claimed that the *Domesday Book* contained an ancient clause which exempted them from taxation and demands made on them by their feudal landlords. Faith in this myth, which, in the absence of Facebook and Twitter, spread on the fourteenth-century platform known as 'word of mouth' was such that at least 40 villages downed tools altogether in the South West and they only picked them up again when swords were pointed in their direction. Events around the Great Rumour are murky – but they do show that when the mood took them, the peasantry were no pushover and the *Domesday Book* continued to be cited long after – much as the *Magna Carta* (1215) or the term 'freemen of the land' were during the 2020 Covid pandemic in order to escape lockdown restrictions.

Life was far from easy. For the first half of the fourteenth century the gulf between the haves and have nots was wider than at any time in history. As spelled out by John Ball in that proto-Marxist Blackheath sermon, the ruling elite lived in luxury, had servants, spoke Norman French and ate meat; the serfs spoke Middle English, lived off pottage, onions, eggs and leeks and dwelt in thatched messuages. The rich spent their days in leisure, playing cards, jousting, hunting, drinking wine and eating swans stuffed with eels. Most everybody else spent theirs toiling in the fields, worrying about inflationary pressure and burying their many children.*

* Some 25 per cent of children died in their first year and about 12 per cent before they reached the age of two.

In 1340s England, about 90 per cent of the population were beholden to their manorial masters. In return for a roof over their head and the right to farm their smallholdings these tenant farmers were obliged to pay hefty tithes and provide unpaid labour, and had an obligation to reap hay and drive their master's goods to market before handing back the profits. But even they weren't at the bottom of the pile because about 40 per cent of the population were unfree serfs who were chattels of their manors and had no titles, property or possessions. Their rights were so limited that in theory, their children couldn't even marry without seeking their feudal lord's permission.

Which is not to say that 'vills' and manorial estates were all oppressive dictatorships presided over by quail-sucking Sheriff of Nottingham types either. Estate management was a fundamentally tedious job and most of the nobility, whether 'lay' or 'clerical', preferred hunting, praying and fighting wars to running their land and hanging out with the hoi polloi.[10] As such they relied on stewards (like William Harrison in Chapter One) to run their estates and manage disagreements through local seigneurial* justice courts. So society was highly stratified, yes, but it had a certain order, and everyone knew – or rather was expected to know – their place in it. And things would have gone on in much the same way had the Bubonic Plague not arrived in England in June 1348 and wiped out an estimated 40 per cent of the population in 24 months.

When you consider that all the wars and pandemics of the twentieth century killed less than 3 per cent of British people across a time span of 100 years, that is one staggering figure.

The Great† Pestilence not only laid bare the disparities of wealth between rich and poor and the imbalance of dependency between one on the other, but it also underlined the utter incompetence of the ruling elite.

The feudal system was soon being questioned and as it was, little unity was forthcoming between the different sides. The people across

* The lowest rank in the landed gentry – just below an esquire and just above a yeoman which was the highest rank of servant e.g. a steward.
† Everything 'bad' was 'great' back then.

the social divide did not put their differences aside and clap for reapers or bang pans for the Black Prince. Nobody summoned up the Siege of Orléans spirit or walked in circles round their smallholding to raise money for sisters of charity. Instead, in the Black Death's wake, everyone tried to make a buck and for those who had survived there was no greater opportunity than the empty spaces left by the dead. Prior to 1348, the feudal system had resulted in a shortage of land for tenants and landowners alike – now, there was a veritable abundance of it. The rich grew richer, the class below grew wealthy too and even those at the bottom made money as the old certainties began to crumble. Depopulation had resulted in increased social mobility, the weakening and even disappearance of the feudal bonds and many serfs began to rise above their station or simply disregard their status in the pecking order and wander off and do their own thing.

Longer term, the terrible disease and its consequences spawned another outcome, as those not-so-dumb villeins started to appreciate that with a labour shortage, they could start demanding better pay. Wages soared and, with them, inflation and soon the ruling elite began to decide that they didn't much like the free market – at least where the labour supply was concerned.

The rabble were, to put it frankly, getting ideas and those at the top started putting pressure on Edward III to impose legislation that would keep them in their place. That was easier said than done though because 'new money' had given another band of people significant and increasing power too. In the City of London, the emerging guilds and livery companies now had, among their ranks, some very wealthy people indeed and, in fact, many a merchant was now richer than their supposed social superior. These prototypical 'nouveau riches' were building grand houses and wearing fur and purple and gold cloth to the point where it was getting hard to distinguish where everyone sat in the artificially constructed social hierarchy. It was not just the merchants either because among the ranks of the franklins (or freemen) and all the way down to the peasantry, people were beginning to wear better clothes and put on airs and graces. This blurring of boundaries irked the upper tiers of the elite so much that in 1363, Edward III was obliged to reissue the 25-year-old 'Sumptuary Laws' which laid down in Latin just how bling you could be.

'Poulaines', which were pimped pointy shoes, were the ultimate outward fashion accessory of the era and very much the equivalent to owning a flashy car or fancy watch today. These bunion-forging footwear Ferraris had long been the pride and joy of the elite, but with changing fortunes, almost anyone with a few quid could now nab themselves a pair and it was all too much. The great poulaine outrage would rumble on for much of the fourteenth and fifteenth century and eventually Edward's great-great-grandson, Edward IV, would feel obliged to introduce his own Sumptuary Laws in 1463 which policed the length of people's phallic footwear. Aristocrats were allowed extensions up to an impressive 24 inches (61 cm), gentlemen* had to make do with half that (30.5 cm) while merchants were restricted to a rather embarrassing 6.5 inches (16.5 cm).[11]

One can imagine that Sigmund Freud would have had a field day.

The penalties for breaking the law could be severe. People caught wearing the wrong clobber could be fined, see their property confiscated and even, in some extreme cases, be put to death.[12]

But back in the 1300s, it wasn't just wealthy merchants who were challenging the order. For beneath the guildsman sat another 'artisan' class which also began to flourish in the wake of the pandemic. Though technically peasants, this rising artisanal class were increasingly influential within their communities. Smarter, sometimes literate and with more money in their pockets than their neighbours, they also became the de facto representatives of their local communities – trade union representatives or unelected town councillors before there was such a thing.

In 1349, in the wake of the Black Death and seeking to restore order and curb inflation, the King issued a decree called the 'Ordinance of Labourers' which sought to put everyone back in their place. These hated laws fixed wages at pre-plague levels, made work compulsory for all men and women under the age of 60 and also made it a criminal offence for those without land to seek better pay or new masters.

The Ordinance led to mass discontent among the working people which was made worse because as soon as the plague had passed, the war with France was back on and needed to be paid for. That saw the monarchy cede more power to Parliament and an ever-greater dependency on those merchants in the City of London who lent them cash, even as the deficit spiralled out of control.

From the early 1370s, England lacked strong leadership. Edward III, who was likely suffering from dementia, became ever more erratic and when he died and was succeeded by his 10-year-old grandson Richard II in 1377, he left an unpopular regent in charge in the shape of his son, John of Gaunt, the Duke of Lancaster. Gaunt was a hugely divisive figure already but a series of catastrophic political and fiscal decisions saw his popularity dip even further. The Duke had little interest in the people and was mostly concerned with getting his hands on money to fight France. In December 1376, even before Edward had died, he convened what would later become known as The Bad Parliament and pushed through a poll tax which demanded 4d (£9 in 2025 money) off every man and woman in the country over the age of 14. Across the country, sheriffs were ordered to levy the tax on Gaunt's behalf and with very little resistance, about £22,000 (£21 million in 2025) was raised from the population of about 2.5 million. Things went off largely without a hitch, which encouraged Gaunt to do it again, and so in 1379, with the Hundred Years War continuing into its 42nd year, he imposed a second tax. This time it was levied on a sliding scale, which took people's means into account, and while this was remarkably progressive in that aspect, it was fundamentally flawed as a result because that scale had 50 categories, ranging from Dukes who paid £6 3 shillings and 6d (about £8,000 in 2025) down to clergy who only had to pay 4d (£9 in 2025).

Bedlam ensued as people started hiding their oversized pointy shoes and mothballing the curtains and pretending that they were something less than they were, and just £18,000 (£17 million in 2025) was raised – a drop in the ocean when you consider Gaunt's war was costing £100,000 (£97 million) a year. So, in November 1380, Prince John tried one last time. Things were a little different on this occasion, not least because there had been a reshuffle at the top and John Ball's sworn enemy, the Archbishop Sudbury, was the new Chancellor. Sudbury wanted to make his mark. When this third poll tax was introduced, it was decided that everyone, regardless of their means, would pay 12d (roughly a week's wages).

When Margaret Thatcher's government made the same mistake with her own 'Community Charge' (which was quickly dubbed the poll tax) in 1990 (just weeks after the fall of Ceausescu), some 130,000 people disappeared off the electoral roll in London alone – and in 1380 much the same thing happened, but on a larger scale.

About one third of the population 'magically' disappeared from the tax rolls of England in the space of a year and this feisty act of non-compliance so infuriated Archbishop Sudbury and his treasurer, Robert Hales, that in February 1381 they appointed a commission to go out and investigate the municipal authorities who were failing to bring in the cash. Sudbury, the very definition of an 'out of touch' elitist, seriously underestimated the burgeoning anger beyond London and was very much responsible for what happened next.

In Essex, where non-compliance had resulted in a 36 per cent[13] drop in the number of names on the tax register, the government's men on the ground included three prominent local dignitaries led by Sir John de Bampton, a former sheriff, and now a justice of the peace. On 30 May in the market town of Brentwood, 27 miles northeast of London, he and his commission summoned representatives of local villages to account for their non-payment of tax.

One by one the men came forward and mumbled their excuses until Thomas Baker from the village of Fobbing stepped up.

In the fourteenth century, nominative determinism was the order of the day. People who thatched roofs were called 'thatcher', meat providers were called 'butcher', people who kept pigeons were called 'culver' and as you might have gleaned from his name, Mr Baker made bread. Some chroniclers later claimed that Baker was spurred to act after his daughter was molested by commissioners – a common story that was also spun around another (probably fictional) revolutionary called Jack Straw. But, whatever his motives, Baker told the commissioners to stick their demands where the sun doth not shineth and taking unction at his impertinence, de Bampton ordered his arrest.

This was to prove a significant error of judgement. The 'peasants' outnumbered the members of the commission by a factor of about twenty to one and when they rallied to Baker's side, the self-important justice of the peace simply made matters worse by ordering his two serjeants at arms to arrest everyone else present.

Shortly thereafter, he and they were obliged to run for their lives.

The revolution had begun.

* * *

Matters moved with considerable momentum and far from being an unruly rabble, the peasant leaders, many of whom may have been former soldiers, demonstrated impressive organisational skills. Proving to be highly capable military planners they exploited rivers, roads and other existing lines of communication between rural settlements. Messengers, carrying coded pieces of parchment, had soon spread out into Essex, Suffolk and East Anglia, promulgating the news of the uprising. Walsingham suggests that in the process some strong-arming may have gone on and:

'Those who refused or disdained to do so, would know that they would have their possessions pillaged, their homes burned down or demolished and themselves be executed.'

Although we can't fully trust him, it's reasonable to assume that a 'whose side are you on' mood prevailed and as momentum gathered, it is likely too that England's underclass, who had suffered through 'history's worst century' had simply had enough of all the misery and rallied willingly to the cause. On 4 June, the Essex rebels convened a meeting in the town of Bocking and drew up a manifesto. No reliable record survives but the chroniclers claimed that those present swore an oath to 'destroy diver lieges of the lord king and to have no law in England except only those they themselves moved to be ordained'.[14]

Nowadays, the Thames estuary, which separates Essex from Kent, is a ferocious channel, dotted with rip tides and swells, but in the era before large commercial shipping carved out its belly, it was quite a different beast. Marshier and far shallower than it is today, the estuary had its own distinct culture too, and the region was a hive of activity and a meeting point between the two counties. Goods, people and gossip crossed back and forth and inevitably news of the events in Essex soon spread south into Kent, encouraging further insurrection there. On 2 June, rebels led by a man called Abel Ker attacked Lesnes Abbey in Erith (modern-day Abbey Wood) where the local tax records were kept. Having broken in, they forced the powerful abbot to swear an oath of allegiance to them before burning the piles of vellum and some of the buildings to the ground.

Three days later, in an on the face of it unrelated incident, a man called John Belling was arrested in Gravesend in a dispute over his status. Belling, who was doing quite well for himself, claimed that he was a freeman, but a local dignitary Sir Simon Burley insisted that he was one of his serfs and thus his property, and it resulted in a stand-off. Serjeants acting for Burley confronted Belling in a market square and tried to apprehend him and when that failed, demanded the enormous sum of £300 (£265,000 in 2025) for his emancipation from feudal bonds.

This blatant attempt at extortion ended with Belling being taken to Rochester, where he was imprisoned in the castle. The next day, 6 June, a mob descended on the fortress and when the gates were thrown open, the crowd surged in. Rochester Castle was supposed to be an impregnable fortress, and its swift surrender hints that the bailiff, Sir Thomas Raven, a former MP, had weighed his options and decided to side with the rebels.

Raven was an unlikely revolutionary and like many a modern populist rabble-rouser, his motives were very far from ideological. This influential tub-thumper just happened to be heavily indebted to powerful merchants in London, and probably saw the uprising as an opportunity to settle some scores, destroy records recording his own financial impropriety and perhaps profit from the anarchy.

Chaos, after all, is a fabulous way for the rich to make more money.

Following the fall of Rochester, Belling and other prisoners were released and with momentum gathering, the next day they advanced on Maidstone where the 'mad priest of Kent'[15] John Ball was being held. At Maidstone, the peasants elected 'a wicked and nasty fellow' by the name of Wat Tyler to be their leader before springing Ball and his fellow prisoners from jail.

'Wat' is an abbreviated form of the name Walter, but can also mean 'commander' and may have been a title rather than his given name. What we know of the historical Wat beyond what he did for a living (obviously he was a 'tiler') and what he stood for is largely lost to time. His name may linger but the details of his life, like those of the mass of ordinary people he led, is otherwise written in water. What is beyond doubt is that he was a natural leader who, like Thomas Baker of Fobbing, was gifted with a very modern disdain for the ruling class and quite probably the gift of the gab. Tyler was almost certainly an experienced ex-soldier – probably the fourteenth-century equivalent of an NCO – and thus an experienced leader.

All the evidence suggests that he proved to be a highly effective 'general' and, from its inception at Maidstone, Tyler's army forged alliances and made full use of those impressive lines of communication between the counties of Southern England. The command of logistics was particularly impressive. They were not about to risk the kingdom either and early in the uprising the decree went out that those within 'twelve leagues' of the sea should stand down from the peasant army lest the French take advantage of the situation and launch an invasion.

Propaganda is key to any successful military assault and Tyler's team was on top of the PR too. The rebels presented themselves as orthodox Catholics and Royalists who were loyal to the boy king and who sought only to rid the country of John of Gaunt, the hated Sudbury and other establishment figures. With his army now numbering tens of thousands of people, Tyler marched on Canterbury.

On 10 June, Tyler's forces stormed the city, raided the castle prison and released the prisoners who were held there before making their way to the great cathedral where in 1170, England's most famous saint, Thomas a Becket, had been martyred by four knights. As high mass continued within the grand Norman building, 4,000 rebels advanced into the cathedral's precinct where a delegation, perhaps led by Tyler himself, entered the great church and demanded that Sudbury be removed and executed:

'For he who is now Archbishop is a traitor who will be beheaded for his iniquity.'[16]

Sudbury was not there but in London and that only served to anger the peasants who promptly began executing perceived 'traitors' in the cathedral precincts in his place. That show of force only ended when local burghers started loudly swearing allegiance to King Richard II. With order restored, the rebel army moved on from the business of violence to the more practical one of burning tax records.

The unprecedented success of the insurgency had caught the Church and the Crown completely off guard, but had probably surprised its own leaders too. The heady atmosphere was getting contagious and on 10 June in Essex, a parallel rebel force attacked Cressing Temple, near Braintree, which was run by the powerful and wealthy order of Knights Templar and whose prior John Hales was the treasurer and sidekick to Sudbury. The site and its records were burned and shortly thereafter, the same group beheaded the Escheator or King's representative in Coggeshall, Essex. Further west in St Albans, another uprising, incited by a long-running local dispute between the people and the local abbot concerning fishing and farming rights, saw the prison broken into, records burned and locals swear allegiance to Wat Tyler, whose name was already resonating well beyond his immediate locale.

Tyler was now the most talked about man in England and as his fame grew, his head undoubtedly expanded with it. The change in his fortunes had been vertiginous and in the space of just a week he had gone from being an anonymous roofer to having knights, bishops and kings tremble at the very mention of his name. The adulation of the mob is as intoxicating as any drug known to humankind and Tyler was now a king among his people. The Chronicles hint at increased swagger and it may have informed what happened next.

On 11 June, Tyler, Ball and their lieutenants left Canterbury and marched up Watling Street (the modern-day A2) towards London.

On the way, they overtook Princess Joan, mother of King Richard II, who had been on a pilgrimage to the shrine of St Thomas in Canterbury and engaged in some ribald and unwanted banter with her and her entourage, which hinted at their confidence. The next day, Tyler's army arrived at Blackheath and camped out on the same common that today plays host to weekend junior leagues, visiting circuses and a popular hot beverage van. The heath sat just five miles southeast of London's only bridge and Tyler's army were hammering at the door of the capital.

Learning of the advance, the 14-year-old boy king left Windsor Castle and travelled by royal barge via the Tower of London to Greenwich just a few hundred metres from Blackheath. His arrival caused a sensation and a crowd quickly gathered on the foreshore. A message was passed to Tyler requesting his demands and when the reply came it can hardly have lightened the mood on board. The rebels wanted nothing less than the heads of the Keeper of the Privy Seal, the Bishop-elect of Durham, John Fordham, Sir Robert Plesington, Chief Baron of the Exchequer, Treasurer Hales, Archbishop Sudbury and the King's own uncle, John of Gaunt.

Others on the list, in the words of the author, Alastair Dunn, hint at the 'interconnection of local and national political grievances'[17] with the names of Bampton and Bealknap, who had sparked the Essex revolt, plus that of John Legge, the serjeant at arms in Canterbury.

The King, of course, was not about to behead anyone to placate some yobbos from Kent and, seeking to delay the rebels, offered to meet them in Windsor, some 65 miles to the west of Greenwich on 17 June before heading back to the Tower of London. Historians disagree over how much of the decision making was being taken by the 14-year-old King, but as events unfolded, he did appear to show remarkable resolve. Richard II was a striking-looking young man. Six foot tall, with blond hair, strong cheekbones and a handsome face, he was also quite effeminate in manner, and he may have been gay.*

Much has also been made of Richard's youth, but in an age when about 40 per cent of the population of England were younger than 15, he was, in a sense, representative of his people.

Tyler's force, now brandishing banners and flags bearing the Cross of St George, advanced on London until, by the following day, they had

* As strongly hinted by the chronicler Thomas Walsingham. However the jury remains out on whether this was true and it may have been politically motivated propaganda.

reached Southwark, which lies on the south bank of London Bridge. This area, which is nowadays famous for overpriced flat whites and bespoke cheeses, was then renowned for being a den of iniquity. Dotted with taverns and brothels including the 'Bishop of Winchester's Geese' which was named after its clerical landlord. The rebels stormed the Marshalsea Prison* just south of the bridge and released the inmates before levelling the 'handsome place' owned by its keeper – John Imworth – whose fate we shall learn later on.

Further along the river, another band of men and women were attacking properties owned by Sudbury and burning them to the ground while shouting: 'A revel! A revel!'

This violent pattern would repeat itself across the long hot days that followed as the city turned into a literal and metaphorical tinderbox. The 'rustici', who had arrived in London with one set of aims, now found their ranks swelled by locals with grievances of their own. In a brilliant propaganda coup, Tyler had made it known that his army did not intend to plunder London but to root out the 'traitors' within and so many a local Londoner joined the cause. As rebels clogged the streets to the south of the river's only crossing, William Walworth, the Lord Mayor of London, was busy calculating what to do next. He had time to think, because in the fourteenth century the bridge was heavily guarded and at the south end had a large drawbridge which had been raised as the 'great noise' of the mob approached.

The City of London then, as now, was a semi-autonomous state. A Vatican to the cult of Mammon it was controlled by 'the Great Twelve' livery guilds whose liverymen were far more interested in commerce and gold than the intrigues of politics. It is however important to add that they also despised John of Gaunt with an absolute passion, not least because in 1377 he had essentially caused a riot in the city after threatening to suspend the city guilds' newly won concessions and trading rights. On that occasion Gaunt himself had been chased out of the Square Mile.

* A later iteration of the jail stood until the 1870s when it was demolished, although a long high wall is still visible. That prison once held Charles Dickens's father, who was imprisoned there for debt in the 1820s.

Gaunt had subsequently demanded that the Aldermen and Mayor make a penitential process to St Paul's in his honour, but they refused and in a display of their growing confidence, offered an apology instead.

Walworth – like many of his peers – thus held Gaunt in contempt and come the revolt in June 1381 he was not about to risk his fiefdom for the King's uncle's neck. A powerful fish merchant and money lender, he was the very definition of the new and wealthy 'upper-middle' merchant class who were in the ascendancy and, like many a largely self-made man, he was no idiot either. He knew that his small militia was no match for Tyler's army and, appreciating that resistance might be counter-productive, instructed the keeper of London Bridge to lower the drawbridge and let the rebels in. As the bridge came down, the rebel army teemed across it and, shortly after that, all hell broke loose.

Making their way up the River Fleet, the peasant army descended on the headquarters of the loathed Hospitallers of the Order of St John at Clerkenwell and incinerated it and its records. They then turned and headed back down the river, ransacking the Fleet Prison before advancing towards the mighty Savoy Palace for the main course. Nowadays, the Savoy is more likely to bear witness to an orgy of cocktails, cream teas and cake than acts of extreme violence, but in 1381 it was the main residence of John of Gaunt and thus a target of the mob. Gaunt had owned the lavish palace since 1360 and according to Walsingham, 'nothing anywhere in the kingdom was comparable in nobility and beauty'. The complex sat astride the Strand – the Middle English word for shoreline – and was then the most desirable real estate plot in England.

Gaunt was in Northumberland, negotiating peace with Scotland. In his absence, his palace was stacked high with furniture and expensive cloth and in the scorching heat of that June week, not much was needed to send the great house up like a pile of dry hay. The torching of the Savoy Palace was quasi-religious in nature – a ritual act of conflagration that sought to cleanse and purify the purpose of the mob. The building was teeming with riches, but the peasant army were ordered not to loot anything on pain of execution and instead all the gold and silver was thrown into the sewers. At least one person present gave into temptation and was cast into the flames. The Chroniclers gleefully recorded that another group of rebels got so drunk that they were subsequently burned alive in the cellars – but such 'urban myths' about dumbass rioters are a common thread for historians of populist insurrections, so we should probably take it with a pinch of salt.

The next day, the rebels moved on Westminster and burned down the house of the under-sheriff of Middlesex before once again freeing prisoners from the prison. Making no attempt to attack the Abbey or nearby governmental buildings, they then moved on to Newgate where they breached the gates of another jail which has led some historians to conclude that London's criminal underworld may have been conniving with Tyler.

In Gaunt's absence the crowd sought out scapegoats, and ordinarily that would have meant killing Jews, but Edward I's expulsion of them in 1290 meant that other innocent victims needed to be targeted instead. First, the mob went after the lawyers, including one Roger Legett, whom they dragged from the pulpit at St Martin's and beheaded on the streets of Cheapside, and then they turned on the 'foreigners'.

London then, as now, was a multicultural city, made up of significant communities of Gascon, Flemish, Irish, Italian, German and Lombardian migrants. Many had grown rich lending money, trading cloth, weaving and brokering deals and lived in expensively furnished homes. Like immigrant communities throughout history, they tended to keep themselves to themselves, and retained their own language and customs, all of which made them figures of suspicion, envy and hate. The textile merchant 'Flemings' were particularly loathed and at least 35 were rounded up and executed at St Martin in Vintry and Cheapside – the favoured killing ground of the peasant army.

Another victim was Sir Richard Lyons, Privy Councillor, MP and, like his friend Geoffrey Chaucer, a member of the Worshipful Company of Vintners, who had made a fortune as a wine merchant. The Chronicler Froissart speculates that Lyons was targeted because he had once invoked the ire of a then anonymous trader called 'Wat Tyler', but more likely this powerful landlord was simply in the wrong place at the wrong time.

Things were turning uglier by the hour and the Royal Party, holed up in the Tower of London, began to fear the worst. Alongside the King were his mother Joan, his half-sister (also Joan), his two half-brothers Thomas and John and his cousin and childhood playmate Henry, the son of John of Gaunt, who would one day rise to become King Henry IV. Also present were Archbishop Sudbury and his sidekick Robert Hales as well as the tax collector John Legge and William Appleton, Gaunt's personal physician.

Much as the Ceausescus dithered in Bucharest in 1989 when they should have fled, so too, by locking themselves in the Tower, the fourteenth-century English elite were now in zugzwang* and every move spelled potential disaster.

The only bluff the King could take advantage of was that the rebels believed he was on their side. So he sent a message to Tyler requesting that they meet to discuss things further and on 14 June he left the Tower for a 7 a.m. rendezvous in Mile End. There, the rebels delivered their revised list of demands which called for the wholesale emancipation of the serfs, a fixed rate of 4d per acre for rents and a general amnesty for anyone who had taken part in the revolt. Buying time, the King agreed to it all and 30 clerks were immediately ordered to draw up the details with a meeting arranged for the following day.

As Richard deceived, Sudbury ran.

Not exactly thrilled at the prospect of being the next Thomas a Becket and calculating that, with the King away, the crowd might make their move on him, the Archbishop sought to escape through the water gate (now known as Traitor's Gate) at the back of the castle but was immediately captured by the rebels. He was dragged to Tower Hill where, eight haphazard blows later, his head was separated his body.

His skull can still be viewed today in a glass case at St Gregory's Church, Sudbury, Suffolk; his body was taken to Canterbury Cathedral where, in the absence of his skull, it rests still with a cannonball atop his corpse.

---

* Zugzwang – a position in chess in which one player can move only with loss or severe disadvantage.

Hales, Legge and Appleton all followed Sudbury to his fate and their heads were taken to London Bridge, stuck on pikes and left to rot.

Although events had thus far been dominated by men, at least one of the revolutionaries storming the Tower and arranging the executions was a woman. King's Bench Court Rolls relate that Johanna Ferrour masterminded the assault, and was also responsible for the ransacking and destruction of the Savoy Palace. She was also judge and jury in the case of Sudbury vs the Mob:

'Together with others, Johanna went as the chief leader to the Tower of London, and she laid violent hands first on Simon, recently Archbishop of Canterbury, and then on Brother Robert Hales . . . and she dragged them out of the Tower and ordered that they be beheaded.'[18]

John of Gaunt's son Henry survived it all – spared, according to legend, by Johanna's near namesake (and possibly her husband) 'John Ferrour' of Southwark, who recognised him and stayed the hand of a fellow rebel. Twenty years later, so the story goes, Henry IV repaid the debt and spared Ferrour's life following a rebellion.

Most of history's well-worn 'good stories' are in fact little more than establishment fairy tales and this too-good-to-be-true destiny narrative is probably just a bit of later Lancastrian propaganda.

Saturday 15 June dawned and, having appointed the Earl of Arundel as his new chief adviser, the young King visited Westminster Abbey in preparation for his meeting with Tyler. After paying homage at the shrine to his patron saint, Edward the Confessor, he headed on to Smithfield, nowadays a famous meat market but then a literal field on the outskirts of the city, and arrived sometime in the mid-afternoon. On the way he probably passed a band of rebels who were heading towards the Abbey with one final execution to tick off their 'to do' list. Their target was the much-hated Marshalsea Prison governor Richard Imworth, who tried in vain to protect himself by clinging to the pillars of Edward's shrine – but it was to no avail, and he was dragged away and beheaded.

At Smithfield, Richard was attended by William Walworth who carried a message to Tyler. Froissart would later claim that Tyler was intent on kidnapping the King and murdering his attendants and, while that sounds like grotesque exaggeration, the man from Kent did now have the upper hand and all the usual bets were off.

The Chroniclers differ on what exactly happened next but, in piecing the various strands together, matters probably played out something like this. When the King and the peasant general met, Richard demanded of Tyler: 'Why will you not go back to your own country?' to which Wat replied that he wasn't going anywhere until he'd got his hands on the charter he'd been promised. Brimming with confidence, Tyler spent the entire conversation juggling a dagger between his hands which unnerved everyone else present. But his respect for his social superior was distinctly lacking too. Having called Richard his 'brother' he declared that he was thirsty and demanded water and when it came, he took one swig and spat it out at the feet of the royal party. This may have been down to him fearing it was poisoned but it was deemed to be highly disrespectful to the monarch and things only got worse from there.

His thirst unquenched, Tyler ordered a flagon (1.1 litres) of beer and when it was brought, necked the lot in one go – which is never a great idea on a scorching hot day. Mildly inebriated and with his army standing shoulder to shoulder just a few yards away, things looked like they were about to turn very nasty indeed so the King sought to cool matters by immediately agreeing to cede to all the rebel demands.

Apparently satisfied that he had got his way, Tyler began to walk back to his men, but in the next few seconds, the Plantagenet dynasty was to almost witness its Ceausescu moment.

Unable to take the indignity of it all any more, a royal valet called Sir John Newton yelled out to the retreating Tyler that he was 'the single greatest thief and robber in all of Kent'. Tyler stopped in his tracks, turned back and with his dagger still drawn, advanced on the King, demanding that Newton be executed. As he moved, William Walworth drew his sword and when Tyler plunged his dagger at him, the blade bounced off Walworth's armoured breastplate causing him to momentarily stumble.

Seizing the initiative, Walworth slashed his sword across Tyler's throat and with his neck bleeding profusely, Tyler staggered towards his horse, mounted it, trotted some yards and fell. As he lay in the mud, his band of archers drew their arrows and the future of English history now hung in the fate of a few dozen bow strings.

Showing remarkable resolve, Richard mounted a horse and rode towards them. Reaching the archers, he appealed for calm and asked them to move away north to Clerkenwell and, perhaps overawed by his presence, they obliged.

Depending on whom you believe, the rebel leader was then either carried away to the nearby St Bartholomew's hospital from where he was later dragged by the King's men, or taken straight to a corner of Smithfield where he was executed. His head was cut off and stuck on a pole and carried off to London Bridge, where it joined the rest of the characters in this chapter – in a gruesome medieval game of top trumps.

The revolt, in London at least, was over.

Beyond the city it was not, and disturbances and skirmishes played out for weeks.

In a famous encounter in North Walsham in Norfolk, the local bishop defeated an army of rebels and on 28 June a retreating band of about 500 Essex peasants were cornered by the King's men at Norsey Wood near Billericay and slain. According to a local legend, their bodies were taken to nearby Great Burstead, where they were buried in a pit in the graveyard.

Two days after Tyler's death, news of the uprising reached York where copycat attacks on local abbeys broke out, as they did in nearby Scarborough. There were further uprisings in the South West too, with a revolt in Bridgwater and the Somerset town of Binegar where yet another troublesome priest called Nicholas Frampton and a local landowner called Thomas Engilby weaponised the mob to settle private scores.

Both men – incredibly – were pardoned by the King, as were the Rochester bailiff Sir Thomas Raven and the archbishop-beheading Johanna Ferrour. But John Ball and Thomas Baker were not so lucky and were hanged, drawn and quartered.

Walsingham claimed that a fourth leader, the mysterious 'Jack Straw', was also executed after first confessing that the revolutionaries had planned to murder the nation's ruling class, the clergy and even the

King. There is however scant evidence to suggest that Straw existed, and Walsingham probably made the story up from a prevailing rumour.

The Mayor of London, William Walworth, was one of the few to do well out of the chaos. His central role in stopping the rebellion did not go unnoticed and his reward was a handsome pension and an increase in his status and renown. Legends were written about him and although his fame did not endure as much as his near contemporary 'Dick Whittington', he remains a celebrated figure among the Aldermen, sheriffs and clerks of the City of London Corporation in the Square Mile today. Walworth may not have his own panto or fictional cat, but he does have a statue on Holborn viaduct and a very significant stained-glass window at Mansion House – home and headquarters to the modern Lord Mayors.

Richard II's mythos did not endure and his leadership in the revolt would come to be seen as the high point of his reign. Ever more erratic, he developed a reputation for being a 'dilettante' and a hedonist and he never went near a battle again. According to Froissart, Richard's relative Thomas of Lancaster (brother of Henry IV) once said of the King that he was 'heavy in the arse, he only asks for drinking and eating, sleeping and leaping about' and that the wearer of the 'hollow crown' was basically a bit of a waster. Imbued with a lofty sense of his divine right to rule, but devoid of any other redeeming characteristics, he was to become an ever more divisive figure. A series of political, diplomatic and military blunders and the imposition of more unwelcome taxes would eventually see him toppled by his own cousin, Henry, son of John of Gaunt – who, having overthrown him in 1399, probably starved him to death in Pontefract Castle in February 1400.

* * *

In the wake of the uprising, establishment forces moved to control the narrative. In Geoffrey Chaucer's *Nun's Priest's Tale*, ostensibly a story about a farmyard full of talking animals, a proud cock and a cunning fox, 'Jack Straw' and the great noise are directly referenced in the passage where the screaming animals and people chase the 'Chauntecleer' out of town.

Chaucer's friend, the poet John Gower, also put nib to parchment and knocked off Visio Anglie as part one of his long poem 'Vox Clamantis' (the voice of one crying out) which sought to demonise and denigrate the peasants in the great revolt. Gower, who may (or may not) have witnessed the uprising, blended violent and bestial imagery with a nightmarish topicality slanted very much in the establishment's favour. His scabrous assault on the character of the peasantry, which (like Chaucer's own work) predates George Orwell's *Animal Farm* by some 560 years, sees the mob metamorphosise into literal animals and that famous 'great noise' becomes the howling and barking of the common horde. Gower's peasants are as ignorant as they are zoic, and have no understanding of what they are doing. The herd are stampeding for the sake of it and are positively diabolic in nature:

'Thus, Satanic force lies defeated by an act of God, yet it hides still in the ungovernable peasantry. For the peasant is always plotting destruction.'

Ochlophobia* and the notion of the 'ungovernable masses' who need to be kept down haunted the establishment narrative for the next 300 years.

From the Elizabethan era onwards, writers revisited the saga and layered it with fictionalised elements and as they did, the 'stupid' or 'threatening' working-class character became a stock feature of literature and theatre. Shakespeare's ordinary people and even his merchant-class characters tend to be unrefined imposters and idiots. They are the light reliefs, the drunks and the thieves; they say dumb things and often exist to be ridiculed. In *Twelfth Night*, the steward Malvolio is roundly mocked for believing that he can rise above his station and more – that the lovely, aristocratic Olivia might return his love. In *A Midsummer Night's Dream*, working-class artisanal weaver Bottom is quite literally transformed into an ass.

By the eighteenth and nineteenth century, the attitudes of radical thinkers like Edmund Burke, Thomas Paine, Friedrich Engels and later Karl Marx saw a shifting of interpretation among the liberal-minded intelligentsia regarding the 1381 uprising and the people involved. Radical pamphleteers and Irish nationalists were inspired by the revolt even as

* Fear of the mob.

'establishment' history and its historians sought to downplay it and villainise the 'peasants' who took part. Well into the modern age, the apocalyptic priest John Ball and the rebel roofer Wat Tyler and those who followed them were depicted as an ignorant swamp of ill-educated countryside dwelling idiots who fell for some insurrectionist populist claptrap.

H.E. Marshall, author of the influential children's history of Britain, *Our Island Story,* published in 1905, like many a chronicler before her, seemed mostly concerned for the welfare of the royals and was particularly upset that Richard's mother Joan was *'nearly frightened . . . to death'*.

And while to her credit, Marshall did accept that the uprising led to *'the beginning of freedom for the lower classes in England'*, not everyone was convinced.

In Volume One of Winston Churchill's influential *History of the English-Speaking Peoples*, begun in 1936 but only published in 1956 during his second term as prime minister, the great man included just two paragraphs on the revolt. And, typically, managed to make it all about himself. In an apparent nod to the social unrest of the 1930s or perhaps the still unfolding populist Mau Mau Rebellion (aka revolution) in colonial-era Kenya which he, as British prime minister, was mishandling daily, Churchill refers to the violence with an 'all this has a modern ring'. Later, he describes how, following the death of Tyler, 'the leaderless bands wandered home and spread a vulgar lawlessness through their counties. They were pursued by reconstructed authority.' Modern fans of the wartime PM would have you believe that Winston was a man of the people, but in truth he was much more a latter-day William Walworth.

Churchill was not alone in his scorn for the common villeins. Well into the last century, even as Britain witnessed the rise of trade unions and socialist movements and saw events like the General Strike of 1926 and miners' strikes in the 1980s play out, the great uprising was sidelined in history texts, even as the myth was encouraged that England did not do popular revolts and insurrections. Mob violence was said to be beneath us and the media propped up the notion that, like sex, olive oil and driving on the right, this was the sort of thing they did on the

'Continent'. In that narrative, Tyler's revolt was a blip – the uprising dated to a time when the country was not fully developed and had French-speaking kings and anyway, it had all been for nothing.

The writers of the 1930 comical history *1066 and All That* played their part by dubbing it all the 'Pheasants' Revolt' and as late as 1970, in the frankly unimaginatively titled 'The Peasants' Revolt of 1381', The University of York academic and historian R.B. Dobson was claiming that the uprising was 'unnecessary' and its impact 'negligible'. Even 'Life in the UK', a short 'official history' pamphlet, which since 2005, those seeking to become British citizens have been obliged to read, reduces the events to: '*There were labour shortages and peasants began to demand higher wages.*'

But the events of that week in June 1381 were no sidebar to history and no insignificant chapter. This was, by any measure, a popular revolution of ordinary people against a corrupt, oppressive and maleficent ruling elite and its impact was seismic. In the immediate aftermath of events, the government and the social classes whose interests it served were royally spooked and gave in to many of the demands. No further poll tax was imposed and the restrictions on wages put in place under the Ordinance of Labourers in 1349 were abandoned. Across the following years, average pay went up by about 40 per cent. Serfs began to gain their freedom, whether by paying for it or simply by wandering off to find better and freer pastures to graze. Those hated records were kept but now they worked much more in favour of the ordinary working people by proving their rights of inheritance and property ownership, and in time a new degree of social mobility came too which allowed everyone to start buying pointy shoes – albeit of restricted length.

But of course it didn't change everything.

While England was one of the first countries in the world to abolish serfdom and though the Revolt signalled the start of that, villeinage still continued well into the Tudor era and the class system and indeed many of the trappings of the ruling elite still remain today. Our unelected head of state is – like all the kings and queens since 1399 – a direct descendant of Henry IV and thus John of Gaunt. In the City of London, there is still a Lord Mayor (distinct from the Mayor of London) and he (or very occasionally she*) still governs it through the Corporation of the City of London, which to all intents and purposes remains a medieval institution. It retains heralds (known as Beadles), three esquires, a Court of Aldermen, Serjeants and a Court of Common Council. The Court of Aldermen still appoints Freemen too and all that has really changed in that regard is that some of them are now women.

Within the City's boundaries, the Great Twelve livery companies still wield enormous power and influence, and retain many of the halls (or at least the sites of them) that stood in 1381 where modern-day merchants, business people and liverymen and women still meet.

And of course, the social divides go well beyond the City of London. The tropes of class and wealth continue to bleed into every facet of politics and life in the UK and lamentably the cap doffing prevails as much as the punching down. Many an aristocratic English family, many a wealthy merchant and indeed many a politician and pundit continue to believe that the 'peasants' should be seen and not heard – lest they start getting ideas. That they are the 'unwashed masses' who need to be kept in check and at arm's length.

History rarely repeats but it does echo and if you lift your head and listen very carefully, you can still catch the reverberations of 1381 everywhere.

* At time of writing there have only been two woman Lady Mayoresses of London.

CHAPTER FOUR

BLOODY MARY

How History Demonises Women

It was a summer's day in 857 CE and John VIII* was processing through the great doors of Old St Peter's Basilica and preparing to make his way through Rome to the Lateran Palace, some 5 kilometres away.

Even in the mid-ninth century, the city was an important site of pilgrimage, drawing in Christians to its many holy sites, shrines and tombs – but these early tourists were not just there for the dead and hoping to catch a glimpse of a living saint too. Two years into the role, John was a draw: one of the A-listers of his age, and his celebrity was such that when the Pope descended the marble steps of the great building, he was greeted with roars of approval and cries of 'Salve Papa!' by the large crowd that had gathered.

But then, something unbelievable happened.

Stopping in his tracks, John began to grasp suddenly and desperately at his stomach and then letting out a terrified scream he collapsed to the floor and gave birth – to a baby.

In the ninth century, it was not unheard of for popes to have children. Until the Second Lateran Council in 1139, the Catholic clergy were not necessarily expected to be celibate and indeed Adrian II, whose papacy preceded John VIII's, lived quite openly with his wife, Stephania, and daughter until their murder in 868 CE. But until that Sunday morning in

* Of 265 popes since St Peter in 67 CE, only Nicholas Breakspear aka Adrian IV (1154–59) was English.

857 CE, no pope had themselves given birth while in office, for the simple reason that to get the gig, you had to be a man.

'John' was now revealed to be a woman and having been so, at least according to the chronicler Jean de Mailly, the crowd turned on her.

The woman was tied to a horse's tail, dragged through the cobbled streets of Rome and then stoned to death. De Mailly, writing in the 1200s, placed events in the eleventh century and did not identify the woman by name, but a hundred years later, the Italian humanist Boccaccio wrote another account in his *De Claris Mulieribus** (*c.*1350) which placed the story in the ninth century and dubbed her 'Giliberta'.

Another friar, the thirteenth-century Dominican Martinus Polonus† added a romantic dimension to the story, describing in *Chronicon pontificum et imperatorum*‡ how:

'*When a girl, she was taken to Athens in male clothes by her lover, and there made such progress in learning that no one was her equal . . . It is said that following her death she was buried at the same place that she was killed (and that) in their processions the popes always avoid this road . . . out of abhorrence of that calamity.*'[1]

And it's true, for hundreds of years, popes avoided Via Sacra – referred to in various sources as Vicus Papissa (Woman Pope Street) – where the baby was said to have been born. This was highly inconvenient, because the route was the quickest way to the Lateran Palace but superstition won over reason and papal processions continued to take the long path home until 1486, when danger-seeking Pope Innocent VIII deliberately went down Via Sacra in defiance of the abject silliness of it all – and survived.

According to Polonus, a stone inscription marked the spot and read: '*Petre pater patrum papissae prodito partum*' ('Oh Peter, father of the fathers, betray the childbearing woman pope'). If it ever existed, it has long gone, along with a statue to the woman pope and her child which once stood near the Colosseum.

* Known as 'Concerning Famous Women' or the 'Book of Famous Women'.

† Martin of Opava was a Polish friar, born in Silesia *c.*1215.

‡ 'The Chronicle of Popes and Emperors'.

Competing accounts of her life followed on from those first chronicles and as they did, her story evolved. No longer killed by the mob, later rewrites claimed that she had died in childbirth, or lived out her life in a closed order of nuns, paying penitence for her sin of deception – while her son went on to become the Bishop of Ostia. In time, 'Giliberta' became 'Agnes' before the chroniclers settled on 'Pope Joan'.

Joan went on to become a significant figure in Catholic folklore and by the fifteenth century, was even being cited in the celebrated heresy trial of the Czech priest Jan Huss. Huss, like John Ball before him, was a proto-Protestant and, like Ball, he was destined to suffer a violent fate. In 1414, the Holy Roman Emperor, King Sigismund, convened the Council of Constance in Germany, ostensibly in the hope of healing the schism that had led to two rival popes reigning side by side – one in Rome and one in Avignon. But as a side hustle, some of the delegates conspired to kill off the troublesome Czech priest who, again like Ball, had acquired a most unwelcome reputation for speaking the truth. Luring Huss with the promise of indemnity, the council promptly arrested him and put him on trial for heresy which is where Joan comes in.

With his life on the line, Huss claimed that the story of Pope Joan was proof enough that the world did not fall apart if you didn't have a 'proper' pontiff on the Vatican throne. This defence didn't go down brilliantly well with his accusers and he was burned alive at the stake as a heretic, before having his ashes thrown in the Rhine.

As time went by, more people came to believe the story and even as events were weaponised by Protestants through the fifteenth and well into the sixteenth century, many of the Catholics continued to embrace it. Joan was name-checked some 500 times in medieval writings and was even included in a collection of papal busts in Italy's Siena Cathedral where Johannes VIII, Femina ex Anglia, was placed between Leo IX and Benedict III. The statue remained there until 1600, when according to Cardinal Baronius, a seventeenth-century Vatican librarian, Pope Clement VIII decided that it needed to go. Not wishing to waste a perfectly good terracotta statue, her name was scrubbed out and replaced by that of Pope Zachary.

Her legend persisted because it served competing, but fundamentally misogynistic, narratives. For the Dominican and Franciscan monks, whose orders had been created in the thirteenth century as a direct response to the corruption of the Vatican, she was a useful means of satirising popes. For the Lollards and later Protestants, she provided clear evidence of the invalidity of the priesthood and the redundancy of Catholic theology. And for the Catholic See itself she served as a 'warning from history': a reminder that everyone with a penis needed to be constantly on guard against women who wanted to 'replace' them.

The paranoia fostered some epic stupidity including the 'porphyry chair'. This purple throne, hewn from a block of the hardest granite on Earth, which is still on display in the Vatican today, has a hole cut in its middle and it supposedly spawned an 'eccentric' tradition – first attested to by the sixteenth-century French philosopher Pierre Grégoire:

'They introduced this cautionary measure, that thenceforth the Supreme Pontiff should be taken to the pontifical seat and not confirmed before, sitting on that seat with a hole, his genitals should be touched. I should think, though, that the Supreme Pontiff is placed upon this low [humili] seat so that . . . he might feel humbly about himself.'[2]

In *Roma Triumphans*, written in 1645, another writer, the Swede Laurens Banck who had witnessed the coronation of Innocent X in September 1644 wrote:

'Afterwards, [the Pope] is taken by [the canons of the basilica] to a marble seat with a hole . . . so that, seating upon it, his genitals might be touched.'

Once convinced that their man had a full set of tackle, the cardinals would announce: '*Testiculos habet et bene pendentes*' which roughly translates as 'he has two testicles, and boy do they hang well' and with that important business concluded, the serious and sacred matter of anointing the pope could begin.

It's a properly weird story and as usual that means that it is (quite literally in this case) bollocks. Despite the claims of Grégoire and the anti-Catholic Banck, no cardinals ever fondled the papal family jewels through a hole in a granite chair. In fact, the familiar shape of this grand throne demonstrates exactly what it was originally – a very blingy Roman emperor's toilet.

And yet, despite being a myth, Joan's legend continues to resonate. Her story featured in a 2009 film by Sönke Wortmann, she is a character in an Xbox game called *Persona 5* and the pop star Rihanna even gave her legend a nod when she turned up at the Met Gala in 2018 dressed as a woman pope. Perhaps her most celebrated cultural depiction comes courtesy of Caryl Churchill's influential 1982 play *Top Girls*, where Joan features as one of the famous women from history that the central protagonist, Marlene, meets in the dream-like opening scene.

But regrettably, Joan never existed. Though the story was repeated for over 700 years as a cardinal truth, the line of popes tells a different tale and the legend was roundly debunked early as the mid-seventeenth century by a Protestant French clergyman called David Blondel. Joan's fable had in truth been a misogynistic parable from the start and it is one which 'teaches' that women only get to the top by cheating, or imitating men, and more that those who seek to upend the patriarchy will suffer the consequences.

For most of history, the place of women in the narrative consisted of nameless wives (like Mrs Harrison in Chapter One), nameless mothers, sisters of important men, sometimes their daughters, or stereotypes. When names were recorded, it was usually because the women in question had either been exceptionally loyal to their husbands or committed some terrible and unforgivable sin against the world of men. Eve, the first named woman in the Bible, is quite literally a subsidiary part, who according to John Wycliffe's first English translation of Genesis in 1382 was made out of Adam's spare rib:

'And Adam said, this is now a bone of my bones, and flesh of my flesh; this shall be called virago, for she is taken (out) of man (she shall be called Woman, for she was taken from Man).'[3]

In recent years, academics, including US scholar of biblical literature Ziony Zevit, have suggested that the Hebrew word '*tsela*' was mistranslated into Greek and that in fact the author of Genesis was intimating that Eve was created from Adam's penis bone – which is hardly a less insulting narrative. Whatever the truth of their anyway entirely fictional mythological origins, women are condemned from page one of the master text of the Abrahamic faiths to be a deific afterthought, built out of bits of man that are just lying about on the floor of the celestial shed. Things hardly get better from then on in, because subsequently almost all the women in scripture are presented as one of three things: stupid, insipid or evil seductress.

Eve sets the ball rolling by defying God, and not only does she eat from the tree of knowledge, but encourages Adam to do so too. In the same book, Potiphar's unnamed wife seduces Joseph, of technicolour coat fame, before accusing him of rape when he rejects her advances. Jezebel is a femme fatale who instigates the downfall of those who cross her and eventually the kingdom itself. Delilah connives with the enemy, then tricks her man into cutting his hair short, causing him to lose his super human strength, resulting in his capture by the Philistines. Both women die in violent circumstances as a result: Delilah is crushed to death when the temple collapses on top of her and Jezebel gets eaten by dogs. The message is clear.

It rarely ends well for other scriptural women too. Lot's wife gets turned into a pillar of salt when she defies an angel and takes a quick peek at the destruction of Sodom. Sarah, wife of Abraham, is 'barren' and when he takes a second wife (Hagar) from a lower social class in order to sire an heir (Ishmael) she is at first supportive but only until she has a child of her own – at which point Ishmael and Hagar get kicked out of the family home.

Later in the New Testament, Herodias, wife of Herod, plots against John the Baptist after he throws shade on her and gets her daughter (Salome) to dance seductively in front of the King. Herod gets so hot under the collar that Salome is able to demand the prophet's head on a plate – which he delivers.

Of the limited roll call of women who feature in the New Testament, the two most famous represent the starkest stereotypes of womanhood: Jesus's mother Mary (17 mentions) is a virgin and Mary Magdalen (mentioned 12 times) is, at least according to tradition, a prostitute.

Women fare no better in other traditions. Those encountered by Odysseus and his men on their ten-year voyage, according to Hellenic tradition, are either untrustworthy and attractive or loyal and dull. Blown off course, the sailors encounter Circe, who invites a group of them into her home before turning them into pigs. At another point, the warriors encounter the Sirens, who try to lure their ships on to the rocks and Calypso, who like the Kathy Bates character Annie in Stephen King's *Misery*, holds the protagonist against his will for seven years before finally letting him go. When Odysseus gets home, he finds that his supposedly loyal wife Penelope has spent his absence amassing a harem of 100 hot suitors and is obliged to kill them all before there can be any happy ever after.

The secular fairy tale tradition ploughs much the same turf. Many of these familiar stories are actually much older than once thought and research conducted in 2016 revealed that Jack and the Beanstalk, Beauty and the Beast and even Rumpelstiltskin have their roots and tropes in the Bronze Age. The revival of the tradition, which began in the thirteenth century and developed in the wake of the Renaissance, didn't do feminism any favours. For the most part, fairy-tale women are hags, crones, spinsters, witches, wicked stepmothers, jealous queens, femmes fatales, ugly and scheming siblings or beautiful, virginal idiots. The common thread throughout finds 'naive girls' or 'good women' needing to be rescued by charming princes, while the bad ones – who seem to make up most of the rest of womanhood – need to be beaten or consigned to dust.

In Chaucer's *The Wife of Bath* and the anonymous *Sir Gawain and the Green Knight*, both written in the fourteenth century, the knights have dealings with 'witchy' elderly women and in each story, the 'old hag' poses an existential threat to them.

In the *Three Bears*, written by the Poet Laureate Robert Southey and first published in 1837, an 'impudent, bad old woman' is punished for encroaching on a man's world. In that original version, there is no character called 'Goldilocks' and her part is played by a diminutive hag who has her inquisitiveness and greed rewarded by being chased away by the bachelor bears. In Hans Christian Andersen's *Red Shoes*, penned in 1845, a vain peasant girl 'Karen' is spoiled by a gullible stepmother who buys her the eponymous footwear. When Karen goes to church and turns the eyes of the men, her fate is sealed and she is eventually obliged to chop off her feet to stop her dancing.

The role of women in the contemporary popular culture narrative has barely improved. Cinematic women are still routinely seen as sex objects, crazies, underwritten wives and vamps and woe betide any 'woman' who dares to get old. In the 1987 film *Fatal Attraction*, 'Alex', played by Glenn Close, becomes a bunny-boiling psychopath for daring to fall in love with a married man and the happy ending only arrives when his wife kills her. In the popular modern fairy tale known as '*The Beatles*', a wicked 'intruder' (also read: 'foreigner') Yoko Ono lures handsome John from his guitar-wielding fellow cavaliers, causing the downfall of the kingdom, the rise of Wings and the penning of 'The Frog Chorus'.

The few women who do prosper in public life, whether they be Angela Merkel, Margaret Thatcher or Queen Elizabeth II, are only grudgingly accepted because they 'act like men'. In both the satirical representations of her in shows like *Spitting Image* and in the eyes of her male Conservative colleagues, the first woman to be British prime minister was portrayed as a masculine figure, and she herself played up to the trope herself by adopting a much deeper voice after she took on the role.

Thatcher was the first British woman to be prime minister – but she was not our first female leader. That honour goes to Æthelflæd, daughter of King Alfred, born in about 870 CE. Long dismissed as a minor figure, who didn't even merit a mention in most history books of the period until the twenty-first century, she ruled as 'Lady of the Mercians'* over a crucial 32-year time frame, first in partnership with her husband, Æthelred (not the Unready), and for the last eight in her own right.

While the West Saxon *Anglo-Saxon Chronicle* would later write her off as little more than the puppet ruler of a client state beholden to her

* In the ninth century England was divided up into seven separate states, now known as the Heptarchy, and of those, Mercia was, along with Wessex, one of the two dominant states.

brother, King Edward the Elder of Wessex, this was very far from the case. In the last two years of her reign, she not only saw off a series of Viking incursions but took the fight to the enemy by extending Anglo-Saxon territory northwards. Between 917 and 918, her campaigning saw the Danish rulers of Derby and York both submit to her and as Æthelflæd led her army northwards, she displayed remarkable tactical verve and was an accomplished diplomat too. At Leicester, having laid waste to the countryside around the city, Æthelflæd made it known that if the locals surrendered everyone would be spared. And she was true to her word.

Her example probably normalised the notion of a woman ruler in the early tenth century because when she died, in 918, her daughter Ælfwynn briefly became the second Lady of the Mercians, which (incredibly) is the only occasion in English history when a mother has been succeeded by her daughter as a sovereign in these lands. The historian, Michael Wood, has suggested that 'without her England might never have happened' and as her nephew, Æthelstan, who was educated in her court, went on to use his unique position in the island to unite the kingdoms of Wessex and become the first king of England in 927, it's a compelling argument. Æthelflæd was a remarkable figure but while other queens regnant* of England followed, they did so with dispiriting intermittency.

In the 1,100 years since the establishment of the unified kingdom of England in 929 CE, there have been 57 English monarchs but just eight of them have been women ruling in their own right. Following Æthelflæd's death, it was almost 200 years until another queen came along and even then, the redoubtable Matilda, who sat on the throne during the 15-year period known as 'the Anarchy', is a contested monarch. From the end of her reign in 1148, it would be another 405 years until not one, but two women reigned in England – and both in the same year.

One of those was the 15-year-old Lady Jane Grey – and her successor and nemesis was the 37-year-old spinster daughter of Henry VIII, Mary.

* A queen in their own right rather than married to a king.

Most of us remember her better as 'Bloody Mary', the childless, wicked, murderous hag. A brief but violent amuse-bouche between the reign of the boy king Edward VI and the glorious Elizabethan age. But her life merits so much more attention than that.

* * *

A mile or so north of Harlow New Town, just off the A414 bypass there is a B road that winds its way to the village of Hunsdon and the Hadhams that lie beyond.

A mile or two along this bendy and ancient track, you come across the Norman church of St Dunstan's. Much is made on the parish's website of a link with Henry VIII, but in fact it is his daughter, Mary, who lived here for much of her adult life. Indeed, if you step into the graveyard, you can glimpse the roof and upper floors of her home, Hunsdon House, which peeks out above the surrounding gardens like an illustration in a children's fairy-tale book.

Princess Mary lived here for two decades in the mid-sixteenth century and it was in these environs, at midnight on 4 July 1553, that she made a decision which altered her life's course and that of English history. Of which more in a moment.

The previous day, Mary had received a message summoning her to the bed of her 15-year-old half-brother, King Edward VI, who was dying of tuberculosis at the Palace of Placentia in Greenwich. After months of deteriorating health, the boy king's hours were numbered and this was more than just a private tragedy. Edward was unmarried and childless and a crisis of succession loomed, which threatened the very stability of the kingdom.

Teenage Edward had spent his brief reign tightening the Protestant Reformation that his father had fomented when he split from the Catholic Church, in part to marry Anne Boleyn in 1533. That had led to Henry's excommunication from Rome and the 1534 Act of Supremacy by which he had made himself and his successors the Supreme Heads of the Church of England. The break with Rome had caused significant social and religious upheaval in the country, as well as in Henry's immediate private life, since his first wife and daughter, Mary, were naturally vehemently opposed to both the divorce and the break. While the King never really took to Protestantism himself, the Dissolution of the Monasteries had one positive side effect in that it made him fabulously rich. His son Edward, the only child of his third wife Jane Seymour, was a different creature altogether and was deeply committed to the cause.

The 1549 Acts of Uniformity, enacted when he was just 11, were a 'hard break with papacy' that had seen the reformist Archbishop of Canterbury impose standardised common prayers and practices that made any path back to Catholicism almost impossible.

Given the King's young age, he had yet to sire a child and this potential problem had been anticipated even before he took the throne. Under the terms of Henry VIII's third Act of Succession, signed in 1543, the King's daughters, Mary and Elizabeth, both previously declared bastards, had been returned to the line 'just in case' they were needed.

Now, as Edward lay dying, that had turned out to be the case.

On paper, the transition from Edward to his eldest sister Mary should have been straightforward, but there was a significant fly in the chrism* because she remained the most prominent die-hard Catholic in the country and there was a risk that she would reverse this sixteenth-century Brexit from Rome. So even as the very life sapped from him, the scheming and politicking began and nobody put in the hours quite like the regent, John Dudley, the First Duke of Northumberland.

Despite reassuring the 37-year-old princess in daily missives that she would become queen when her brother died, Dudley was plotting something altogether more beneficial to his own interests and had already conspired, with the dying Edward, to change the King's will in favour of his 16-year-old daughter-in-law, Lady Jane Grey, who was a great-granddaughter of Henry VII.

Edward idolised Northumberland and taking his advice, dictated letters patent from his deathbed which decreed that:

* Anointing oil at a coronation.

'I am convinced that my sister Mary would provoke great disturbances after I have left this life, and would leave no stone unturned, as the proverb goes, to gain control of this isle, the fairest in all Europe. My resolve is to disown and disinherit her together with her sister Elizabeth, as though she were a bastard and sprung from an illegitimate bed . . .'[4]

The King's other advisers, including Sir Edward Montagu, the Lord Chief Justice, harboured considerable concerns about the consequences. But given the King's frail condition and Northumberland's belligerence, Montagu and fellow councillors acquiesced and the letters patent were issued, sanctioning Lady Jane Grey's accession to the throne.

On 4 July 1553, the plot to crown Jane hit a rather significant snag when Mary, while preparing to leave Hunsdon for London, received intelligence that Northumberland's invitation to come to Greenwich was a trap. That left the 37-year-old princess with three options. Flee and forfeit her right to the throne, stay put and wait for Northumberland or fight on – and that evening, in the precincts of St Dunstan's, she chose the final course.

Ordering her party to follow her, she turned right on to that winding road and galloped north towards Cambridge.

With the unfortunate moniker of 'Bloody Mary' and her regrettable reputation for burning people alive at the stake, the future queen would later go down in history as one of monarchy's greatest villains. In fact, as both princess and queen, she had her lighter side too and, in addition to a great love of dancing, was an inveterate card player, who delighted in outwitting opponents at the table. Now those gambling instincts came to the fore as she treated her predicament like an elaborate hand of Primero*.

Her first move was to dispatch two letters: the first to the ambassadors of her cousin and ally Charles V, the Holy Roman Emperor, the most powerful man in Europe, forewarning him of her intention to declare herself queen. The second was a bluff, designed to buy time, by

* Mary's favourite card game. Although the rules do not survive it seems to have been an early form of poker which involved bluffing your opponents into submission with the aim of gaining the highest hand.

telling Northumberland that her personal physician had come down with plague and that she was moving her court to Norfolk to give him space to self-isolate. It was a cunning move but Northumberland was no idiot and sent armed men north to intercept her at the Cambridgeshire home of Sir John Huddlestone where she was believed to be staying. Arriving at the house the following afternoon, the duke's posse were told that Mary was long gone and responded, in predictable fashion, by burning Huddlestone's home to the ground.

That same day, 6 July, at around 6 p.m., young King Edward died and with the rogue 'queen' in East Anglia, Northumberland appreciated he now had a very serious problem on his hands. Mary was not only better known in England than Z-lister Lady Jane Grey, but she was also far more popular too. If she could raise an army and move on London she would have every advantage.

With this firmly in mind, on 8 July, Northumberland dispatched messages across the east of England warning that Mary with her 'ungodly pretenses' was plotting with foreign powers to seize power illegally. Mary had moved decisively, however, and had already reached the safety of her home in Kenninghall, Norfolk, where news of her brother's death – which was still being withheld from the wider public – caught up with her. Sending out messages of her own, she swiftly summoned support and began to amass an army.

Back in London, Northumberland played his own cards and, in an attempt to get the political upper hand, summoned Lady Jane Grey to his residence, Syon House, where he told her that she was now queen. Completely overwhelmed by the unwelcome news, Jane had a rather epic meltdown in front of him and her bewildered courtiers and her inconsolable state continued until her parents turned up and convinced her that everything would be OK. Jane was an intelligent young woman; well versed in Latin, Greek and antiquity, she may have already worked out how things were going to end.

Two days later, on 10 July, the new queen, her teenage husband Lord Guildford and their entourage processed on barges to the Tower of London to await her coronation – as was then the tradition. As the boats entered through the Lion Gate, there was little fanfare and the official proclamation of Jane's ascendancy, made by heralds across London the following day, went down like an offer of lukewarm tripe for breakfast. As her messengers marched about vainly shouting 'God save the Queen!', it was left to an apprentice called Gilbert Potter to point out loudly that nobody had ever heard of Lady Jane Grey and that everyone knew the rightful heir was Mary. For his services to truth, Gilbert was marched to Cheapside where his ears were nailed to a plank of wood and cut off.

That same Monday evening, Mary's messenger, Thomas Hungate, reached London and interrupted a royal banquet to deliver a letter to the senior churchmen and nobles who made up the Privy Council – effectively the government of England at the time. Mary's message, read aloud to the throng, demanded their loyalty:

'You know, the realm and the whole world knoweth; the rolls and records appear by the authority of the King our said father, and the King our said brother, and the subjects of this realm; so that we verily trust that there is no good true subject, that is, can, or would, pretend to be ignorant thereof.'[5]

This was their last chance and as Hungate trotted her words out, disquiet hung ever heavier in the air. For ruining the party, the messenger was ordered to be taken to the Tower – and as he was marched away, the Privy Council pushed their plates aside and called for the scribes to attend. The banqueting hall now became much like any modern political war room and, seeking to justify 'Queen Jane's' ascendancy, Northumberland and his advisers began knocking up a dodgy dossier which was then signed by the 23 councillors present. Though everything now appeared to be nice and legal, nobody could really have been convinced of that and in the centre of it all, the reluctant teenage queen sat in stony silence, her face drawn of colour – as she contemplated the poisoned chalice that had been thrust into her hands.

Like any contemporary power-broking, iPhone-wielding mandarin, Northumberland was fire-fighting on multiple fronts and seeking to seize back both the initiative and the narrative. Firing off a letter to

Charles V, the Holy Roman Emperor, he informed Europe's most powerful monarch of Edward's death and passive-aggressively told him that, in line with the late King's wishes, Jane was now Queen of England.

Simultaneously, Mary was writing letters of her own, to the very same people, and telling her cousin Charles that she was in fact the true queen. Away from London and ensconced in her Catholic Norfolk stronghold, she may already have been confident that momentum was on her side. That optimism was only slightly dashed when her cousin and former fiancé the Emperor wrote back seeking to talk her out of it. Seriously underestimating his cousin and believing that she was on a suicidal trajectory, he tried to convince her to accept Jane as queen but Mary was having none of it.

The following day, 11 July, the Privy Council gathered again and concocted another letter to Mary. Pointing out to her that her brother had signed 'letters patent' and that everyone who was anyone agreed with the late King that the teenager was the rightful heir, they argued that Mary had no right to the throne and that she was, in short, a bloody awkward woman who should leave the men to get on with running the country.

'You will upon just consideration thereof . . . and for the just inheritance of the right and godly orders taken by the late king our sovereign Lord Edward the 6th and agreed unto by the noble and great personages aforesaid, cease by your pretence to vex and molest any of our sovereign lady queen Jane's subjects, drawing from them the true faith and allegiance due unto her grace.'[6]

The council assured her that if she was *'quiet and obedient'*, no harm would come. But it was a lie as 400 cavalrymen under the command of Northumberland's son, Robert Dudley, were already scouring East Anglia for the errant princess, while back in London, his father was mustering troops. By the afternoon of the 12 July, he had a force of about 2,000 men made up of Yeomen of the Guard, German and Spanish mercenaries and detachments of cavalry and infantry, but a great big question mark hung over who would lead them. In his youth, Northumberland had been a renowned military commander, but now aged 48 and in failing health, he sought to pass the buck to Lady Jane's father, the sprightly 37-year-old Duke of Suffolk. Jane once again descended into tears and pleaded with Northumberland to leave her father at her side and do it himself and he bent to her command.

That same day, Mary marched her army, numbering 15,000 men at arms to Framlingham Castle, one of the most impressive strongholds of the day, and as she progressed, the good news just kept coming. Robert Dudley's 400 cavalrymen had been routed and forced to retreat to Bury St Edmunds. Norwich had come out on her side and so too had other towns to the west and south. All of this made the Privy Council even more jumpy and the following day, as Northumberland prepared to march his army north, the imperial ambassadors were secretly invited to a meeting with them. Most, quite obviously, had already switched their allegiances to Mary and Northumberland's grip on power was ebbing away.

Northumberland himself was a usurper. His rise to power (as John Dudley and later Earl of Warwick) had come on the back of his impressive military record and following the death of Henry VIII he had been appointed to the Regency Council which was led by his mentor, Edward Seymour, the Duke of Somerset as the Lord Protector. However, in 1549 and partly as a result of liberal agrarian policies that were supported by Somerset, popular unrest had broken out – and Dudley, now known as the Earl of Warwick, had seized the opportunity to oust him.

In July 1549, the people of East Anglia rose up against landowners who were fencing off common land and soon – and much like events in 1381 – another rebellion was afoot. This time the populist leader was a former tanner called Robert Kett, a yeoman farmer of the town of Wymondham in Norfolk, whose quarrel with another landowner called Flowerdew wound up with him leading 16,000 people in an armed revolt against the state. Kett's rebels, like their forerunners in 1381, gained significant momentum and having drawn up a list of fairly reasonable demands, they delivered them to the regent, Somerset, who was known to be sympathetic to their cause.

Dudley wasn't having it though and eventually defeated Kett's army at 'Dussindale' in Norfolk in August. At the end of play some 2,000 rebels were dead and that December, Kett swung from a rope off Norwich Castle.

In October 1549, Dudley toppled Somerset in a *coup d'état* and though he later sought to reconcile with him, the former Lord Protector was soon back behind bars. Charged with treason, he was executed for felony on 22 January 1552 and interred, as so many people in this chapter were destined to be – in the church of St Peter ad Vincula which lies within the walls of the Tower of London.

Though chaotic, Somerset had at least been popular and while Dudley, who made himself Duke of Northumberland in 1551, did rein in the spending and curb the nation's economic woes – the same could never be said for him. Distrusted by his councillors in London, it was widely assumed that he had one eye on the throne.

Northumberland, in short, was not a man who attracted loyalty and as Mary's momentum grew in July 1553, what support he had melted away. By Friday 14 July, Sir William Paget, an influential figure in the courts of both Edward VI and Henry VIII, was openly siding with Mary and suggesting that he was prepared to lead his own militia south.

Three days later on Monday 17 July, Northumberland reached Suffolk and was advancing on Bury St Edmunds, but with Mary's forces now numbering 30,000, his Ceausescu moment had come. With the regent out of town, the Privy Council deserted him and that same day they gathered at Baynard's Castle, home of William Herbert, the 1st Earl of Pembroke, where the Duke of Arundel read out a group statement to the assembled councillors:

'This crown belongs rightfully, by direct succession to my lady Mary, lawful and natural daughter of our King Henry VIII.'[7]

Northumberland's fate was sealed. The councillors left and made their way to Old St Paul's to give thanks, in an explicitly Catholic Mass, for England's deliverance from 'the wicked duke' and for the reinstatement of the rightful queen. Northumberland, encamped at Cambridge, was told the news by a party led by the Earl of Arundel who then arrested him. Realising the game was up and hoping to save his own and his family's necks, Lady Jane Grey's father Henry immediately left the Tower of London and loudly pledged his loyalty to Mary on Tower Hill. The following day, the disgraced Northumberland was paraded through the streets of London, alongside his sons, as the crowds threw human excrement at them. Amid fears that he might be lynched before he could be executed for treason, the Duke was then bundled into the Tower, while his eldest son stood sobbing in the street.

On Thursday 3 August, with Princess Elizabeth at her side, Mary rode into London in triumph as crowds greeted her and church bells rang. The Marian Age had dawned and Lady Jane Grey, queen for just 13 days*, got in fast with the excuses. In a remorseful letter, she accepted her own role while laying blame squarely at Northumberland's feet.

'I can have no hope of finding pardon . . . having given ear to those who at the time appeared not only to myself, but also to the great part of this realm to be wise and now have manifested themselves to the contrary. {They} have made a blamable and dishonourable attempt to give to others that which was not theirs . . .{and my own} lack of prudence . . . for which I deserve heavy punishment . . .'

Displaying remarkably un-Tudorish compassion, perhaps because she too had spent a life being manipulated by men, Mary showed mercy and although Jane was found guilty of high treason in November 1553, the Queen granted her and her husband a reprieve that allowed them to live on at the Tower with heads intact.

Once again, however, the ambitions of old men got in the way and when Jane's father was found to have been heavily involved in the Protestant Wyatt's rebellion that came early in Mary's reign, the teenage girl and her husband's fates were sealed.

Even then the Queen sought to save them one last time, promising that their lives would be spared if they converted to Catholicism – but it was not to be. Having both declined the offer, on 12 February 1554, Guildford was taken to Tower Hill where he was publicly beheaded in

* Jane was technically queen for 13 and not (as is popularly supposed) nine days. Unlucky for some.

front of a baying crowd. Later that afternoon, Jane was spared the same indignity and led in private to a place of execution within the Tower's walls. Offered a blindfold, she tied it herself and then stumbled forward, reaching for the block.

Not wishing to facilitate her end, those present held back until, in tears and agony she begged someone to help her, asking 'Where is it? What shall I do?' and was guided to her fate.

Having asked the axeman to 'dispatch me quickly', her end followed swiftly. Jane had just turned 17. Her body and that of her husband were taken to the Church of St Peter ad Vincula and buried without ceremony alongside the graves of the other high-profile traitors.

* * *

In order to make sense of Mary's reign we first need to examine her, at times, distressing childhood.

Princess Mary Tudor was born on 18 February 1516, the only surviving child of the 24-year-old King Henry VIII and his Spanish bride, Catherine of Aragon, then 31.

Mary's older brother, Henry Duke of Cornwall, born in 1511, had only lived a few weeks before dying, like so many other babies of his age in infancy. Catherine had had five further pregnancies which had all resulted in miscarriages and stillbirths, until Mary was born – an event which occasioned national jubilation.

Though pleased, Henry was not exactly cracking out the best mead because he not only wanted but really needed a boy. The King's father Henry VII, great-grandson of John of Gaunt on his mother's side, had seized power at the conclusion of the War of the Roses following the defeat of Richard III at the Battle of Bosworth in 1485 and many had viewed his legitimacy as tenuous at best. The disquiet had continued into Henry's own reign and to secure his dynastic ambitions and the future of the kingdom, a son was required.

Catherine may have thought rather differently. In stark contrast to the arriviste Tudors, Spanish-born Catherine descended from veritable A-list European royalty and was the product of a strong tradition of powerful women, including her mother, who was none other than Isabella I, Queen of Castile and Aragon. Isabella reigned in her own right and later in tandem with Catherine's father, Ferdinand II of Aragon in the dynastic alliance known as 'The Catholic Monarchs' and, until her death in 1504, was living proof that women could rule every bit as much as the men. Isabella was a hugely capable monarch who, after years of political turmoil and social chaos under her brother, Henry the Impotent, had brought relative peace and prosperity to her realm. That, of course, does not mean she was 'good' by our own standards as much of her wealth and power sprang from the subjugation of other people; it was Isabella and Ferdinand, after all, who financed a violent, navigationally illiterate thug Italian called Christopher Columbus on his first voyage west in 1492.

Isabella and Ferdinand had ruled during the 'Golden Age' of Spanish global imperial dominance that would make their dominion the unquestioned superpower of the fifteenth and sixteenth centuries, with all that entailed. But while the Golden Age may have been great for this fifteenth-century power couple, it wasn't much fun for most everyone else. For in addition to their many colonial conquests, the King and Queen were also responsible for the Spanish Inquisition, the expulsion of the Jews and Muslims from Spain in 1492 and the subjugation, murder and enslavement of the people of the Americas under the Spanish crown.

At the time, however, history had yet to judge them for that and the Spanish side of Mary's family were undoubtedly among the most powerful people in Europe at the time. Courtesy of her mother's side, Mary would also have known the fate that awaited strong-willed women who crossed the powerful men in their lives.

Following Isabella's death in 1504, Mary's aunt, Joanna, had become queen of Castile and Leon only to be horribly gaslit – first by her appalling husband Philip of Flanders (aka Philip the Handsome), whom she had married aged 16, and then by her own father. Joanna was not meant to be queen and had only got the gig by default when the line of succession above her died out one by one. A highly educated woman, as her power grew her errant husband Philip attempted to control his wife by using her personality against her. Philip the Handsome was a wrong 'un who repeatedly cheated on Joanna, and when his wife decided that she had had enough and attacked one of his lovers with a pair of scissors, he began to whisper that she was mad.

There are signs that Joanna may have been suffering from depression. Having six children, all born in less than ten years, would have put both physical and emotional pressure on anyone, but there had been other difficulties in her life too. In childhood, in the midst of the Spanish Inquisition, Joanna was tortured, on her mother's orders, for 'religious rebellion' and likely never recovered from the experience. Philip's cruelty, infidelity and reckless spending simply made a bad situation worse, but he had private ambitions of his own too and was plotting to usurp her.

Through his marriage to Joanna, Philip was the consort and not the King of Castile and Leon in his own right, but according to her mother Isabella's will, if she was to become 'unable to rule' then her father, Ferdinand II, had the right to take over. In June 1506, just two years into her reign, her husband and father conspired to push her off the throne, citing 'infirmities and sufferings, which for the sake of her honour are not expressed' and Philip took over. Two months later, he died unexpectedly, perhaps from typhoid but more likely as a result of having been poisoned by Ferdinand and subsequently, so it was claimed, Joanna went mad. According to later chroniclers she refused to part with her dead husband's body until her father removed her to the castle at Tordesillas, where she remained a prisoner for the rest of her life.

Whether Joanna was really 'mad' or a victim of the men in her life, or a bit of both, remains a matter of debate. Writing about her in the *British Journal of Psychiatry* in 2020, the psychiatrist Greg Wilkinson[8] suggested that there was no real evidence to support the case that she was mentally ill. Correspondence concerning her at the time of Philip's death makes no reference to her harbouring his body, or signs of insanity, and likewise when she visited England in 1507 to see her then widowed* sister Catherine of Aragon, no mention was made of her mental incapacity.

* Aged 15, Catherine had married Prince Arthur (also aged 15), older brother of Henry, in 1501 only for him to die a year later.

Throughout history, again and again, powerful men have sought to dismiss the women around them as 'hysterical', 'mad', 'vengeful' or 'irrational'. This trope of women being simultaneously threatening and inferior to men stretches from Eve to modern online misogynists. Joanna fits firmly into the pattern and whatever her truth, Joanna was certainly no 'madder' than her 'colourful' brother-in-law Henry VIII.

On account of her mother's heritage, Mary was raised speaking Spanish and from an early age was also schooled in Latin. Accounts of her childhood remark on her intelligence and acute awareness of what was going on around her – although, as with any gushing splash about the brilliance of contemporary royal princes and princesses, we should always take toadying with a pinch of salt. Whatever the spin, Mary was clearly bright and was doted on by her father who dubbed her the 'pearl in my world'.

The princess served as a useful diplomatic tool too and on 5 October 1518, aged two, was betrothed to the French Dauphin as part of the process of Anglo-French rapprochement known as the Treaty of London. The French signed on the condition that Mary was sole heir to the throne, but Catherine was secretly pregnant, and Henry hoped that a boy might be on the way. His hopes were dashed when the Queen gave birth to a stillborn girl some months later.

Mary never met the Dauphin and the arrangement was later annulled. By the age of five she was anyway betrothed to her 22-year-old cousin, Charles V of Spain, who 12 years later would become the Holy Roman Emperor.

In 1525, nine-year-old Mary was sent to live at Ludlow Castle in Shropshire, where a court had been established for her in view of her role as the symbolic ruler of Wales. Though this sounds like a negligent bit of parenting, it was common at the time for members of the royal family to live apart and operate separate courts. Though often referred to as the Princess of Wales, she was never formally given the title but either way, was taking on a position that had, for 50 years, been held by men. Her appointment suggests that Henry viewed her as his heir apparent – despite, by now, having sired a longed-for son.

Henry Fitzroy*, born in Essex in 1519, was the King's child by his mistress Elizabeth Blount, and, though kept out of the public eye, was raised in the court nursery until 1525, when Henry considered legitimising him for the purposes of succession. Fitzroy was given Durham House, now the site of the Adelphi Theatre on the Strand and at an elaborate state occasion at the Bridewell Palace, on 18 June 1525, was made Duke of Richmond and Somerset by his doting father. This was the first time in almost 200 years that a king had recognised an illegitimate child as a potential heir and it instilled considerable disquiet in Henry's queen, Catherine, who had not only been very publicly humiliated, but had also been made to look inadequate for failing to produce a son.

Richmond later became Lord Lieutenant of Ireland, but by the time he married Lady Mary Howard in 1533, aged 14, his moment had passed and Henry VIII had a new preoccupation in his life, in the shape of Anne Boleyn. In the traditional narrative of Henry's dynasty, the arrival of Anne on the scene heralds the start of that famous cycle of the *divorced, beheaded, died, divorced, beheaded, survived*. But that does Catherine and her daughter Mary considerable disservice, because they did everything in their power to frustrate the wayward King's attempts to mute and block them from his story. The rhyme is inaccurate too, for Catherine was never formally divorced, since Henry argued they had never been married in the first place.

Anne Boleyn was a strong woman and from the moment Henry set eyes on her in 1526, when she was in her mid-twenties, she refused to be – as her sister had been before her – just the King's 'bit on the side'. In order to get her into bed, Henry would have to put a ring on her finger, so he petitioned Pope Clement VII for an annulment of his first marriage, arguing that as Catherine had been wed to his late brother, the 24-year-long partnership had been incestuous and thus illegal.

Catherine did all she could to frustrate that narrative and her nephew Charles V leaned heavily on the pope to put pressure on England's most important primate, Cardinal Wolsey, to stand up to the King. But Henry

* Fitzroy means 'son of the king'.

and his mistress were not ones to be cowed into submission and eventually, with the connivance of Archbishop Thomas Cranmer, they plotted to break with Rome altogether. The English Reformation that followed had repercussions that would resonate for centuries and affect millions of lives – but in the short term it also brought very personal misery to the door of Henry's teenage daughter.

In 1531, Catherine was evicted from the Palace of Placentia and moved to Kimbolton Castle in Cambridge where she became a virtual prisoner. Two years later, on 1 June 1533, having stripped both his first wife and his daughter of their titles and reduced Mary to the status of a 'cursed bastard', Henry married Anne in an elaborate ceremony at Westminster Abbey. But if he thought he had won he had another think coming because 17-year-old Mary was not about to let Henry get away with his toxic, alpha-male bullshit.

Much of what we know about what followed comes courtesy of the correspondence of Eustace Chapuys, a Savoy-born French diplomat in the service of Charles V who worked as his imperial envoy to the court of King Henry. Chapuys had fought Catherine's corner in the row over the legitimacy of her marriage and he continued to be a stout defender of both her and her daughter against the machinations of Anne, whom he referred to as a 'whore'. Following the birth of Princess Elizabeth on 7 September 1533, a girl whom Chapuys called the 'little bastard', moves to reduce Mary's status intensified as Anne sought to drive her to irrelevance and Chapuys, with a ringside seat, witnessed it all, and reported that:

'A rumour is afloat . . . that her household and allowance are to be shortly reduced. May God in his infinite mercy prevent a still worse treatment! Meanwhile the Princess, prudent and virtuous . . . has taken all these things with patience, entrusting entirely in God's mercy and goodness. She has addressed to her mother, the queen, a most wonderful letter full of . . . comfort.'[9]

Mary's refusal to accept her lot ended with her being sent to live at Hatfield (old) House, where under the watchful eye of Anne Shelton, Anne Boleyn's paternal aunt, she essentially became both a prisoner and Elizabeth's nanny.

Hatfield nearly killed her and Mary's health went into steep decline as she became ever more withdrawn and sickly. She deteriorated so rapidly that Chapuys became convinced that she was being poisoned and, in a sense, she was because taking the 'medicine' that was proffered by apothecaries in the sixteenth century could often have lethal consequences.

In the absence of proper medical reports, it's unclear what exactly was wrong. For most of her childhood, Mary had had fairly robust health and apart from a bout of smallpox in 1528, there had been nothing much to write home about. But as she entered puberty, she began to suffer terribly from menstrual pain and irregular cycles, which were diagnosed by her mother's apothecary as 'strangulation of the womb'. Mary – like her aunt Joanna the Mad – was probably depressed too and, frankly, who could blame her? Abandoned by her father, unable to see her beloved mother and reduced from the status of heir to the throne to a bastard servant, she had fallen just about as far as it was possible to go. Friendless and alone, her one companion was Anne Shelton who was obliged to slap her violently if she ever suggested she was a princess. Royal families are rarely functional but this one was in another league.

Mary had also been denied her last great pleasure as she was now refused permission to ride horses, for fear that she might try to escape. Her already slim chances of marriage had also been reduced further as tales of her supposedly erratic behaviour spread.

As the months passed, her health only deteriorated and in addition to those often debilitating menstrual cycles, she suffered intense toothaches, vomiting, neuralgia and bouts of fever.

In January 1534, on a whim, Henry decided to visit Mary and his baby daughter Elizabeth and set out to Hatfield some 25 miles north of London. As soon as he left, Anne started to fear that her stepdaughter might try to wrap him around her teenage finger and ordered Thomas Cromwell, Henry's chief adviser and friend, to intercept the King and dissuade him from meeting Mary. Cromwell duly caught up with Henry and suggested that he should meet Mary in his place. But when Cromwell encountered the young woman, she was in no mood to be told what to do. 'Lady' Mary told Cromwell she had no intention of giving up her birthright and that if her father and Anne thought that bullying her would break her spirit – they had another think coming.

Mary then sought permission to meet her father and kiss his hand but was refused. As the King and his adviser left later that day and trotted away back towards Ermine Street, Henry turned momentarily and saw Mary, on the terrace above the hall, kneeling in his direction with her hands clasped together in silent prayer. Her father tipped the edge of his hat at her and rode back to London. Later he would tell Chapuys that the princess's obstinacy was down to her Spanish blood and when the envoy remarked that she had been wonderfully brought up, 'tears came into (Henry's) eyes and he could not refrain from praising her'.[10]

The battle of wits continued but by the start of the following year, the King had lost what little reserves of patience he had left and Mary was told to submit to the Acts of Succession and Supremacy passed the previous year and ordered 'on pain of her life . . . not to call herself Princess or her mother Queen and that if she does, she will be sent to the Tower'.[11]

The King meant business and if any further proof of that was needed it came when he executed John Fisher, Bishop of Rochester, and Thomas More, his former Lord Chancellor, for refusing to submit to the act. Fisher's naked headless corpse was displayed at Tower Hill under his command and while More dodged the traditional death meted out to the traitor he was beheaded and interred without ceremony at St Peter ad Vincula. His head was then poached until it had softened adequately to be impaled on a spike before being taken to London Bridge, where it was reduced to bone by ravens.

Such extreme violence meted out on such a famous and celebrated figure, who had once been a key adviser to the King, sent shock waves around Europe, in much the same way that the executions of French aristocrats were to terrify their English counterparts in the 1790s. The general consensus was that Henry VIII had completely lost his mind – and naturally his bride got the blame for that too. Wicked Anne was clearly urging him on to ever more heinous atrocities and Chapuys wrote that the King was fulfilling his destiny, 'that is that at the beginning of his reign he would be as a gentle as a lamb, and at the end, worse than a lion'.

Filled with disquiet, Mary began making plans to flee to Europe.

On 7 January 1536, fate intervened when Catherine of Aragon died at Kimbolton Castle in Norfolk. Twenty-two days later she was buried at Peterborough Cathedral and even as Mary mourned her loss, the tide began to turn in her favour.

On 24 January 1536, while jousting in full armour at Greenwich, the 44-year-old king was nearly killed when he was knocked from his horse, only for the huge animal to fall on top of him. Henry suffered significant trauma to his head and was initially thought to have suffered a fatal injury.

Anne collapsed on hearing the news, had a miscarriage and lost a baby boy.

It was the beginning of the end and by the late spring, Boleyn had fallen spectacularly from favour. Apophenia, the human tendency to tie together disconnected and random events into one conspiratorial whole, may have played a part. After all – at least if you were superstitiously minded – it all made sense. Catherine's death had been followed by the King's near fatal accident and Anne's miscarriage of a potential male heir. The Tudor preoccupation with superstition and sorcery went into overdrive and some began to whisper that Anne was a witch who had cast a spell on her husband and the kingdom. In any other circumstances, Anne could have relied on Henry to defend her, but having suffered trauma during his jousting accident, the King was behaving oddly and unpredictably and had fallen out of love with Boleyn.

The consequences for Anne were fatal. In May 1536 she was accused of high treason for engaging in adulterous relationships with five men, including her own brother, George, the Viscount Rochford and Henry Norris, who she had flirtatiously suggested would make a good replacement husband. The charges were ridiculous as it could be proved that Anne and the men she was accused of having sex with were in different places, often many miles apart, when they were allegedly committing the acts. But unfortunately, in Tudor England, you were guilty until proved innocent and Anne's fate was sealed. The prosecution also charged that she and her co-defendants had formed a Boleynite caucus that was frustrating the schemes of Thomas Cromwell including his plans to introduce the Act of Suppression, which would lead to the Dissolution of the Monasteries. Anne had also disagreed with his moves to forge an anti-French alliance with the Holy Roman Empire.

In short, this 'bloody difficult woman' needed to go.

Henry had probably grown tired of Anne even before he had his accident. The marriage had led to the break with Rome; the execution of some of his closest friends including his 'father figure' Thomas More; he had been excommunicated from the Catholic Church; and nearly died in the accident which had seen Anne suffer a miscarriage. His previous relationship with Anne's sister, Mary, may also have caused him to believe that he had himself committed incest and that his lack of a male heir and near death was down to God's general displeasure. By this logic, Anne's execution would be a form of atonement that would wipe the slate clean and allow him to wed Jane Seymour – the latest woman to catch his eye.

On 17 May 1536, Thomas Cranmer annulled Henry's marriage to Anne. That same day, George Boleyn and his fellow defendants were beheaded on Tower Hill. Two days later, Jean Rombaud, generally agreed to be the greatest celebrity executioner of his time, was brought over from Calais by Henry VIII as a 'favour' to his condemned wife. Rombaud removed her head with a single swipe of his custom-made, Toledo-forged sword and headless Anne Boleyn and the other plotters were taken to St Peter ad Vincula and added to the pile.

Eleven days later, Henry married Jane.

Mary now sought to reconcile with her father and found an ally in her new stepmother. Finally submitting to her father's demands, she was now brought back into the fold.

The following year, in October 1537, Edward, the much longed for son and heir, was finally born. But tragedy followed and two weeks later Jane died as a result of complications from giving birth. Mary was now propelled back into prominence, taking her place as her father's hostess and de facto queen, while becoming her baby stepbrother's godmother. With a solid male heir on the scene, the pressure was off and Mary was free to retire to Hunsdon and indulge in her love of gambling – while courtiers set about proposing a line of unsuitable suitors for her to marry. One of those candidates, as suggested by Thomas Cromwell, was the Duke of Cleves, a powerful German prince who in 1539 inherited his father's lands and was, at 23, the same age as Mary. The arrangement came to nothing, but the duke's older sister Anne was single and Cromwell – with fateful consequences – arranged a match between her and the King.

In the well-known story, the renowned portraitist Hans Holbein was dispatched to knock off a portrait of her and when he saw it, the King was bowled over by her beauty only for their first meeting, in December 1539, to descend into disaster.

The by now decidedly eccentric king thought that a good way to greet his betrothed would be to jump out at her in disguise. This ill-advised strategy seems to have seriously annoyed Anne, who didn't recognise the irritating personage who was leaping about and that caused the King to start shouting:

'I like her not; I like her not.'

Popular history, to its shame, has propagated the sexist myth that Anne was 'ugly' and that the King was repelled by her, but in fact this was not the case. The evidence suggests that Anne's portrait was accurate, that she was indeed very attractive and strong-willed with it and that it was the obese and unhinged king who was a turn-off and not the other way around. The marriage went ahead but was never consummated. On their wedding night, Anne deserted her grotesquely obese husband and his festering leg ulcer and slept elsewhere which was just about the worst insult that Henry could suffer.

While not the entire cause of Cromwell's subsequent downfall, the Cleves debacle was the first tottering domino that would lead to his execution in July 1540 and after three botched hacks by the incompetent executioner, he too was laid to rest in St Peter ad Vincula.

Anne of Cleves and Henry had divorced three weeks earlier – and, though now very much an ex-wife, she had managed to dodge the fate that had met so many others who caused Henry displeasure. The 'great survivor' went on to be an influential figure in Tudor England. Granted the title 'the King's sister', she was given ample estates including Hever Castle and Richmond Palace while working hard to further reconcile her friend, Princess Mary, with her father the King.

Two more wives followed. Catherine Howard, a mere teenager, was bullied into being the wife of a 28-stone (178 kg) man who was more than 30 years her age. Shortly after Henry's 50th birthday she began an affair with a courtier and when they were caught, both their fates were sealed. The twice widowed Catherine Parr, Henry's last wife, survived him when Henry finally died in 1547.

The ascent of Mary's teenage brother and his meddling Lord Protectors upended Mary's life. Henry VIII may have dissolved the monasteries and broken with Rome, but England had otherwise remained to all intents and purposes a Catholic country and most rituals and observances had gone unchanged. With Edward now on the throne, the Reformation stepped up a pace and under the guidance of Thomas Cranmer, things turned positively puritanical. As moves were made to introduce the English language *Book of Common Prayer* and abolish High Mass, 31-year-old Princess Mary responded by becoming increasingly devout in her faith.

In doing so, she posed a threat to the authority of her young brother and the plans of his Protestant advisers, and on at least one occasion she again considered fleeing England and going to live under the protection of Charles V. But she prevailed and outwitted her enemies and on Sunday 1 October 1553, was crowned Queen at Westminster Abbey in the presence of her younger sister Elizabeth. It was the pivotal moment in her life. Her defiance had won through and more to the point, she had secured her place, as a woman, in the historical narrative.

Next up on her to-do list was an heir and that meant that she needed a man.

Courtiers and ambassadors began casting their eyes about for a suitable candidate until they came to rest on Philip II of Spain, King of

Naples and Sicily, heir to the Spanish crown and the son of Charles V. The Holy Roman Emperor approved of the match, not least because he realised it would extend Habsburg influence across the entire continent of Europe.

The notion of a Spanish king meddling in England's affairs was the source of much disquiet and in November 1553, a parliamentary delegation, led by the Speaker, Sir John Pollard, approached Mary and begged her to choose an English suitor instead. Their preference was for her kinsman, Edward Courtenay, but Mary had been sent a picture of Philip and found him easy on the eye. Having listened to Pollard witter on for hours about her duty, she then told the assembled throng that it was:

'Entirely vain for you to nominate a perspective husband for me from your own fancy but rather let it be my free choice to select a worthy husband for my bridal bed, one who will not only join with me in mutual love but will be able with his own resource to prevent an enemy attack from his native land.'[12]

News of her betrothal went down badly and anti-Spanish sentiment, whipped up in popular broadsheets and ballads, began circulating in London and elsewhere. In early 1554 it resulted in the Wyatt's Rebellion, an uprising whose leaders included the eponymous Thomas Wyatt, William Thomas (a religious scholar), Henry and Edward Courtenay and Henry Grey, the Duke of Suffolk himself. Having set the ball rolling at Maidstone, Wyatt and his men marched on London and before you could say 'Wat Tyler' they were at Southwark trying to cross the River Thames.

On 1 February, with the fate of her reign hanging in the balance, Mary delivered a barnstorming speech to the hustings at the Guildhall in London, where she waved her coronation ring and, in a calm, rational and deliberately deep voice, declared:

'I love my people as a mother loves a child.'

The revolt quickly collapsed and few of the rebel leaders were spared. Somewhat predictably, Wyatt himself was hanged, drawn and quartered.

Nine months after her coronation, in July 1554, Mary, now aged 37, got her wish and married Philip of Spain. At 27, he was a full decade younger than her and, to add to the general complications of 'keeping it in the family', referred to her as his aunt. To placate Parliament and any other nascent rebels, including her own sister Elizabeth, who was suspected of involvement in the Wyatt's Rebellion, Philip was appointed *jure uxoris** and not crowned king of England and Ireland in his own right.

The joy that had greeted Mary when she had first processed into London had now, however, been replaced with general unease. Philip, like his wife, was a devout Catholic and while Mary sought to reassure her council that she was not about to mimic her grandparents and conduct her very own 'English Inquisition', there were fears among proponents of the new Protestant orthodoxy that she would seek to reverse the Reformation.

* * *

The Marian Age was brief and a period of decidedly mixed blessings – which is why, perhaps, Queen Mary is not as celebrated as her sister Elizabeth.

But as rulers of the era go, she was far more capable and stable than her brother, or for that matter her late father, and a significantly better monarch than occult-obsessed James I who would eventually take over from her sister in 1603. Henry and Edward's reigns were characterised by upheaval, violence and futile wars and by contrast, the start of Mary's five-year reign saw some improvements in the general condition of the nation. The economy stabilised, spending was curbed – and to begin with, at least, she sought to be a conciliatory figure.

Promising to uphold religious tolerance she insisted that she would not force her own faith on the nation and appointed a council of ministers made up of both Protestants and Catholics. Unfortunately, those early good intentions didn't last long and soon she was seeking to reverse everything her brother and father had done. Frustrated in her attempts to reclaim the lands of the lost monasteries and their treasures, in 1554

* Literally meaning 'by right of his wife' so a king consort and not a king of England.

she reinstated the Heresy Laws with the Act of Repeal, and in doing so, put the lives of just about every powerful Protestant in the land in jeopardy.

Henceforth it was now a crime, punishable by death, to deny papal supremacy and by dint of that the Catholic Church was now once again the top dogma in town.

Through the move, Mary had basically declared open season on Protestantism and hundreds of wealthy families upped and fled for the safety of German and Swiss religious enclaves taking their money with them. When the Queen moved to confiscate their estates the following year, Parliament blocked her and, frustrated in her mission, she started to burn people instead. The Act of Supremacy, passed in 1555, reimposed Papal predominance on England and those who would not submit faced the consequences.

Archbishop Cranmer was the first senior figure to fry. Cranmer had supported the break from Rome and had been critical in annulling Mary's parents' marriage and declaring her a bastard and quite obviously this was why his fate was sealed.

Convicted of heresy and condemned as a traitor, Cranmer publicly recanted his belief in the Protestant cause – but after two years in prison, he was sentenced to be burned alive at the stake anyway.

On 21 March 1556, the pyre was ready and Cranmer was led from his cell to meet his end. This was to be a powerful and symbolic moment and proof that Catholicism was now firmly back in town in Marian England, but on the day the 66-year-old Cranmer ruined everything by displaying extraordinary bravery. Sensationally disavowing his previous recantation, he condemned the pope and transubstantiation and reasserted his belief in Protestantism, before sticking his right arm, with which he had signed the proclamation, into the fire.

In a literal flash his death relit the Protestant reformers' cause while Mary's former popularity went up in flames, like so many martyrs.

Mary's reign was in fact far more 'burny' than 'bloody' but, semantics aside, certainly the crimes against humanity carried out in her name were appalling. In total some 300 Protestant martyrs met their end in her reign and in the execution of Cranmer and others she proved herself to be as violent and vengeful as her father. This was all succour to the Protestant cause and the theologian and historian John Foxe, who himself had been forced into exile by her, would subsequently compile a book called *The Actes and Monuments* (1563), better known as *The Book of Martyrs,* which chronicled the atrocities carried out in her name. Foxe's compendium was hugely influential and would go on to become the second-biggest-selling book of the sixteenth century, after the Bible – sealing her notoriety in the process.

One of Foxe's tales, the story of the Guernsey Martyrs, who were executed in the Channel Islands for their heresy in 1556, is typical.

Three women – two sisters Guillemine Gilbert and Perotine Massey and their mother Catherine – were arrested for stealing a goblet but during their trial it transpired that they were heretics. Subsequently, all three were ordered to be burned alive in public. Perotine was eight months pregnant and as she suffered her terrible fate her baby burst from her womb. The infant was taken to safety, only for the island's bailiff to order that the newborn be thrown back in the fire.

We, in Western Europe, live in a broadly secular age so it can be a challenge to comprehend that even our very recent ancestors viewed the world in extremist religious terms, and while we should never make excuses for it, a sort of perverted logic was at play. In the sixteenth century, Christians, on both sides of the Reformation, believed that heresy was a contagious illness that could only be contained through the literal incineration of those infected and further, by being burned at the stake, those who suffered the disease had the opportunity to experience the torment of the hellfire that awaited them and thus repent before meeting God.[13]

It's also worth bearing in mind that while Mary's brief reign – spanning just five years – was peppered with such horrors, it was hardly dissimilar in that to those of her siblings and her father. Henry VIII, who was king for 37 years, not only beheaded two of his six wives but also ordered the execution of many of his closest friends. During his reign at least 81 people were burned at the stake and an estimated 72,000 others were executed. His son Edward VI, monarch for five years, oversaw the killing of 5,500 Catholics, while Elizabeth, Mary's successor and queen regnant for 44 years executed 800 Catholic rebels at the conclusion of the 1569 Rising of the North and had 183 mostly Jesuit Catholics hanged, drawn and quartered for daring to practise their faith during her reign.[14] None of them were given a cartoonish sobriquet for their efforts and that's simply because the Protestant England that followed was forged out of their legacy, not Mary's. Ultimately, England's first queen regnant was demonised because it suited Anglican propaganda.

The legacy of any reign is also as much about good fortune as anything. Those, like our own late non-executive Queen Elizabeth II, who reign in quiet, prosperous and largely peaceful times, tend to be more popular than those who rule through chaos and disaster.

Mary was an executive monarch and though the many problems that plagued her time on the throne were largely beyond her control, the buck stopped with her.

In 1557, a flu pandemic struck England and an estimated 2 per cent of the population died as a result; but in some rural settlements the pandemic claimed upwards of 60 per cent and in London around 7 per cent out of a population of a little over 100,000 died. At the same time, an extreme weather event saw scorching heat and droughts precede unprecedented rainfall that destroyed crops across England. Famine, wage hikes and (our old friend) rampant inflation came hot on the heels of each other and were all blamed on the Queen; but even greater calumny, at least for England's flailing self-esteem, ensued when the country's last French possession, Calais, was lost in January 1558.

Things were no better in her private life either. Philip spent much of his brief time in England exerting what influence he had in trying to further the interests of Spain and to the detriment of everyone else. Besotted as she was with her much younger husband, the Queen still hoped that he would sire the child she so desperately needed to secure her legacy; but the affection was one way and nature, like so much else in her life, was not on her side. Twice she believed herself pregnant and twice ridicule ensued when, after months of sequestering herself away at the

Palace of Placentia in readiness, no baby arrived. The second pregnancy may in fact have been an advanced stage of cancer as, several months after the baby failed to appear, on 17 November 1558, the by now very frail queen died.

She was 42 years old.

* * *

Elizabeth now became queen and, refusing to marry the many men who were pushed her way, went on to eclipse her sister's legacy completely. Her 44-year rule secured the Protestant future with all the good and bad things that that entailed. England, the religious outsider, found in its break with Rome the green shoots of an identity which had previously eluded it. Culture flourished, overseas trade and colonial expansion followed and Little England became a needle in the side of mighty Spain from the time of the Armada (1588) onwards.

Meanwhile, Foxe's *The Book of Martyrs*, first published in March 1563, sealed Mary's place in history as the great villain of the age. Henceforth, the country's first true queen regnant was destined to be remembered as an unhinged, spinsterish witch.

Bloody Mary we remember; Mary I we forget.

In most standard history books and TV documentary series that cover the era, Mary merits little more than a passing mention or a walk-on role. Despite her extraordinary story, Mary not only failed to get her own Ladybird book but was not even afforded the dignity of her own grave either. In 1606, James I had Queen Elizabeth's body moved and buried in the same spot as her older sister, with the later greater monarch now very much trumping Mary's place in the Westminster Abbey ranking of famous tombs.

A plaque on the spot reads: *Partners both in throne and grave, here rest we two sisters Elizabeth and Mary, in the hope of one resurrection.*

Most of our monarchs do not deserve the exaggerated place in history that we afford them and far too many are given a free pass for their deeds. Henry VIII was a violent and frankly unhinged dictator and not some handsome rogue, and while the Elizabethan Age was later forged (largely by Victorian hagiographers) into another golden era, it was, in truth, a time of nascent imperialism and slavery which only benefitted a very small number of people.

None of us controls the manner in which we are remembered, and if you are famous or powerful then you have even less mastery of its course. Mary's story is no exception – and though her brief reign was unexceptional, there has to be a sense that her treatment in the narrative is no small part down to her being a strong and opinionated woman who sought to get her own way in a world of men.

Commit that cardinal sin – and history will condemn you or seek to sideline you altogether.

CHAPTER FIVE

GANGSTERS

The Enduring Appeal of the Outlaw

It was late on the bitterly cold night of 28 November 1926 and while the rest of Illinois slept, the lights were on in the basement of the Hawthorne Hotel on West 22nd Street, Cicero where Tony 'the Greek' Anton and his friend Mr Brown were shooting the breeze.

Tony, 35, was a former boxing champion, not long retired from the ring, who ran a string of concerns on the block, including a smoke room, two hotels and the basement restaurant itself. Brown, 26, was an entrepreneur who lived in a suite of apartments on the top floor of the Hawthorne and his ever-expanding paunch served as testament to the wealth he had accrued in the second-hand furniture market – then booming in Illinois.

The two men enjoyed each other's company and liked nothing more than to smoke cigars and exchange banter over a bottle of bourbon and this night had been much like any other – until suddenly the restaurant doorbell rang.

Hearing the chime, Tony raised himself wearily from the table, telling his friend:

'Customers! I'll get their orders and be back in a second.'[1]

But Mr Brown was never to see him again.

A little under a week later, on 4 December, Tony's bloodied coat was discovered in a patch of snow and a month after that, on 6 January 1927, the *Chicago Herald Examiner* broke the terrible news. The former boxer's frozen corpse had been discovered in a shallow grave in Burnham, Illinois with a lime-filled paper bag tied over his head; two rounds had been plugged into his face – the hallmark of a gangland execution – before 'an inflammable liquid (had been) poured over the body and set aflame'. The hotel owner was also missing the third finger on his right hand, sawn off to extract a hefty diamond ring that had once been wedged on it.

Chicago had seen its fair share of violence across the decade but the murder sent shock waves through the city, and nobody was more affected than Tony's friend, Mr Brown. As he and other mourners followed the coffin to its final resting place at the Elmwood cemetery, the businessman seemed inconsolable as he dabbed the tears from his eyes. But even as he gathered with fellow mourners at the graveside, some were doubting his sincerity; which was fair enough, because everyone present knew that the second-hand furniture dealer 'Mr Brown' was really called Alphonse 'Scarface' Capone and he had never sold so much as an antique commode in his life.

But had Capone really whacked The Greek? After all, the two men had been on very friendly terms and in some respects, Tony had been Al's number one fan. The restaurateur loved to regale customers with tales of the big man's generosity and in particular that time when a bedraggled newspaper boy had appeared at the boss's table trying to sell him an evening paper on a rain-drenched night. Taking pity on the kid, Al had handed him a $20 bill and bought all the papers before telling him to 'run along home to your mother'.[2]

It was typical of his legendary largesse and Tony had benefitted from it too because Al paid well above the going rate to live in his hotel suite, which was known locally as Capone's Castle, and in addition, kept an entire phalanx of bodyguards on the floor below. The arrangement had made the former boxer a whole heap of dough, but then again, by the time of his disappearance, Tony was known to have been having second thoughts about his guest – on account of the dangerous company he kept and the attraction he drew.

The problems had started two years earlier, in January 1925, when Capone's boss and mentor, Johnny Torrio, had been gunned down outside his home at 7011 Clyde Avenue. Having been hit five times, he only narrowly escaped death, when his would-be executioner's gun jammed, and it had been a sobering and somewhat transformative experience. The mobster had subsequently quit the game and high-tailed it to Sicily, leaving Al as de facto CEO of the South Side Gang – aka 'the Outfit' – then the biggest racket in Illinois. But the promotion to senior management had made Al and his fortified 'castle' suite in Cicero a prime target for every hoodlum in the city.

Prior to that ambush, Torrio had been a conciliatory figure among the rival gangs slogging it out for supremacy in the Chicago 'beer wars'. Arguing that there was more than enough business to go round, he had sought to bring peace to the various mobs, arguing that violence was a distraction from the real business of making money. But the rival North Side Gang had other ideas and its leader, Dean O'Banion, had repeatedly tried to encroach on Torrio's territory and take over his business. To his credit, Torrio had responded to the aggression with remarkable sangfroid and, in magnanimous fashion, had even cut O'Banion in on some of the action, but the North Side leader repaid the favour by betraying him to the cops and it became clear that O'Banion was a liability.

Shortly after Torrio's release from custody, while arranging chrysanthemums in Schofield's – the downtown flower shop that served as his HQ – O'Banion was taken out and in revenge, his successor, Hymie 'The Pole' Weiss, had then ordered the hit on Torrio which resulted in him fleeing to Sicily.

Weiss, like O'Banion before him, wanted to be the biggest hood in town and, emboldened by Torrio's departure, he determined to seize control of the South Side empire now being run by Al Capone. On 20 September 1926, a convoy of eight cars drove down West 22nd Street, parked up in front of Tony the Greek's premises and emptied a thousand rounds into the restaurant while Capone was eating his lunch. Al only survived because his quick-witted bodyguard, Frank Rio, threw him under a table and lay on top of him.

The heat was on and soon the cops had descended on Cicero and were raiding Tony's premises, causing him to get jumpy and perhaps it was that which led him to seek a way out of the partnership. Following his death, the suspicion among his friends was that he had asked Capone to leave, that Al refused to go and that was why he had been killed.

Al was already a well-known figure in Illinois in 1927 and had been since May 1924 when 'Alphonse Caponi' had made headlines after being accused of firing six bullets into a small-time hoodlum, Joe Howard, at Heinie Jacobs' saloon. On that occasion the many witnesses to the killing had suffered a contagious bout of amnesia when called to give evidence and that had led a publicity-hungry, crusading 24-year-old assistant state attorney, William H. McSwiggin, going after the hoodlum only for him to wind up dead too.

McSwiggin's murder on 27 April 1926, while out drinking with the notorious 'McDonnell gang' in Cicero, had briefly catapulted 'Caponi' into the national press, and the matter was only concluded when Al surrendered to US agents in the safe knowledge that they had nothing on him. But now, nine months later and in the wake of Tony the Greek's murder, all eyes were focused on him once again, and with questions swirling about the threat he posed to public safety, Al responded by doing something incredible. On a Sunday afternoon in January 1927, he invited a group of pressmen to his house on Prairie Avenue and when they arrived at the door, they were greeted by Capone, in bright pink apron and clutching a wooden spoon from which he was eating freshly made bolognese. Having invited them inside he served a splendid lunch, accompanied by fine Italian wines, before proffering his opinions on a host of subjects ranging from sport to the murder of his friend Tony Anton. Al insisted that he was innocent. Tony was his friend and anyway he did not approve of violence because it was bad for business and all he wanted to do was make money.

By the time the journalists left, Scarface Capone had metamorphosed, Cinderella-like, into a lovable, wise-cracking media 'personality' called Al Capone. One part businessman, one part romantic outlaw in the grand Western tradition of Butch Cassidy or Billy the Kid. The kind of guy who sticks it to the man while giving the public what they want – cheap booze.

Later in his life, Al would come to bitterly regret that press conference, but in 1927 with his most prominent enemies six feet under, millions in the bank and the press singing his praises – the world was at his feet. In the words of the contemporary author and journalist F.D. Pasley, 'Capone emerged supreme and unchallenged as Chicago's bootleg boss – the John D. Rockefeller of some twenty thousand anti-Volstead filling-stations.'[3]

It had all begun quite differently.

* * *

Like so many other tales of the American dream, this one starts as a story of immigration.

In 1894, five years before Capone was born, his parents Gabriele and Teresa left Angri, the small town 25 kilometres northwest of Salerno in southern Italy, and set out with their two small children for the promised land. The young couple were ambitious people and they wanted to make a better future for themselves and their growing family. Gabriele was an artisan, a baker and a *pastaio** who, unlike most of his fellow southern Italians at the time, was able to both read and write. He was adaptable too, so when his attempts to find work as a pasta maker in New York failed, he took itinerant jobs on building sites before reinventing himself as a barber. While he grafted and studied at night school, Teresa, who was pregnant with her third child when they arrived, was obliged to stay at home and raise an ever-expanding brood of kids on what scant income they had.

In addition to Vincenzo (later James) and Raffaele (later Ralph) who had both been born in Italy, the couple had Salvatore (Frank) – the first child to be born in America before Alphonse, aka Al, arrived in January 1899. Other kids followed with John, Albert, Matthew and the baby sister, Mafalda, all being born between 1899 and 1912. Another daughter, Ermina, died before her first birthday.

Frank and Ralph would later become key players in their brother's outfit, but in a downright bizarre twist, James turned out to be the 'white sheep' of the family. Having spent his early years in rural Italy, James

* Pastaio – a maker of pasta.

hated the big city and having become obsessed with the Wild West decided that he wanted to become a cowboy instead. Aged 16 he ran away from home and joined the Miller Brothers' Wild West Show – a travelling circus that was touring the Midwest.

Later claiming to have fought in the war (he hadn't), by 1919 he was living as 'Richard James Hart' and serving as a town marshal in Homer, Nebraska. A year later, with the introduction of Prohibition in 1920, James became a special agent in the Bureau of Indian Affairs, stationed in South Dakota, and waged war against bootleggers, at the very moment that his brothers were making money out of organised crime. According to his biographer, Jeff McArthur, James went on to become 'the most feared name among bootleggers in the Midwest'.[4] Sporting a ten-gallon hat that screamed 'Wild West chic' he adopted the moniker 'Two Guns' and befriended members of the Native American Lakota people, with whom he seems to have been on good terms, despite them choosing to call him 'Big Hairy Thing'.[5]

In a curious echo of his younger brother Al's career trajectory, 'Two Guns' already had one eye on his myth. James was a handsome and stylish man and the early photojournalist, Frank Fiske, captured him in a series of flattering photos, dressed in clothes that seemed to hark back to the lost, mythical age of nineteenth-century cowboys and incorruptible lawmen. His heroic moment was not to last, however, and having been accused of murdering a man in cold blood, he lost his job. Reconciled with his brother Ralph in the 1930s, he eventually joined the family business, before dying aged 60 in 1951.

But back in the early 1900s, that parallel Capone narrative was yet to play out and as the hard-working and respectable Teresa and Gabriele Capone built lives in America, their fortunes rose and fell.

Migration then, like now, was a divisive issue in immigrant USA. Between 1890 and 1929, the population more than doubled, growing from 63 million to 127 million as people moved to the promised land. This wave was largely driven by migration from Central, Eastern and Southern Europe and supplemented the existing population made up largely of those of British, Irish, French and German descent, as well as the Indigenous Native American people. By 1890, a record 14.8 per cent of the entire population had been born elsewhere, and even in the years that followed, it rarely dipped far below that peak. The Capones were one family among the 60 million other people who crossed the Atlantic in the era and like fellow immigrants from Southern and Eastern Europe they arrived into a climate of hate.

Italians in fact fared worse than almost any other immigrant group because the white Anglo-Saxons who ruled the roost saw these 'Catholic' peasants as lesser in every way. At the turn of the century the false, racist 'theory of eugenics' had gained considerable traction in America. Obsessed with the supposed purity of the 'gene pool', the bigots who promoted this pseudo-scientific nonsense believed that the very presence of Italians risked polluting it. As the popular press rallied to bad science, the politicians cowed before them and in 1921, in a classic piece of knee-jerk legislation, the Harding Administration introduced the 'Emergency Quota Act'. Initially presented as a temporary measure, this law sought to explicitly reduce and limit the number of immigrants from Eastern and Southern European countries while boosting those from the United Kingdom and Germany.

Though Italians did not suffer quite the same appalling segregation or 'Jim Crow Laws' suffered by African American people, they were often associated with the same racist stereotypes. Prejudice maintained the lie that the Italians were inherently 'untrustworthy' and 'criminal' and their status as 'white people' was regularly questioned.[6]

By dint of an example, at an 1890s Congressional hearing, a mine foreman was asked why he did not refer to Italians as 'white men', only for him to reply that of course he did not because an 'Italian is a dago'.

Italophobia was, in short, rife and as Capone's star rose across the 1920s, a very familiar trope of 'immigrants are responsible for all the crimes' dogged his narrative. In the 1932 film *Scarface*, based closely on the life of the gangster, there is even a scene where a concerned group of Chicagoans call for the repatriation of Italians and a halt to immigration in general to stem the violence. In a trope familiar to readers of modern British tabloids, the unease is articulated by an immigrant who says words to the effect of 'even I think immigration has gone too far'.

Italians as a group were, in fact, no more responsible for criminality than any other minority at the time – as contemporary statistics clearly demonstrate.

Al Capone was anyway not an immigrant. 'I'm no Italian, I was born in Brooklyn,'[7] he once told a journalist and it was true, although as the son of immigrants, he nonetheless grew up in an immigrant community. Brooklyn, the Bronx and Queens all had significant Italian migrant communities but they, in turn, were segregated along regional lines. In Manhattan's 'Little Italy', for example, families from Calabria tended to live on Mott Street, Sicilians settled around Elizabeth Street, and Northern Italians resided along Baxter Street. The Capones were fairly unique in that when they arrived in New York they didn't know anyone and, seeking not to sequester themselves among fellow Neapolitans, they found lodgings on Park Avenue (although, to be clear, this was Park Avenue in Brooklyn and not its more desirable namesake on the Upper East Side).

Their neighbours included Poles, Slovaks, Irish and Germans, as well as fellow Italians, and 'Donna Teresa', despite her very limited English, quickly became a respected local matriarch. Though a strict disciplinarian, who insisted that her boys be home by ten, with so many children under her wing it was impossible to keep an eye on them all and it must have been a relief when Al was sent to school aged seven.

In the classroom, Capone faced the same institutionalised racism that Italian Americans experienced everywhere else, but he proved himself to be an above-average student who did well at maths and English. In other circumstances and handed better opportunities, this boy from Brooklyn might have gone on to become a businessman or stockbroker who could then have robbed people legitimately. Instead, he began to bunk off school and hang out on the mean streets where, as a member of a 'kids' gang', he engaged in petty theft, pickpocketing, vandalism and regular fights with rival outfits.

Recollections of the youthful Capone differ. Some remembered him as a bruiser and a dreamer, forever scrapping or thinking up get-rich-quick schemes. By contrast his biographer, Deirdre Bair, quotes the screenwriter Daniel Fuchs, who grew up in his neighbourhood, as saying that young Al was 'something of a non-entity: affable, soft of speech and even mediocre'.[8] However, as Fuchs was born in 1909, some 14 years after Capone, we should perhaps take the childhood reminiscences of a professional storyteller with a degree of scepticism.

Seeking to keep his sons on the straight and narrow, Gabriele Capone tried and failed to get his older boy, Frank, into shoe-shining and when the kid lost interest, the brushes and wax were passed on to Al. Things didn't go as planned though, for from the moment young Al set up shop under the Gair concrete clock tower in Brooklyn, he began to notice Don Batista Balsamo.

Balsamo was the original 'Godfather of Brooklyn': a smartly dressed gangster who ran every protection racket on the west and south side of Long Island. Both feared and respected in equal measure, he wore swanky clothes and fine jewellery and drove flashy cars. Swiftly appreciating that shoe-shining was a mug's game and that 'protection' was where the money was, Al diversified his business strategy. Soon his own gang, the South Brooklyn Rippers, were extorting money from fellow street vendors rather than doing any hard work themselves – and young Capone was raking it in.

Unfortunately, as the shoe-shine racket got ever more successful, it came to the attention of Balsamo himself who, with an admiring wink and a nudge, kicked Al and his gang out of the area and into the arms of another group called the 'Forty Thieves Juniors' where he came on to the radar of Johnny 'The Fox' Torrio.

Torrio, like Balsamo, was an alluring role model for a kid with no respect for the law. Always wearing the best clothes and driving the fanciest cars, he was a smooth operator with it. By 16, Capone was running money and errands for him and the two became quite the Brooklyn Fagin and Artful Dodger. Torrio had his fingers in all the usual pies. Prostitution, gambling, extortion rackets, loan sharking, drug running and, most of all, the 'numbers game', an illegal lottery in which punters made bets on three numbers that gave them a chance of winning a cash prize.

More intelligent than most of his rivals, Torrio worked hard to present himself as a respectable member of society who always went home to his wife for dinner and it gained him some standing among the ordinary people of New York.

Organised crime was, after all, more than just about the money. It was about respect. It was a means by which people from the bottom of the pile could matter. In the 1931 gangster movie *Little Caesar*, the central character, 'Rico' Bandello, played by the actor Edward G. Robinson, summed it up:

'Money's okay, but it ain't everything. I want to be somebody. Look hard at a bunch of guys and know that they'll do anything you tell them. Have your own way or nothing. Be somebody!'[9]

Ralph, Al's brother, worked for Torrio too and the two Capones often shot pool and frequented the dance halls of Lower Manhattan together. As the money came in, Al started to dress stylishly and as he was an exceptionally good dancer and charming with it, he was a hit with a lot of women that he met and embraced 'every opportunity for sex that came his way'.[10]

By the age of 16 he had contracted gonorrhoea and that same fateful year, Torrio loaned his protégé out to a racketeer called Frankie Yale who owned a joint on Coney Island called the 'Harvard'.* Capone worked as Yale's enforcer, bouncer and all-round hard man. That might seem a little incongruous as we often think of Capone as short and stocky and that is down to the phenomenon known as 'cinematic alief', where the actor portraying a real-life person becomes conflated with them. As Capone has been memorably played by Edward G Robinson, 5 ft 3 in (1.63 m) and James Cagney, 5 ft 4 in (1.65 m) as well as the 5 ft 7 in (1.75 m) Robert De Niro it is perhaps unsurprising, but in fact he was 6 ft (1.82 m) tall and weighed around 250 lb (113 kg).

In a celebrated interview with him in *Liberty* magazine in October 1931, Cornelius Vanderbilt Junior described him thus:

'Much taller than I imagined, and much broader; a fellow with a winch-like handshake . . . and (a) winning smile.'[11]

* Yale called it Harvard as a joke.

In conversation, Capone spoke with a soft, effeminate voice, and Nova Stucker, a warden on Alcatraz during Al's incarceration there, would later tell interviewers and friends that he 'sounded like a woman'.[12] But it was deceptive because he could play as rough as any other tough guy.

Al's time at the Harvard ended when he was glassed down the left side of his face by a patron and the wounds were so serious that he ended up spending considerable time in hospital. The permanent facial lesions gave birth to his hated nickname 'Scarface' and he went to considerable effort to disguise them by wearing thick make-up and only being photographed in profile. If they came up in interviews, he would claim that he had received the scars as a result of war service. But it was a lie. When America entered World War I in 1917, Capone neither volunteered nor was drafted into the American Expeditionary Forces. Instead, and perhaps cowed by the attack on Coney Island, between 1915 and 1917 he worked as a box-cutter in a factory in New York on a salary of $3 a week ($100 in 2025 money) and tried to keep out of trouble. This stab at legitimacy may also have been due to a Catholic Irish girl called Mary 'Mae' Josephine Coughlin, who worked for the firm as a time-keeper and with whom he fell hopelessly, headover-heels in love.

The couple married on 30 December 1918, three weeks after the birth of their only child, Albert Francis, known to all as Sonny. Mae was two years older than Al and, as an Irish girl from a good family, was thought to be 'marrying down' by throwing in her lot with the Italians. Despite all that followed, including Al's many sexual and criminal indiscretions, the marriage would last the rest of his life.

Quite what Capone did for a living between 1917 and 1919 remains a bit of a mystery and while there are mythical tales of him running a candy shop or working in a bowling alley, the truth is that he probably stayed at the factory while working for Torrio on the side. All of that changed when two life-altering events came at him in quick succession. The first was the sudden death of his father from chronic myocarditis in his barber's shop in November 1919, as a result of 'the Spanish Flu'. The second followed two months later, when, on 16 January 1920, the Volstead Act came into force and the manufacturing, sale and supply of alcohol was outlawed overnight in the United States of America.

* * *

Prohibition is as old as civilisation itself. The Babylonian *Code of Hammurabi*, written *c.*1750 BCE, decreed the amount of beer that could be consumed by citizens, limiting it to two litres a day – and five if you were a priest. And across the centuries that followed, rulers tried to ban all manner of nice things, including sport. In 1314, amid growing fears about the popularity of a game being played by the peasants, the Mayor of London, Nicholas de Farndon, with the backing of Edward II outlawed football proclaiming:

'*We command and forbid on behalf of the king, on pain of imprisonment, such game to be used in the city in the future.*'

Efforts to prohibit the beautiful game came and went for the next 500 years but during the latter period, frustrated fans could at least console themselves with a nice refreshing glass of laudanum. You could purchase commercially produced opium in British and American apothecaries well into the late nineteenth century and it wasn't the only drug on sale. In the 1890s, cocaine was considered to be a wonder drug and manufacturers added it to everything from cigarettes to shampoo and even in its earliest iteration 'cola' and numerous other soft drinks.

The British politician William Gladstone, prime minister four times between 1868 and 1894, put opium in his tea before speeches, and Queen Victoria liked nothing more than a lovely opiate tincture to liven up her morning. Meanwhile heroin, patented by an English physician C.R. Alder Wright in 1874 and subsequently mass produced by Bayer, was the go-to cough syrup in genteel homes across the West, even as there were moves to outlaw the real social menace – beer.

The anti-alcohol movement in the US, which sprang up from Protestant, Baptist and Methodist churches in the early 1830s, began with calls for moderation – but by the early 1900s, campaigners were lobbying for an outright ban and on the face of it, there were good reasons to be concerned. Americans had long had a mighty thirst and by 1850, the adult population were drinking an average of seven gallons of pure alcohol a year. That's roughly four pints a day per person and more than three times what the average American drinks in 2025. This rampant alcoholism fuelled all manner of social ills and domestic violence, in particular, was a considerable issue.

As the crusade against booze gained momentum, it attracted some properly eccentric characters including Carry Nation aka 'Hatchet Granny', who, like so many other extremists in history, believed herself to be on a mission from God. Having lost her first husband to drink and having married a second who was singularly underwhelmed by her proselytising efforts, in 1900, and aged 54, Carry received a message from heaven telling her to 'Go to Kiowa (a small town in Kansas) and smash up the bars.'[13] Never one to refuse a deific request, she hotfooted it to the town and having stormed into Dobson's saloon declared:

'Men, I have come to save you from a drunkard's fate!'

Before throwing rocks at the bar. On her release from jail, her husband sarcastically suggested that the next time she did something so idiotic she should first arm herself with an axe and, taking his advice literally, she purchased a hatchet from a local hardware store and began to do just that.

Within a few short years she had become a national figure and as her celebrity grew, this one woman armed wing of the temperance movement diversified the act into rants against tobacco as well. Heckled by a cigar vendor on Coney Island in 1902, she paused mid-sermon to take her axe to his display case and having chopped it to smithereens was arrested for the umpteenth time. In the ensuing tussle with law enforcement one of her fingers was broken, leading her to proclaim:

'Never mind, you beer-swelled, whiskey-soaked, Saturn-faced man, God will strike you.' And God delivered because: *'Six weeks from that time this man fell dead on the streets of Coney Island.'*[14]

Had she lived 200 years earlier, Carry would have been burned as a witch. Instead, she became a national celebrity and influencer and effectively turned the cause of Prohibition into a headline-grabbing movement that began to gain significant traction.

Two religious groups, the Women's Christian Temperance Union and the Anti-Saloon League, joined the charge and they had some very powerful allies indeed. By the early 1900s, many of America's biggest business leaders were on board, including Andrew Carnegie, Henry Ford and J.D. Rockefeller who all believed that perceived industrial inefficiency was down to the feckless peasants drinking too much.

Oh and the Ku Klux Klan were all in favour too.

The original KKK was a 'secret society' that had been formed in the 1860s in the wake of the Civil War by a group of white supremacists in the south. That 'movement' swiftly fizzled out but 40 years later, in 1905, a bestselling book called *The Clansman* by Baptist preacher Thomas Dixon Jr, reawakened interest in the men in hoods and when D.W. Griffiths portrayed the KKK as crusading heroes in his racist 1915 film *Birth of a Nation*, the group sprang back to life. The Klan promulgated the false notion that alcoholism was exclusively a disease of foreigners and black people and that the influx of Catholics from southern Europe was a particular source of the evil that was now ruining the USA. By their warped and nasty logic, Prohibition would be an act of national purification that would make America great again.

The US entry into World War I on 6 April 1917 furthered the temperance cause too. As young men marched off to war, anti-German sentiment ran rife and the country swiftly turned on the 10 per cent of the population who could trace their origins back to Germany. Sauerkraut was rebranded 'liberty cabbage', 14 states banned German teaching, vigilantes raided libraries and burned German books, dachshunds were renamed 'wiener dogs' and as most of America's biggest breweries were owned by German families, beer boycotts became commonplace too.

The suitably named John Strange, 21st Lieutenant Governor of Wisconsin, summed up the Prohibitionist mood:

'We have German enemies across the water. We have German enemies in this country, too. And the worst of all our German enemies, the most treacherous, the most menacing, are Pabst, Schlitz, Blatz and Miller.'

Panicked politicians soon jumped on the Prohibitionist bandwagon and in December 1917, Congress passed the 18th Amendment, which would eventually ban the manufacture and sale of alcohol, by a majority of 65 votes to 20. Despite President Woodrow Wilson vetoing it, in October 1919 the Volstead Act was passed and Prohibition was set to become law.

Three months later on 16 January 1920, America witnessed the biggest party in history as towns and cities across the country drank everything dry. In saloons and bars across the country, mock funerals were held and black curtains and papier-mâché decorated the walls as the nation's drinkers cavorted for one last time.

The following morning, the country awoke to a blistering hangover that would last 13 years and given that the nation had just been through a war and a global pandemic the timing could not have been worse for those in dire need of a stiffner. As four million weary US servicemen returned from Europe, a popular song 'How Dry Am I' lamented their predicament:

I've got the blues, I've got the blues,
I've got the alcoholic blues.
No more beer my heart to cheer;
Goodbye whiskey, you used to make me frisky.

The policy, later dubbed 'the noble experiment' by President Herbert Hoover, did initially have some positive impact. Domestic violence plummeted and there was an immediate uptick in the nation's health, with cases of cirrhosis markedly declining.

The ban wasn't total either and there were plenty of loopholes. Doctors were able to prescribe 'whiskey' and on a visit to the US in 1931 Winston Churchill procured a doctor's note that allowed him six shots at mealtimes – and more 'should it be required'. Though homebrewing was technically banned, vineyards began selling 'home kits' of boxed grape juice, advising in big letters that it should not be left lying about lest it 'ferment'. The winks and nudges came at no extra charge.

It was not illegal to drink alcohol if you could get your hands on the stuff. Many wealthier families had stockpiled supplies and, as alcohol was allowed for 'industrial purposes', many a bottle of ethanol was known to go missing too.

Churches and synagogues were exempt as well and as a result, it was said that some congregations swelled as converts found a new path to salvation.*

Prohibition had some surprising cultural and social side effects too. In the illegal speakeasies that sprang up in its wake, white people and black people began to mix freely for the first time, and it revolutionised the musical landscape. The bar rooms of America, once the preserve of men, saw women enter them too and rich rubbed shoulders with the poor.

The Volstead Act had a big impact on cinema too and the 'nightclub scene' became a set piece in many a period film and it also influenced the literature of the time – most notably in F. Scott Fitzgerald's Jazz Age masterpiece, *The Great Gatsby*.

Volstead also radically changed the nation's habits, as millions of Americans were encouraged to turn to hard liquor and even hard drugs. Prior to 1920, most of the nation's drinkers had consumed beer, but as it was large in volume and hard to smuggle, ale and lager provided only a slim profit margin for bootleggers at considerable risk to themselves. Whiskey and other spirits could be far more easily transported and sold at a far heftier margin and the same was true of cocaine which had also been effectively banned in 1920 by the Dangerous Drugs Act.

This phenomenon whereby consumers end up hitting the harder stuff when alcohol and narcotics are banned is called the Iron Law of Prohibition (ILP) and it goes like this: the harder the enforcement, the harder the substance. In essence, smaller, stronger doses make life easier for the racketeers.

Prohibition also helped spawn the popularity of cocktails for as the quality of the spirits on offer was decidedly iffy, speakeasies started mixing it with other drinks to make it palatable. The Cosmopolitan, the Sidecar and the White Lady all have their roots in the Jazz Age.

* I have found no evidence to back this up and it was probably a myth.

There were fatal consequences too, for as unregulated liquor flooded the market, people started to get poisoned by it. By 1928, an estimated 1,000 people were dying annually as a result of drinking tainted hooch and quite soon, all those initial gains in public health were all but wiped out.

And then of course there were the economic ramifications too. On 1 January 1920, there had been 13,000 breweries in the USA – by the morning of 17 January 1920, there were just over 100 left. The nation's distilleries largely shut too with just six left up and running for medicinal purposes when the act came into force. Thousands of people lost their jobs as a result and the US State lost $482 million in tax revenues (equivalent to about $9 billion in 2025) in a single year.

In the end, just two sectors enjoyed a significant boom. For as organised crime and bootlegging took off in the nation's biggest cities, homicide shot up by 78 per cent[15] while undertakers had never had it so good.

Even before the Volstead Act passed, Johnny Torrio had grasped the business potential that Prohibition would bring and calculated that Chicago, with its reputation for hard drinking, hedonism, individualism and corruption, was the ideal place to set up shop. Torrio already had established links to the city where his cousin, Victoria Moresco, was a successful 'Madam', running a string of brothels that were fronted by her husband, Giacomo 'Big Jim' Colosimo, who was a huge figure in every way. Colosimo was in fact living, breathing proof of the rampant corruption in the city at the time, for despite being the biggest brothel owner in town, he had also been appointed 'crime czar' by the city's mayor Big Bill Thompson – with special responsibility for prostitution.

Back in 1909 and having had some local difficulties with the notorious 'Black Hand gangs' – an early iteration of the Sicilian mafia – Colosimo had brought Torrio in to protect him and by 1919 the two men had become business partners. The arrangement had been mutually beneficial until Volstead came along, at which point Torrio began pressuring Big Jim to move away from prostitution and into booze and speakeasies instead. The Chicago 'crime czar' was reluctant to do that as, having recently divorced Torrio's cousin Victoria, he had now remarried a much younger woman called Dale Winter and he wanted to keep his nose clean.

The two men fell out spectacularly and an impasse ensued until May 1920 when, while Colosimo was dining in one of his restaurants, a lone hitman resolved the problem and shot Big Jim in the back of his head. Despite the establishment being thronged with paying customers, nobody saw a thing and nobody was ever charged, although it was whispered that Coney Island hard man Frankie Yale had popped Big Jim, on Torrio's orders.

Torrio himself arranged the lavish funeral and elaborate bouquets of flowers adorned Colosimo's hearse as he made his final journey.

Prior to his untimely death at just 42, Colosimo had managed to consolidate the crime syndicates of Chicago into a loose affiliation and the city was ripe with opportunity and just waiting to be exploited. Within days, Johnny Torrio had consolidated his hold on the firm and 'The Chicago Outfit' was born. As with any other business takeover, the new CEO brought in his own talent and chief among them was his trusted lieutenant, Al Capone, later to be made the chairman of the board. Capone was on the run after nearly killing one of Frankie Yale's enforcers, Arthur Finnegan, in New York and the move suited him.[16]

Mae and Sonny followed in mid-1920 and Al worked as a bouncer and general enforcer at the notorious 'Four Deuces' gambling den and brothel on 2222 South Wabash before getting promoted to manager. Business was soon booming and so, under the name 'Mr Al Brown', he opened a fake store next door to the Deuces and printed off business cards which claimed that he was a 'second-hand furniture dealer'. The shop was one of many fronts that he was to open across the next decade – although the myth that he also ran a string of launderettes and thus gave rise to the term 'money laundering' is just that: a myth.

As Capone rose in prominence and power, he brought his mother and brothers Frank and Ralph, aka 'Bottles', over from NYC too and set them up in a house on 7244 South Prairie, which he bought for $5,500 ($90,000 in 2025). While bookish Mae raised Sonny, a sickly child who was nonetheless every bit as cheerful as his name suggested, Teresa ran the house like the traditional Italian matriarch that she was. There were frequent run-ins between the two women and though they eventually declared an uneasy truce, they never really got on, not least because Teresa didn't learn English and Mae could not speak Italian.

Despite him being a fifth grade dropout, Al was big on learning and the opportunities that it provided and obliged his younger siblings and nephew to stay at school, while seeking to provide his own child with the best education available. Sonny was sent to a succession of expensive private schools and though kept in the dark about his father's business activities, everyone else knew and he was constantly bullied.

Capone's conservative instincts where education was concerned are illustrative of the many paradoxes at play within the man: while he was quite happy to use sex workers, for example, he in fact intensely disliked having brothels in his business portfolio and was forever seeking to get rid of them. His ethics could best be summed up as 'hypocritical' and when not bribing every cop, every politician and every hack in town, he was in the habit of making grandiloquent pronouncements that could easily pass for those of a modern conservative politician.

In a 1931 interview with Cornelius Vanderbilt, he offered the following hot take:

'We must keep America whole and safe and unspoiled. If machines are going to take jobs away from the worker, then he will need to find something else to do. Perhaps he'll get back to the soil. But we must take care of him during the period of change. We must keep him away from red literature, red ruses; we must see that his mind remains healthy. For regardless of where he was born, he is now an American.'[17]

Prior to that attempt on his life that saw him flee to Sicily, Torrio travelled a lot and frequently left Al in charge, who in turn promoted his brothers to the board. Both siblings brought particular talents to the organigram. Frank was much like Torrio and presented himself as a respectable and diplomatic figure, who was drawn to the political wing of the operation; Ralph, put simply, was a thug. It was the ideal mix of skills and together they made a killing, both literal and metaphorical, with the enterprise turning over millions of dollars a year, from just about any racket you can think of.

Not everyone was willing to be bought off though and that caused no end of headaches. In 1923, in a significant setback for the Outfit, the unappreciative voters of Chicago kicked corrupt mayor 'Big Bill' Thompson out of office and elected a Democrat called Michael Dever in his place. Dever not only promised to rid Chicago of violence but take on the rackets too and in a further unwelcome turn of events, he actually set about delivering. Soon he – and his similarly 'untouchable' Chief of Police, Morgan Collins – were upsetting Torrio and Capone's expansion plans and making life distinctly uncomfortable.

Both gangsters managed to stay out of custody thanks to the bent cops and many spies they had on their enormous payroll, but the interference was unwelcome and so they moved their operation to Cicero where Capone set up his HQ at Tony 'the Greek' Anton's Hawthorne Hotel. Cicero was chosen for the simple reason that while it was adjacent to Chicago it remained politically independent of it. In April 1924, having ensured that potholes had been filled on the main streets and that the incumbent Republican candidate had been pushed aside in favour of their own man, Joseph Z. Klenha, Capone moved into politics and set about rigging the local elections.

Unfortunately, those nebulous voters could still not be counted on and significant violence and intimidation followed as the Outfit sought to get its way. Come election eve on 31 March, Capone's men were out menacing polling stations and prowling the streets, making sure that citizens 'voted the right way', while the Democratic Party's local offices were ransacked, with at least one candidate being violently assaulted.

While cruising through town in their fleet of sedans that night, Capone, brother Frank and associates drew the attention of a police patrol, and when they were pulled over a gun battle erupted, which ended with Frank lying dead in the road. His lavish funeral would follow on 4 April, with tens of thousands of dollars' worth of floral tributes provided, inevitably, by Schofield's Flowers which was run by the florist gangster Dean O'Banion. Frank's death was not in vain because Klenha won the election, meaning Capone and Torrio now ruled Cicero. The town would remain their principality until Al's downfall eight years later.

Despite suffering several attempts on his life, Capone prospered and following Torrio's retirement he became one of the most famous Americans of his age. One part mobster, one part political player, one part concerned local businessman and one part celebrity, he was a gift to journalists who came from as far away as Britain to interview the colourful and affable gangster. Capone was a highly adept businessman who used his charm, intimidation and violence in tandem with modern innovations like telephones, typewriters and ticker-tape to control his empire. All run with impressive efficiency from his base in Illinois.

Capone was also adept at exploiting the hypocrisy that was at play in Prohibition America saying: 'They call it bootleg while it's in the trucks . . . but when your host . . . hands it to you on a silver tray, that's hospitality.'[18]

'What's Al Capone done?' he later asked. 'He's supplied a legitimate demand. Some call it bootlegging. Some call it racketeering. I call it business. They say I violate the prohibition law. Who doesn't?'[19]

In a 1966 introduction to a Capone biography, the British historian Andrew Sinclair perfectly summed it up:

'Al Capone was to crime what J.P. Morgan was to Wall Street, the first man to exert national influence over his trade . . . Had he not been born a Neapolitan, in the Brooklyn slums, he might have used his ruthlessness and organising powers to make his pile in legitimate business.'

Such sentiments were widely shared and Capone made a fortune in the process. By 1929 his annual turnover was about $100 million – some $1.8 billion at time of writing – and like any other businessmen who want to appear to have a social conscience, he gave back too. Capone tipped generously and often and paid well over the odds for basic services. When the Great Depression hit in 1929, he set up a soup kitchen in Chicago, which served breakfast, lunch and dinner to about 2,500 people a day through the winter of 1930. Some viewed this largesse cynically but the *Bismarck Tribune* gave it context, arguing: 'A hungry man is just as glad to get soup and coffee from Al Capone as from anyone else.'[20]

Capone was remarkably popular across the colour divide too. In 1971, his biographer, John Kobler, conducted a series of interviews with ordinary Chicagoans who had encountered him 50 years earlier. An elderly black doorman who had befriended Capone in his prime told Kobler that, 'these folks round here never knowed [*sic*] who paid the rent but it was Al'.

Louis Armstrong, who moved from New Orleans to Chicago at the same time as Capone, knew the gangster from the clubs and, according to his own biographer Laurence Bergreen, once described him as 'a nice little cute fat boy . . . like some professor who had just come out of college to teach or something'.[21] Capone also supposedly crossed paths with another famous jazz musician when Al's 'Boys' supposedly kidnapped Fats Waller and drove him to the Hawthorne Hotel, on the night of the boss's 27th birthday in January 1927. Having just buried his friend, Tony the Greek, Al needed cheering up so, according to the story, Waller was deposited at the piano, handed a drink and instructed to play – which he did, for the next three days. Waller's son later claimed that the party only ended when Al stuffed $1,000 ($20,000 in 2025) in the exhausted jazzman's pockets and ordered his henchmen to take him home.

It's a great anecdote and that probably means it has been exaggerated over time.

Tall tales aside, what can be said without any doubt is that for thousands of ordinary working people in 1920s America, Capone was that most alluring of stereotypes, the *good guy-bad guy,* and many would later attest to how loved he was.

While conducting research for his biography in the early 1970s, Kobler met a waitress who had also known Capone back in the Prohibition era; she stated quite simply that this 'wonderful person' had 'taken from the rich and given to the poor'. In short and quite literally, he was Chicago's Robin 'Hood'.

F.D. Pasley agreed: 'To the upright dries he was anathema, to downright wets a public benefactor, to the politicians, Santa Claus.'[22]

The notion of the romantic outlaw who takes from the rich and gives to the poor sits in a tradition which stretches back to the outlaw of Sherwood Forest, first referred to in the Middle English work, *Piers Plowman*, probably written in the 1370s by William Langland. Robin's legend persists because it has a subversive appeal. Hood and his imitators are the ultimate romantic rebels who live on the margins of society and sock it to the man.

In late 1800s America, the idea got a reboot and dime novels and magazines turned many of the Wild West's 'most wanted' into celebrities.

Much as a modern pop star might adopt an alter ego, they had epic pseudonyms too, and Henry McCarty became 'Billy the Kid', Robert LeRoy Parker reinvented himself as 'Butch Cassidy' and Harry Longabaugh becoming the 'Sundance Kid'. The likes of Butch and Sundance were also extremely PR savvy too and they actively courted the press to put their own spin on their narrative while building up a cult of fandom.

Tales of the two men and their Wild Bunch gang appearing out of nowhere, robbing banks and trains before disappearing into thin air, catapulted them on to the front pages of the nation's newspapers and turned them into folk heroes. Their exploits made them a target and eventually a consortium of business interests pooled their resources and hired the Pinkerton Detective Agency to take them down. But in many ways their early, violent deaths in Bolivia only added to the mystique and to this day, and thanks in no small part to the romantic portrayal of them in films and TV series, both men remain celebrated figures.

Billy the Kid, shot in cold blood aged 21 by his erstwhile friend and biographer Pat Garrett on 14 July 1881, is another case in point and contemporary dime novels, ballads and early silent films raised him to the status of America's first 'bad boy' superstar of crime – the Elvis Presley of outlaws.

If Billy the Kid, Butch and Sundance were the criminal equivalent of folk music or early rock and roll – then Al Capone was rap.

With his feuds, his bling, his flashy cars, his love of expensive clothes, his posse of mobsters and beautiful women, Capone's streetwise outlaw extravagance embodied the live-fast-and-make-it-while-you-can ethos of hip hop, a full 50 years before the music exploded on to the scene. Some of the more traditionally minded lawbreaking brethren couldn't keep pace:

'There used to be some adventure in crime,' one ageing bandit told the *New York Times* in the 1930s, 'in the old days a criminal took a chance and gave the other fellow a chance . . . Nowadays when a man goes out with a machine gun, there isn't any thrill.'[23]

Despite the difference in approach there were however similarities and much like the cowboy outlaws before him, Capone swiftly became part of the entertainment landscape. With the invention of talking films in 1927, a whole new genre of gangster movies featuring fast-talking, working-class anti-heroes was born and for the next seven years and until the introduction of the Hays Code* in 1934, the image of the modern mobster was honed off the back of his and others' examples. The effect was interactional with the fictional gangsters influencing their real-life iterations and vice versa and while the movie makers were obliged to pretend that they were making 'moral lessons' or 'calls for action' against the scourge of organised crime, they in fact deliberately glamorised the gangster lifestyle and in the process helped turn Capone and his imitators into a cultural phenomenon.

The most celebrated examples of the genre, *Public Enemy* (1931), *Little Caesar* (1931) and *Scarface* (1932) all feature dynamic and hugely attractive performances at their heart and the films remain very watchable today.

As played by James Cagney, Edward G. Robinson and the early method actor Paul Muni respectively, these men have risen from the streets and they not only know what they want but they know how to get it. They are witty and urbane. They hang out in fancy nightclubs, sleep with beautiful women, ruthlessly dispatch their enemies, have their own code of honour, dress exquisitely, enjoy the best things in life, embrace

* Hays Code – a set of self-imposed movie industry codes which between 1934 and 1968 censored depictions of violence, nudity, criminality, homosexuality, substance abuse and sex on screen.

culture and drive about the place in modified cars that are chock-full of gadgets.

Ian Fleming, who would later write about Chicago's gangster-land in his 1963 travel guide *Thrilling Cities*, had a fascination for organised crime that long preceded it, and his fictional Spangled Mob appear in three of the James Bond books. But watching those pre-code films it is striking that many of the tropes that inform the amoral 007 were clearly lifted from the gangster genre and we will see why that may have been the case in a moment.

The extreme violence of early 1930s gangster films and the sexually liberated content within them eventually sparked moral outrage and censorship followed. But while the public moralists feigned indignation, many Americans found solace in the rebellious example of these big screen bad guys. Following the Wall Street Crash in 1929, the country had descended into the Great Depression and the gulf between the haves and the have-nots widened to a chasm. In that environment, the vision of these everyday Joes getting rich quickly gave audiences a degree of comfort and even hope.

In *Public Enemy*, the central character, Tom Powers, played by Jimmy Cagney, states of his goody-two-shoes brother, who has fought in the war and is now struggling to keep his head above water, as '. . . that sucker. He's too busy going to school. He's learning to be poor.'

Gangsterism offered a fast track to the dark side of the American Dream – and with it power.

By 1931, Capone was at the peak of his fame and fortune and more to the point was no longer simply an American cultural phenomenon but a worldwide sensation. His global notoriety was such that he even appeared, that year, as a character in *Tintin in America*, the only real-life person to ever feature in one of Hergé's books and in an interview that same year in *Liberty* magazine, sounded every bit the concerned public figure:

'Virtue, honour and the law have all vanished from our life,' he told Vanderbilt. 'Crooked bankers who take people's hard-earned cash for stock they know is worthless would be far better clients at penal institutions than the poor little man who robs, so that his wife and babies may live.'[24]

Many a contemporary reader may have nodded along to those words but by then and, aged just 32, time and momentum were no longer on his side.

* * *

Capone's problems started in 1927 when the US Assistant State Attorney Mabel Willebrandt came up with the idea of prosecuting criminals for tax evasion. That same year, the Supreme Court upheld her suggestion and while Al snorted with derision at the very idea, his canny bodyguard, Frankie Rio, began to get very twitchy indeed. Capone had good reason to think himself untouchable. He was, after all, the undisputed king of organised crime and all he surveyed, and things got better still when the corrupt Republican Big Bill Thompson was swept back to power with Capone's help in 1927. Al was so emboldened by the win that he left Cicero and moved back to Chicago, first to the Metropole and from July 1928, the Lexington Hotel with 'a double walled fortress of meat' (i.e. henchmen) to protect him.

Capone's bodyguards were provided with cards, signed by the corrupt mayor, which read:

'To the Police Department: you will extend the courtesies of the department to the bearer, signed Mayor Thompson.'

Now known affectionately as 'Snorky', since nobody dared call him Scarface any more, Capone was starting to get bored with the whole gangster thing. The carousing was not as fun as it had once been and the ever-present threat of assassination was getting him down. Capone increasingly fantasized about giving it all up and retiring to his house in Miami, but feared that if he climbed down from the tiger he was riding, he'd get eaten.

Despite all the money, the big houses and the celebrity, Capone could barely move without putting his life at risk. The American dream ultimately is to have so much money that the ordinary rules of life do not apply, but having achieved unimaginable wealth, Capone himself now discovered that he was trapped, Midas-like, by the very spell of his success.

'It's a tough life to lead,' he said; 'you fear death at every moment, and worse than death, you fear the rats of the game who'd run around and tell the police if you don't constantly satisfy them with money and favours.'[25]

Capone was now 'the most shot-at man in America'.[26] When not living in his heavily guarded and fortified suite at the Lexington, which had gigantic metal shutters, he was driven about in a 1928 armoured Cadillac whose 25mm thick bulletproof windows were so heavy that they needed a complex winching system to lift them up and down.

Snorky had killed an awful lot of people himself and so perhaps it was only to be expected. Chicago's decade-long turf wars resulted in an estimated 700 murders and roughly 200 of those killings were directly or indirectly carried out by Alphonse Capone and his gang.

Nobody was immune and in a line of work not renowned for its human resources departments, gangsters dismissed employees through the barrel of a gun or the blade of a knife and even Frankie Yale, Al's erstwhile employer, fell victim to his erstwhile protégé. Yale, who had double-crossed Capone one time too many, had an armoured sedan of his own but had neglected to upgrade to bulletproof windows and on the night of 1 July 1928 he was to regret it. Chased through the streets of Brooklyn by Al's hitmen, the side window of his car was blasted with a shotgun before he too was then blown away with a Thompson machine gun.

For all Capone's affable outward charm, it should never be forgotten that here was a man whose business dealings rested ultimately on intimidation and violence although, as with any legend, there are countless myths too. In Brian de Palma's hugely bowdlerised 1987 film, *The Untouchables*, which purports to tell the story of FBI agent Eliot Ness's battle to bring Capone to justice, there is a famous scene where Al, played by Robert De Niro, bludgeons one of his henchmen to death at a gang dinner using a baseball bat. It's a disturbing moment which contrasts the fine surroundings of the fancy restaurant with the savage reality of gangsterism, but despite the story being oft repeated down the decades, it almost certainly never happened. Performative killing was not Capone's style and anyway, by 1930 he was very much delegating the violence, not delivering it himself.

Innocent people got caught in the crossfire too and as the Chicago turf wars waged on, dozens of innocent people were shot or blown up.

The reluctance of the authorities in Chicago to act was in no small part down to the fact that many of them were on the payroll. In 1926 alone the Outfit was turning over about $105 million a year ($1.6 billion in 2025) and Capone was forking out about $300,000 a week ($4 million) in salaries and pay-offs. Almost everyone who mattered in Chicago was in his pocket, including the crooked Republican mayor Big Bill Thompson, who had been re-elected in 1927, with his help.

Thompson, like Capone, was as performatively conservative as he was corrupt and was greatly concerned with the shape of flags and the teaching of 'proper history' in schools. A big fan of George Washington, whose photograph adorned Capone's office walls, Thompson was appalled at the way in which children had been encouraged to examine the president's true history. So, one of the first things he did on taking back power was to sack the superintendent of schools, in order to counter 'the treason and propaganda which insidiously have been injected into our schools and other educational institutions'.[27]

When not promulgating fake history, Thompson busied himself taking bribes and like Capone, he undoubtedly thought himself beyond the reach of the law. But by 1929, the tide was beginning to turn.

Following Hymie Weiss's murder in October 1926, the diminished North Side Gang had been led by Bugs Moran, whose personal animosity towards Capone was well-known and the mutual beef between the two men was to culminate in one of the most infamous atrocities of the era. On Valentine's Day, 14 February 1929, Moran got 'a tip off' that a truckload of whiskey needed to be offloaded quickly and it was going for a bargain price. The offer was too good to ignore, so he sent seven men to the garage on North Clark Street to take the delivery; but Moran's people had walked straight into a trap. Two armed assassins dressed in cops' uniforms and another two purporting to be plain clothes detectives 'arrested them', ordered them to stand up against a wall and then machine-gunned them in cold blood – before calmly walking away.

Just one man, Frank Gusenberg, lived long enough for the real cops to arrive but he then refused to reveal what had happened and died shortly thereafter.

The only surviving witness was 'Highball', a German shepherd who, as a dog, was unable to help the police with their enquiries. Highball was deeply traumatised by what he had seen and was subsequently put down which only piled further public revulsion on to the existing horror.

Nobody knew for sure if Alphonse Capone was responsible for the crime (and we still don't), but by now that wasn't the point and the authorities moved against him.

Capone in fact had a cast-iron alibi as he had been visiting the DA's office in Miami on the afternoon of the killings, and having turned up expecting to be questioned about Frankie Yale's murder was somewhat bemused to be questioned about his lack of income tax payments instead.

Three days later, Capone faced further difficulties when he was subpoenaed to go to Chicago to face bootlegging charges. Claiming he was sick and had been in bed since January with influenza, Al even got a doctor's note to back him up but unfortunately, there were new sheriffs in town in the shape of the Bureau of Investigation (BOI) and J. Edgar Hoover's federal agents didn't mess about. The BOI* quickly proved that Capone had attended races in Miami, made a plane trip to Bimini and been generally cavorting around Florida in good health when he was meant to be sick in bed. On 27 March, the mobster completed a week of testimony in front of the grand jury in Chicago and when he left to return home was immediately arrested for contempt of court. Bail of $5,000 was posted and he was released pending trial – but the net was closing.

On 13 May, Capone attended a celebrated meeting in Atlantic City, where America's biggest mobsters gathered, much as the 'great nations'

* The FBI from 1935.

had at the Berlin Conference in 1884, to carve up the spoils of Prohibition and cool tensions between the warring parties. All the big names were there including Lucky Luciano and Bugsy Siegel, and it was hosted by another crook, Nucky Johnson, who was – coincidentally – the sheriff of Atlantic County. No minutes were taken, so the outcome remains a mystery; however, on 17 May, Capone and his bodyguard Frank Rio were arrested in Philadelphia for carrying concealed, unlicensed weapons and, following a lightning-quick trial, both men were sentenced to a year inside.

Al probably arranged the arrest and imprisonment himself, calculating that some time behind bars might show public penance for the Valentine's Day massacre while being good not only for his image but also for his personal safety. Despite brokering a truce with rival outfits, he now not only had the BOI but also the Sicilian mafia on his case and the latter had put a $50,000 price tag on his head, so a spell at the Eastern State Penitentiary, at the taxpayers' expense, was a cost-efficient way to keep the security bill down.

'I want peace and I am willing to live and let live,' Capone told Lemuel Schofield, his interviewing officer. 'I'm tired of gang murders and gang shootings. With the idea in mind – of making peace among the gangsters of Chicago – I spent the week in Atlantic City, and I have the word of each of the men participating that there shall be no more shootings.'[28]

Capone served seven months in some comfort. Teresa and Mae arranged for the delivery of his own mattress, lamp and easy chair, and Al and fellow inmates were entertained by his $500 state-of-the-art radiogram. Capone was largely at liberty inside and treated the warden's office as his own, in between reading a lengthy book on the life of his hero Napoleon, whom he dubbed 'the original racketeer'. Capone's incarceration coincided with the onset of the Great Depression, and when those respectable gangsters on Wall Street brought the global economy to its knees on 24 October 1929, the roaring twenties quite literally crashed to a halt.

Released on 17 March 1930, Capone stepped into a different world and like entrepreneurs everywhere, he faced an evolving business environment. As cash-strapped Americans tightened their belts, not only were proceeds from prostitution, alcohol and gambling all significantly down on the first quarter of the previous year but now his public image was taking a hit too. A week after his release from jail, the man who had once been dubbed the 'Unofficial Mayor of Chicago' was named 'Public Enemy Number One' by the newly created Chicago Crime Commission – and the label stuck.

Enraged by this perceived harassment, Capone decided to move to Miami, telling the press that: 'I need the sunshine . . . I shall take a little trip to Florida after I get things straightened out here. You see, I haven't had much sunshine for the last 10 months.'

But that didn't work out either because the moment he arrived in the Sunshine State he was promptly arrested for 'vagrancy' on the orders of Governor Doyle Carlton. The new vagrancy law had been passed the previous year, specifically to target Capone, and allowed the cops to arrest anyone suspected of being 'a crook or gangster' and escort them back north. It was clearly unconstitutional and Capone's lawyer's appealed, but it fell on deaf ears and Al was constantly rearrested and taken back across state lines.

As if all that wasn't bad enough, a secret society, controlled by some of the wealthiest and most powerful men in Chicago, was now on his case too.

In February 1930, a building contractor called Phil Meagher, working on the site of the University of Chicago hospital, was shot and though he survived, this incident motivated a group of anonymous businessmen to set up 'The Secret Six', a consortium of powerful business interests dedicated to taking down organised crime in the city. To this day, nobody is entirely sure who these six men were, or even if they were just six, but the consensus is that the group was led by Charles G. Dawes, who had won a Nobel Peace Prize for his post-war 1923 Dawes Plan. The Secret Six operated as a sort of a freelance intelligence gathering arm to the BOI using their considerable resources to fund the prosecution of Capone and fellow mobsters. At the same time, the IRS

Bureau of Internal Revenue under Elmer Irey, alongside publicity-hungry Special Agent Eliot Ness of the Bureau of Prohibition, were all after Capone too.

Al had in large part become a victim of his own celebrity, which had all started with that press conference that had followed Tony 'the Greek' Anton's killing in 1926. In doing so he had broken the first rule of organised crime and made himself famous – and having realised the mistake he was now telling anyone who would listen that he would be the 'happiest man alive' if he could simply retire to anonymity in Florida. But he knew that was just wishful thinking:

'Once you're in the racket, you're in it for life. Your past holds you in it. The gang won't let you out. Murder, murder, murder that's all this racket is. I'm sick of it'.[29]

In December 1930, Al's little sister Mafalda, who had long complained that she couldn't get a husband because of who she was, married her singularly reluctant suitor John Maritote in flamboyant fashion in front of 4,000 guests. Capone resisted the urge to attend and stayed hidden away in Miami but the endgame was looming.

Throughout the following year, as Eliot Ness raided breweries and posed for photos, fellow agents George Johnson, Frank J. Wilson and the undercover Irish cop Michael Malone, working under the alias Michael Lepito, did everything they could to take Capone down.* A significant breakthrough eventually came when Leslie Shumway, Al's accountant, was turned by Wilson and having been arrested, very publicly, in front of Capone's men, he set about dishing the dirt.

The trial began on 6 October 1931 and – apart from failed attempts to menace the jury and a brief distraction, when one of his bodyguards, Phil D'Andrea, was found to be carrying a gun in court – the case proceeded smoothly. The prosecution counsel proved that Capone, with his many properties, his two yachts and lavish spending, was quite obviously living beyond the means of legitimate income streams and was

* Although *The Untouchables* (1987) is largely a work of fiction, screenwriter David Mamet used Malone for the character played by Sean Connery.

thus guilty of tax evasion. The defence witnesses meanwhile turned out to be hapless idiots whose every word simply made matters worse for Capone, whose legal team let him down as well. At one point, his counsel Michael Ahern actually compared Al to Sherwood's most famous son, declaring that the law was seeking to convict him on the sole basis that he resembled 'the mythical Robin Hood you read so much about in all the newspapers'. Proceedings then descended into something approaching farce when the prosecuting attorney, George Johnston, shot back that Capone was a weird kind of Robin Hood – as he quite literally wore a diamond-studded belt.

On 24 October 1931, Capone was sentenced to three sentences of five years each on tax and Prohibition charges. At the courthouse door, Al complained that he had been treated 'unjustly, especially by the press', adding 'publicity, that is what got me'.

Deposed King Alphonse was driven straight to Cook County jail to start his 11-year stretch.

* * *

Capone's appeal came to nothing and in May 1931 the 32-year-old was moved to a federal prison in Atlanta. When jailed previously, Capone had been treated like a celebrity and afforded the run of the joint. This time, things were very different indeed and the Public Enemy Number One was set to be treated just like everyone else.

Having passed the psychiatric assessment, Capone was examined by doctors who found that the patient was suffering from latent and untreatable syphilis. It was to be that and not a rival's bullets which would get him in the end, but in the meantime prisoner 40886 was taken to an eight-man cell where he became the target of every tough nut and wise guy in the penitentiary. Al in fact proved to be a model inmate who kept himself to himself and spent hours each day replying to the large sacks of mail that arrived addressed to him in the prison mail room. When not replying to his fans, Capone earned $10 weekly working in the shop stitching shoes and counting out the days to his release.

But despite his good behaviour things were about to get a whole lot worse for him.

Following his inauguration, in March 1933, President Franklin D. Roosevelt entered the White House on the explicit promise of enacting his New Deal. Though the series of policies, programmes and reforms that followed are now chiefly remembered for the way in which they sought to address poverty and inequality in the USA, there was a huge focus on law enforcement too and with the Volstead Act repealed, just in time for Christmas 1933, FDR determined to go after violent crime and the misery it spawned.

A new breed of 'romantic outlaws' – including 'Bonnie and Clyde', John 'the killer' Dillinger, Charles Arthur 'Pretty Boy' Floyd and 'Machine Gun Kelly' – were hitting the headlines and the new administration was determined to show that crime did not pay.

At the same time, considerable effort was poured into the BOI's image management and in tandem with the new mood there was a significant shift in the broader cultural representation of gangsters and federal agents as America swung behind the good guys. The most celebrated example of this was Warner Brothers' *G-Men*, a box office hit in 1935, which had James Cagney, who had risen to fame playing the public enemy, cast as a reformed gangster turned (the recently rebranded) FBI agent – who takes down the hoods. The smart, wise-cracking, hard-drinking lone cop now displaced the gangster as the hero protagonist of the hour and it was this new template of 'gangster-like cop' that influenced everything from 007 to Dirty Harry across the decades that followed.

Now relegated to the role of bad guys once more, the era's outlaws started to drop like pins in a bowling alley. Having murdered nine police officers and four innocent people during their violent 21-month crime spree, Clyde Barrow and Bonnie Parker met their ends in a police ambush in May 1934. Two months later, John Dillinger was killed by agents in a shootout outside a movie theatre in Chicago. And in October the same year, Pretty Boy Floyd also met his end when he was killed by Bureau agents in Ohio.

Machine Gun Kelly – whose image had largely been moulded by his publicity-hungry wife Kathryn and who, in fact, hated machine guns and loud bangs – had been captured the previous year after begging the G-Men not to shoot him and in retrospect, probably counted himself lucky.

To underline this new zero-tolerance approach it had been decided, in August 1933, that the military prison on the island of Alcatraz 1.25 miles off the coast of San Francisco would be turned into 'a prison of last resort' for America's most dangerous men. Machine Gun Kelly would soon become prisoner 117 and the former Public Enemy Number One, Al Capone, prisoner number 85. By any measure, the decision to move Capone to the Rock was a publicity stunt and one which very nearly backfired. Interest in Scarface had dimmed following his imprisonment but now he was being moved, he returned to the headlines once more and it flattered his ego. As Al was taken across the country by train, that August 1934, crowds gathered at railroad junctions to catch sight of him and by the time he reached the Federal prison he had renewed swagger.

Having been processed he even sought to order the governor Warden James Johnston around, only to be put firmly back in his place.

In those early days, Alcatraz was every bit as miserable and tough as its later reputation deserved. Everyone on the island, no matter who they had been on the outside, was known by their number and that included the crime artist formerly known as Scarface. A British inmate and former drug dealer, William Henry Ambrose, who was deported from America by order of the president in August 1935, gave an insight into what life was like inside, telling *Time* magazine journalists:

'Not a word can be spoken by the convicts . . . at the table or at work in their cells. We got to talk once a week, on Saturday afternoon from 1 to 3.30, when we were allowed in the yard . . . everyone who's caught is punished.

'Capone is burning up at the restrictions. He's been in the hole [solitary confinement] several times for talking. But whoever the convict was that said Al was losing his mind over it was absolutely wrong. He's not cracking up. He worked first in the dry-cleaning shop and then, I think, in the shoe shop. Now he's in the library.

'The hopelessness of it gets you. Capone feels it. Everybody does. You know you'll never get parole. There's no chance there for anybody—only that God-awful silence.'[30]

Capone was set to work in the library where he offset the loneliness by reading Walter B. Pitkin's bestselling *Life Begins at Forty* and teaching himself the banjo.

Music was a hard-won privilege on Alcatraz and Capone, who had always loved jazz and opera, found considerable solace in his instrument. There are nearly as many legends about Al Capone's side hustle on the banjo as there are about his criminal activities and many a tall tale has been told about 'The Rock Islanders', Alcatraz's very own inmate band, of which Capone was said to be a member. Ever suspicious of such 'good stories', I went looking for proof and having initially failed to find substantial evidence for Capone's role in the group, by chance made contact with an American film-maker called Steve Davis, who has a long-running interest in Alcatraz. Through him, I was privileged to be introduced to Chuck Stucker, who grew up on the island and whose uncle, Nova Stucker, was an associate warden there. In his archive, Chuck has a programme for a concert that was held on the island on Sunday 28 April 1935 and among the artists listed as performing that day, we find Alphonse Capone on 'tenor banjo'.

So, it's true. The once-feared gangster Al Capone really was in The Rock Islanders although another story – which claims that Machine Gun Kelly was on drums – unfortunately seems to be baseless and that Sunday in April 1935, they were played by one Alfred Loomis, a professional counterfeiter.

The vocalist was Charles Richard Kray, one of many gay military men imprisoned on the Rock for the 'crime' of engaging in same-sex relationships. Indeed, in a much-neglected bit of LGBTQ+ history, many of Alcatraz's first prisoners were incarcerated there simply because they were homosexual and prisoner number one, Frank Bolt, and four others out of the original ten were serving convictions for 'sodomy'.

The programme that April day included 'Cinderella's Honeymoon Parade', '12th Street Rag' and another Jazz Age favourite, 'High

Society' by Porter Steele. And as the band played songs that had once entertained Capone in his favourite clubs, at the height of his powers, perhaps a little part of him drifted away to memories of happier and better times.

But it was not all concerts, self-help books and banjos and on 23 June 1936, James Lucas, aka prisoner 224, attacked number 85 and stabbed him in the back with a pair of scissors. The motive for the attack may have been down to Capone's perceived friendliness with the guards and general compliance, but once Lucas had struck him, the streetfighter of old kicked in and the guards had to intervene to save the assailant from the gangster's violent wrath.

Lucas was sent to solitary while Capone spent several days in the hospital wing.

On his release and in declining mental and physical health, Capone poured out his heart in letters to Mae and also sent her songs that he had transcribed on to sheet music. Two of those, 'Madonna Mia' and 'Humoresque', were long thought to be original Capone compositions and in 2018 the musician Jack White bought the latter and recorded a version of it for his album 'Boarding House Reach'. In doing so, Capone posthumously added plagiarism to his charge sheet, as musical detectives soon worked out that 'Humoresque' was really the original work of a little known Czech composer caller Antonín Dvořák, while 'Madonna Mia' was copied from an existing songbook.

Despite efforts to treat the syphilis that was eating away at him, his condition worsened and having found God by 1938 he was often to be heard speaking to 'angels' in his empty cell. We looked at the impact of solitary confinement on prisoners in earlier chapters and while that too may have played a part, the primary cause for these delusions was probably the disease that was now attacking his brain.

By his release on 16 November 1939, the once-feared Scarface had a mental age of seven. His wife Mae, who was in deep denial, had to be encouraged to bring in a full-time nurse, Gertrude F. Cole, to look after him and while she searched for a miracle cure, Capone spent his final years in a state of cognitive decline that had been denied his many victims. Al liked singing and fishing but spoke less and less and died on 25 January 1947, just a few days after his 48th birthday.

His death certificate noted that he was 'retired from his usual occupation'.

In the years that followed, his notoriety only rose. Capone became easily the most notorious gangster in history and, like many a famous Tudor monarch, hoteliers cashed in on his name. While writing this book, I have met people who have told me that they have slept in rooms where he once slept and eaten in restaurants where he once ate across America. Few of these claim have any grounding in truth.

His cultural impact lives on and he has been portrayed at least 25 times in films and TV series by everyone from F. Murray Abraham to Tom Hardy. In fact there is probably not a gangster film out there that does not owe something to the legend. Songs have been written about him too by everyone from Michael Jackson to the Prodigy and he even appears as an NPC (non-player character) in *Empire of Sin*, now available on a gaming console near you. Few people live up to their legend, but Capone transcends his. He was in fact everything you might have thought of him to be and that is why many of the biographers who come to bury Little Caesar end up praising him instead.

Popular culture continues to worship 'romantic outlaws' in a manner that no other criminal group is revered. Nobody ever made a sympathetic serial killer film or tried to get a stalker on to a chat show – but gangsters and outlaws are viewed, if not sympathetically then at least with broader empathy. In the 1990s the likes of the Kray Twins, the thug 'Mad' Frankie Fraser and the drug smuggler known as Mr Nice even became celebrities in the UK. Films like the *Godfather* trilogy, *Goodfellas* and *The Untouchables* are a staple of cinema and bookshops positively groan with tales of the Mafia and organised crime.

In his own time, Capone's popularity rested in large part on the singular unpopularity of Prohibition. This 'bad law' had criminalised everyone who wanted a drink and as such he was cast as a hero. If one were to be positively revisionist one could even go as far as to argue that Hatchet Carry and her fellow travellers were in part responsible for the violence and mayhem that followed and the myth of the American Dream must be held culpable too. The false hope of its impossible promise gave those who believed it every reason to pursue a life of crime. That is not to condone Capone – or Torrio or their fellow mobsters – but it does perhaps explain them.

The movie studios probably deserve blame too. By romanticising hedonistic criminality and aspirational violence and by making audiences fall in love with the men who perpetrated it, they created an enduring monster.

It is possible to be nostalgic for just about anything and Prohibition America for all its many horrors rests easy in the collective imagination. The jazz, the cars, the style and the movies that sprang from it can make an enticing cocktail that belies the darkness of it, and in that atmosphere the larger-than-life Florida-loving man of the people Capone may even seem like an appealing figure.

But though it may be tempting to glamorise and even idolise this man who rose and fell on the dark side of the American dream, we should never forget that like every other gangster in history, Alphonse Capone was primarily a self-serving parasite.

CHAPTER SIX

THE ILLUMINATI

The Secret Societies that Really Run our World

On 1 May 1776, four students from the University of Ingolstadt in Bavaria gathered together in their 27-year-old professor Adam Weishaupt's study and leaned in as he explained how they were going to take over the world.

Weishaupt, a philosopher and lecturer in canon law at the Jesuit-controlled university, had chosen May Day deliberately. The date heralded the traditional end of spring and the start of summer and the young academic saw his nascent movement in similarly symbolic terms. Together these five intellectual saplings would grow and branch out and, in time, their metaphorical forest of enlightened thinking would creep into every corner of the Earth. As his students listened intently, Weishaupt told them that he was the guardian of ancient knowledge and that soon the old order would be swept away to be replaced with something better: *them*.

Adam dubbed the group *Bund der Perfektibilisten* or the 'Order of Perfectibilists' and proclaimed the Owl of Athena (Minerva in Roman tradition) as their emblem. Athena was the virginal Greek goddess of wisdom and her all-seeing bird had been a symbol of sagacity since the age of the Minoans. The notion of the 'wise old owl' has continued through the era of Gothic novels and Beatrix Potter to that of her near namesake Harry – and that despite owls in fact being no wiser and actually a little dimmer than most other birds of prey. But let's not allow the pedantry of ornithology to get in the way of a nice metaphor.

From the start, Weishaupt was as obsessed with secrecy as he was with symbolism, and told his followers that:

'The great strength of our order lies in concealment; let it never appear in its own name but always covered by another name and another occupation.'[1]

Each of his five apostles were given code names and Herrs Sutor, Merz, Bauhof and Massenhausen became Erasmus, Tiberius, Agathon and Ajax respectively, while Adam dubbed himself 'Spartacus' after the legendary Thracian gladiator who rose up against Rome.

In truth, Weishaupt made for an unlikely Spartacus – let alone an embryonic Doctor Evil. Despite bursting with big ideas and madcap ambitions he was a bit of a loner and in some ways very much the prototypical basement-dwelling blogger 200 years before such a thing existed. Despite churning out letters and essays in a never-ending stream of consciousness that would put any modern sub-stacking influencer to shame, even he must have appreciated that he had one hell of a hill to climb where the whole world domination endeavour was concerned. After all, it's one thing to boast about how you're going to dismantle nation states, destroy the established church and form a world government – but it's quite another thing to actually do it; although, to his credit, Weishaupt did have a rather cunning plan.

In order to take over the world, the Perfectibilists would first engage in wholesale entryism and having joined existing societies with large established networks they would then take them over. Less owls and more cuckoos.

The good news was that in the mid-1770s you could barely move on a Bavarian university campus without stumbling upon some secret sect that was knee-deep in conspiracy. One of the biggest were the Rosicrucians, an esoteric movement that had first emerged over a century earlier following the publication of three mysterious 'manifestos': *Fama Fraternitatis* (1614), *Confessio Fraternitatis* (1617) and *Chymical Wedding* (1617). These peculiar works, addressed to 'the learned of Europe' and made up of cryptic poems, parables and quasi-religious passages, were said to have been inspired by the work of a fourteenth-century influencer called Christian Rosenkreutz, who gave the movement its name. Rosenkreutz was claimed to have been a seeker of enlightenment and while in his own era his order had numbered just eight virginal males (we shall meet quite a few of those in this chapter), they in turn had taken a vow to recruit and pass on their knowledge until such time as other celibates were ready to take over the world.

Much like 'bitcoin', the true founder of this viral movement was shrouded in mystery and – again like 'bitcoin' – much of the philosophy of Rosicrucianism was based on frankly unintelligible bullshit that relied entirely on gullible people buying into it, while others made hay. Rosenkreutz most certainly never existed and much of the founding literature seems to have been written by seventeenth-century theologians Johann Valentin Andreae, Michael Maier and Thomas Vaughan. Andreae later admitted penning the *Chymical Wedding* and even went as far as to dismiss the entire movement as an elaborate parody – although this itself may have been a cover for the propagation of the philosophy or just a poor excuse for wasting everybody's time.

Max Heindel, another exponent of Rosicrucianism, freely admitted that the faith was a hotch-potch of other people's ideas, saying: 'Our origins are Egyptian, Brahminic, derived from the mysteries of Eleusis and Samothrace, the Magi of Persia, the Pythagoreans and the Arabs.'[2]

Certainly, the philosophy was a mosaic of fairly abstract and random stuff but by cunningly passing Rosicrucianism off as 'ancient knowledge' that had been handed down across the ages, it garnered unwarranted credibility – a trick that would be borrowed by both the Perfectibilists and the Order of Freemasonry whom Weishaupt also sought to infiltrate.

Freemasonry was actually a bigger and far greater prize than Rosicrucianism which it had both copied and to some extent eclipsed. Claiming to trace its roots back to the stone cutters who built King Solomon's Temple in 900 BCE and further to Euclid, the fourth century BCE father of geometry, the brotherhood hinted that it had been been responsible for every major construction project in history from the Pyramids to Stonehenge. In fact, by the time Weishaupt set up his own society it was only 60 years old, having been formally established in a London pub called the Goose and Gridiron in St Paul's churchyard in 1717. For all its weird and wacky rituals and associated conspiracy theories and funny handshakes, early Freemasonry actually had much to say for it. The society provided an opportunity for open-minded men from different backgrounds to meet and share ideas and was a sort of quirky LinkedIn, but with booze, aprons and purpose thrown in.

Across Europe, the growing network had swiftly became a hotbed of freethinking and the organisation encouraged recruits to live by codes of integrity, honesty and a love for all humankind. While decidedly agnostic in nature its members were expected to believe in a 'supreme being' and Freemasonry attracted some very big names indeed including Wolfgang Amadeus Mozart, John Locke, Voltaire, Joseph Haydn and Benjamin Franklin.

By the late eighteenth century, the movement was particularly flourishing in the German states and Great Britain, and with everyone enjoying themselves, naturally the Catholic Church set out to suppress it. In 1738, Pope Clement XII delivered a papal bull, which banned membership and ordered:

'Bishops and prelates, and other local ordinaries, as well as inquisitors for heresy, (to) investigate and proceed against transgressors . . . and punish them with condign penalties as being most suspect of heresy.'[3]

It didn't work, largely because by then Freemasonry had grown so much in influence that its members could effectively snub their nose at the Vatican. And that enduring irreverence for authority impressed Weishaupt who saw the movement as a shortcut to the fulfilment of his dream. Here, after all, was an existing 'secret society', chock-full of prominent and powerful people and a network that he could hijack and exploit.

He knew that in order to do that, the Perfectibilists had to be 'better' than the group they were seeking to infiltrate – a sort of paid content 'Freemasons Platinum' – and he realised too that he needed to be exceptionally selective as to whom he brought on board. Weishaupt thus ordered his people to recruit the crème de la crème of the era's intelligentsia and to keep the riff-raff out. Writing to one follower concerning a potential conscript in October 1776 he instructed:

'If Winterhaltern is to become one of us, he will have to be refined quite a bit. In the first place, I do not care at all for the way he walks, his

manners are crude and unpolished, and I have no idea how he thinks. Most of all, I would recommend that he change his uncouth nature. He must become a completely different person, and so far, he is not of much use . . . Look for clever young people and not such coarse fellows.'[4]

Later he added:

'Seek out the nobiles, potentes, divites, and doctos quaerite.'

Before adding a little snippily about another prospective draftee:

'I don't know about Agathon; I have my doubts that we will keep him. He has a good head, but a corrupt and malicious heart.'

Weishaupt's pickiness eventually paid off and having dropped their awkward and forgettable original name, and having rebranded themselves the 'Illuminati' the group really would go on to take over the world.

Kind of.

* * *

1776 was a crucial year, in a decade of change, that sat atop the very high point of the century and though he did not know this at the time, Adam really could not have picked a better moment to make his bid for global domination. Two months after Weishaupt formed his secret society, on 4 July, the Continental Congress in North America adopted the Declaration of Independence and in a moment the next 200 years of history were set upon a different path.

The roots of that revolution lay in the 70 years that had preceded it.

The eighteenth century had begun in a baptism of fire. The War of the Spanish Succession (1701–14), like the Great War (1914–18) 200 years later, was an era-defining conflict that had caused an irrevocable shift in the tectonic plates of power in Europe, and once again it was in part down to a hereditary monarch failing to produce an heir.

Charles II, the last Habsburg king of Spain, had, like so many other kings and queens before him, spent much of his brief miserable life attempting to sire a child. Taking the throne at the age of four, he was a sickly boy with significant mental health challenges and a hugely pronounced 'Habsburg jaw'. Erratic and eccentric to say the least, he became known as El Hechizado or The Bewitched and, among other traits, was later claimed to have slept with the body of his long-deceased father, in the hope that close proximity might cure his impotence.

You don't need a degree in reproductive health to guess that it didn't and, while it's tempting to conject that the lack of an heir may have been down to the presence of a dead body in the marital bed, there was in fact a different explanation. Following his death, aged 38, in 1700, a post-mortem revealed that Charles only had one testicle and it had atrophied; the modern medical opinion is that he was intersex.[5]

Charles's passing left a vacancy on the Spanish throne and a power vacuum in Europe, and when his nephew Philip of Anjou was declared king, potentially uniting France and Spain, the other European powers got the jitters. The move threatened the balance of regional power, and war with England and Scotland (soon to be Great Britain), as well as with Austria, became inevitable. The conflict raged across the next 13 years and dragged practically every major regional power into the vortex. This was the first modern 'world war', with all the recognisable reverberations that such a conflict prompts. The carnage saw 500,000 killed in battle and an additional 750,000 die as a result of illness and disease and while events mostly played out across Europe, it went global too. The Anglo-French 'Queen Anne's War' which waged in North America concurrently was really part and parcel of the same event, making this a truly intercontinental conflict.

With the Treaty of Utrecht (1713),* both Spain and France were politically and financially enfeebled, and a newly energised Great Britain emerged in the ascendant. Under the military command of John Churchill,† the 1st Duke of Marlborough, the country had demonstrated that, alongside Austria, it was now one of two major regional superpowers. Britain and her allies had achieved their key objective too and while Philip V was recognised as the new King of Spain, he was removed from the French line of succession. Utrecht granted control of Gibraltar and Menorca to the British, giving them effective naval control

* Austria and the Holy Roman Empire fought on until the Treaty of Rastatt in 1714.

† Ancestor of Sir Winston.

of the Western Mediterranean. Utrecht also gifted British merchants the rights to the Asiento, a 30-year-long monopoly which allowed them to supply 4,800 enslaved African people to Spain's South American colonies every year.

This egregious public-private partnership, built on the exploitation of African people, was dubbed the South Sea Company and having opened offices in Argentina, Venezuela and Cuba it began expanding the country's trade, influence and power into the region and laying the ground for Britain's future empire.* Queen Anne invested heavily and eventually held about 22.5 per cent of the stock and although the company ceased to trade in human life in 1739, its legacy endured. George I, II, III, IV and William IV all either profited from or supported the continuation of the slave trade.

Back in 1714, there were huge cultural, social and religious ramifications too, and a bruised and humiliated France was now obliged to formally recognise Protestant Anne as the rightful queen of England. This was a huge moment since across the sixteenth and seventeenth centuries, Catholic kings and notably Charles V and Philip II, husband of 'Bloody Mary', had tried to suppress or dilute the ideas of the Protestant Reformation through Inquisitions, Counter-Reformations and marriage. As long as Catholic Spain and France had the upper hand, they had some success in pushing back the tide; but now, that changed and a new set of beliefs went mainstream.

Key among them was the notion that God was transcendent and that, in essence, his realm was wholly separate from humanity and the natural world. By dint of that, the very notion of an Earth-bound hierarchy was itself challenged and people once again had to ask themselves the same question that John Ball had posed back in 1381:

'When Adam delved and Eve span, who then was the gentle-man?'

As the ideas of the Reformation spread, they mixed with those of the Renaissance and collided with radical innovations in technology and

---

* The South Sea Bubble burst in 1720 as a result of greed, corruption and over-inflated stock. The 'slave trade' was seen as a route to easy money but many investors lost everything. The company survived.

science to forge a new atmosphere known as the Age of the Enlightenment or *Aufklärung*, a term coined by Immanuel Kant in his 1784 essay *What is Enlightenment*, which opens with one of the greatest mission statements in history:

'Enlightenment is man's emergence from his self-imposed immaturity. Immaturity is the inability to use one's understanding without guidance from another. This immaturity is self-imposed when its cause lies not in lack of understanding, but in lack of resolve and courage to use it without guidance from another. Sapere Aude! "Have courage to use your own understanding!" – that is the motto of enlightenment.'*[6]

The long days of university life can loom large and academics love nothing more than a good old spat over when things started, ended, reached their middle – or even happened at all. The *Aufklärung* has provided fertile ground for such time-filling ruminations, and for centuries the cloisters of Europe and America have reverberated to the sound of irate professors shouting dates at each other.

Some place its start at the Peace of Westphalia, which concluded the Thirty Years War in 1648 and its end with the Fall of the Bastille in 1789, while others insist it began with the death of Louis XIV of France in September 1715, two years after the Treaty of Utrecht and continued well into the nineteenth century. In truth, historical eras are rarely any neater than anything else in life and given that the ideas of the Enlightenment have yet to fully illuminate the world, there's a case that it has never ended. But let's dodge that theoretical rabbit hole for the moment and simply agree that throughout the 1700s, philosophers, clerics, writers, poets, academics, pamphleteers, coffee house proprietors, dreamers, revolutionaries and literary salons had never had it so good – at least where tossing ideas about was concerned.

It was not such great news for the Vatican or indeed the royal houses of Europe, however, because as reason, science and human progress were championed, those fusty old institutions began to look ever more

* Sapere Aude: 'dare to know' or 'dare to be wise'; i.e. 'have the courage to use your own reason'.

redundant and silly. And matters were made a whole lot worse because courtesy of mass printing, they could no longer control the message and that caused all manner of headaches for the control freaks at the top.

Just as we tend to look back somewhat patronisingly on our fourteenth-century peasant forebears, it can be tempting to think of our slightly more recent ancestors as a bunch of illiterate cider-drinking yokels, tending cows and sucking on bits of straw. But in fact, by the late 1700s, millions of people across Europe were able to read and write, and in countries where the ideas of the Reformation had taken seed, this was particularly the case. The Protestants put enormous store by education and from the time of Martin Luther and his 1524 treatise *An die Ratsherren aller Städte deutschen Landes*, parishes in emerging enclaves actively preached that pedagogy was akin to God-ology.

John Locke's *Some Thoughts Concerning Education*, published in England in 1693, and Jean-Jacques Rousseau's *Emile, or On Education* printed in France in 1762, both promoted the notion of educating rich and poor alike.

Literacy rates across Europe varied wildly in the period, with a significant disparity between the north and south of the continent – and, as we have seen in the early life of Capone, it remained rock bottom in parts of southern Italy and elsewhere well into the twentieth century. But as the ideas of Locke and Rousseau took off and as the volume of printed matter went through the roof, elsewhere an ever more literate populace increasingly spent what leisure time they had reading. Book production (by volume) in the sixteenth and seventeenth century was in the region of 150 to 200 million copies,[7] which though an impressive figure was positively dwarfed by the 1,500 million books that were churned out across the eighteenth century.

The number of pamphlets printed at the time can only be fathomed at and while by the early 1700s they were being eclipsed by newspapers, the sheer quantity of available reading material was staggering. Daily and weekly papers had first appeared in German states in the 1600s but by the 1750s, with the cost of paper falling, they were being churned out across Europe. While books and periodicals remained relatively expensive, for the first time in history news and information was theoretically within the reach of everyone who could read.

Something else changed too. Prior to the eighteenth century, those who could read often did so out loud, meaning that reading was a collective, social activity. Villagers would gather in pubs or barns to hear stories, Bible readings, ballads or news reports and then discuss what they had heard. Now, with the rise in literacy, all of that started to evolve. By 1750,* about half the population of England were literate, while in London the figure was 90 per cent, and across the German states, the figures were even higher. As people picked up printed matter and devoured it, a literal revolution went on inside their heads and, for the first time in history, ordinary individuals cultivated an interior, intellectual world and began to look afresh at the universe about them.

We know, because we have lived through something very similar in the internet age, that mass information does not equate to 'good information' and that was as true for the eighteenth century as it is today. It is no coincidence that the rise of printing in the seventeenth century coincided with the emergence of many ridiculous ideas, dumb belief systems and on occasion downright dangerous conspiracy theories – including the wiccaphobia that resulted in the execution of the Perry family back in Chapter One. Some of the stuff that passed for thinking – well into the eighteenth century – was as loopy as anything that exists on social media in our own era, and while the age gave posterity the writings of Voltaire, Rousseau, Kant and David Hume, it also saw a revival in that age-old condition called stupidity. Mysticism and pseudoscience flourished and men like Franz Mesmer, who promoted the theory that animals, humans and even Brussels sprouts contain 'magnetic energy', grew rich on fake science.

In times of revolution, ignorance has an unnerving habit of thriving in the same atmosphere as progress and as mindless, ill-informed pre-clickbait nonsense flourished, the 'verified' science of the era did too. The principles of cosmology, for example, first set out by Copernicus in the early 1500s but expanded on by Sir Isaac Newton in the late

* Literacy rates differed between men (60 per cent) and women (40 per cent).

seventeenth century, now not only explained why apples fell out of trees but redrew the universe altogether. By the late 1700s, many who stared up at 'the heavens' now saw an infinite chasm of emptiness instead and it must have blown countless minds.

Critical thinking was not new. Pre-Socratic philosophers like Xenophanes, Thales and Heraclitus were on the search for something akin to absolute truth as far back as 500 BCE and Heraclitus's epigrams, which include 'if you change the way you look at things, the things you look at change' and that 'there is nothing permanent, except change', very much chimed with the thinking of the Enlightenment. Many of the eighteenth century's big thinkers deliberately name-checked the Greeks and particularly Socrates, because once again they knew that their own ideas would be given more credence if they could demonstrate that they were building on the shoulders of giants.

The Enlightenment saw the emergence of the first public libraries and, just as notably, public spaces dedicated to the pursuit of knowledge like the British Museum which opened in 1759 and the Louvre in 1793. Although both buildings would eventually be stuffed to the rafters with items plundered from both countries' empires, these were, at first, a genuine attempt to democratise the understanding of the world and take the notion of the cabinet of curiosities to the masses. Modern art galleries and public spaces like the Natural History Museum, Science Museum and the National Gallery (which we will visit later) in London are thus an enduring product of the Enlightenment and so too are books of general knowledge. In 1751, under the editorship and guidance of Denis Diderot the first edition of the radical 28-volume *Encyclopédie* was published in France. This hugely ambitious undertaking was created with the specific aim not only of educating people but radicalising them too by 'changing the way they think'. It was a cultural and intellectual phenomenon whose impact was such that some would even end up blaming it for the French Revolution and while many of the contributors to the project were not themselves revolutionaries, the work was undoubtedly revolutionary; a rough guide to those seeking to navigate the big ideas of the era.

Diderot was a fiery figure who had been arrested and incarcerated for nascent revolutionary activity before his grand project came out. For a flavour of his radicalism, take this line from his *Poésies Diverses* written in 1875:

'Men will never be free until the last king is strangled with the entrails of the last priest.'

With its full title *A Systematic Dictionary of the Sciences, Arts and Crafts* the radical encyclopaedia featured many of the big names of the day including Voltaire, Jean-Jacques Rousseau and Montesquieu and for those who got their hands on a copy, it was a sort of upmarket eighteenth-century Wikipedia with the red meat of revolution thrown in for free. Though it only had a total print run of about 4,250 copies and had to defy repeated attempts to ban it, many of the surviving editions found their way into the universities of Europe including the one at Ingolstadt, where young Adam Weishaupt was busy seeking enlightenment in his godfather's extensive library.

Prior to 1776, the young Weishaupt had led a fairly unexceptional life. Born in 1748 in Ingolstadt, later to become famous as the home of the fictional Dr Frankenstein, Weishaupt was the scion of an academic family and his father Johann had been professor of imperial institutions and criminal law before dying suddenly at 36. His mother, Anna, had also died – probably in childbirth – and so the five-year-old Adam was adopted by his godfather Johann Freiherr (aka 'baron') von Ickstatt, who was the director of the university.

In the 1750s, Ingolstadt was a hotbed of clerical activism and anti-Reformation ideas. Founded in 1472 by Louis IX, the Duke of Bavaria, from the sixteenth century onwards it had been infiltrated by Jesuits who, in a classic display of entryism, ended up effectively taking over the university to the point where Ingolstadt became the de facto headquarters of the Counter Reformation in Southern German states.

The Jesuits were a hierarchical and secretive Catholic sect and knew, like so many other cults before and since, that if you want to control the narrative and the future direction of the world, a good way to do that is to influence young minds.

Raised in an environment that was positively infused with their methods and educated at the university which they essentially controlled, Adam witnessed these machinations up close while always staying one step apart. His was a life of contrasts since his powerful and influential godfather, Baron Ickstatt, though dean of the college, was not himself a Jesuit and indeed was a liberal, pro-enlightenment figure, who maintained an impressive library that was stocked full of banned books. While studying law at the university, Weishaupt, perhaps inevitably, developed a curious love–hate relationship with the Jesuits and, while appalled by their lack of reasoning and somewhat unsubtle approach, was nonetheless impressed by their organisational skills, their loyalty, their hierarchy and their rituals.

From the early 1750s, the Jesuits had began to suffer setbacks as they became ever more out of step with the times and their power and influence diminished. Their deliberate meddling in state affairs had led to their expulsion from the Portuguese Empire in 1759 and they were subsequently kicked out of many other countries too until in 1773 Pope Clement XIV felt obliged to issue a brief *Dominus ac Redemptor*, which effectively closed the order altogether. That drove them underground and as they were expunged from Ingolstadt and elsewhere, they left many a vacancy, including the post of professor of canon law, which was filled by Adam Weishaupt who, by 1775, had been appointed dean of the faculty of law.

Ickstatt died in August 1776, a month after the American Declaration of Independence and three months after the creation of the Perfectibilists. The timing could not have been better and his protégé and executor now had both money in the bank and a growing sense of confidence that he was in tune with the zeitgeist. Soon his agents were out and spreading his creed and beginning to get noticed which was very risky indeed, for while Bavaria may have been a hotbed of radical thinking it was certainly no modern liberal democracy. Appreciating that risk and in order to ward off potential infiltration by state actors, Weishaupt set up a system of individual cells whereby 'insinuators' (recruits) were brought in by 'scrutators' (handlers) who would then educate them in the mores, means and objectives of the society. Everyone was kept in the dark about the further links in the chain and that way, nobody ever knew who else was involved.

Two additional benefits to this system were that it created both a sense of mystery and a hierarchy and that incentivised members to stay in the organisation and get promoted to the next level. Members went from being an entry grade Novice to a Minerval to an Illuminated Minerval in a hierarchy that was essentially a straight up copy of the Jesuit order. Weishaupt, aka Spartacus, placed himself atop the pile and beneath him established a sort of Politburo made up largely of the original members of the outfit – which he called the Areopagite. He also claimed that a mysterious council of 'Most Serene Superiors' sat above him in the order of things and that they were the real hand (or hands) that guided the movement and suggested, like the Freemasons and Rosicrucians, that the order had ancient roots that had been passed down through the ages. Weishaupt promised that those who climbed to the very top would have these mysteries revealed to them.

Over the next two years, the five original members grew to 27 with lodges in five German cities, which were also given their own code names. Ingolstadt was Eleusis, Ravensburg was Sparta, Munich became Athens, Freising was Thebes, and Eichstaedt was dubbed Erzurum, while simultaneously Weishaupt and his team set about trying to infiltrate the Freemasons. Adam had tried to join them prior to creating his own order but had failed to make the grade. By 1777 he was now a figure of some influence and a dean of the university at Ingolstadt so he was welcomed in, and having been so, he set about selling his organisation as a purer form of Freemasonry to potential recruits.

In late December 1777, Maximilian III, Elector of Bavaria, died of smallpox aged 50 triggering the decidedly underwhelming War of Bavarian Succession that resulted in his distant cousin, Charles Theodore, taking his place. Charles, aged 53, saw himself as a bit of a thespian and was initially viewed as a breath of fresh air by the region's intelligentsia but it rapidly transpired that he was preternaturally lazy and suggestible too, and soon the new Elector's advisers were taking advantage and pushing him towards restricting liberal and potentially subversive movements.

As is so often the case, the clampdown in fact had the opposite of the desired effect and potential recruits began lining up to enlist in Weishaupt's organisation.

Among them was a 27-year-old diplomat called Adolph Knigge, who joined in 1780. Knigge was a bright and ambitious young man who had used a modest inheritance to put himself through college. Having graduated in law from Göttingen University, in 1772, he had become a 'Court Squire' (essentially private secretary) to Friedrich II in the Landgrave of Hessen-Kassel before being head-hunted by the Weimar Court where he rose to become Chamberlain in 1777. Having joined the Freemasons, he caught the eye of Costanzo Marchese di Costanzo, one of Weishaupt's recruiting sergeants.

The meeting of minds was serendipitous as Knigge had himself been making plans to form a secret society of his own and now, in the existing organisation, saw a shortcut to the fulfilment of his own ambitions. Knigge was useful to Weishaupt too as he not only knew many of the most influential people in Germany but was affable and gregarious with it and under his code name – Cato – he became a one-man recruiting drive as he rose to prominence in the organisation.

One of the great attractions of the Illuminati was that as members moved through the ranks, new layers of understanding were revealed to them. It was a bit like gaming where you get better stuff as the journey progresses – except that the prize here was not a virtual spirit goblet or *Fortnite V* bucks but the receipt of ancient wisdom. The ultimate goal, or the final level if you will, was to meet the mysterious 'Most Serene Superiors' who sat above Weishaupt and find out what they knew. But nobody ever got there and there was a reason for that. The problem with any multi-layered, pyramid scheme – whether it be Scientology, Apple products or indeed the Illuminati – is that eventually you run out of both goodwill and divine revelations. And Illuminism's ultimate divulgence of knowledge could only ever be as good as Adam Weishaupt could come up with . . . because he had made the whole thing up. Knigge was no idiot and had probably worked this out long before Adam was obliged to admit it to him. And when he confessed, Knigge was delighted because, with the ficticious council gone, Knigge realised that he and Weishaupt could innovate and become the top rank themselves and make some necessary changes.

The inherent problem with revolutionary movements made up of cells is that they invariably indulge in both 'groupthink' and favouritism and Weishaupt's outfit was no exception with his original student recruits now occupying all the senior ranks of the Areopagus. Most of them had remained loyal to Spartacus but as the society had grown some heads had swelled with power, while others had become heretics and nascent Judases who thought that they could do things better. Weishaupt himself could not abide dissent and was a grudge-bearer of epic proportions and this simply made things worse. Knigge, by contrast, was a skilled diplomat and conciliatory figure and having established a degree of cohesion, he encouraged his fellow Illuminati to stop behaving like a bunch of bickering schoolboys even as he sought to recruit older and wiser minds.

Weishaupt's original order had not only banned Jews, Jesuits and women from its ranks but also anyone over the age of 30 and that had turned the Illuminati into a sort of 'incel' heaven. While Knigge continued to keep the Jews, Jesuits and the women out, he did at least raise the age barrier and began recruiting more senior and seasoned Freemasons into the ranks which had two major consequences. Firstly, by making itself attractive to Freemasons, many of the core principles of the original Illuminati and, in particular, its antipathetical attitude to any concept of a 'higher order' were watered down. And secondly, by its very expansion the group broke cover.

Knigge's rise to prominence also annoyed many existing members because as he set about restructuring things, a lot of core traditions including a decidedly bizarre initiation ceremony were binned. Weishaupt's schtick about the Illuminati being an ancient order, whose traditions, including the initiation rites, had been handed down from ancient times, was core to the movement and as it was all stripped away, inevitably many existing members started to question everything else as well.

In October 1781, the Illuminati held a mini-convention at Wilhelmsbad and Knigge got his way. Older people were in and weird stuff was out and by 1784, the ranks had swollen to 650 members and included powerful men like Count Pálffy von Erdöd, the chancellor of Hungary, Karl August, Grand Duke of Saxe-Weimar-Eisenach, Ernest II, Count Metternich of Koblenz, the Duke of Saxe-Gotha-Altenburg, Duke Ferdinand of Brunswick-Wolfenbüttel and Friedrich Nicolai, a leading figure in the *Aufklärung*, who took one look at the collection of weirdos and aristocrats gathered about him and promptly sought to resign.

Meanwhile, the rival Rosicrucians started to plot against them and knowing that Elector Charles Theodore's advisers were unsettled by secret societies, began spreading rumours about their 'secret hand' being at work. Although arguably nobody did more to bring down the Bavarian Illuminati than the Bavarian Illuminati itself, because as Knigge and his influence over everyone else had grown, Weishaupt had become pathetically jealous of him and was now doing everything in his power to bring him down and reassert his own authority.

The two men fell out and at the peak of the Illuminati's powers, in July 1784, Knigge quit and went off to write a book on etiquette called *Über den Umgang mit Menschen* ('On How to Deal with People') – which detailed how to treat others with respect. The future bestseller would go on to become his legacy and the modern German word *knigge* is nowadays synonymous with 'etiquette'.

Without Knigge at the wheel the Illuminati was left all at sea and when the Elector of Bavaria issued a decree banning all secret societies, the hapless Weishaupt immediately panicked and complied with the request. The academic revolutionary who had once sought to take over the world was now more concerned with maintaining the influence and the platform he had built for himself and started lobbying Charles Theodore for a change of heart, but it was too late because the Minervan Owlets were coming home to roost. In the spring of 1785, a group of four disgruntled Illuminati members came forward and handed the Bavarian authorities a list of names that belonged to the 25 most important people in the society, before divulging that Weishaupt himself was seeking to overthrow both the church and the monarchy.

'Spartacus' promptly fled to a neighbouring state where things now took a decidedly weird turn. On 10 June 1785, while out walking with Weishaupt through the streets of Regensburg, Johann Jakob Lanz, a Catholic priest and Illuminati member, was struck by a lightning bolt, which killed him instantly. When removed to the local morgue, a small leather satchel was discovered, sewn into his vestments, and inside it was a list of Illuminati members, along with plans on how the movement intended to continue the struggle. The documents were sent to Bavaria where Charles Theodore ordered the total suppression of the organisation.

Notable members of the Illuminati were promptly arrested and Franz von Zwack – a diplomat and former student of Weishaupt's who had risen to be a senior figure in the group – was put under surveillance in Munich.

In October, Zwack's home was raided and though he was not in, documents praising atheism and suicide as well as notes on how to 'sexually arouse women' and make lethal poisons were also found. The police handed it all over to the four apostates who compiled it into a book and in 26 March 1787, the 400-page tome, *Einige Originalschriften des Illuminaten Ordens* ('Some Original Writings of the Order of the Illuminati') was published, causing an immediate sensation in the German states.

As members of the group were rounded up, a handful managed to flee and Weishaupt himself was saved courtesy of Duke Ernst II of Saxony-Gotha, a member of the Illuminati, who appointed him as an attaché at his embassy in Regensburg, thus granting him diplomatic immunity.

Adam's revolutionary days were however over, and while he continued to write books prodigiously, including a long self-pitying justification for his failure to take over the world, the Bavarian academic all but faded from the limelight and died in Gotha, aged 82, in 1830. That should have been the death knell of the Illuminati.

But, in many respects, things were only just warming up.

* * *

Five years after the collapse of the Bavarian society, in July 1789 the French Revolution began and three years later, in 1792, the old ruling order was toppled once and for all as Louis XVI and the *Ancien Régime* were replaced with the First Republic. On the face of it, this new order seemed to represent the very pinnacle of High Enlightenment ideals. The stuffy old order was gone, egalitarianism had taken its place, a new rationalism would follow and everyone – or at least all men – would be equal (kind of). The ideas behind Diderot's first *Encyclopedie* had come to be. Religion was banned and as a process of de-Christianisation followed, the French state established the atheistic Cult of Reason before having second thoughts and replacing it with the very Masonic sounding Cult of the Supreme Being.

Churches were soon converted into Temples of Reason and the scripture of Voltaire briefly replaced that of Jesus Christ.

With the old order gone, the midwives of the French Revolution had achieved something truly extraordinary. The doors of reason had been flung open, heralding a better and brighter future. Of course, it couldn't last, and almost immediately, the revolution began to eat itself as the people who had once embraced the high ideals of liberty, equality and fraternity started killing each other like it was the beer wars in 1920s Chicago.

Matters reached a crescendo during the so-called Reign of Terror, which ran from roughly September 1793 to July the following year as state-sanctioned violence saw around 42,000 people executed. These mass killings were not without logic and were an attempt to draw a line under the revolution and stamp out factionalism and resistance once and for all. It was hoped that a final violent lancing of the boil of resistance would restore order to the revolution but it backfired spectacularly and across the Channel, conservative forces soon saw an opportunity to weaponise the madness as the nefarious Illuminati was reborn.

In 1797, a Scottish author called John Robison published a book called *Proofs of a Conspiracy* which accused Adam Weishaupt and the Bavarian Illuminati of being the architects of the French Revolution. According to Robison, while Freemasons were fronting it, the (non-existent) Most Serene Superiors and Weishaupt and his cells were behind everything playing out in France and if nobody stopped them then Christianity would be eradicated and the masses tyrannised in a new era which he dubbed 'darkness over all'. Robison had once been a hugely respected professor of natural sciences at the University of Edinburgh who had contributed to the *Encyclopaedia Britannica* as well as writing dozens of books of his own – and on the face of it was no crank and that gave him considerable and undeserved credibility.

In times of uncertainty many frightened minds hanker after simplistic answers and turn to populist seers who they believe will make sense of the chaos. In our own age, social media teams with libertarian professors and bestselling academics who have risen to prominence by seeking to explain that all the problems in our world stem from 'mass migration', or 'wokeism' or 'globalist conspiracies' that are seeking to undermine our way of life.

Much the same was going on in the eighteenth century.

The causes of the French Revolution were immensely complex and went far beyond the ideas of Enlightenment or indeed anything that could really be grasped or articulated at the time. There is not the space or time to go into them here either but suffice to say they included the usual round of: incompetent government, an out of touch elite, high taxation, inflation, crop failure, starvation and a rising bourgeoisie who wanted a bigger say in things.

The one thing that did not cause the French Revolution was a shadowy cabal of elites in Bavaria guiding everyone's hand – but this was an attractive lie and unfortunately people are eternally susceptible to those, and Robison's barking mad hypotheses provided simple yet sensational answers for those uninterested in complexity. The confirmation bias gave order to the chaos and distilled the whole terrifying set of events down to a single nefarious plot – fomented by Germans, no less. The revelation was a sensation and his book sold out in weeks.

It is a truth, which is unfortunately rarely acknowledged, that the bat-shit beliefs of hard-core conspiracy theorists tend to be the outward projection of personal failure, private woes and inner self-loathing and Mr Robison was no exception.

In his youth, the academic had been a celebrated figure who had invented the siren[8] and worked on an early steam car with his friend,

John Watt. But by his late forties Robison had grown bitter and angry and – at the risk of being a little inelegant – his unfortunate case of ball ache had made matters a whole lot worse. The extreme groin pain, which came out of nowhere in 1785 and plagued him for the rest of his life, not only left physicians baffled but had a profound effect on his personality. As the once-brilliant academic self-medicated on the then freely available opiates he fell into a torpor of addiction, paranoia and bad thinking.

In his youth, Robison had travelled widely, been a Freemason and even met Rosicrucians and members of the Illuminati along the way. But rather than having his mind opened by the encounters, their decidedly continental behaviour had rather shocked him and as he lay writing feverishly in his bed, the latent bitterness found fresh form as a grand conspiracy theory. Weaving youthful experience and exaggerated reports coming out of France into one apophenic whole, his opiate-fuelled exercise in paranoia took readers on the express steam car to crazy town, before finding its way across the Atlantic and into the newly independent USA.

There, the Scottish academic's book sparked an Illuminati panic which strongly resembled the 'Red Scare' and McCarthy era 'witch-hunts' which would follow in the 1950s. Americans began seeing Adam Weishaupt's group everywhere and a rumour spread that the 'Eye of Providence' – aka 'the all-seeing eye'– which was incorporated into the Great Seal of the US in 1782, was proof of their existence. It was all just a coincidence. The symbol, which can trace its origins right back to the Sumerians and Egyptians, had long been common in Europe and in the Age of Reason many saw it as a symbol of enlightened thinking. Its esoteric and ancient nature appealed to writers and artists who incorporated it into their work and it was, in essence, a sort of 'emoji' or meme of its time among smart-thinking people. But now, courtesy of a drugged-up Scottish academic, it took on a fresh and terrifying symbolism as it proved, quite obviously, that 'they' were everywhere and 'they' were leaving signs for all to see. Indeed, 'they' were so bold that 'they' had even put 'their' symbol on the US $50 bill.

George Washington and Thomas Jefferson were both dragged into the fray and were now obliged to waste precious moments of their brief lives denying a lot of nonsense.

One citizen, a Reverend G.W. Snyder, of Frederick Town in Maryland, was particularly triggered by Dr Ball Ache's hypothesis and on 22 August 1798 wrote to Washington including a copy of John Robison's book and a list of green ink questions familiar to anyone who has ever been obliged to correspond with a lunatic conspiracy theorist.

Washington was a Freemason, the first of 15 presidents who belonged to the order across the next 230 years,* and having read in Robison's book that the Illuminati had infiltrated masonry, Mr Snyder was determined to warn him against a cult that:

'*. . . endeavours to eradicate every Idea of a Supreme Being, and distinguish Man from Beast by his Shape only . . . some of the Lodges in the United States might have caught the Infection . . . They use the same Expressions and are generally Men of no Religion. Upon serious Reflection I was led to think that it might be within your Power to prevent the horrid Plan.*'[9]

The resulting correspondence, in which the American president gives the distinct impression of a man politely batting off a loon, concludes with Washington telling Snyder:

'*It was not my intention to doubt that, the Doctrines of the Illuminati, and principles of Jacobinism had not spread in the United States . . . The idea I meant to convey, was, that I did not believe that the Lodges of Freemasons in this Country had (been infected.)*'[10]

Publishers love a success story and Robison's book inspired many copycat publications. One of the most celebrated was Jesuit cleric Augustin Barruel's *Memoirs Illustrating the History of Jacobinism,* which appeared in England in 1799. Barruel, like Robison, didn't think much of the French Revolution and thought it signalled the end of times. In his version of events, the same nefarious Enlightenment intellectuals (the philosophes) working in tandem with the Freemasons and Weishaupt had plotted the French Revolution from the start in order to enslave everyone into atheism.

* The last was Gerald Ford, president from 1974 to 1977.

Barruel's book also crossed the Atlantic and a year after its publication, while fighting the 1800 US presidential election, the Democrat-Republican candidate, Thomas Jefferson, was obliged to put pen to paper to deny accusations, spread by Theodore Dwight, leader of the Federalist Party, that he was an agent of the Illuminati.

Having taken time to read Barruel's book, Jefferson went on to dismiss it as the 'ravings of a Bedlamite' and correctly identified that the author was an agent of conservatism who hated progress.[11] Ultimately, and satisfyingly, the whole thing exploded in his opponent's face when a preacher called John C. Ogden decided that it was Dwight and his team who were the real members of the Illuminati and that this was all a cover for their own conspiracy. Writing anonymously in a Philadelphia-based newspaper called the *Aurora*, Ogden dubbed Dwight the Pope of New England – and suggested that he was seeking to poison young minds. Jefferson romped home on a landslide win with 62.5 per cent of the vote.

But the Illuminati conspiracy did not die. On the contrary it only grew and prospered and within 30 years it had spread to the four corners of the globe.

In January 1831, two months after the death of Adam Weishaupt in Gotha, Yakov Ivanovich Sanlen, head of Nicholas I of Russia's Secret Police, was summoned to meet the Tsar. Pacing about in his chambers, the agitated monarch showed him a report that detailed the attempts of the Illuminati to infiltrate his predecessor (and brother) Tsar Alexander's court and suggested that he too may have been a member of the order.[12] Nicholas had bought wholesale into the conspiracy and believed that across Europe the Illuminati had infiltrated churches and the governments of France and England, and that only Russia by virtue of its innate moral probity could hold back the tide.

Nicholas's mind had further been poisoned by one of his key advisers, an antisemite called Mikhail Magnitsky, who convinced him that the sect was financed by the Jewish Rothschild family of bankers, who were spreading the virus of Illuminism under the cover of their business affairs. Nicholas, who already harboured strong antisemitic feelings, had his biases confirmed and began to actively go after Jewish communities in Russia, forcing them to assimilate while banning books by Jewish authors.

The Bavarian Illuminati, which had itself been decidedly antisemitic, had now bizarrely taken on an afterlife as an explicitly Jewish conspiracy, funded by Jewish bankers, and as the twentieth century dawned, the Russia-spawned forgery 'The Protocols of the Elders of Zion' began propagating the lie that the guiding hand of 'globalists' secretly controlled the world. This fake document was thoroughly debunked, first by *The Times* in 1921 and then in the *Frankfurter Zeitung* in 1924, but all the fact checking had come far too late and to nothing and many racists continue to believe this nonsense even today.

The trouble with any conspiracy theory is that once it gains momentum it garners credibility and a sort of alternative truth along with it. With Tsars, courtiers, fake dossiers and Scottish academics all on board, it was not exactly surprising that gullible members of the public should start to believe it all too and as it snowballed, nobody did more to conflate the Illuminati conspiracy theory with the antisemitic 'New World Order' hypothesis spawned by the 'Protocols' than British banking heiress Nesta Webster. Webster was the product of extreme wealth and privilege and inherited a fortune from her father Robert Bevan, when he died in 1890. Nesta used some of her inheritance to go travelling in style and, having met and married Arthur Webster in India, settled down to a life of wedded tedium.

Believing, on Rizla-thin evidence, that she had talent as a writer she penned a book *The Sheep Track – An Aspect of London Society* and when it failed to sell, cast around for something else to fill her time. While visiting Switzerland, aged 38, Nesta had experienced a bizarre 'mystical experience, which led her to believe that she was the reincarnation of a late eighteenth-century countess (the Comtesse de Sabran), whose daughter had been imprisoned and son-in-law guillotined during the French Revolution.'[13] Having read the 'Protocols', Barruel and Robison, this dangerous and entitled fool tied the threads together and forged a grand conspiracy theory which pointed the finger for the death of the

Comtesse's family squarely at the Illuminati and the Jews. Had she been anyone else she would have been ignored or simply dismissed as a lunatic. But Webster was very rich and well connected and like stupid yet gilded people throughout time she positively oozed entitlement and certainty. So people who should have known better afforded her lethal nonsense a platform and it spread like a malignant cancer.

Her first attempt to make sense of it all was the sanity-busting *World Revolution: The Plot Against Civilisation*, which came out in 1921. *Secret Societies and Subversive Movements* followed in 1924 and put her firmly on the map as the key conspiracy influencer of her time.

The book repeated the 'blood libel' myth that had sprung up in the Middle Ages but which had found new life in fascist literature spawned by the Protocols, and the heiress claimed that Jews indulged in ritual murder and cannibalism to secure the blood of Christian children for the Feast of Passover. Webster also suggested that Adam Weishaupt – whom she wrongly claimed to have been Jewish too – had been the invisible guiding hand throughout the revolutions of the nineteenth century and long after his group had disappeared. Webster also argued (although I use the word very loosely) that socialism and communism were modern offshoots of the 'deep-laid conspiracy' and that it was all there to be seen in the (debunked) 'Protocols of the Elders of Zion'.

Her 15-chapter book ends with the chillingly stupid:

'It is evident then that the complete story of the Protocols has not yet been told, and that much yet remains to be discovered concerning this mysterious affair.'[14]

Throughout the 1920s, this very rich and very deluded woman flourished while her powerful friends propagated her dangerous lies. Nesta had friends in British Freemasonry, including her chum Winston Churchill, who had been initiated into Studholme Lodge No. 1591 on 24 May 1901[15] and as such, she deliberately differentiated between British Freemasons, who were obviously a good thing, and Continental Freemasons, who were a secretive globalist cabal. The toadying paid off and even before her books appeared, Churchill was citing her ideas – most famously in an article in the *Sunday Herald* on 8 February 1920. In the piece, the future PM repeated Webster's theories about the Illuminati being a global anti-nation-state conspiracy. Name-checking Weishaupt (Spartacus) and also wrongly claiming that he was Jewish, Churchill added that the Illuminati had:

'Played . . . a definitely recognizable part in the tragedy of the French Revolution and has been the mainspring of every subversive movement during the Nineteenth Century; and now at last this band of extraordinary personalities from the underworld of the great cities of Europe and America have gripped the Russian people by the hair of their heads and have become practically the undisputed masters of that enormous empire.'[16]

Over the next two decades, Webster wrote a further seven 'history' books, and in the 1930s penned a column for the fascist news-sheet *The Patriot.* A supporter of Oswald Mosley's British Union of Fascists, she remained committed to his and Adolf Hitler's cause right up until the moment in 1939 when it suddenly became unfashionable, although her words and deeds undoubtedly helped build the pyre upon which six million Jews were killed. The Holocaust served as evidence, if ever it were needed, that the promulgation of baseless racist conspiracy theories can only lead to one destination.

But the collective memory is short and even in the wake of the horrors of World War II, the Illuminati conspiracy theory refused to die.

* * *

In 1958, a millionaire confectionery magnate called Robert W. Welch Jr, whose life's work thus far had consisted of giving America Sugar Babies, Junior Mints, Sugar Daddies, diabetes and tooth cavities, decided that it was time to retire from Candy World and fight global communism instead.

Born in North Carolina in 1899, Bob had been a child prodigy. Educated at home by his strictly Baptist mother he had gained admittance to the University of North Carolina aged 12 – the youngest student in the college's history – and things had only got more miserable from there. Launching himself on the academic world by loftily seeking to convert fellow students to the Baptist movement, he swiftly became something of a pariah among his peers and spent most of his education sulking in his room. Following a similarly bitter experience at Harvard Law School, he set up a candy business and when it failed, went into partnership with his brother James instead.

The new venture made both men rich and gave Bob time to indulge in side projects, which included fringe journalism and the war on socialism. Bob was something of a Nesta Webster superfan[17] and boy did he hate commies. Indeed for Welch, pretty much everything he didn't like was communism. So, FDR's Great Depression-busting 1930s New Deal was communism, and the defeat of the 'lost cause' of the racist Southern Confederacy in the American Civil War was communism and Catholicism and immigration were communism too. World War II was a bit problematic for the patriotic Welch, since he thought that anti-communist Hitler had actually got a lot of things right, but it was all over by 1945 and so he was able to start getting upset about 'the reds' all over again. While visiting the UK in the late 1940s, he was appalled to witness the 'red' Labour government providing affordable homes, a free health service and educational opportunities to ordinary working people and all for free – and having returned to America he vowed to stop the fiendish virus of human progress before it spread across the Atlantic.

In 1952, Welch published a book, *May God Forgive Us,* which railed against the treatment of General MacArthur who had been sacked at the start of the Korean War, as well as the blunders of US foreign policy, the rise of Chinese communism, the fall of Chiang Kai-shek and the infiltration of the US state with red ideas.

Having tried and failed to set up a political party, in 1958 he instead established a secret group called the John Birch Society which took its name from that of an American Baptist missionary who had become a special forces officer in China during the war before getting killed by communist guerrillas in August 1945. Welch promulgated the (likely false) notion that Birch was the first victim of the Cold War and wrote a hagiography of the dead missionary called, imaginatively enough, *The Life of John Birch* which turned the life of the 'great man' into a template of what Bob thought America should be: traditionalist, macho, square-jawed, Baptist and of course anti-communist. Welch also believed there had been a cover-up regarding the facts of his murder by Maoist guerrillas and that this was proof that the Illuminati-backed global elite had already seized power in Washington DC.

Welch was convinced that 'the deep state', under the guise of the United Nations, was plotting to create one massive country that would marginalise the old order, suppress business interests and, significantly, make super-rich people like him a thing of the past. All of this, as Bob was eager to point out, could be traced back to Adam Weishaupt and his Bavarian Illuminati, which he dubbed the 'ancestor of communism'.

A man not naturally imbued with the gift of awareness, Bob then set about turning his organisation into a secret society, chock-full of very powerful, very rich and very well-connected people who would take on the '*furtive conspiratorial cabal of internationalists, greedy bankers, and corrupt politicians*'[18] who (he thought) really controlled both the USSR and USA, and who were seeking to create that one-world socialist government. Once again, and much like Nesta Webster, his enormous wealth bought him a platform and credibility that was utterly undeserved, and somewhat incredibly all sorts of people rallied to his conspiratorial cause simply because it had an awful lot of money to play with.

Welch's original 11 recruits were all very rich white men and included Fred C. Koch, the chemical engineer whose Koch Industries would go on to be one of the wealthiest companies in the world.

Obsessed with secrecy, Welch then went positively Weishauptian and split the JBS into secret cells and chapters. The movement attracted right-wingers and small business leaders and grew in strength and influence during the McCarthy era although unlike Nesta Webster, Welch was no antisemite and was willing to let Jews in. Later on, he allowed Mormons, Muslims and even Catholics in too, but mostly it was because they weren't 'commies' so were deemed to be OK.

Welch portrayed himself as an ordinary guy who was socking it to the deep state and the elites and many an angry American middle-aged man rallied to the cause as the list of enemies ballooned. Across the 1960s that roll call of nemeses grew to include: the civil rights movement, the

Kennedys, the Warren Commission (a 'communist' conspiracy), rock and roll, folk music, hippies, homosexuals, lesbians, women's rights activists, IRS agents, atheists, abortionists, public (state) schools, people who had sex lives that were not for the purposes of procreation, tattoos, tattooists, public school teachers, overseas aid, university professors, agnostics, progressives, free museums, affordable healthcare and most of all the wicked United Nations which was hell-bent on establishing that one-world government that would eclipse the super rich. Welch had no time for the 'left wing and liberal press'[19] either which he believed was just a mouthpiece for the invisible New World Order.

When not plotting to expose the global elite, Welch developed some 'interesting' side theories too. He believed that one-time Republican presidential nominee Robert Taft had contracted cancer because commies had hidden a bar of radium in his chair, thought that Martin Luther King was a KGB agent and claimed that the government had put fluoride in the water as part of a mind-control plot to make the masses compliant to their will.

Clever people laughed and in his 1962 protest song 'Talkin' John Birch Paranoid Blues' Bob Dylan sang:

I wus lookin' for them Reds everywhere,
I wus lookin' in the sink an' underneath the chair.
I looked way up my chimney hole,
I even looked deep inside my toilet bowl.[20]

But all the mockery did not make him go away and thousands if not millions of people would eventually buy wholesale into the JBS lunacy. At its peak, the society had an estimated membership of 100,000 members[21] and though it never fulfilled Welch's aim of recruiting 'one million fervid patriots and loyal citizens',[22] the organisation gained massive traction, particularly within the Republican Party, which saw its crazy ideas seep into the mainstream from the dawn of the twenty-first century onwards.

Robert Welch may have died in January 1985 but his society still exists and you can hear its talking points everywhere in MAGA ('Make America Great Again') America and beyond. Infowars conspiracy theorist Alex Jones has claimed that 'Donald Trump is more John Birch Society than the John Birch Society'[23] and indeed, the president's father Fred was, like many other tax-hating millionaires, a fan of Welch.

The theories that Welch promoted don't so much live on in the USA today but thrive and Bircherist (what passes for) thinking and its associated and often paranoid right-wing fantasies have never had it so good. Tech billionaires trot them out as truth on the platforms that they own while their acolytes suck it up and in a very real sense, under the reign of Donald J Trump, the sweet magnate's crazy anti-progressive paranoia drove the most powerful country in the modern world.

Meanwhile, the spectre of the long dead Illuminati and the New World Order lingers on too, although in the interests of balance we need to lay some of the blame for that at the door of acid-dropping hippies.

* * *

In 1968, a group of wacky free thinkers, who were members of a satirical religion called the Discordians, had a far-out idea (man). They would single-handedly defeat conspiracy theories by deliberately spreading disinformation – and seriously how could that *possibly* go wrong?

Their plan, dubbed 'Operation Mindfuck', was part prank and part art project and it went like this. The group's co-founder, Kerry Thornley, would write letters to *Playboy* magazine where two other members of the outfit, Robert Shea and Robert Wilson, worked as staffers. In the correspondence, Thornley would attribute every bad thing in history to 'the Illuminati' and Wilson would publish the letters thus propelling the nonsense into the mainstream. At the same time, they would take out adverts in the underground press and spread rumours about everything from the space race to the JFK assassination.

But here was the smart bit. Having done so, they would then write again to the same publications and debunk it all thus encouraging readers to engage critical thought and more enlightened thinking. The Discordians, in essence, hoped that their project might make the world a better place – but this was the late 1960s when a lot of people were very stoned indeed, and Operation Mindfuck turned out to be a fucking disaster.

The Discordians' main target was the District Attorney, Jim Garrison, whose mission to uncover the 'truth' about the JFK assassination had led him to conduct a state-sponsored witch-hunt against a gay man (and war hero) Clay Shaw. Shaw, quite obviously, had nothing whatsoever to do with the death of Kennedy and was indeed a fan of the young president, but the publicity-hungry Garrison managed to get him put on trial for conspiracy to murder in 1969 anyway.

In the late 1950s, Kerry Thornley had served alongside Kennedy's assassin Lee Harvey Oswald while doing his national service and somewhat bizarrely had even written an unpublished book, *The Idle Warriors,* about Oswald's defection to the USSR a year before the disturbed young man killed Kennedy. Knowing the real assassin as he did, and convinced of his guilt, he had been utterly appalled by the trial of the innocent Clay Shaw and felt compelled to act – only for his counter-conspiracy theory plan to go very astray when everyone started to believe the nonsense.

Shea and Wilson went on to write novels about the Illuminati, which, though satirical in nature, only made things worse because they fed the dangerous nonsense of the 'invisible hand' and the false notion of the deep state.

In fact – and courtesy in no small part to the internet – more and more people across the world continue to believe this absurd nonsense today and worst of all, it has bled into the mainstream. If you ever hear a politician of the far left or far right talk about the 'deep state', well that is code for 'the Illuminati conspiracy theory'. The notion of 'globalists' or 'the New World Order' or plotting of Bilderbergers, Rothschilds, Clintons or Davos attendees is all the same stuff.

But then again, according to those who buy into this stuff, academics, journalists and the authors of history books are all part of the conspiracy. So, I would say that – wouldn't I.

* * *

It's late morning on an early summer's day in 2024 and my student son and I have set out to infiltrate the headquarters of the United Grand Lodge of England and the Supreme Grand Chapter of Royal Arch Masons of England near London's Covent Garden. I've told him to comb his hair and look respectable and I myself have donned an ill-fitting suit so nobody stops us as we trot up the steps to the imposing HQ and right into the heart of the operation.

It doesn't last.

'May I help you?' a voice pipes up from behind a desk in the reception area and when I say that we'd 'just like to look around!', the friendly woman points ahead, advising 'museum up the stairs to the left . . . library on the same floor . . . gift shop next door, bar and café back down the stairs,' adding, 'they do a lovely flat white.'

In my bag, I'm carrying a book called *The Illuminati: The Cult that Hijacked the World* by Henry Makow and it is frankly explosive stuff. You see, in between inventing the party game 'Scruples', Makow has dedicated his life to the destruction of the deadly Illuminati conspiracy in the hope of revealing 'the truth' – although suddenly, remembering I have it on me, I am briefly concerned that my bag might get checked by security and we will get no further.

But there's no check and James and I breeze in.

The exhibition is, it has to be said, a teeny bit eccentric. There are elaborate aprons and chains everywhere you look and a great glass case that contains a comically outsized golden chair. There is also a fairly straightforward and detailed history of Freemasonry and while it is all very informative – on the conspiracy theory front at least – it frankly all feels like a bit of a let-down.

We pop into the gift shop and buy a notepad and a key ring and then head on to the bar for a coffee. All about us, middle-aged men in suits are chatting and laughing in a decidedly non-megalomaniacal way and it's all rather convivial. I strain to listen but only get snatches, which is unfortunate because according to Henry Makow PhD's book, lodges like this are the headquarters of 'a small Satanic cult of Cabalistic bankers and Freemasons that controls the world's finances and our media.

Our leaders are junior members of this International Cult called the Order of the Illuminati . . .'

Many 'leaders' Henry continues, 'are kept in line by having them indulge in horrifying occult rituals, including human sacrifice, sexual orgies, paedophilia, rape and murder.'[24]

Maybe we've missed all that or been distracted by those lovely aprons while all the disgusting activity was happening behind us. Or perhaps it is going on, even now, behind the door marked 'fire escape' so I strain to hear the cries of pain – but all I get is the tinkling of spoons on teacups and some joviality from an adjoining table and while my son suggests we take advantage of the cheap beer on offer, instead we leave and walk out into Great Queen Street and back towards Charing Cross.

It's a lovely afternoon and London is abuzz with people and life so I suggest we pop into the National Gallery. Soon we are walking about the galleries contemplating Matisses, Brueghels and Cezannes and eventually we stumble into a small dark room that houses the museum's prized Da Vinci – aka The Burlington House Cartoon. As we sit in the semi-light, gazing upon this remarkable image of St Anne and St John the Baptist, Madonna and child, it strikes me that we are gathered together at an altar to culture in a temple dedicated to the cult of the Enlightenment. Here we are together, with a random assortment of ordinary people from all over the world and we haven't paid so much as a penny to get in and look at this masterpiece of Renaissance art. It's remarkable and more to the point, it's reassuring because in a way, the Perfectibilists really did get what they wanted and the late Robert W. Welch and even his modern disciples would have hated every single thing about it.

Here at least, the *Aufklärung* has won.

Later, on the train home, I take out Makow's book and re-enter his world of conspiracy once more. Across the closely typed pages I 'discover' that despite having warned about the Illuminati in the 1920s, Winston Churchill was in fact an Illuminati tool (clever huh) and that the Nazi henchman Martin Bormann was a 'Soviet Agent' hell-bent on the destruction of the world. Hitler, at least according to Dr Makow, may have been an Illuminati agent too, as were hundreds of other random people from history. Despite its bright red cover the book is repetitive and banal and I'll be honest, a bit frightening with it because not only do people believe this guff – some of those who do have actual influence on our world.

Those modern myths so frequently promulgated by populist politicians of the globalist New World Order or the 'deep state' or the scare stories you might see on social media about how we are going to be locked in '15-minute cities' and forced to eat bugs, are but an extension of the nineteenth-century Illuminati scare. And they serve the exact same purpose because ultimately, the cult of anti-illuminism was only ever anti-intellectualism and anti-progress, dressed up as something else; a flagrant attempt by regressive forces to keep the 'peasants' in their place, to keep their own hands on the reins of power and to hinder the fomenting of a better and more equitable world for the majority.

As our train rattles through the South London suburbs, I take out my freshly bought Freemason notebook and put it all down – until eventually James looks up from his phone and asks me what I'm doing.

'I think I've got it,' I say. 'You see, this is a case where the conspiracy theory *is* the conspiracy – and everything is the opposite of what everyone thinks.'

'Well, you would say that, wouldn't you,' he says benignly before turning and gazing out of the window at the world passing by.

CHAPTER SEVEN

MONSTERS

The Demons Inside Us

Despite the best efforts of Enlightenment thinkers and those mighty rationalists of the nineteenth and twentieth centuries that followed in their wake, a good proportion of people in our modern world continue to believe in abject bollocks.

Britons, living as they do in one of the most agnostic nations on Earth, might comfort themselves that they are broadly reasoned, but a 2023 YouGov poll found that about a third of my fellow citizens believe that spilling salt, breaking a mirror, or opening an umbrella inside their home will somehow bring them bad luck. Many more instinctively reach out to touch a piece of wood for good fortune, or avoid a ladder in the street for fear of the worst and even highly respected academics, presidents and queens have been known to make a wish after blowing out their birthday candles or cutting a piece of cake.

Magical thinking – the cognitive notion that we as individuals can control the world and its outcomes by obeying illogical rituals and reading apophenic signs still – affects the 4 per cent of Britons who apparently suffer from 'extreme superstition' and my late mother Hannah was most certainly in that camp. In fact, you could barely move without triggering her dismay. The numbers 13 and 7, magpies, cracks in the pavement, rabbit feet, crossed cutlery – in fact any cutlery – all daily intruded into her life. People singing at a meal was a sign of disappointment. Forgetting what you had just been talking about suggested that you were a liar and she had a particular thing about shoes on a table. Like earworms, herpes and stupidity, superstition can be highly contagious and as magical thinking is memetic and is thus passed down the generations, my sister and I spent much of our early lives saluting black and white birds or dodging cracks in the pavement or chucking handfuls of salt at people sitting behind us in the Little Chef; even today I start to get decidedly twitchy if someone puts shoes on a table.

Most things in life have some sort of evolutionary purpose and superstition is no exception. It's fairly easy to comprehend why walking under ladders or even opening umbrellas inside might be deemed unlucky as the former is quite obviously dangerous, while the latter is liable to take out someone's eye. But in order to understand why someone might be afraid of a pair of shoes on a static piece of furniture, we need to dig a little deeper into the human experience.

Throughout our history, people have feared what we cannot control and sought to impose order where none exists and in my mother's case, her curious belief system probably stemmed from the exceptionally dangerous environment in which she had been raised. Hannah's early life, you see, was spent in a Staffordshire mining village, where potential disaster loomed with every breaking dawn. Some years before her birth, in March 1924, the local colliery was flooded with dozens of miners inside and it was considered a miracle that every one of the 72 men down in the pit had walked out alive. Twenty years later, when Hannah would have been about ten, workers in another nearby pit at Sneyd were not so fortunate. Locals believed that it was unlucky to work in the colliery on New Year's Day – but with the war on, such considerations were ignored and on 1 January 1944, 57 men and boys were killed when an explosion ripped through the mine.

Though we would later laugh at my mother's terror of table-placed footwear, it undoubtedly went back to that childhood in Staffordshire. For there was a tradition that when miners died, their boots were taken and placed on the kitchen table out of respect. To do so at any other time was to show a lack of respect or worse, risked incurring the wrath of the unspoken mystical forces that protected the community. As fundamentally irrational as these beliefs may seem to us today, in such an unpredictable environment they provided a valuable defensive mechanism that gave my mother's community solace and hope. By trusting in magical thinking, the miners and their families felt they had control over nature – just as our Paleolithic ancestors had believed that tapping trees* protected them from the monsters that lurked in the forest beyond.

Ancient mythology positively teems with tales of magic, omens – and terrifying creatures. In the third century BCE, Mesopotamian Epic of Gilgamesh, the eponymous hero, battles numerous beasts including the demon Humbaba. In Minoan legend, the bold prince Theseus tackles the bull-headed Minotaur and frees his people from a tribute of human sacrifice. In Greek mythology, Cerberus is the multi-headed hound of Hell who guards the Underworld and stops anyone leaving and across the world – even today – tales of monsters persist. In Britain alone we have the Loch Ness Monster, the Black Shuck of Suffolk and the gigantic headless horseman of Butterton Moor – who rides the back lanes around Leek and who is often spotted by people returning from the pub. From the Yeti of the Himalayas, to North America's Bigfoot, to the European Bogeyman or Wewe Gombel – the Javanese monster who steals children in the night – every place on Earth has its fiend.

While nowadays such stories seem to be little more than scary bedtime tales – or a means of drawing in tourists to the lochs around Inverness – they have a purpose too.

Humanoid monsters – whether they be zombies, ghosts or vampires – tend to frighten us more than anything else. A 2023 survey carried out by One Poll in 2023 placed Freddy Krueger of the *Nightmare on Elm Street* series as the 'scariest monster of all time', with Jigsaw (from the *Saw* movie) and Chucky from *Child's Play* coming in second and third. All three are distinctly human or human-like and there is a good reason for that, for while Freddy Krueger and friends might seem, on the face of it, to simply be part of our entertainment landscape, horror stories and films may also be a means by which humans prime ourselves against danger.

* Probably the origin of touching wood. It is thought that ancient hunters knocked on trees to awaken the spirits to protect them and to ward off monsters.

Modern psychologists and sociologists believe that when ancient people told scary stories around the campfire they were really engaging in primitive health and safety briefings and through storytelling were warning the children about the dangers lurking in the bestial world beyond. In the same way, when we are watching a horror movie, in safe surroundings, we are simultaneously training ourselves, albeit subconsciously, to the real-life threats that exist beyond our comfortable cinema seat. Terror of imaginary monsters and even scary puppets is primal and it is hard-wired into us. In a 1919 essay titled '*Das Unheimliche*' (or 'the Uncanny'), the Austrian psychoanalyst Sigmund Freud made a distinction between things that could be homely (*heimliche*) or unhomely – and therefore frightening. Freud's idea gave rise to the 'uncanny valley effect' – a term coined by the Japanese roboticist Masahiro Mori in his 1970 essay '*Bukimi no Tani*' to explain why people can be repelled by bad waxworks or human-looking robots that are not quite human enough. Arguments continue to rage as to the exact nature of 'the uncanny valley effect' but for the purposes of this chapter it could explain why we are repelled by zombies, scary-looking china dolls, doppelgangers, CGI that doesn't quite work and men in cloaks with exaggerated canine teeth or tall fellas with bolts in the sides of their heads.

Mary Shelley's *Frankenstein*, which is ostensibly an Enlightenment fable about the dangers of the encroachment of science on the human world, is a case in point. In her book and the films that it spawned, the monster looks human but isn't and it is that 'recognisable monstrousness' that triggers a terror response in reader or viewer.

In our own age of rapidly evolving technology, we have become positively preoccupied with the notion of replicants and in films from *Blade Runner* (1982) to the *Terminator* series, to *Ex Machina* (2014) and AI pictures the 'uncanny valley effect' lives on.

Human-like monsters terrify us most of all because they are able to blend into our realm – while being alien to it. The word 'monster' is itself rooted in contempt. Derived from the Latin word *monstrare* which means 'to warn' and 'to show' it is believed to come from the ancient

Greek and Roman notion that babies born with 'defects', whether they be extra digits or missing limbs, were bad omens, signs of divine displeasure and harbingers of doom. And this might be why a distinctly ableist bent runs through the long tradition of monstrous villains stretching back in time.

Hephaestus, god of blacksmiths, masonry and fire and the first disabled character in Greek mythology, gets flung from Olympus (by his own mother) for being born 'lame' and 'unsightly'. Though Hephaestus was an important figure in mythology, his disability, his banishment and his association with the suspect worlds of fire, forges and trade set him well apart from the beautiful and perfect gods who surrounded him. To be imperfect was, in short, to be a monster. And that tradition has continued into the modern age. The scheming, craven, Wife of Bath in Chaucer's *Canterbury Tales* is deaf, William Shakespeare's Richard III is hunchbacked and, in the eighteenth and nineteenth century as 'freak shows' monetised the fear of 'difference', the association between 'the monstrous' and 'disability' grew. Charles Dickens's disabled characters tended to be either 'innocent victims' like Tiny Tim and Miss Mowcher, the dwarf hairdresser in *David Copperfield*, or stock villains like Daniel Quilp, the unhinged, one-eyed, violent dwarf who is the main antagonist in *The Old Curiosity Shop*.

In Robert Louis Stevenson's *The Strange Case of Doctor Jekyll and Mr Hyde* (1886), the mild-mannered, intelligent and cultivated Jekyll drinks a serum which transforms into his monstrous alter ego who is described as being 'pale and dwarfish (and giving) an impression of deformity'.[1] By the late nineteenth century 'evil disabled' characters veritably abounded in literature. Long John Silver, the main antagonist in Robert Louis Stevenson's *Treasure Island* (1882) is missing a leg and Captain Hook in J.M. Barrie's *Peter Pan* (1902) is missing a hand. But it was only in the twentieth century that the two became inexorably intertwined and henceforth, the 'baddies' in popular culture almost always had some sort of disability.

In Hitchcock's original 1935 movie version of John Buchan's *The 39 Steps*, the arch-villain Professor Jordan is identified because he is missing half a finger. Dr No, the eponymous villain in the first 007 film in 1962 has mechanical hands; 'Oddjob' in the 1964 movie *Goldfinger* is mute, and in the book, written in 1959, he has a cleft palate too. And so it goes on. Marvel's original Doctor Doom has a hideously scarred face, which he tries to hide out of vanity, and DC Comics' Joker in his various iterations has acid burns and facial disfigurement. In the *Star Wars* universe, the most famous villain, Darth Vader, has a horribly burned head and prosthetic arm too.

Mental health has also long been fertile ground for novelists, filmmakers and history's chroniclers when seeking to take a shortcut to demonisation and many, if not all, of the characters above have mental as well as physical health issues too.

Now of course 'real-life monsters' do exist – because, and as we have seen, history veritably teems with them. Henry VIII, the Spanish Inquisitors, Matthew Hopkins (the Witchfinder General) and countless others who have featured in this book were clearly 'monstrous' people and TV streaming services bulge with stories of psychopathic serial killers and mass murderers whose example serves to remind us of the actual threats that can be posed to our world.

But throughout history people have turned mortal enemies into fantastical monsters for no other reason than that it is a means to quite literally monster and other them. Few figures from the past serve as a better example than Dracula.

* * *

In the winter of 1463, visitors to the court of the Holy Roman Emperor, Friedrich III, then residing in Vienna, were in for a treat. The emperor had recently signed Michel Beheim, the most famous European Meistersinger of his time and Michel had a new work waiting to be launched on the world. The Meistersingers were the rappers of their day: virtuosos of rhyme and metric, who performed their poems accompanied by a pared-back musical ensemble. The court poet's new piece, rendered in the rhyming formula AAB was titled 'The Story of a Bloodthirsty Madman called Dracula of Wallachia' – and the term 'parental advisory recommended' could have been coined for the 1,070 lines that follow.

Beheim's poem told the tale of Vlad Tepes, otherwise known as Vlad III, the very real and recently deposed *voivode* (military overlord) of Wallachia, a region of 77,000 square kilometres (30,000 square miles) which lies north of the Lower Danube and beneath the Southern Carpathian Mountains in modern-day Romania. A year earlier, Vlad had been kidnapped by Matthias Corvinus, the King of Hungary and Croatia, and taken to Visegrad, north of the Hungarian capital where – even as Beheim recited his work – he was being held prisoner for plotting with the Ottomans to overthrow the King. Out of sight and thus out of mind, the Meistersinger told it as it was – or at least how his audience wanted it to be – and by his account, Vlad III was one badass Wall-a-chia-er:

'It was his pleasure and gave him courage
To see human blood flow
And it was his custom
To wash his hands in it
As it was brought to the table'

The poet portrayed the deposed voivode as an agent of heresy and repeatedly used the term *wutrich* meaning 'bloodthirsty monster', which he had previously deployed with great effect while writing about the powerful, contemporary Ottoman Sultan Mehmed the Conqueror.[2] All the best artists repeat their material.

'Dracula' meant 'Son of the Dragon' and Vlad Tepes had earned his sobriquet courtesy of his father, Vlad Dracul II, who had been inducted into the 'Order of the Dragon' by his mentor Sigismund of Luxembourg, Holy Roman Emperor until 1437. The order was chivalric and militaristic – and was awarded to those who had sworn to defend the cross of Jesus and the bastion of Hungary against the Islamic 'heathen' from the Ottoman East.

It is commonly held that sequels never live up to the original but in a rare departure from tradition – and much like *Toy Story 3* – Vlad III was to become the defining instalment in the saga.

At the time of his capture, Vlad III (Dracula/Tepes) had been one of the most influential figures in the region, but fortunes can change and as Beheim recited his poem he was now the most reviled man in Europe. According to Beheim, Dracula was an agent of terror of 'Bin Laden' like proportions but you didn't just have to take the poet's word for it because others were saying much the same thing. A year earlier, in 1462, when Pope Pius II had sent an ambassador to investigate his arrest, the King of Hungary had also laid the atrocity propaganda on thick. Indeed, by the time the papal emissary had met Dracula he believed he was encountering the very devil himself and his report back to Pius related how Vlad had boiled and skinned people alive, impaled babies and stuck entire families on stakes in between murdering an estimated 40,000 people.

The Meistersinger would not have yet had access to such papal sources but he had plenty of other material to feed his rhymes. They included a widely circulated dodgy dossier of tales, whispers filtering in from the East and a first-hand account from a decidedly biased monk known as Brother Jacob, who spilled the beans to him at the Abbey of Melk in Austria. The (later) St Gall manuscript, so-called because it was compiled at a monastery in the canton of St Gallen, Switzerland, also contained positively juicy, first-hand stuff.

Between 1457 and 1460, Vlad III had purged the 'Saxon' settlements of Transylvania and as he did, the clerics and monks had fled to Switzerland where they churned out horror stories about Tepes.

The 32 anecdotes should not be read on a full stomach:

'Once he had a great pot made with two handles and over it a staging device with planks and through it, he had holes cut, so that a man could fall through them with his head. Then he had a great fire made underneath it and had water poured into the pot and had men boiled in this way.'

Another time:

'Several Ambassadors were sent to him. When they came to him, they bowed and took off their hats and under them they had brown and red berets or caps, which they did not take off. He asked them why they had not taken off their caps or berets and they said: "Lord, it is not our

custom. We never take them off before our ruler." He said: "Well, I wish to strengthen you in your custom." And as they thanked his grace, he had them take good strong nails and had them nailed around the caps into the head, so that they would not take them off.'[3]

Sarcastic, sadistic and inventive with his means of execution, Vlad III's crimes forged him into the original pitiless supervillain.

In history, like comedy and sex, timing is everything and Vlad's rise in the annals of villainy coincided with a revolutionary new invention. Johannes Guttenberg's printing press, first assembled in Mainz in Rhineland-Palatinate in 1439, swiftly took off and by 1500 there were 250 towns with presses across the German states producing all manner of materials.

Beheim's poem ended up at the University of Heidelberg and soon Vlad's evil deeds were being forged into a cottage industry of horror stories that were well known far beyond Wallachia, Hungary and Germany. A report by Frederick III's ambassador, Nicolas von Popplau, who encountered that other literary monster King Richard III at Pontefract Castle in 1484, suggests that within a decade of Tepes' death (in 1476) even the distant English monarch was well versed in his deeds.[4]

Dracole Waida, a pamphlet first published in Nuremberg in 1488 by Ambrosius Huber, which relied in large part on the Saxon atrocity stories from St Gallen, is the best known of near contemporary accounts and details more of Vlad Tepes' crimes against humanity:

'Here begins a very cruel frightening story about a wild bloodthirsty man, Dracula the voivod. How he impaled people and roasted them and hacked them into pieces like a head of cabbage. He also roasted the children of mothers and they had to eat their children themselves.'[5]

In another section, the pamphlet describes how he 'had people ground to death on a grindstone'. *Dracole Waida* is famous for its woodcuts, including one which depicts one of his most heinous acts. In the image, Vlad, resplendent in dapper clothes and dashing beard, sits with a nice goblet of wine and table full of food before him, while one of his henchmen hacks limbs off lifeless corpses with an axe.

Hands, heads and limbs are scattered about the place while just to the right of him and well within screaming distance, dozens of men and women have been skewered on gigantic wooden stakes in what is dubbed, 'the forest of the impaled'.

This – according to the text – is a representation of the voivode's night-time attack on the Saxon city of Brasov in April 1459, when:

'Dracula had the entire suburb burned. Also . . . all those whom he had taken captive, men and women, young and old, children, he had impaled on the hill by the Chapel and all around the hill and under them he proceeded to eat at table and enjoyed himself in that way.'[6]

Books and pamphlets detailing Dracula's cartoonish degrees of violence prevailed across the following century as reports of his depravity only grew with time. In an age where we daily witness appalling human rights violations of our own, these grotesque images do not seem wholly beyond the bounds of possibility, but likewise it is an unfortunate fact of history that atrocity propaganda has a habit of turning mere men into demons.

So just how much of it was true?

* * *

Vlad (Dracula) Tepes was born in 1431 at Sighişoara, Transylvania, the second of four sons of Vlad II Dracul and his second wife Cneajna, a Moldavian princess.

Vlad II was the illegitimate son of Mircia the Elder, voivode of Wallachia and though details of his early life are sketchy, it is assumed that he grew up at the court of the Holy Roman Emperor Sigismund, where he probably resided as a hostage under the King's protection. There were no clear lines of succession for medieval voivodes and so when his father died in 1418, there was essentially a chaotic free-for-all as rival claimants tried to seize control of the throne – which was eventually taken by Mircia's only legitimate son, Michael.

These were extremely turbulent times and the region bore witness to ever-shifting balances of power. Wallachia was sandwiched between the Holy Roman Empire to the west, the expanding Hungary to the south and the encroaching Ottoman Empire to the east, but that was the least of problems for those at the top. Ruling Wallachia at the time was akin to juggling explosive porcupines on a unicycle, while reciting the nine times table backwards.* Once in power, voivodes were embroiled in a constant struggle to hold on to the reins and everything could fall apart very quickly indeed. Repeatedly usurped or murdered, the throne changed hands with wearisome regularity and in some ways was a bit like a prolonged, extremely violent, tennis rally with the ordinary Wallachians obliged to look on from the stands as the spiked ball of sovereignty was slammed back and forth across the net.

To give a flavour of just how complex and chaotic things could get, let's very briefly consider Vlad II's (that is Dracul's, father of Dracula) path to power.

Following the death of their father, Mircea, Dracul's half-brother Michael I sided with the Hungarians but that only caused the Ottomans, under Mehmed I, to invade and demand tribute. Michael agreed, largely because he had no choice, and then changed his mind once they had gone – a common theme in the Wallachia box set series. In retaliation, Mehmed backed Michael's cousin Dan II as he sought to seize the throne, and Dan invaded and subsequently killed Michael in battle. Between 1420 and 1427, the voivodary then changed hands four times as Radu II, Mircia's son, took back and then lost the throne – each time either relieving or being replaced by Dan II. In their final encounter Radu II was killed but victory was short lived because in 1432 the Ottomans invaded and murdered Dan II before putting his cousin, Alexander I Aldea, on the throne instead.

I hope you are keeping up.

Alexander promptly repaid his sponsors by siding with the Hungarians and in 1432 helped stall the Ottoman advance into Moldova. But then – in part out of frustration with Sigismund – he renewed the treaty with Murad which lasted until Alexander died of natural causes in 1436. On his passing, his half-brother Vlad II, aka Dracul, finally took over, thus taking everyone through to the next round.

* Please do not try this at home.

Complicated isn't the half of it, and if you found it impossible to keep up with that brain-knotting slough of events then fear not; suffice to say being the top guy in Wallachia was extremely perilous and not very much fun at all.

Six years after Vlad II (Dracul) came to power and when the future Vlad III (Dracula) was about 11, he and his brother Radu joined their father on a diplomatic visit to the court of Murad II in Edirne (in modern-day Turkey) only for everyone to get banged up abroad. The invitation had been a trap and the party were kidnapped, with the boys' father Vlad II only released on condition that he left his two sons, Vlad and Radu, behind as hostages. Murad II was a canny and manipulative man, who was not only the de facto leader of the Sunni Muslims but also the head of the expanding Ottoman Empire, and as such young Vlad Tepes' time at the court saw him come into contact with a different faith system and culture and knowledge distinct from his own.

It would have been character-forming too but not in a positive way.

Victims of childhood kidnapping more usually than not suffer long-term psychological damage as a result of being separated from home and family. The impact on mental well-being can impact them for the rest of their lives and leave them suffering PTSD – and although this was the fifteenth century, we must never forget that these children were people like us and not some distinct group that was somehow preternaturally disposed to put up with such desperate and terrible experiences. Radu (nicknamed 'the handsome') had a better time of things than his brother Vlad and was celebrated as a charming and charismatic presence at court which probably did not help matters between the two teenagers either.

The Greek chronicler, Laonikos Chalkokondyles* suggests in his contemporary ten-volume *Demonstrations of Histories* that while Radu fell under the spell of the court and perhaps even its faith system, Vlad (Dracula) maintained an icy aloofness. Whatever went on, the uncertainty and constant paranoia that they might be poisoned must have messed

* Chalkokondyles was an Athenian-born scholar who wrote ten volumes of Histories which were inspired by those of Thucydides and Herodotus. Unusually for the time he was fairly even-handed and wrote at length about the customs and habits of the Ottomans and attempted to take a balanced approach.

with both of their minds. The psychological torture went far beyond the realms of the Ottoman Empire too. From about 1444 and in a narrative that curiously echoes the English legend of the Princes in the Tower, a rumour began to circulate that Murad had murdered the two boys in his charge and, declining to put Vlad II's mind at ease, Dracul lived out his days not knowing the truth of his children's fate.

During his period of captivity Vlad (Dracula) may have witnessed the means of execution which would later be associated so closely with his own legend. The Ottomans certainly used impalement as a psychological weapon and we know for example that they deployed it at the Siege of Constantinople in 1453 although crucially that was after Vlad had returned to his ancestral homeland. A long Islamophobic trope has it that the 'European' Vladimir Tepes was somehow dehumanised by his time in the Ottoman Empire and that impalement was all the fault of the Muslims. It is an idea which buys into that notion of 'corruption from the east' and the infection of European purity by association with Islam, but impalement was certainly not unique to the Ottomans and its history stretched back in time. The Babylonian *Code of Hammurabi* (*c.*1772 BCE) ruled that the method was the preferred means of execution for women who had murdered their husbands and even before it was deployed as a punishment for infanticide in the Holy Roman Empire in the sixteenth century, it was being used elsewhere in the world too.

Indeed it was even used by one of England's most celebrated figures in the same year (1462) that Vlad (Dracula) 'the Impaler' would start using it too.

John Tiptoft, the First Earl of Worcester, born in 1427, was a brilliant scholar and a much-admired nobleman of the Yorkist Tudor court. Having visited the Holy Land in 1458, he returned via an extended sojourn in Italy, where he studied at the University of Padua, before coming back to England to take on a number of high-profile roles including Lord Deputy of Ireland and Lord High Treasurer. However, in the wake of the Battle of Tewkesbury in 1461, when his sponsor, the Earl of March, defeated and usurped Henry VI to be crowned King Edward IV, Tiptoft's worst traits came to the fore. As Lord High Constable from 1462, he presided over the prosecution and execution of the defeated Lancastrians who were not only hanged, drawn and quartered, but impaled too.

Warkworth's chronicle of 10 May 1470 relates that:

'Gentlemen and yeoman were hanged and drawn and quartered and beheaded; and after that they (were) hanged up by the legs, and a stake, sharpened at both ends . . . was put in at their buttocks and the other end went out through their heads. For the which the people of the land were greatly displeased, and ever afterwards the Earl of Worcester was greatly hated.'[7]

Tiptoft eventually met a sticky end himself when he was beheaded on Tower Hill on 18 October 1470, full of faux piety and excessive self-regard to his very end, a large crowd turned out to jeer.

Twenty-five years earlier things were not going swimmingly for the rest of Vlad (Dracula's) family in Wallachia. In 1445, Vlad II's (Dracul's) relationship with the legendary 'White Knight' John Hunyadi, father of Matthias Corvinus (whom we met earlier) and Regent of Hungary disintegrated. Hunyadi seized the initiative, swiftly moved to usurp him and, seeking to put his own man on the throne, advanced on the capital. In November 1447 the arrival of that army on the outskirts of Târgovişte triggered an uprising of the powerful, aristocratic, warlord class known as 'the boyars' and Dracul fled the city while his eldest son Mircea was captured, blinded with hot pokers, put in a coffin and buried alive.[8]

Hunyadi's men later caught up with Dracul in North West Wallachia and he was killed following a melee in swampland near the village of Balteni in the commune of Peris.

The White Knight (Hunyadi) installed his puppet, Vladislav II (no relation), as voivode and having seen off one irritation, set about dealing with the Ottomans.

In 1448, with momentum seemingly on his side, Hunyadi crossed the Danube alongside protégé Vladislav II and led 10,000 men into Turkish-occupied Serbia before engaging the enemy at Kosovo Polje.* The usual time frame for such engagements in the fifteenth century was in the order

* Now in the District of Pristina in modern day Kosovo.

of a few hours, but this battle rumbled on for days until the tide turned and the White Knight fled only to be captured by Đurađ Branković, the Serbian Despot* who took him hostage.

That presented an opportunity for the teenage Vlad (Dracula) Tepes who was still a captive in the Ottoman Empire and, having been provided with cavalry and infantry by Sultan Murad II, he marched west and straight into Wallachia before taking back Târgovişte unopposed.

He was just 17 years old.

With the White Knight captured and with Hungarian and Wallachian soldiers still fighting the Ottomans to the east, this *coup d'état* was the last thing the regional boyars needed and he found little support from the elite. Diplomatic moves were made and Hunyadi's deputy, Nicholas Vizaknai, urged Vlad (Dracula) to be reasonable and negotiate but the young hothead thought he had it in the bag and refused to comply. He could not have been more mistaken. A month later, Vladislav II and his army returned from the front and Vlad fled back to the Ottoman Empire.

The following year he returned to the region once more – and moved to Moldavia where his uncle, Bogdan II, had just become king. In a letter, dated 6 February 1452, he requested permission to move to the Saxon stronghold at Brasov, but the White Knight (Hunyadi), who had returned from captivity and was now back in control of Hungary, refused.

Vlad waited for his moment to come which arrived when, in 1456, the usurper Vladislav II, who had grown tired of Hunyadi, began making overtures to the Ottomans. Dracula got the nod from Hunyadi and invaded Wallachia once again. In late July 1456, on the outskirts of the settlement of Târgşor, he and his army of exiled boyars came face to face with those of Vladislav – the man he held responsible for the cruel, slow execution of his elder brother and the death of his father. According to legend, the two men agreed to settle the matter in a duel and, in the words of one biographer, Radu Florescu, Dracula then 'had the satisfaction of killing his mortal enemy and his father's assassin in hand-to-hand combat'.[9]

The new voivode, now aged 25, had witnessed enough in his young

* Hence the modern term.

life to know that the prize was only his as long as he could hold on to it and, to that end, immediately sought to take out any potential usurpers. The greatest threat to his reign was now posed by the boyar warrior class – and concluding that something drastic needed to be done before they once again turned against him he moved. On Easter Sunday 1457, he invited the boyars and their families to a grand banquet at Târgoviște and when the meal was concluded, posed a riddle as to how many princes had ruled Wallachia. The post-prandial parlour game quickly turned sour however as every answer they gave him was declared wrong. According to some accounts, the body of Dracula's dead brother had recently been unearthed and he had witnessed for himself the desperate scratch marks on the inside of the coffin lid where his suffocating brother had strived to prise it off. While we ever need to be wary of such 'good stories' whatever his motive, clearly he was in no mood for party games.[10]

According to the 'Saxon stories' some 500 boyars and their families were dragged from their tables and impaled on waiting stakes in the courtyard outside. Those women and children who were not killed were then marched in chains 100 kilometres northwest to Poenari where – again, according to Saxon sources – they were worked to death rebuilding and repairing his castle. Where fact ends and fiction begins is always hard to divine in a time of such limited and biased sources and the numbers have almost certainly been exaggerated.

Impaling people is actually a very impractical means of execution and very difficult to achieve, because even once you have managed to insert the person on the spike which you have to push up through their behind, there is the not inconsiderable problem of keeping the impaled victim upright. In addition to being hard work for executioners you require space for them to work and the available square footage in the still standing courtyard at Târgoviște is simply not large enough to accommodate all the bodies that the Saxon sources claim were put there. So, while impalement certainly took place, that figure of 500 is probably grossly inflated. It is perhaps more likely that some victims were impaled and left to die – in order to spread fear – while others were perhaps killed using more conventional means. Either way I hope you're not reading this on a full stomach.

Saxon propagandists would subsequently claim that in that one atrocity, Dracula wiped out the boyar class entirely, but that is probably not true either. As any smart revolutionary or invader knows, if you eradicate an entire tier of administration there is nobody in place to govern and that can create more problems than it solves. Perhaps Dracula made an example of those who posed the greatest threat to him and cowed the others into submission. Although we do know that a fresh class of boyars did rise at the time and they were largely made up of Vlad's most trusted men, many of whom (it was said) came from the lowest agricultural class. This gave rise to the popular Romanian legend, much beloved of the later communist dictator Nicolae Ceausescu, of Dracula's peasant army taking on the elites.

The murder of the 500 boyars was not the end of the violence and having dealt with them the voivode now cast around for further scores to settle. Having previously sought to ingratiate himself with the 'Transylvanian Saxons' in the towns of Brasov and Sibiu, only to be rebuffed, Vlad now turned against them too. These town-dwelling Saxons were an easy target. An exclusionary elite, made up of merchants and wealthy traders who kept themselves apart from the rest of Wallachian society, their only interaction with the peasantry was to invite them in on market days and employ them as servants. They paid almost no taxes and, in many ways, resembled modern-day 'expats' in Asia and elsewhere who live behind gigantic walls in guarded enclaves. They were widely hated and when Vlad (Dracula) attacked them, the move would have been popular with the broader Wallachian peasantry. The Saxon purges would be critical to Dracula's legacy because as these wealthy German merchants fled into Hungary and Austria, they carried tales of his atrocities with them.

Having asserted his power and put the fear of God into his enemies, a rare peace now came to Dracula's Wallachia. Trade and commerce briefly flourished – and Vlad underlined his authority by building a grand in-yer-face court at Târgovişte.*

* Just a 15-minute walk across the city from the schoolyard where the Ceausescus would one day be shot.

All the while, and to the east, the Ottomans were continuing to expand their territory and encroach on the interests of Hungary and the neighbouring Holy Roman Empire. In 1453, the long-diminishing Byzantine Empire had finally collapsed when Constantinople had fallen to the Muslim Sultan Mehmed II and that event sent shock waves across Christian Europe that would resonate for the next 400 years. The Ottoman Empire would go on to inspire fear, awe and envy in equal measure across Europe right up until the moment in 1922 when it crumbled into dust.

Vlad III (Dracula's) reign now played out in a climate in which the Ottoman rulers, whom he knew personally, were the heads of the expanding regional superpower.

In September 1459, Pope Pius II ordered a new crusade against the Turks but it largely fell on muffled ears and when he set out his plans the following year, only Dracula was willing to step up to the mark. Sensing division among his enemies, Mehmed advanced once more and stormed into Serbia and Greece before sending envoys to Târgovişte demanding tribute of 10,000 ducats and 1,000 young men to be trained as janissaries. Vlad fobbed him off with excuses and only changed his mind when the Ottoman leader started advancing on his dominion.

A truce of sorts was brokered, only for the voivode to change his mind once again when his unwelcome guests had gone back home.

In frustration, Mehmed sought to lure Dracula into a trap but, receiving a tip-off, Dracula turned the tables on his enemy and the Ottomans were overwhelmed at the city of Giurgiu. Nobody understood the enemy better than he did for the simple reason that he had grown up among them. As the tit-for-tat escalated, the Sultan decided that it was time to topple the troublesome Wallachian prince once and for all, so he raised an enormous army and headed west. Knowing that Vlad was now in a secret alliance with the Hungarian King Matthias Corvinus, Mehmed knew too that a blow against Wallachia would considerably weaken Hungary – his main obstacle to regional domination.

Mehmed planned to put Dracula's brother, Radu the Handsome, who had remained behind in the Ottoman lands all these years, in his sibling's place and as the vast invasion force marched West:

'The whole sky seemed to move,' wrote the historian Chalkokondyles, *'the army looked like a great wave in the sea.'*[11]

The Ottomans crossed the Danube on 4 June, and having done so, may have felt like they had just marched through the very gates of hell. Dracula had resorted to a scorched-earth policy and burned every last thing to the ground.

Despite that, the Ottomans marched on the capital and by 17 June, they were 20 kilometres from Târgovişte. Having made camp, Mehmed ordered his men to stay in their tents to prepare for battle the next day and hearing word of this, Dracula took advantage. In the middle of the night, in an unprecedented act, the warrior prince launched an audacious stealth attack on the camp. Knowing that the enemy were in their tents, he hoped to gain the advantage by either killing or kidnapping Mehmed but despite the success of this surprise and daredevil assault, his men couldn't find the Sultan and were forced to flee empty-handed.

Mehmed was undeterred and continued to march on until some miles outside Târgovişte, the army stumbled upon a truly shocking scene.

According to Chalkokondyles:

'(In) a field about three miles long and a mile wide, there were large stakes on which they could see impaled the bodies of men, women and children, about 20,000 of them . . . the Sultan himself in wonder kept saying that he could not conquer the country of a man who could do such terrible and unnatural things and put his power and his subjects to such use . . . And the other Turks . . . were scared out of their wits. There were babies clinging to their mothers on the stakes . . . from whom they were attempting to suckle.'[12]

The victims not only included Ottoman hostages and captives but also Dracula's own people. The scene was made all the more horrific because, according to Chalkokondyles, nesting crows had made their homes in the human entrails. When the Ottoman army arrived at Târgovişte, the gates to the city had been flung open and the streets were empty.

Vlad had plundered his own city, massacred his own people and fled.

Mehmed marched on to Brăila, leaving Radu behind to try to defeat Vlad's remnant forces and Radu proved to be a very different man to his brother. Rather than fighting and impaling his way across the territory, he sent messengers across the region, reminding the Wallachians that more horror would persist if regime change didn't happen. The diplomacy paid off and peace followed.

Vlad, meanwhile, had retreated to the Carpathian Mountains with his remnant forces. Seeking to regroup while awaiting reinforcements from his allies in Hungary, he may have been hopeful that he could launch a counter-attack and turn the tables once again, but those reinforcements never arrived and his messages to Corvinus in Hungary went unanswered.

The Hungarian king now saw his erstwhile ally as a liability and receiving intelligence that Dracula had sought to make overtures to the Ottomans and even offered to convert to Islam – he turned decisively against him. The intercepted missive, which he later showed to the emissaries of Pius II, were forgeries, knocked up by Vlad's Saxon enemies in Brasov – but it was enough to convince the Hungarian king that he needed to arrest the Impaler. Vlad was tricked into a meeting and then taken to Hungary as a prisoner – while his monstrous legend took off.

For the next 11 years, Radu the Handsome ruled Wallachia and it was not until three years after his death in 1476 that Vlad III managed to stage a comeback. Reforging an old alliance with Stephen III of Moldavia, he was crowned King of Wallachia for the third and final time in late November 1476 but his reign lasted just one month. While marching to engage Turkish forces in December, on yet another ill-fated mission, he was ambushed and killed. Some sources claim his head was taken to Constantinople, where it was stuck on a spike. Others insist his body was taken to the monastery at Snagov* and buried near the altar. In the 1930s a tomb was identified – but when archaeologists opened it the grave, rather ominously, was empty.

The complex saga of the real-life Dracula is not so unlike those of

* The island monastery is still there and sits just a few hundred metres across the lake from the country palace, where 500 years later, the communist Dracula Nicolae Ceausescu and his wife Elena fled.

other European warlords of any time. If you are English it's comforting to think 'that sort of thing never happened here' but of course it did. In the ninth century alone, the Kingdom of Northumbria went through 15 rulers in 100 violent years and the so-called 'medieval era' – which ran from roughly 1066 to 1485 – was a period of extraordinary tumult, chaos, revolving monarchs, civil wars and anarchy.

It's possible to have some sympathy for Vlad III too. The childhood years in exile, the murdered father and the brother who was buried alive would have left their mark on anyone and here too was a prince forever caught in the maelstrom between the Ottoman Scylla and the Hungarian Charybdis and forced to appease them both. We can give him some credit as well. Vlad brought a brief degree of order to his dominion and not only built grand castles but showed great tactical nous while securing Wallachia's independence from Hungary. But of course he was not doing any of the above out of a deep love for his people or from altruistic intent. The voivodes of Wallachia, like the gangster kings of Chicago, may have shown occasional largesse – but only because it made for good optics and in seeking to understand Vlad Tepes we must never lose sight of the fact that fundamentally, he was a murderous tyrant.

Propaganda can dent the reputations of the best of people, but that does not mean that it cannot shine a light on the worst of people too. And despite his strong leadership, Vlad III was most certainly one of those. Here was a man who was willing to carry out the most heinous acts imaginable in order to cement his power and while we might quibble about the scale, or methods of execution, or make comparisons with other tyrants of the era, or simply say 'well, that's just what they did back then' – there is no escaping the terrible truth. In his 46 years on this Earth, Vlad III (Dracula) visited unspeakable horror on the people he encountered and scorched the very earth upon which his people trod. If we shy away from that truth, or make excuses for it, then we are simply doing the work of an egregious tyrant. Albeit one who had a lovely line in facial hair.

The legend of Vlad III serves as a warning. It reminds us that even the very worst people can have their heinous deeds repurposed into elaborate fairy tales and more – that we should ever be on guard against them both.

* * *

In August 1890, a 42-year-old Dublin-born former civil servant turned theatrical agent called Abraham Stoker arrived in the Yorkshire whaling town of Whitby on the suggestion of his employer, at the start of what would be a life-changing holiday.

'Bram' was a man of inherent geniality but it had been tested to the limit in the previous month as his histrionic boss, the era's most renowned actor Sir Henry Irving, had conducted a hectic tour of Scotland. Irving, born John Brodribb in 1838, had come from nothing to make his breakthrough, aged 33, in a Victorian horror melodrama called *The Bells* (1871) before going on to seal his reputation as a Shakespearean actor and in the words of a later obituarist he had been:

'Famous alike as tragedian, comedian, and character-actor; he was the leading interpreter and producer of Shakspere's [sic] *plays. But to none of these qualifications did he owe the special position which be occupied in public esteem – a position which, it is scarcely too much to say, no other actor has ever won.'*[13]

But there were two sides to the celebrated thespian: the public-facing philanthropic 'national treasure' Sir Henry and the real-life aloof, grudge-bearing, histrionic John Brodribb – who was frankly a bit of a monster. Despite that, Stoker idolised him and that was because Bram had two sides to his personality too. For despite being married to Florence Balcombe, a famed beauty who had briefly been Oscar Wilde's fiancée, he was at the very least bisexual and probably gay – and was certainly somewhat in love with his boss. Irving and Stoker's mutual friend, the author Hall Caine, later wrote that Bram's affection for Sir Henry was 'the strongest love that man may feel for man'.[14] But the sentiment was not reciprocated because Sir Henry was very straight and very much in love with the actress Ellen Terry and Stoker was way beneath his orbit anyway.

So having checked into Mrs Veazey's guest house at 6 Royal Crescent that August of 1890, Stoker was not only physically and mentally drained but emotionally rinsed out as well. He was probably in something of an artistic torpor too, for in addition to being Irving's lackey he was also a frustrated author with six distinctly unremarkable books under his belt and he was looking to start a seventh.

In that first solitary week as he waited for his wife and baby son to join him, Stoker wandered about the town making notes and reading. He spoke to the local coastguard, who told him the story of the *Dmitri,* a Russian ship that had run aground on sands in 1885. He may also have heard a tall story of a huge black dog that had been seen leaping from the wreck – before shooting up the 199 steps to St Mary's graveyard that lies near the ruined Whitby Abbey. Bram visited the graveyard and jotted down some names – including 'Swales' who would later become a character in his finished book – and he visited the subscription library where he took out an 1820 book called *The Accounts of Principalities of Wallachia and Moldavia* by William Wilkinson, who had been British consul in Bucharest in the early nineteenth century.

In its first chapter, there is a very brief account of the reign, across just a few lines, of the voivode Dracula who:

'. . . *with an army crossed the Danube and attacked the few Turkish troops that were stationed in his neighbourhood; but this attempt, like those of his predecessors, was only attended with momentary success.*'[15]

While the details were sketchy and there was no description of him impaling babies or any of the other assorted egregious acts attributed to Vlad III, Stoker was taken with the name 'Dracula', which in modern Romanian now meant 'son of the Devil' and given the Victorian fashion for Gothic settings, he was probably inspired by the exotic location in Wallachia too.

Stoker's choice of Whitby as the vampire count's English entry point has intrigued literary detectives ever since *Dracula*'s publication in 1897. Some have speculated that he went all that way to the town simply to read Wilkinson's book, while others have conjectured that the atmosphere of the place and its ruined Gothic abbey were a trigger that inspired him to start the work. In fact, once again, Stoker's employer Sir

Henry may have played a major part in it as Irving was an early method actor who believed in blending surroundings into his performance and taking what modern dramaturgs might call a 'holistic' approach. Having knocked off those rather forgettable romance and mystery novels, Stoker wanted to create something more enduring and as Irving was the major artistic influence in his life, he copied his approach. Five years later, during another seaside sojourn at the Kilmarnock Arms in Aberdeenshire, Stoker would, according to his wife Florence, terrify fellow guests by sitting 'for hours, like a great bat, perched on the rocks on the shore, or wandering alone up and down the sandhills thinking it all out', and this positively 'method writing' style seems to have started in Whitby.

Killing time in the town while waiting for his family to join him, Stoker played off the scenery around him and looted what resources and stories there were to hand to start work on a project that was already taking form in his head.

The line – often misattributed to T.S. Eliot – that 'bad writers borrow and great writers steal' also played a part in the inception of the book and Stoker undoubtedly plagiarised elements of fellow Irishman Sheridan Le Fanu's lesbian vampire novella *Carmilla* for his epistolary work. Stoker's interest in fifteenth-century Wallachia may also have been sparked by an encounter in London with the distinctly humourless Hungarian diplomat and travel writer Ármin Vámbéry. The two men had met first in 1890 and, according to Stoker himself, it was from Vámbéry that he first heard the legend of the real Dracula's life as well as tales of the seventeenth- and eighteenth-century vampire scares in Eastern Europe, and which – much like the witch-hunts in Western Europe of the same era – were rooted in fear, superstition and social anxiety about death and disease and 'other'.

That paranoia had also spawned a book *Dissertations sur les apparitions des esprits et sur les vampires,* written by a French monk, Dom Augustin Calmet in 1756, which examined real-life vampire stories and described the methods used to kill them – or actually stop them coming back from the dead in Romania, Hungary and elsewhere. Calmet was seeking to apply rigour to the discipline and was trying to explain the phenomenon, but his accounts provided a rich source of material for writers of vampire stories and Stoker may have consulted them while researching ideas in the British Library.

Progress, however, was painfully slow and from its inception in Yorkshire in 1890, the book would take a further five years to take form, with Stoker repeatedly trying and failing to find his way into the story until further inspiration was triggered by another event close to home which unleashed something within him. That event was the imprisonment, in 1895, of his friend and fellow Irishman Oscar Wilde, who was convicted of 'gross indecency' and sentenced to two years hard labour for the crime of being a 'gay man'. The psychological impact on Stoker was immense.

Wilde's incarceration was, in the words of the American academic Talia Schaffer:

'*. . . an earthquake that destabilised the fragile, carefully elaborated mechanisms through which Stoker rooted his desires. Stoker's careful erasure of Wilde's name from all his published (and unpublished) texts gives a reader the impression that Stoker was ignorant of Wilde's existence. Nothing could be further from the truth.*'[16]

Within a month of Wilde's conviction, Stoker had broken out of his writer's block and was furiously penning the book that positively brimmed with inner paranoia, repressed homoerotic desire and the monsters and fears that lie both beyond and within ourselves. *Dracula* (the novel) encapsulates the Victorian terror of 'transgressive' sexuality and the notion – as represented by the metaphor of vampirism – that it can be 'catching'. The central protagonist Jonathan Harker's time at the count's castle in Transylvania thus reads as a homoerotic parable of temptation while feeding into very homophobic cliché of the time: for quite clearly Dracula and his three brides (a harem of vampire witches) are seeking to tempt and convert their victims and failing that kill those who will not come over to their side.

In the American version of the novel, things are even more explicit and the count tells the female vampires:

'Wait! Have patience! Tonight (he) is mine! Tomorrow (he) is yours.'

Stoker also took other latent Victorian fears and placed them into the story too. So in addition to those repressed homoerotic elements in the story, the notion of the night-stalking predator may have come from tales of 'Jack the Ripper' whose crimes, committed between 1888 and 1891, were playing out as he first attempted to write the book.

The lingering evocations of childhood monsters played a part too. As a boy, young Abraham had been bedridden and it had led him to be a voracious reader with a highly developed internal world. Stoker had devoured stories of Irish folklore, including the legend of Leannán Sídhe, the beautiful, vampiric fairy monster who takes human lovers and then destroys them. He had also read Mary Shelley's Ingolstadt-set *Frankenstein*, which his mother, Charlotte Stoker, would later refer to in correspondence with him.

And Mrs Stoker's own reminiscences played their part too.

Charlotte, you see, had borne witness to mid-nineteenth-century Ireland's many sufferings, including the potato famines of 1845 to 1852 up close – although arguably an even more chilling event from childhood haunted her most of all. In 1832, aged just 14, she had lived through the cholera epidemic that had wiped out at least half the population of her native Sligo. In her own extraordinary account of the event, written with her son's encouragement in 1872, she described how the contagion had 'come from the East' and then explained what had happened as it spread:

'The rumour of the great plague broke (and) gradually the terror grew on us as we heard of it coming nearer and nearer. It was in France. It was in Germany, it was in England, and (with wild afright) we began to hear a whisper pass "It was in Ireland."'[17]

When it arrived in Sligo, a waking nightmare played out in the streets of the town and people began to get sick and die in horrifying numbers. Those who could flee 'the miasma' – including the clergy 'of all denominations' – did so and the one Catholic priest who remained was left to preside over scenes of unspeakable horror. Charlotte tells the story of a very tall local man, 'Long Sergeant Callen', who, having died, was taken to the morgue, where it was found that his great height meant that he couldn't fit into a coffin. As such the undertaker took out a sledgehammer and began to break his legs, only for Callen to scream:

'The first blow roused the sergeant from his stupor, and he started up and recovered.'[18]

Cholera causes dehydration and fluid loss, which can lead to kidney and circulatory failure and that can cause victims to turn blue. If treated properly it has a 99 per cent survival rate, but in the absence of knowledge, the people of Sligo had no idea what was happening to them and, believing that the illness was carried through the air, failed to address its causes. As it spread, hundreds of Sligo's citizens died while superstition took hold. Just as in my own mother's childhood village, the inhabitants of Sligo tried to make sense out of something none of them could possibly understand and believed that invisible forces or perhaps God's vengeance was at work.

The outbreak had occurred in the immediate wake of a huge and violent storm and that was taken as an omen. It was also noted that the 'miasma' did not affect everyone. Some families – including Charlotte's own – went entirely unaffected while others were wiped out. Were the untouched protected by black magic? Was this some biblical plague? Was God's hand at play? In the absence of understanding, it was anyone's guess. And it would be years before anyone worked out that the reason that Charlotte's family survived was down to the fact that they had their own water supply. It wasn't magic – it was good fortune.

Sligo's cholera epidemic filled Bram's head and fed into all those other fears of monsters that Victorians harboured including the dread of being buried alive, terror of 'the East' and trepidation at the modernity that was shaping a rapidly changing world.

In the late nineteenth century, the world was once again in flux and the old order was ever more in conflict with the new. Motor cars, bicycles, trains, typewriters and telephones filled the cities even as they filled people's heads with fear about what was to come. The works of Darwin and Marx challenged traditional orthodoxy and for many, faith in gods and magical thinking was being replaced with trust in machines and modernity.

Dracula was spawned at that crossroads and in addition to its repressed homoeroticism is preoccupied with a fear of changing gender roles too. For the women in the story are monsters as well. Lucy, married to the positively wet Jonathan Harker, is an enlightened 'new woman' who at one point poses the positively polyamorous brain teaser, 'Why can't they let a girl marry three men, or as many as want her?', only for that to effectively happen when she is seduced by Dracula. Her 'infection' (which is really a sort of liberation) by the predatory foreign monster means only one thing: she must be killed to restore order, and the only solution is to drive a stake through her heart.

Stoker's male protagonists, by contrast, are emasculated and at a bit of a loss, and neither Jonathan Harker nor Arthur Holmwood are up to the task of saving their women. It is left to the swashbuckling vampire slayer Van Helsing to save the day and he only manages to do so by navigating a path between old and primitive knowledge and superstition and the tools of modernity before teaching Harker and his associate Quincy Morris how to slay the beast.

Bram's mother, doting Charlotte Stoker, loved it and, in a letter to her son, told him:

'It is splendid, a thousand miles beyond anything you have written before and . . . it should make a widespread reputation and much money for you.'[19]

It didn't. Though a muted success when it came out, when Stoker died in London, in 1912, aged 64 from that other monster, syphilis, he was mostly celebrated for his work as a theatre manager.

Bram's fame – like the cadaver of his most famous creation – only rose from its grave long after his death. The 1922 German expressionist masterpiece *Nosferatu,* directed by F.W. Murnau plagiarised the book ruthlessly and it too was very much a creature of his time. Made in the immediate wake of World War I and the pandemic that followed it, the movie was informed by the mass slaughter of a generation and fear of what came next. Its central character, Count Orlok, also appears – like so many other cinematic baddies of the twentieth century – both disabled and deformed in that familiar ableist trope that we discussed earlier in the chapter and represents with it all the worst representations of the othered human 'monster'.

The producer Albin Grau and the director Murnau had both experienced the trenches and all the fear and superstition they had spawned. Though set in 1838, the film also sees the Eastern European count quite literally as a vector who carries the plague from the East to Germany. Made, as it was, in the immediate wake of the 'Spanish Flu', that xenophobic fear of the 'other' would have fed into every prejudice of its contemporary German audiences, who now saw viruses both biological and existential everywhere.

Florence Stoker was singularly unimpressed with the infringement of her late husband's copyright and sued. A document was produced which proved that a theatrical version of *Dracula* had been performed on Tuesday 18 May 1897, and this 'copyright performance'* had established his estate's intellectual rights to the story.[20] Murnau was ordered to destroy the prints of his film and desist from showing it but some reels survived and the film went on to be a classic.† Those that exist now credit Stoker with the story and 'Orlok' has become Dracula.

In 1931, Universal Studios released the first in a series of films featuring the actor Bela Lugosi in the title role of *Dracula* and the character went on to be a staple of cinema screens for the next 70 years. Sometimes camp, sometimes threatening, sometimes downright hilarious – whether intentional or not – *he* was always of the 'other'. A monster from the East. He has been reimagined well into our own age and in many and various ways.

Prior to his death Nicolae Ceausescu, the Romanian dictator, promoted the fake history of the fifteenth-century voivode, recasting him as a nascent communist who loved his people, and after his fall there was talk of a Dracula theme park – which was wisely abandoned. Whitby too has latched on to its links with the vampire and if you visit the Yorkshire

* A means to protect the intellectual property of books against those seeking to plagiarise them for the purpose of film and theatre. Rendered unnecessary by the Copyright Act of 1910.

† Remade by Robert Eggers in 2024.

town today you can pop into the Dracula Experience or stumble into one of the many events hosted as part of the biannual Goth-fest.

The most famous monster in Anglo-Romanian culture is undoubtedly here to stay, but in many ways our obsession with this blood-sucking, shape-shifting count and his real-life alter ego tells us much more about ourselves than our collective propensity for high camp and extreme violence.

We human beings are inconsistent creatures who though born out of nature are forever in fear and at war with it. Both 'Draculas' allow us to explore that eternal paradox and the cinematic horror stories of Freddy Krueger, or those ancient tales of fiends and ghosts, allow us to push at the envelope of our civilised world and ponder the darkness both beyond and within our realm.

By contemplating 'the monstrous' – we scrutinise ourselves.

CHAPTER EIGHT

THE DISEASED

The Spanish Flu and the Disinformation Plague

Dawn was breaking and the *fajr adhan** was echoing across the rooftops of the ancient desert capital of the Australian 10th Light Horse pounded into Damascus.

Throughout the night, Arabia's most famous city had been rocked by explosions and a carnival of mayhem as the desperate Turk and German forces had blown up ordinance and burned documents before fleeing north towards Aleppo.

But now all was quiet, bar the rumble of hooves and the calls to prayer, as the cavalry, quite literally, arrived in town.

The Light Horse's 27-year-old commander, Major Arthur Olden, met Governor Emir Said at the town hall and having accepted his surrender on behalf of the Entente Powers remounted his steed and led his men north in pursuit of the enemy. It was 1 October 1918, and 400 years of Ottoman rule in Greater Syria had just come to an end, courtesy of a dentist from Perth, Western Australia.

Thirty minutes later, a battered Rolls-Royce, surrounded by Bedouin irregulars, careered into the main square. At the wheel sat Major Walter Stirling, an affable man in his late thirties and at his side, dressed in Arab robes, was Lieutenant-Colonel T.E. Lawrence, the famous English hero of the Arab Uprising. Lawrence immediately grasped what had happened and began to rage about what might have been. He, Stirling and their

* The call to prayer.

friend Prince Feisal bin Hussein were supposed to have liberated Damascus from the Turks. The upstart Aussies were pencilled in as the supporting cast – at best – and now a dentist of all things had ruined the narrative.

Lawrence had his contacts in the British press and quickly went to work, and by the time the news was reported in London the following day, the Australians had either arrived 'at about the same time'[1] as Lawrence and Feisal, or had turned up hours later. Eight years later, when Lawrence (TEL) rewrote events again in his privately published memoir, *The Seven Pillars of Wisdom* (1926), the 10th Light Horse didn't so much as merit a mention vis à vis the surrender of Damascus. Indeed, the Australian army now only featured when their commander General Harry Chauvel pitched up later on (as he really had done) to seek permission from the British officers to 'make a formal entry with his troops on the morrow'.[2]

Lawrence agreed but only to keep Chauvel at bay. The English colonel had promised Feisal Greater Syria and wasn't about to do himself dishonour by giving it away. In fact, Lawrence knew that under the terms of the secret Sykes-Picot Agreement, drafted in 1916, the French and British had already determined to carve up the Middle East between themselves. Under their deal, the prince got little more than a few million handfuls of sand. So by stalling, Lawrence was either (rather naively) giving Feisal the opportunity to take charge before General Allenby arrived, or more likely was behaving performatively in order to save face.

Either way, Lawrence's attempts to stop the Australians coming into Damascus caused anarchy. Liberated people invariably turn on the traitors in their midst and with the Ottomans gone, those members of the former administration who were left behind were suddenly very vulnerable to attack. Many police officers and government officials shed uniforms and melted into the background, and as they did bedlam erupted as vigilantes went after remnant Turkish collaborators. Hospitals were prime targets and stories soon abounded of wounded and sick patients being thrown out of windows. News of the violence quickly spread to the Australians who were camped on the city outskirts and on

2 October, Chauvel took matters into his own hands and marched his troops into town unannounced. The 'effect was electric . . . the turbulent city was instantly awed into silence'[3] and order was restored.

Chauvel's decisive action did not go down well with Colonel Lawrence, who rewarded the general by portraying him in his book as a meddling, bumptious brass hat and this was not the only bit of nifty postwar editing that he indulged in when penning *The Seven Pillars*. According to the memoir, on the same day that the Australians took control of the city, a doctor approached Lawrence and asked him to inspect one of the Turkish hospitals 'for the sake of humanity' and with nothing better to do, Lawrence agreed and walked straight into a scene of damnation:

'I stepped in to meet a sickening stench and, as my eyes grew open, a sickening sight. The stone floor was covered with dead bodies side by side, some in full uniform, some in underclothing, some stark naked. There might be 30 there and they crept with rats who had gnawed wet galleries into them. A few were corpses nearly fresh, perhaps only a day or two old: others must have been there for long. Of some the flesh, going putrid, was yellow and blue and black. Many were already swollen twice or thrice life width, their fat heads laughing with black mouths across jaws harsh with stubble. Of others the softer parts were fallen in. A few had burst open, and were liquescent with decay.'[4]

Those orderlies who remained spoke of 'fifty-six dead, two hundred dying and seven hundred not dangerously ill' – but having got over the initial shock, Lawrence, at least according to his narrative, appears to have been remarkably sanguine about it all. In the book, he explains how he began bringing Anglo-Saxon order to Ottoman chaos and, having set up a working party from among the less sickly patients, cleaned the hospital top to bottom, ordered a large trench to be dug so the dead might be buried and then ordered all the beds to have their mattresses turned over.

Lawrence was positively imbued with self-regard, verging on omnipotence, and from his description you get the strong impression that everything was pretty much fixed by nightfall. But clearly, it was not.

The following morning an Australian medical major approached him and took him to task as to what was going on. Lawrence, dressed in Arab robes, responded by laughing contemptuously in the other man's face and was rewarded with a slap across his own. In his book, he put the assault down to the major mistaking him for an insubordinate Arab – but it seems highly unlikely. Though Lawrence fancied himself as a master shape-shifter who could pass easily between Arab and English worlds, he actually stuck out like a sore thumb as he was blue-eyed and blond-haired and spoke with a refined aristocratic English accent. Though he had undoubtedly behaved heroically in the Arab Uprising, Lawrence was really not that different to many other public-school gap year boys who 'go native' while travelling about the world. And that Australian major who slapped him might in fact have been the hero of the saga, because he alone had perhaps realised what was going on.

In *The Seven Pillars*, Lawrence puts the hellish scenes in the hospital down to a mix of TB, cholera and 'mostly dysentery'. There is no mention of the second wave of the 'Spanish Flu' (H1N1) – which was running rife across the region and killing thousands. In mitigation, Lawrence left Damascus on 4 October and the first case of the H1N1 virus was only recorded in the city on 6 October so theoretically, he could have 'missed it', and TB, malaria and dysentery (but not cholera) were certainly burning through Syria in late summer of 1918. But by the time he wrote his book in 1926, everyone knew that it was the influenza that had resulted in those scenes of devastation.

Spanish Flu had a very particular calling card. Victims suffered 'heliotrope cyanosis', a term coined from the flower *heliotropium arborescens* which has a purple hue; as their lungs filled with fluid and deprived bodies of oxygen, the influenza turned faces from red to a blueish-black and as life was sapped from its victims they had distended torsos too. As Laura Spinney writes in her book, *Pale Rider*:

'Inside the chest, at autopsy, pathologists found red, swollen lungs that were congested with haemorrhaged blood, and whose surfaces were covered in a watery pink lather. The flu's victims died by drowning, submerged in their own fluids.'[5]

Lawrence's description of the blue-black faces and swollen bodies hints that influenza was running rampant in the region, but then Lawrence was no more a virologist than he was an Arab prince.

The second of five boys, he had been born in Wales in 1888 to an eccentric and doting father, Thomas, and his much younger wife, Sarah, who was a devoutly religious Episcopalian and a strict disciplinarian. Reputation was everything to Mrs Lawrence and TEL's youngest brother, Arnold, would later say that the effect of his mother's religious regime was 'worse than the war'.

By the time TEL was about 18, he had an awful lot of chips on his shoulder. Physically short, a bit of a loner, almost certainly gay* and uncomfortable with it, he sought succour in fantasy and many who knew him well described him as a sort of Peter Pan figure. Having studied history at Oxford and gone to work in the Middle East as an archaeologist, his recruitment into the army in 1914, without a single day of military training, provided an opportunity to reinvent himself as one of those medieval knights he had loved reading about as a child. He saw the war in Arabia as a distinctly heroic narrative with himself, 'Lawrence of Arabia', at the centre of it all – a sort of crusading Arabist warrior poet. And unfortunately, his 'white saviour complex', combined with a sense of inimitability, seriously clouded his judgement.

Romantic men make reckless soldiers. White knights exist to battle dragons and demons, to befriend Arab princes and deliver the people from the forces of evil, and there was no room in his internal epic for Aussie dentists or airborne influenza or doctors who understood the world better than him. So, he ghosted them, rewrote them – or edited them out.

Lawrence was not the only person to ignore the second wave of the Spanish Flu as it tore through Greater Syria in the autumn of 1918. Contemporary Muslim and Christian Arab, as well as Jewish sources, either barely took note of the virus or deliberately disregarded it and that was because at a time of war, it served no purpose. Civilian deaths from

* Debate continues.

conflict and famine were useful propaganda tools that could be used to dehumanise the monstrous Turks. Flu – a non-human agent, carried into the region by all sides – was meritocratic and indiscriminate in nature and could not be blamed on anyone. As clandestine rebel newspapers and anti-Ottoman propaganda leaflets, bulging with tales of Turkish atrocities, came out of Egypt and spread among the literate classes of Arabia, H1N1 was studiously brushed aside as all those deaths were blamed on the enemy.

To their credit, the British-led Egyptian Expeditionary Force (EEF), made up of French, Italian and British Empire forces, did take notice – at least on paper – of the unfolding health crisis and the doctors among them appreciated that the situation was serious. But the military top brass, like the historians who followed, had a distinct *gallantry bias* and viewed 'proper' casualties only as those who had been blown up, shot or otherwise killed in battle. No monuments were ever erected to the 'glorious flu dead' and no books were written by retired army generals of their happy days in the desert campaigning against H1N1.

What historical record there is of the pandemic in Greater Syria is made up of a mosaic of numbers, medical reports, diary entries and snippets of private correspondence.

One Australian sergeant-major wrote:

'Where the divisions had been spared the ravages of shell and machine gun fire during the advance, they were destined to have their ranks decimated by the influenza epidemic that swept over the whole of Syria early in October. Men died like flies. In some of the Australian regiments there were three and four horses to every trooper.'[6]

Detailing his experiences in Syria for his old boy's magazine, former British army major John Hutchinson told of encounters with Lawrence of Arabia and the fateful Battle of Megiddo before adding – almost as an afterthought – that:

'After Damascus the Spanish 'flu played havoc with the Division, which had been severely strained by being kept in the Jordan Valley during the summer – one of our officers died of it, and about thirty men . . .'[7]

By the middle of October, the pandemic had put almost half of the ANZAC Desert Mounted Corps in hospital, and overall four times as many Australian and New Zealand men died from flu as were killed by the enemy.

And the Ottomans were suffering too:

'The Turks in the main hospital died at the rate of 70 or 80 a day, and were buried by their fellow countrymen in a great continuous trench. Of about 20,000 Turkish prisoners of war, 3,000 to 4,000 died from diseases.'[8]

We don't know how many Syrians and other civilians in the region were carried off, largely because the way death was recorded was perfunctory. Best estimates put the number of dead at a relatively conservative 25,000 for all the Central Arabian cities[9] and once the region came under British and French control, from November 1918 onwards, the book-keeping barely improved. Influenza was deemed by the Entente powers to be a 'non-notifiable' disease and thus did not have to be reported to the authorities. As a result, tracking was practically non-existent everywhere.

Across its three major waves between 1918 and 1920, the so-called Spanish Flu infected an estimated one in three of the global population – roughly 500 million human beings. Between its first recorded case on 4 March 1918 and the end of the last wave in March 1920 it killed between 50 and 100 million and while the real figure likely lies towards the top end, we simply do not know how many lives were lost. Those places that did not keep records simply ended up burying a lot more people – and those which did missed an awful lot of incidental deaths.

No corner of the Earth (with the exception of Antarctica) went unaffected and I could have begun this story anywhere. We could have started on the Labrador coast in Canada, where the virus wiped out the entire population of Inuit adult males at the largest settlement, Okak, before going on to kill one third of all indigenous people in the region. Or in the trenches of Flanders, where H1N1's arrival was so devastating that the Allies at first assumed that the Germans had developed a lethal biological weapon. Or on the other side of the wire where the German general Erich Ludendorff became convinced that its effects were costing him the war. Or in Washington, where panicking number-crunchers noted that by early November 1918, 340,000 military men had been hospitalised in a pandemic, which had killed 30,000 US servicemen before they even reached France. Or at one of the many military cemeteries in Europe and America, where more US service personnel of the Great War lie in graves as a result of the influenza (63,000) than ever died in battle (53,000).

Or even at the home of a 49-year-old German immigrant, former brothel-keeper and hotel owner called Frederick Trump, who was one of the first casualties of the pandemic in New York City on 30 May 1918. The surname might sound familiar and that's because on his death, his real-estate assets and the generous life insurance policy he bequeathed to his widow allowed her and his eldest son, also Frederick, to go on to create a business empire. A little over 100 years later, Frederick Senior's grandson would be president during another epidemic.

But I digress. Suffice to say that we begin in Damascus in October 1918 for the simple reason that this is where England's most famous soldier was forging his mythos even as the second wave hit. Lawrence's failure to acknowledge the disease both at the time and in his memoir was certainly not unique and demonstrates that for many it was a sideshow to the main event; a deadly inconvenience that was not really worthy of mention. For a hundred years or more, as generations pinned poppies to their lapels and indulged in solemn remembrance of a bowdlerised narrative of doomed youth, they failed to remember the virus that had claimed more lives globally than both World Wars put together. The war dead were easy to glorify. The parameters of their mission could easily be understood. The 228,000 people – from these islands alone, mostly young and many in uniform – who died of flu could not be made sense of, and were thus forged into a sidebar of history in what amounted to a conspiracy of silence.

In culture, the gigantic black shroud of the Spanish Flu was eclipsed by the bigger and more appealing romance of war poets, plays, books and movies. In politics, the weaponisation of war suited generations of political leaders in a way that the dimly remembered pandemic did not.

'Those who forget the past,' as George Santanaya, the Spanish-born philosopher, so pertinently pointed out in 1905, 'are doomed to repeat it.'

* * *

During World War II, in an effort to mitigate the chaos created by different hurricanes swirling about in the Atlantic at the same time, the US Navy and Air Force took to giving them names on the basis that it was easier to track cyclones called 'Susan' or 'Edith'. By 1953 they had formalised the process and henceforth storms were all named after women.

Tropical Storm Alice passed through the USA between 25 May and 7 June that year causing minimal damage to property – but the policy had another consequence which became apparent in August 1969 when Hurricane Camille hit the Gulf coast of Mexico and weathercasters started to do their worst. In scenes reminiscent of the 2004 Will Ferrell film *Anchorman,* newscasters declared that the storm was 'no lady' and when it switched direction, further opined that 'like all women she can't make her mind up'.

The language was so deeply misogynistic that the feminist campaigner Roxcy Bolton called for an end to the practice and when her complaints were ignored, she took to fighting fire with fire. Popularising the term 'himmicane', Bolton soon demonstrated that men in power only enjoyed 'a harmless bit of fun' when it was aimed at women and by 1979, the National Weather Service was naming weather systems after men too. Storm Bob made landfall in July 1979 and didn't stick around to tidy up the mess he had made.

While hurricanes are named to avoid confusion, the labelling of diseases routinely causes it.

Monkeypox, for example, which is endemic to Western and Central Africa, has nothing to do with 'monkeys' and is in fact a largely rodent-oriented pathogen and only got its name after researchers in Denmark injected it into Asian macaques in 1958. Chickenpox has nothing to do with domesticated fowl and is labelled on account of the symptoms, which make human skin look like it has been pecked. Lyme disease caused by the bacterium 'borrelia' which is transmitted to humans by ticks, has nothing to do with the perennial grass that bears its name, or the fruit of which it is a homophone, or even the royally endorsed Dorset seaside town. The name instead derives from a small settlement in Connecticut where an outbreak occurred in 1975, first raising awareness of the disease, which prevails across Europe, Asia and the Americas.

Ross River Fever, a mosquito-borne infectious illness, is not limited to the delta in Queensland where it was first identified in the 1950s and though endemic to Australia, it has been diagnosed in Papua New Guinea, Indonesia, Japan, Samoa and elsewhere in the Western Pacific. Rubella, aka German measles, did not originate in Germany but was first identified there in the early nineteenth century. Ebola, etymologically a derivative of the Ngbandi word *legbala* meaning 'white water', is named after the river in Zaire where it was originally observed in 1976. West Nile Virus has nothing to do with 'the Nile' and is in fact named after the district in Uganda where it was first diagnosed in a patient in 1937.

The autoimmune illness lupus vulgaris may derive its name from the Latin term for 'wolf' but got its epithet on account of a thirteenth-century physician called Rogerius, who compared its tell-tale facial lesions to animal bites. Japanese encephalitis is so called because the infection, which is found across East and South East Asia, was first identified in – yes, you guessed it – Japan in 1875.

In our own time, we have witnessed the consequences of misnaming and localising deadly illnesses.

In March 2020, as the Coronavirus pandemic swept across the world, Donald Trump, the 45th president of the United States of America, then serving his first term, took to referring to the pathogen as the 'Chinese Virus'. Despite immediate condemnation from the World Health Organization (WHO), which pointed out that the term could lead to racial discrimination and a dangerous, false association that the virus was localised and not global in nature, the millionaire former television host persisted. By his logic, the description was 'factual' because the Coronavirus had first been identified and reported there. But there was a typically petulant angle to his association too because the Chinese had claimed that the virus had been 'caused by American soldiers' and in Trump's own words, 'I can't let that happen, it's not *gonna* happen as long as I'm president.'[10]

Trump was actually telling the truth. The Chinese government had indeed sought to blame America for the contagious disease and, while condemning the White House for dubbing Covid-19 'The Chinese Virus', the authorities in Beijing were actively promoting a conspiracy theory through media channels that US servicemen had brought it to their country. In October 2019, some two months before the strain was first identified in China, hundreds of US military athletes had converged on Wuhan province for the Military World Games. Clearly – by the twisted logic of the CCP – the Americans must therefore have brought the virus with them and perhaps deliberately.

Whipping up conspiracy theories about 'lab leaks' through their many state-sponsored propaganda outlets, the Chinese then went on to say that they had evidence and as both sides descended into a childish game of tit-for-tat, hundreds of thousands of people started to get sick and die.

Almost exactly 100 years earlier, the world had been here before.

As that previous pathogen swept across the globe, from its first wave in the spring of 1918 it was – depending on where you were on the planet – dubbed 'The German Flu' (Brazil), 'The Bolshevik Flu' (Poland), 'The Brazilian Flu' (Senegal), 'The Naples Soldier' (Spain), 'The Portuguese Flu' (Spain), 'The Flanders Flu' (UK) and of course 'The Spanish Flu', by which it came to be known globally.

The story of how that last name stuck and how it impacted on what played out in the months and years that followed is sobering – and perhaps even critical for our understanding of how a notion of collective villainy can be created and propagated. As scapegoats were sought, as nations descended into a recrudescence of denial and as the press sided with the politicians to downplay the seriousness of the crisis – millions died while millions more simply stuck their heads in the sand.

* * *

Quite how unbothered Europe's leaders were when the first cases of flu arrived on the continent, in the spring of 1918, is evidenced by the fact that, at first, pretty much everyone ignored it.

The world had been through a major pandemic well within living memory and everyone should have known better because the Russian Flu (now widely believed to be a coronavirus) which had raged across the world from 1889 to 1894* had killed about 125,000 people in the UK alone. That virus had hit London, then the most populated city in the world, harder than anywhere else globally and memories of it lingered. The Russian Flu had in fact become something of a case study in the nascent science of virology and, while discussion over the nature of pathogens was still in its infancy, when the next virus reared its head in early 1918, scientists in the UK and elsewhere did take note. The problem was that practically nobody else did. To some extent that was understandable because at first, there didn't seem to be anything to worry about and moreover, the deadliest war in European history was playing out on the continent.

The Entente and Central powers had bigger things to worry about than a few cases of the sniffles and so even as the disease started to spread across Europe during the spring and summer of 1918 and even as people began to be hospitalised, the decision was taken, pretty much everywhere, to downplay the risk.

For those seeking to do that, the apparatus was firmly in place because press censorship was just about as tight as it had ever been. In Britain, the Defence of the Realm Act, introduced just four days after the country had entered the war, on 4 August 1918, provided the state with a whole raft of powers which could be used to suppress anything not deemed to be in the national interest, stating:

'No person shall by word of mouth or in writing spread reports likely to cause disaffection or alarm among any of His Majesty's forces or among the civilian population.'

* The years in which Bram Stoker was making his first notes for *Dracula* which may also have been partly inspired by the pandemic.

The act was not a blanket ban on free speech. Legitimate criticism was tolerated and prior to Field Marshal Lord Kitchener's death in 1916, Lord Northcliffe's *Daily Mail*, in particular, led a sustained campaign against him, calling out his incompetence in the 'Shells Crisis'. But by 1918, with four years of war behind them, most newspapers, including the left-leaning *Manchester Guardian*, had fallen into line. The act had turned Britain into a 'commissary dictatorship . . . hidden in plain sight'[11] granting the government unprecedented powers and obliging newspaper editors to either censor themselves or be censored.

In fact, Britain was not really impacted by the influenza's first wave until that late spring, when soldiers and sailors disembarking from Europe introduced it into Scotland and then England. Even then, cases were relatively mild and almost everyone who caught it recovered. Between May and June, Royal Navy doctors noted 10,313 cases among those who had been sent to the sick bay, but just four died, so it was understandably not considered to be that big a deal. And even when the numbers began to climb and its severity increased, the authorities' main preoccupation was the threat it posed to morale and motivation. Concerned that news of the 'bug' might be used as an excuse to bunk off the important business of sacrificing their lives in muddy fields, and equally aware that the other side might take advantage, the government did everything in their power to suppress the story. Which again was understandable, because in the spring of 1918, as the Allies waited for the Americans to turn up in large numbers, it looked like they may be losing the war.

On 21 March, the Germans launched 'Operation Michael', the first in a series of major counter-offensives that, in the words of Field Marshal Haig, put Allied 'backs to the wall' and which the Germans hoped would win them the war. The initial assault, in two phases, saw 47 Divisions punch a hole through the Allied lines and pour in through the breach. In just a few days, they made deeper advances than either side had achieved since the conflict had begun four years earlier and some 250,000 Allied men were killed, wounded or captured. The Germans now seemed to have the upper hand and there were fears that they might now make it all the way to Paris, but then, just as they seemed to have momentum firmly on their side, the enemy ground to a halt.

'The expected third phase of the great German offensive gets put off from day to day,' the American neurosurgeon, Harvey Cushing, wrote in his diary. 'When it will come off no one knows . . . (but) . . . I gather that the epidemic of grippe which hit us hard in Flanders also hit Boche worse and may have caused the delay.'[12]

German general Erich Ludendorff knew where the fault lay and later wrote:

'It was a grievous business having to listen every morning to the chiefs of staffs' recital of the number of influenza cases and their complaints about the weakness of their troops.'[13]

In fact Ludendorff may have retrospectively been blaming his own failure on the convenient arrival of the disease. The operation had been a victim of its own initial success and had even taken the Germans by surprise. As they advanced further and further into France, they began to suffer the classic curse of the invader: supply chain issues. But the influenza certainly did not help matters.

Looking on from London, and totting up their own sick-bay figures, the British government was suffering similar disquiet. The flu may not have been fatal in that first surge but it was certainly a most unwelcome setback to the war effort. So, as the wave passed through the population and as the public began to notice that something 'was going round', the government sought actively to ignore it.

In June 1918, *The Times* suggested that the ailment that so many were complaining of was in fact 'war weariness'.

The UK did not yet have a Ministry of Health, let alone a National Health Service, and responsibility for the nation's well-being rested with local Medical Officers of Health, charitable foundations and the Education Board. Consequently, there was no joined-up response to the growing health emergency and as the Allied Hundred Day Offensive began in August 1918, the state's attempts to render the illness inconsequential simply made matters worse. That very month and believing it was all over, the Chief Medical Officer of the Local Government Board, Sir Arthur Newsholme KCB FRCP, went as far as to cancel what pandemic preparedness plans there were – including schemes to ban large public gatherings and limit numbers on public transport.

Although he may sound like it, Sir Arthur was no fool and had actually been something of a seer in terms of improving public health. A long-term advocate of state-run healthcare and pandemic preparedness, as far back as 1916, he had warned that all those men moving about created the perfect environment for contagious disease to fester and spread. But having spent time as Medical Officer for Health in Brighton and being a man of advancing years, and entrenched opinions, he had also come to the unfortunate conclusion that the new science of epidemiology was fundamentally flawed. Like many other health professionals at the time he held that it was unclear as to how the virus was spreading and that there was little that could be done – apart from letting herd immunity run its course.

Later in the year, as the pandemic visited its worst in November 1918, Newsholme would double down, telling a meeting of the Royal Society of Medicine (RSM) that while quarantines and border controls might have an impact on slowing cholera and plague, influenza's mode of transmission was impossible to track and, as such: 'I know of no public health measures that can resist the progress of pandemic influenza.'[14]

Long before that, he seems to have become genuinely irritated at all the fuss and declared privately that all the talk of the flu was unpatriotic nonsense that would only encourage munitions workers to stay in bed. Had that first wave been it, history would have ignored the influenza outbreak of 1918 as stoutly as Newsholme was seeking to do. But as twenty-first-century citizens know to our cost, you can't just will a pandemic to go away.

By late 1918, developments in science and technology had allowed the human race to wage war on an unprecedented scale. By Armistice on 11 November 1918, 40 million people had been killed more efficiently and mechanically than ever before. As machines spun through the sky raining death on the trenches and cities below, as armoured tanks crushed wire and bones beneath them, and as 1.5 billion shells were hurled across the skies of the Western Front, Northern Europe was turned into an apocalyptic wasteland of mud, smashed-up cities and broken human beings.

Nations had unleashed the power to destroy each other on a massive scale, but were powerless to stop an influenza virus and now – just as in Bram Stoker's *Dracula* – the medieval world of plague and modernity collided. As millions carried the H1N1 with them, it was left to the adults in the room to raise the alarm and there were very few of those left. By 1918, there were just six neutral countries remaining in Western Europe: Sweden, Switzerland, the Netherlands, Norway, Denmark and Spain, and neutrality had largely inured them to the censor's stamp. Spain, by coincidence, was one of the first nations to feel the full force of the disease in that first wave and, with a relatively free press, was thus one of the first to actually report it.

During April and early May of 1918, the Basque city of San Sebastian experienced an outbreak of influenza that left officials baffled. Lying as it does, just 20 kilometres from France, local doctors surmised that it may have come across the border but to their bewilderment the French newspapers and local government officials were entirely silent on the matter so the Spanish concluded that the 'miasma' (literally 'bad air') may have come, quite literally, out of nowhere. As it spread west along the coast and south by rail and road, thousands fell ill, as others sought to come up with a name for it. Two years earlier a popular *zarzuela*, essentially an early form of popular musical, had opened in Valencia. *The Song of Oblivion* by José Serrano was set in late-eighteenth-century Italy and featured a particularly memorable earworm called 'The Naples Soldier'. So, 'catchy' was the tune that the Spanish dubbed the virus 'The Naples Soldier'. And the laughs pretty much ended there.

On 22 May, the populist *ABC* newspaper in Madrid carried the first reports:

'It is really rare to find a parent, executor or friend who does not mention the effects of the grippe or who are convalescing from the ailments thereof . . . in the asylums, in the alleyways and in the tenement houses – the fever runs wild.'[15]

Though the Naples Soldier affected people of all ages, Spanish clinicians found that its effects were particularly pernicious among those aged 20 to 40.

On 28 May, the British press, which had been studiously ignoring Britain's own outbreak at home, leapt on the story and the *Hull Daily Mail* reported 'The Spanish Plague' for the first time:

'Practically all Spain is affected by the mysterious epidemic resembling influenza which is raging and causing many deaths. So many workers in Government offices are down with it that public business is greatly hampered. Many private firms have had to close for want of staff. Two-thirds of the tramway staff are laid up, and the service has had to be greatly curtailed.'[16]

Two days later, the *Liverpool Echo* added that half of the parliament in Madrid had fallen sick and that the Spanish King Alfonso XIII himself, then aged 32, was seriously ill. Then – as now – the failing health of a member of a royal family made for better copy than the far bigger story of millions of mere 'peasants' taking to their beds and it guaranteed front page coverage in many European papers that were themselves sick – of constantly reporting on the war. As the Spanish PM went down with it too and as the local press started alerting the public to the seriousness of the illness and began giving advice on how to avoid contagion, back across the border, Dr Rene Legroux of the Pasteur Institute in Paris began downplaying the 'hysteria':

'The Spaniards made a great fuss about it,' he said, *'but for that it wouldn't have been noticed.'*[17]

Neutral countries may have no enemies, but at time of war, that means they have no allies either and even the presence of an English Queen consort, Eugenie, granddaughter of Victoria, didn't help their cause. The British establishment had a long history of barely contained contempt for Spain, running right back to the sixteenth century and now it was all laid bare. The English press's liberal use of 'The Spanish Plague' across its pages tapped into all those sixteenth-century 'black legends' put about by the Elizabethans, which demonised the Spanish Empire even as it conquered the world rather more successfully than them. By admitting that the monster was among them, the Spanish had unwittingly made themselves a scapegoat.

'No-one loves the messenger who brings bad news,' wrote Sophocles in his 441 BCE tragedy *Antigone*, and it was ever thus. Fifty years earlier, in 491 BCE, the Spartans had thrown a Persian emissary down a well after he came bearing demands of 'earth and water' from the powerful King Darius and as we have seen – messengers had a frankly rubbish time of it whether visiting the court of Lady Jane Grey or popping by to deliver news to the voivode Vlad Tepes III.

Traditionally news had been carried about by heralds – or shouted out by criers in town and village squares – but by 1918, politicians had to rely on the press to inform the public and as they had minds and agendas of their own they could both shape public opinion and not always be relied upon. The good news was that they could also be flattered and even bought. Alfred Harmsworth – Lord Northcliffe from 1905 – who was very much the Rupert Murdoch of his time, owned 40 per cent of the UK's daily papers, and as his stable included *The Times* and the *Daily Mail* he exerted massive sway on the population and their view of the war. It was his influence that essentially toppled the Prime Minister Herbert Asquith in 1916 as a result of the 'Shells Crisis' which led to the populist David Lloyd George becoming leader that same year. Lloyd George had a distinctly love–hate relationship with Harmsworth but was canny enough to keep him onside and in 1918 would make him a viscount for services to the war effort. A year earlier, having offered him a cabinet role, he appointed him Director of Propaganda – meaning that henceforth the state and the fourth estate were largely working in tandem and could thus put all the blame for the virus on Spain.

Britain was not alone in that and indeed, one hugely significant paradox of the naming of the 'Spanish Flu' was that for once, the warring nations actually agreed on something. In sounding the klaxon of the health tsunami, the Spanish press had inadvertently turned their country into a pariah and that suited everyone . . . apart from the Spanish who had problems of their own already.

Though neutral, the war playing out across the border had rekindled existing problems and spawned new ones inside the country. Much as modern-day Europeans might be divided over politics in the USA, or Palestine, or Ukraine, the Spanish people were split between those who supported the Central Powers and those who backed the Entente Allied nations, and particularly their neighbour France. This was very much 'culture war' territory and those who wanted Berlin to prevail tended to be more conservative and Catholic in nature, while the rest, who in fact made up the majority, were more liberal, forward-thinking and of a more republican bent. Several thousand Spanish men fought as mercenaries during the course of the war and almost all of them served in the French Foreign Legion – so there was a sense that they had skin in the game too.

Even before the pandemic came along, 1918 had been a particularly bad and chaotic year for Spain. The elections held in February and March for Congress and the Senate were conducted in the wake of a series of major crises that had simply compounded the broader fractures within the country. As there was no clear winner either time, the voting had only added to Spain's woes and, prior to catching the influenza, there had been talk of Alfonso abdicating. As calamity piled on top of catastrophe, a government of national unity was formed under veteran former Prime Minister Antonio Maura, but as is so often the case when consensus is sought, it lacked purpose and direction. In already troubled times, the arrival of the pestilence was taken as a 'bad sign' by the then very many superstitious people in the nation and when the King fell gravely ill, and then gave it to the ageing prime minister too, the outbreak became a deadly metaphor for the many other ills besetting the country.

Seeking to shake off blame and in mounting despair, the sickly Spanish government sought scapegoats of their own. The obvious choice was Portugal, which was very unfair indeed since, if anywhere in the world had a legitimate claim to have been impacted by the literal Spanish Flu, then it was their Iberian neighbour.

Portugal was theoretically fighting in the war on the Allied side in 1918 – as it had done since 1916 – but the unpopular conflict had gone badly for the country's politicians and they had domestic problems of their own as a result. With so many French soldiers fighting at the front, the war had also drawn in Portuguese agricultural workers too and, as they made their way across Spain and into France and back again, they became unwitting vectors. The coughing and spluttering of Portuguese workers in trains led to much finger-pointing among their fellow Spanish travellers and in the midst of a reputational PR crisis, Madrid took to performatively blaming Lisbon for the disease. The Spanish even set up cordons at train stations near the border, where Portuguese citizens were sprayed with a foul-smelling disinfectant and by late summer all trains coming into the country were being sealed to protect the Spanish people from the unclean Portuguese neighbours.[18] Eventually, they shut the border altogether.

None of this helped the actual people of Spain and having been clobbered by that first wave, when the second arrived in September, the country was hit even harder. At least 260,000 lives were lost with 45 per cent dying in October 1918 alone. In total, about 1.25 per cent of the population lost their lives – a devastatingly high statistic although as in other places around the world, wealth directly affected chances of survival with high-income groups suffering an excess mortality rate* of about 29 per cent compared to 62 per cent in mid- and 69 per cent in low-income groups. And though the virus visited its worst among that same 20-to-40-year-old age bracket, you were more likely to get off lightly if you resided in an urban environment where you were more able to self-isolate than in an overcrowded agricultural dwelling.[19]

The author Beatriz Echeverri would later point out: 'Spanish flu had nothing Spanish about it at all.'[20] It was true although in fairness, it had nothing to do with the rest of Europe either.

Although this would not be understood for decades, in fact, the 'Spanish Flu' pandemic had really started in earnest in America although the Americans also sought to blame others, and specifically the British.

One of the great challenges for the British in World War I was a lack of continental space. While the Central Powers had a mass of land

* Excess mortality – a higher than usual degree of mortality during a specific period.

behind their lines in which troops and supplies could be billeted and stockpiled, British Empire troops were obliged, due to the limits of geography, to pack everything into just a few hundred square kilometres down the Atlantic coast. To that end, the fishing port of Étaples, which sits on the Pas-de-Calais just across the English Channel from Portsmouth on the northwest seaboard of France, was transformed into a major hub and by 1917, the entire area was one gigantic military training ground and medical facility. In addition to vast stockpiles of supplies, there was a huge practice field (known as the Bullring) as well as 12 hospitals with 23,000 beds. The base served as a temporary home to 100,000 men and women[21] and in 1917 the camp had experienced a major epidemic of seasonal flu, so when the 'Spanish' variant came along a year later, America started pointing the finger at the camp.

Epidemiologists who first studied the pandemic agreed and long believed that the outbreak at Étaples could have been H1N1 but it is now widely assumed that the American troops alone were responsible for bringing it into Europe, where it was supercharged by the existing smorgasbord of illnesses running rife. The lessons that could have been learned at the overcrowded camp at Étaples during the 1917 flu epidemic were not heeded either and that just made matters worse but the 'Spanish Flu' could more accurately be called the 'Kansas Virus'.

It was there, in January 1918 in a sparsely populated Haskell County, that a doctor called Loring Miner first recognised that a powerful strain of flu was on the loose and felling some of the strongest and most robust farm workers in the area – but when he sought to warn the public via the local *Santa Fe Monitor* they were reluctant to print the story for fear of denting wartime morale.

As such, the first documented victim was Albert Gitchell, an army cook, who presented himself at the medical station at the unfortunately named 'Camp Funston' in Kansas (300 miles east of Haskell County) on 4 March, complaining of a headache, a sore throat and a high temperature – which measured 104°F (40°C). By early afternoon, that same day, over a hundred others had followed him to the bay, presenting similar symptoms, and matters got worse from there. Failing to appreciate the nature of the problem, when the first US troop ships left for Europe the following month, they were essentially cargoes full of H1N1, transporting the virus en masse into France and straight into a gigantic simmering pot of existing misery.

* * *

Lt. Col. Philip Doane, head of the Health and Sanitation Section of the Emergency Fleet Corporation, knew whose fault the pandemic was and in September 1918, voiced his theory that the Germans had put ashore spies from U-boats and released vials of lab-manufactured toxins in public spaces. According to Doane:

'It would be quite easy for one of these German agents to turn loose influenza germs in a theatre or some other place where large numbers of persons are assembled. The Germans have started epidemics in Europe, and there is no reason why they should be particularly gentle with America.'[22]

The theory of German maleficence spread to other countries, including Brazil, where the veteran politician Rodrigues Alves had been re-elected president on 99 per cent of the vote in March 1918. There, the Rio de Janeiro *A Careta* claimed that German submarines had secretly been travelling the world spreading the disease and this was why so many were 'falling victim to the Germans' treacherous bacteriological creation'.[23]

And if it wasn't the Germans, it must have been the neutral Norwegians. On 12 August 1918, a Norwegian freighter called *Bergensfjord* arrived in New York – where its sickly captain informed the port authorities that he had been obliged to bury four men at sea.[24] Almost all of its 200 passengers were ill and had to be transported to hospital but Royal Copeland, a former eye surgeon and homeopath, who was now head of the New York City health department, reassured New Yorkers that they would not be affected and insisted that the Norwegians had got ill because the people there didn't eat hamburgers.

There was 'not the slightest danger of an epidemic', he said, since the flu rarely harmed 'a well-nourished people'.[25]

This was news to millions of sick Americans already struggling with ailments similar to those being experienced by the passengers on the *Bergensfjord* and to those – including the Trumps – who had buried loved ones. So, quite naturally, if America was immune to the 'Spanish Flu' then that 'thing' doing the rounds must all have been the fault of 'aspirin'. It made sense if you 'did your research', because symptoms such as these had not existed before the new 'wonder drug' had appeared on pharmacy shelves a decade earlier and, after all, it had been invented by Big Pharma . . . in Germany.

Pandemics are terrifying. They come out of nowhere and are beyond our control. And as much as inhabitants of coal-mining villages might start to put store by signs and pairs of shoes on tables out of fear for their loved ones down the pits, it is understandable that so many caught up in this terrible flu sought to make sense out of something that was essentially senseless. Denial and superstition are both protective mechanisms. So too are barmy conspiracy theories, and blaming 'aspirin' for the pandemic was a classic apophenic* response to the disaster.

In our own, recent pandemic, similar unscientific theories ran rife. Some argued that the promulgation of '5G', whose development and launch in many countries in 2020 coincided with the arrival of the illness, had somehow caused or 'charged' the virus. In 2020, BT Openreach reported 50 cases of abuse, harassment, assaults and intimidation in April alone, as engineers sought to install the necessary cables. Workers were spat at, kicked and even forced to flee as mobs of conspiracy theorists turned up to confront them. In London, there was a case where a woman blocked an engineer in with her car and began haranguing him for having '5G on his roof' which turned out, in fact, to be nothing more menacing than a storage rack.

Conspiracy theories are very much like viruses. Much like pathogens, they don't need food or energy or oxygen to sustain them, or sex to reproduce. They do not spawn independently and as they mutate, they rely on human beings to carry them about with them and spread their

* Apophenia being that innate human tendency to find meaning where there is none.

poison. They have existed throughout time and tend to repeat themselves. Some are relatively benign and others are lethal.

The 5G conspiracy of 2020 was really not so different from the belief in the fourteenth century that the Black Death was caused by the wrath of God, or people in 1918 believing that they were all dying as a result of 'German made' aspirin.

Bayer – who had first patented the drug in 1899 – were eventually obliged to put out press releases assuring Americans that 'the manufacture of Bayer-Tablets and Capsules of Aspirin is completely under American control'; which, of course, made things worse because nothing feeds a conspiracy theory quite like corporate denial. In fact, just as a stopped clock tells the correct time once every 12 hours, the conspiracy theorists had accidentally got something right. A 2009 paper by researcher Dr Karen Starko concluded that large doses of aspirin may actually have made matters worse, as high amounts of the drug can cause pulmonary edema and hyperventilation in certain patients. So, aspirin may have exacerbated matters for some, but it was not the cause of the illness and it most certainly was not at fault simply because it was 'German'. This attempt to blame everything on 'the enemy' was undoubtedly an extension of the wider efforts to monster 'the Hun' in wartime.

There were conspiracy theories about vaccinations too and, although one was never developed to fight the H1N1, in the swell of paranoia, a rumour started circulating that inoculations for smallpox and typhoid, which were given to US troops as a matter of routine, were plots to poison the boys and may even have started the pandemic.

'They arrested one of the head nurses here today, she is a German spy,' one woman wrote to her sister in the autumn of 1918. *'She is the cause of more than half of the influenza in the camp . . . there was bound to be something wrong when the boys began to die by the hundreds.'*[26]

Another correspondent wrote to the US Department of Justice tipping them off to a story 'near Boston', She summarised the story as follows:

'The teller has a "friend" who has another friend who is a nurse at

Camp Devens during this influenza epidemic. This nurse says that a doctor at Devens has recently been shot for having injected the influenza germ instead of the antitoxin.'[27]

It wasn't true but as Winston Churchill never said, 'A lie can get halfway around the world before the truth has got its trousers on.'

Other theories doing the rounds included the one where mustard gas on the Western Front had fused with those emitting from decomposing bodies to forge a highly toxic miasma in France. Or that all those explosions had forced it out of the soil. Or that jazz, coal dust, fleas on cats and dogs, and even dirty dishwater were to blame. Or that it was travelling tinkers who spoke with German accents. Or perhaps the fault of 'war bread' which lacked the nutrients of the pre-war variety.

And just as in the fourteenth century many thought that this might be the judgement of God. In churches across Spain, France and Italy, in particular, congregations were told that the war and human depravity had brought vengeance upon the Earth, with the priests not realising that by continuing to encourage attendance in the first place, they were themselves spreading the virus.

Once again, it was the Spanish newspapers that tried to warn against the consequences of social mixing – including the dangers of going to pray. September, then as now, was a month of fiestas and religious gatherings in the country and, while some local authorities half-heartedly sought to curb them, the church was simply too powerful an entity to be stopped. In despair at it all, the Madrid-based *El Liberal* began arguing that the government should enforce nothing short of a sanitary dictatorship and suggested that closing houses of worship and other public spaces would be a good place to start. By October, with people dropping like flies, the Spanish government finally took heed and introduced a new set of social distancing rules that prohibited large gatherings and public spectacles. But few in the church took notice and masses continued to be held for the living as well as the mounting roll call of the dead.

By the end of the year, Spain had started to run out of coffins, grave diggers and priests. Clearly new scapegoats were needed and, failing to find them, Europe and America fell back on the old ones. In the USA, recent immigrants made a perfect whipping boy since, as you may remember from the Capone chapter, the years leading up to 1918 had seen some of the highest immigration in US history and immigrants from the south of Europe were viewed not only with contempt, but as carriers of disease. From the previous century, 'nativist' Americans had associated certain illnesses with particular ethnic groups and TB was dubbed 'the Jewish disease', while cholera had been blamed squarely on the Irish.[28] In 1916, Italians were held liable for the polio epidemic that swept along the Eastern Seaboard that year and when the 'Spanish Flu' followed in 1918, they got the blame again. Widely and wrongly believed to be an inherently slovenly and unhygienic people, their non-Anglo-Saxon ways made them a focus of state censure. One health official told the *Denver Post*:

'When an Italian or Austrian is taken sick, a physician is seldom called, but all the relatives and friends immediately flock into the house to call on the sick person.'

Another official told the same paper, *'The foreign element gives us much trouble when an epidemic occurs.'*[29]

'Foreigners' made excellent whipping boys elsewhere in the world too. The first flu fatality in Great Britain was an Indian sailor called Nane Zuella, whose death was recorded in Dundee on 28 June 1918. Obviously, the fact that he was an 'Indian' made him both a bringer of disease and more susceptible to it, and the same applied to the many thousands of Chinese people who were now present in Europe. From 1914 onwards, as the British threw their own people into the military meat grinder of the Western Front, they began to run short of labourers and the government were obliged to look elsewhere for manpower to build and maintain infrastructure – finding it, eventually, in neutral China. There, the British had an existing network of missionaries who were used as recruitment sergeants to drum up around 335,000 men, who were then enlisted into the 'Chinese Labour Corps' and taken to the Eastern and Western Fronts.

In 1917, as they were transported across Canada in tightly packed trains, many fell ill and fearing these 'coolies' were carrying 'infectious illnesses' from Asia into the pure Canadian air, the authorities put them into quarantine where they all started catching illnesses off each other. The following year, when the pandemic broke out, memories were reawakened of the 'Chinese coolies' who had got ill and for many years East Asia was deemed to be the true source of the outbreak. However, Frank Macfarlane Burnet, the Nobel laureate who first investigated the roots of the pandemic, concluded that it had all begun in Kansas, most likely in a pig farm near Camp Funston, and that its spread was 'intimately related to war conditions and especially the arrival of American troops in France'.[30]

History shows us that it is always easier to blame Norwegians, 5G, pills, submarines, Italian immigrants, God, the Indian diet, Chinese people, black people and those who can't answer back, than to face the unfortunate truth.

* * *

Around the time that T.E. Lawrence was leaving Damascus in the early autumn of 1918, the Western world was finally taking the crisis seriously. In San Francisco, on 22 October, a mask ordinance made it compulsory by law to cover your face in public and attempts to encourage mask-wearing there and elsewhere included the punchy pre-social media meme-poem:

'Obey the laws and wear the gauze, protect your jaws from septic paws.'

People were increasingly guilt-shamed into wearing them and the American Red Cross put out a statement saying that:

'The man or woman or child who will not wear a mask now is a dangerous slacker.'

At the same time the US state made efforts to explain why it was important to cover faces and wash hands – while imposing fines of up to $200 on those who refused to comply.[31]

Such measures were, naturally, unpopular among those who thought 'they' didn't need masks or that they didn't work because someone had told them and – just as in the 2020 pandemic – mandates engendered both anger and fear. In San Francisco, local 'libertarians' set up 'Anti-Mask Leagues' and began parading about with signs demanding the right to catch flu even as the protesters caught it off each other.

Even as late as January 1919 and with an estimated 500,000 Americans already dead and the number rising, a rally was being held in the Dreamland Rink in San Francisco, where 2,000 maskless attendees heard speeches on how health measures were against their constitutional rights. A meeting of local councillors in Portland, Oregon, also held in January 1919, saw W.T. Vaughn, a prominent local Democratic politician, declare in an impassioned speech that mask-wearing was 'autocratic and unconstitutional' and he added that he was not about to be 'muzzled like a hydrophobic dog'.[32]

That same report in the *Oregon Daily Journal* demonstrates that the general sentiment, egged on by local populist politicians and vested interests who knew nothing of science, had turned firmly against the messengers – in this case the 'experts' – who actually understood the risks and how best to mitigate them. The people of Oregon were particularly incensed that only nine to twenty people were allowed to ride trams at any one time depending on the size of the cars. Indeed, they seemed to be far more upset about travel inconvenience than the 48,146 reported cases and 3,675 deaths from influenza in their state that year alone.

Urban myths and outright bollocks abounded. The *Los Angeles Times* reported that a woman from Chicago went '*insane from sheer fright when she stepped from a Santa Fe Train and beheld the masked city*' of Pasadena.

'The hospital physicians say there is no doubt that fear engendered by the masks temporarily unbalanced her mind.'

In New York, the homeopath Royal Copeland, who had caught the flu and nearly died as a result in late September, had now decided that the virus might actually pose a risk to well-fed, healthy people too, and on 4 October officially acknowledged that there was a health crisis in the city. But nobody likes the messenger who brings bad news and as Copeland attempted to shut the door on the long-bolted horse, he attracted the considerable ire of business interests that were being impacted by the economics of it all.

One of those, Harold Edel, the 26-year-old manager of Times Square's Strand Theatre, then the largest movie playhouse in the world, was particularly perturbed by all these unnecessary restrictions, and that may have had something to do with the fact that he was about to host a major event. On 20 October, his cinema was due to screen the premiere of the latest Charlie Chaplin comedy *Shoulder Arms*, and the last thing Harold wanted was to turn audiences away. So, he praised those buying advance tickets with the words:

'*We think it most wonderful . . . that people should veritably take their lives in their hands to see it.*'[33]

On 2 November, the *Buffalo News*[34] reported his death from pneumonia.

Two days later, Chaplin would be affected further, when his first great love – the Irish dancer and actor Hetty Kelly – died of the flu at her home in London, aged 25. In the UK, the British government had now woken up to the threat and it was surely just coincidental that the moment only came after Prime Minister Lloyd George had contracted the virus and nearly died while on a trip to Manchester in September. Despite having a scoop on their hands, the Fleet Street press downplayed the event and the prime minister's friend C.P. Scott, editor of the *Guardian*, simply recorded that Lloyd George had caught a 'chill' and was 'now a prisoner of Manchester's not too kindly climate'. It wasn't the climate. It was the flu and having recovered from his near brush with death, the populist, philandering* prime minister set about trying to get the pandemic done. Mines and factories were closed along with a large number of schools and by late October, theatres, shops and dance halls were shut too.

Meanwhile, Sir Arthur Newsholme, who had also contracted the disease and belatedly decided that maybe it might be worth worrying about, declared a health emergency in London and began issuing guidelines,

* Though married, Lloyd George, then 54, was having an affair with his pregnant personal secretary Frances Stevenson who would become his second wife in 1943.

while commissioning a film (*Dr Wise on Influenza*) which appeared the following year. The short 'public health' picture advised maintaining social distancing, cleanliness, ventilation, mask-wearing and all the other sensible things that should have been suggested earlier.

As deaths mounted, capitalism sought to make a killing of another kind and many companies rebranded products which they claimed could ward off the flu. Bauer's 'formamint' was marketed as a 'germ-killing tablet', said to be an effective cure for symptoms and proudly boasted that it contained formaldehyde, which can actually kill if ingested in large amounts. 'Chymol', a delicious-sounding tinned spread made out of bone marrow and egg yolk and 'Lifebuoy soap' were also both sold to the public as cures or preventatives for 'Spanish Flu'.

By late October, the peak had hit and just as the worst was receding, the war ended with spectacularly bad timing. On 11 November 1918, as the guns fell silent, people celebrated and London bathed in a blaze of light as the four-year blackout ended and huge crowds gathered to party. Bonfires were lit, including a gigantic one at the base of Nelson's Column on to which a group of men later tossed a captured German artillery gun. The heat it generated was so intense that it caused the granite at the base of the column to crack, and the fissures there are still visible today. Stolen air-raid maroons were set off in the parks and streets and pandemonium ensued as tens of thousands of people partied. Though wartime alcohol restrictions were still technically in place, Londoners gamely disregarded them and as caution was thrown to the wind it was like tossing gasoline on a centenarian's birthday cake and H1N1 burned afresh once more.

As football ratchets whirred, as corks popped and as thousands indulged in the joy of the moment, not everyone was celebrating. Back on the Western Front, the guns may have fallen silent, but thousands of young men were lying in hospital beds coughing up blood. The roll of honour of one boys' boarding school in Northamptonshire tells a story of its own: Lionel Russell Wilford, died Marseilles 8 November 1918 – influenza; Joseph Roland Grummitt, died Chelmsford 14 November 1918 – influenza; his brother Hugh Cecil Grummitt, died 25 March 1919, aged 20 – heart attack, brought on by influenza; Herbert Markham, died

10 November 1918 – German hospital in Namur, Belgium – influenza; Clive Burrell, died 23 November 1918, Valenciennes – influenza; Captain Gilbert Kennedy, died Sangatte, 11 December 1918 – influenza.[35]

Christmas came and New Year went and, though the war was over, there was no let-up in the pain. The third wave arrived early the following year and a weary world looked on as millions more died.

The peace talks held in Versailles, attended by T.E. Lawrence, King Faisal and representatives of every major power began in January 1919 and continued for months. One morning in April, the US President Woodrow Wilson awoke in his rooms in Paris with a fever of 103 degrees F (39.4 degrees C) and subsequently nearly died. Wilson was diminished physically as a result and some have theorised that he may have suffered an undiagnosed case of encephalitis – which causes a swelling of the brain – as a result of catching the flu. Later in the year, he suffered a stroke, which was covered up, but which left him largely incapacitated for the rest of his term in office. He died three years later in 1924, aged 67.

Wilson's brush with death briefly made the flu a front-page story again – but it soon dwindled on to the back pages and in Britain, as elsewhere, people started to pretend it was all over. It wasn't, and in its final act, the pandemic would fuel social unrest.

For decades afterwards it was claimed that the African-American community dodged the Spanish Flu in a way that many white Americans did not. Some suggested that this was because they got hit hardest in the first wave and thus had immunity or that it may have been a result of their being effectively 'quarantined' by the Jim Crow Laws and general apartheid in America at the time. That narrative is now contested and it's increasingly thought that the lower figures were down to misreporting and a lack of healthcare provision for minorities at the time. Black Americans suffered predictable discrimination and finger-pointing during the pandemic and in one appalling incident, white gravediggers in Baltimore refused to dig graves for black victims in case they caught something off the bodies.

By 1919, the mood among many African-Americans had shifted. Black military personnel had been radicalised by their experiences in the trenches of World War I and were rightfully angry at the way they had been treated by the country they had risked and in some cases sacrificed their lives for. Though sent to the front as 'Americans', the 200,000 black men who fought in the US Expeditionary force were often relegated to secondary duties, were paid less and in many cases were poorly trained. Many had taken part believing that participation in the great undertaking would win them respect and more equal rights back home. But it was not to be and they returned to a country that had essentially exorcised their contribution.

Worse still, black American soldiers now returned to a climate in which the resurgent Ku Klux Klan was actively promoting the notion that they were responsible for all of society's ills. Lynchings and attacks on black people by white racists led to postwar civil unrest across America, peaking in the so-called 'Red Summer', at the very moment that the third wave passed through the country.

From 1910 onwards, the black population of the northern states had swelled dramatically as the Great Migration had witnessed (by 1918) an estimated 500,000 African-Americans move north to escape the racist Jim Crow Laws in the south. There, unfortunately, many found that they were treated no better, but postwar and with a growing sense of empowerment, sentiment was shifting and there was a distinct feeling of 'we aren't going to take this any more' within the black community. When W.E.B. Du Bois, the black rights activist and historian, called upon returning African-American veterans to not simply 'return from fighting' but to 'return fighting', many took him at his word.

White racist paranoia seized on this and soon the KKK and others were promulgating hysteria that radicalised black people returning from the front would now seek to imitate the Russian Revolution of October 1917. That fear in fact went right to the top and in the White House Woodrow Wilson, a man who had instigated explicitly racist 'apartheid style' legislation in his first term, was whispering to aides that black soldiers would be the perfect vector for Bolshevism. Come the blistering hot summer of 1919, the perfect storm of the enduring pandemic, the social injustice it had exposed and the rising wave of black resentment and white racism was ready to explode.

A series of incidents in Georgia, Texas and Charleston in South Carolina between May and late June saw white racists commit arson against black homes with scores of people injured and at least a dozen killed in the process. But come Saturday 19 July, the tinder went up.

That Saturday, a perpetuating false rumour that a white woman had been raped by a black man saw mobs made up of recently returned white soldiers and sailors attack random black people in the streets and on public transport, and soon the violence had spread to African-American neighbourhoods and businesses. As the police refused to act, a four-day riot ensued and the increasingly energised black community organised and fought back.

In the ensuing violence, hundreds were injured and at least 15 people died. This was the only time in the history of US race riots that more white people (10 in total) had been killed than black people but it was just the start. Two days later in Norfolk, Virginia, a week-long celebration of returning black soldiers was interrupted when, following reports of a punch-up, white police overreacted and went in to make arrests sparking a riot which ended in the military being deployed; in the ensuing carnage two people were shot dead and six others wounded.

A few days later, on a baking hot Sunday summer's day, 27 July 1919, a 17-year-old Chicagoan hotel porter called Eugene Williams decided to go paddle boarding with friends on Lake Michigan. Inadvertently straying across the invisible line from 'coloured' 25th Street beach and into the 'whites only' 29th Street area, his very presence enraged white people on the beach who responded by throwing stones at him. Eugene fell into the water and drowned and as friends from the 'coloured only' side went to retrieve his body, the police were called. Once again, instead of arresting the white suspects who had been throwing stones, they handcuffed the black men trying to apprehend them and bundled them off to jail – and now all hell broke loose.

Across the following days, demonstrators took to the streets demanding justice for black lives. Most of Chicago's African-American population lived in the so-called 'black belt' on Chicago's South Side and soon white mobs were descending on the area and setting fire to homes and businesses.

Al Capone's new friend, the corrupt, recently re-elected Mayor William Hale Thompson, responded by deploying 2,800 of the metropolis's 3,500 cops in the neighbourhood. That made matters considerably worse because hardly any police were left to enforce the law anywhere else and across the following 24 hours, violence and vigilantism reigned. In total seven people were stabbed, four black men were shot dead, one white man was killed and 37 others were seriously injured and, in response, more protesters in the black belt came out to fight back.

Come Monday 28th, with the mayor and police having failed to contain the disturbances, Governor Frank Lowden sent in the state militia and across the next two weeks, one of the worst race riots in American history played out. By its end, hundreds of homes had been destroyed, shops and properties had been looted by white gangs and 38 people were dead with 537 injured. The pandemic, following so closely as it had on the heels of war, had only added to the tension as it had underlined the disparity between communities in terms of social justice and exposed failures of public health.

And that was the case elsewhere too.

In India, the 'Spanish Flu' took an estimated 15 million lives – more than anywhere else in the world. South Asia had lost 75,000 to the war too and their sacrifice on behalf of the British Empire was already being written out of the narrative as studiously as that of African-Americans in the USA, causing further discontent that would lead irrevocably to independence in 1947. In the meantime, the British authorities introduced the Rowlatt Act, aka the Anarchical and Revolutionary Crime Act in March 1919 – an emergency law which gave the police the power to arrest pretty much anyone they pleased. The ensuing protests and appalling overreaction by the imperial authorities informed the Jallianwala Bagh (Amritsar) Massacre on 13 April, when General R.E.H. Dyer ordered soldiers to fire on hundreds of peaceful demonstrators killing between 379 and 1,000 children, women and men. That huge disparity in estimated figures is down to propaganda and counter-propaganda – by both sides – but either way, this was an appalling human rights atrocity.

By April 1920, the pandemic was over and while few people in the world had gone untouched, almost immediately everyone conspired to forget it.

Some of the reasons for that are obvious.

For those who had fought in the war it was easier to fetishise and romanticise all the glory, tragedy and lingering antipathy it entailed than to linger on a flu virus that could not be explained. Artists, novelists and film-makers, like the general public, tended to revisit the Somme or Gallipoli or the great romantic saga of 'Lawrence of Arabia' rather than the enervating truth of the influenza virus that took so many more lives.

But in multiple ways, the pandemic altered the course of the century that followed.

Firstly, many nations were spurred into setting up proper pandemic preparedness schemes as a result and there is a strong case that the pandemic resulted in the subsequent establishment of the first state healthcare systems. It informed slum clearances across the world too and led to governments pumping money into medical research and immunisation programmes. The study of viruses and their classification into 'A' and 'B' classes and the innovation of the first flu vaccines, first used in 1944, which all resulted from the event, have saved an estimated 150 million lives and extended life expectancy globally by about 35 years. But people rarely notice progress until it is taken from them – and beyond those hugely significant effects, the impact of the two years of hell was largely imperceptible to the public at large.

Some art was inspired by the pandemic too. T.S. Eliot wrote most of his masterpiece, 'The Waste Land', while recovering from its assault on his immune system in December 1918. The line 'I had not thought that death had undone so many', lifted from Dante and repurposed to describe the new hell, along with:

'He who was living is now dead,
We who were living are now dying.'[36]

This clearly speaks of the fevered experience of flu and survival. The

Norwegian artist Edvard Munch produced two works 'Self Portrait with the Spanish Flu' and 'Self Portrait after the Spanish Flu' in response. Fellow artist Egon Schiele, then just 28, began working on his own response, 'The Family', which showed himself and his wife (in fact portrayed by an ex-lover) glumly sitting in the early stages of illness, but she died before he finished it – and he followed her three days after that.

A handful of novels, biographies and even some films made passing mention of the event. Robert Graves, who got the virus twice, touches on it in his wartime reminiscence *Goodbye to All That* and even claimed to have seen the ghost of his mother-in-law, who had herself died from the influenza, before coming down with it a second time. Graves was writing a poem, 'The Troll's Nosegay', at the time and would later claim that the work saved his life, for despite having a temperature of 105 degrees F (40.6 degrees C), he was determined to finish it.

He succeeded and lived until 1985.

* * *

On 31 January 2020, a huge crowd of thousands of people gathered in Parliament Square in the heart of Westminster in London to celebrate the United Kingdom's departure from the European Union. The UK had voted, by a margin of 52 per cent to 48 per cent, to leave the EU almost four years earlier but political infighting and drawn-out negotiations had meant that it was only happening now. As the clocks counted down to the departure and as a recording of Big Ben's bells rang out across the square, the moment was met by the popping of corks, a blast of 'Rule Britannia' off some speakers and much merriment among the assembled Brexiteers.

In a televised address, Prime Minister Boris Johnson called it 'a moment of real national renewal and change . . . the dawn of a new era'.

And he was inadvertently right, for that very afternoon, doctors in London had tested two members of a family and confirmed that they were the first cases of the novel Coronavirus (Covid-19) in the country. Within days, thousands and then tens of thousands were falling sick and some ended up on life support. As cases mounted across the next two weeks, Conservative politician and former MEP, Daniel (soon to be Lord) Hannan, penned an article for *Conservative Home* magazine which he shared on Twitter on 19 February saying:

'The Coronavirus isn't going to kill you. It really isn't.'

He was wrong. On 5 March a woman in her seventies became the first confirmed victim of the pandemic in the UK and by the end of the month, over a thousand people a day were dying of Covid-19; as it burned across Britain, even the 55-year-old prime minister was struck down with the illness too.

As a result of the Spanish Flu crisis 100 years earlier, pandemic preparedness plans were in place in most countries, but as experts sought to warn and advise, their words were disregarded by populist politicians, press barons, right-wing news presenters and self-styled experts on Facebook, who suddenly knew more about pathogens and the safety of vaccines than the entire collected forces of mainstream science. As governments sought to impose mask mandates and social distancing measures, many a president and prime minister seemed more worried about the optics and the impact it would have on their poll ratings than the safety of the public. And much the same went for many a business leader too.

And once again, nations started to performatively close their borders – as the blame game intensified and scapegoats were sought.

As in 1918 and 1919, there were conspiracy theories, race riots, coffin shortages and those who said that there was nothing to worry about or, worse, that the virus had been created in a lab and spread by enemy agents or those working for the deep state. There were even people who compared face masks to 'muzzles' and who set out to protest against the health measures and social distancing that had been put in place to stop the spread of the disease and save lives.

The story of our pandemic is therefore a familiar one. Like every plague before it, it is also a tale of the best and worst of us. A story of misinformation, of head-in-the-sand populism, of bad politics, poor leadership, denial of evident truths and the dismissal of expertise, and as in 1918, matters were only made a whole lot worse by vested commercial interests, the scapegoating of minorities and rampant ignorance and stupidity. But extraordinary things happened too and good things may well have come out of it. We are so close to events that it is not up to me to say what they are yet, but undoubtedly this pandemic has revolutionised the way millions of people work and many of us too were reminded of the important things in life. Beneath all the fear-mongering and paranoia, it showed the inherent good within our species from the science that developed an mRNA vaccine in record time to our ability to act collectively to adapt and cope when a global catastrophe hits.

It was another kind of lesson too. And more specifically one that demonstrated the importance of understanding the past.

History's purpose is to warn and to guide and without it, we are but blinkered naïfs, stumbling about, lost in the dark.

CHAPTER NINE

ILLEGAL IMMIGRANTS

The Enemy Within

About 75,000 years ago, a group of perhaps just a few hundred people stepped off the coast at what is modern-day Djibouti and swam, waded and drifted across the narrow strait to the other side until they reached the place now called Yemen.

Why they left Africa remains a matter of speculation. They may have been forced out by droughts, caused by an extreme climate event or some other natural or human disaster which led them to go looking for a new home, or maybe driven by that innate instinct we call wanderlust, they simply hit the coastline, looked at the water, figured it was shallow enough to cross, and kept going. What happened next is a matter of ongoing debate and conjecture, and while Yemen is broadly assumed to be the 'ground zero' point for the departure from Africa, even that is contested. However, DNA plotting suggests that in time the descendants of this first group of migrants headed east and throughout the Upper Paleolithic era they dispersed along the Asian coastline. As they went they continued to eat the same diet of berries and fruits they had enjoyed back home in Africa. They gazed at the stars. They invented superstitions. They began to formulate complex language. They laughed, cried, fell in and out of love, had children and grandchildren and buried their dead. And as they pushed onwards, they and their descendants and their descendants' descendants kept diverting from each other until about 45,000 to 60,000 years ago, a group reached the modern-day Indonesian archipelago.

Back then 'South East Asia' was one gigantic land mass and the islands of Borneo, Java and Sulawesi belonged to a bloated peninsula we now call 'Sundaland'. To the east sat Nusa Tenggara and beyond that lay another continent – Sahul – consisting of Australia, Tasmania and New Guinea and the islands of the Torres Straits. Having paddled across the sea, perhaps in dug-out canoes, these ancestors of modern-day Aboriginal people were then prevented from going any further by the Pacific Ocean – and stopped.

At roughly the same time, another significant migration of humans, descended from that same original bunch of African people who had crossed the Red Sea 40,000 years previously, started arching back the other way and entered Europe from around 42,000 BCE onwards. The oldest human remains discovered thus far on this continent were found in the Peştera cu Oase, or 'Cave with Bones', a remote underground river system in southwestern Romania, in 2004. They date from about 33,000 years ago and there is evidence that these migrants overlapped and interbred with Neanderthals, who had lived on the continent for the previous 350,000 years.

The first modern humans planted their feet on Britain about 40,000 years ago but did not hang about. The islands of the archipelago were then a gigantic tundra and the ice ages had rendered everywhere north of the Watford Gap a frozen wasteland of glaciers and snow. The Neanderthals had long been driven out of the region by the freezing conditions and it wasn't until about 10,000 years ago that people started to come in any numbers, via Doggerland, which until 6500 BCE connected the modern-day island to the rest of the continent.

'Cheddar Man', the fossilised skeleton of one of these first Britons, discovered in a cave in the Cheddar Gorge in Somerset in 1903, lived in the region in *c.*8000 BCE and courtesy of his high-quality preservation, we know quite a bit about him. DNA extracted from his bones reveals that he was of Middle Eastern extraction, had blue eyes and may have had very dark or even black skin. That last revelation and the subsequent discussion around it, when first revealed in 2018, caused predictable outrage in some quarters in Britain, with some suggesting that it was impossible to estimate the colour of skin tone from DNA and others insisting you could at least make an educated guess. Quite why anyone would care so deeply about the colour of an ancient ancestor's skin is anyone's guess, but either way, a comparison with the genomes of modern-day humans with British ancestry suggests that Cheddar Man's people contributed their DNA to ours and we retain around 10 per cent of it.[1] In other words, around one in ten people of British descent may share an ancestor from among his people.

About 4,000 years after Cheddar Man died, Britain experienced its first proper wave of human migration, as Neolithic farmers from Europe moved here and started leaving tantalising traces of their culture, including Stonehenge, which was built *c.*3100 BCE. About 650 years after it was erected in *c.*2500 BCE, the so-called 'Beaker people' pitched up in Britain by boat from Western Europe and began a new era in our island's story. These people, like those Neolithic farmers before them, probably had lighter shades of skin and eye colour[2] than Cheddar Man, but, again, that currently remains a bit of a guessing game.

If you are of British descent then these Bronze Age 'Bell Beaker people' – so called because they made bell-shaped pots – are likely among your more distant ancestors. The Bell Beaker people originated in the Iberian Peninsula but ended up just about everywhere in Western Europe too so if you wanted to get highly creative with the family history, you could probably claim that you're a little bit Portuguese too.

From thereon in, British history very much resembles comedian Stewart Lee's famous 'Comin' Over 'Ere' comedy sketch, but in reverse. The Beaker people were followed by those of the 'Atlantic Bronze Age Culture', which saw Western Europe exchange ideas, people, languages and goods, and a remarkable degree of homogenisation across the region. They intermingled with and were possibly usurped by Iron Age 'Celts', a broad term given to people who shared a common culture, language and belief system. Those people then witnessed Romans, Anglo-Saxons and Jutes, Vikings and Normans arrive before European Jews, Flemings, enslaved African people, French Protestant Huguenots, Poles, Germans, Russians, South Asians, Chinese, Ugandans, Jamaicans, Russians and people from just about everywhere else added to the melting pot in varying degrees and numbers. And for most of history they came here by boat.

Many of those movements were of course fiercely resisted. The Saxons, most famously under King Alfred, took up arms against the Norsemen who were encroaching on their land, but 400 years earlier the Saxons themselves had clashed with the Romano-British, who in the early fifth century sought military help from Emperor Honorius to repel them, and when it failed to come, deposed their local Roman leaders.

William the Conqueror's invasion of England and defeat of Harold Godwinson in October 1066 is generally seen as the start of the new era of 'English' history – but William himself did not exactly arrive to a shower of confetti and the granting of the keys to the nation. In an early display of cross-cultural misunderstanding, his men also burned down surrounding buildings and massacred hundreds of his new subjects in London on his Coronation Day – 25 December 1066 – because he and his men had yet to learn the language and didn't understand that the locals were shouting his praise.

Despite William being the very definition of an 'illegal immigrant' who explicitly came here to displace the 'indigenous' people who had in fact supplanted the other people who had superseded those before them, many people continue to openly boast about being descended from him. King Charles III is not alone in claiming lineage from the man who was known in his time as 'The Bastard', and former prime minister David Cameron, the comedian and television presenter Alexander Armstrong, former president Bill Clinton and the *Guardian* journalist John Crace[3] are among those who have established a link. In fact, millions of other people alive today are also his direct descendants too but simply don't know it. That's because most of us only tend to look in the rear-view mirror of our family history and do not consider the much longer journey that went on before it. Most of us know who our grandparents or even great-great-grandparents were, but beyond that, things get a little hazy and very few Britons will know for certain, for example, who all (or any) of their (probably eighteenth century) 64 great-great-great-great-grandparents are or where they all came from.

We may seek to define ourselves by our near present and a couple of key names – but in human terms this is the thin film of moisture on top of the colossal iceberg of our family history that lies below.

And while we may have forgotten who the vast majority of our antecedents are, all we can say with any certainty is that we are all descended from fighting-age immigrants and invaders who came here on boats.

* * *

Britain declared war on Germany on 3 September 1939, but in the next eight months of the 'phoney war' that followed, nothing much happened – and quite frankly it was all a bit of an anti-climax. As the novelty of night-time blackouts wore thin and the nation's petrol tanks ran dry, the British people began to endure the combined offensive of rationing*, conscription and unalloyed boredom. Contemporary wags dubbed it '*sits-krieg*' or the 'Bore War' and these were particularly tough times in Fleet Street, where newspaper editors had to make do with what little excitement they could find. So they made much of the undeniably important but frankly underwhelming French and British naval blockade of Germany and a big deal about the first air raid on Britain in November 1939 – when the Luftwaffe dropped four bombs on a peat bog near the remote village of Sullom in the Shetland Islands and claimed their first victim: a rabbit.

The news cycle livened up briefly when on 8 November, a German carpenter called Georg Elser tried to assassinate the Nazi leader by concealing a bomb in a pillar at the Munich Bürgerbräukeller beer hall. But unfortunately, Hitler left earlier than planned and the device killed unintended targets instead. Elser was taken to a concentration camp where he died five years later.

What Fleet Street needed, more than anything else, was a good war story and they found it finally in the dramatic pursuit of the *Admiral*

* Petrol was rationed from the start of the war. Staples like bacon, butter, sugar and eggs followed in January 1940 and across the next five years, chocolate, sweets, silk and clothing all followed.

Graf Spee in December 1939. The mighty 'pocket battleship*' had sunk nine cargo ships in a three-month killing spree in the Atlantic before a squadron of British warships chased it down to a final confrontation near the mouth of the River Plate – just off the coast of Argentina and Uruguay. The story was breathlessly reported by the British media and the scuttling of the ship on 17 December and the fate of Captain Hans Langsdorff, who shot himself in the head in a Buenos Aires hotel room several days later, made for sensational copy.

Unfortunately, with the *Graf Spee* half-submerged at sea and Langsdorff dead, the excitement was over and as the new year loomed, papers began casting about once again for something to fill the pages. And it was only in January 1940 that the problem was finally solved courtesy of the 'fifth column scare'.

The term was relatively new at the time, having been coined three years earlier in 1936 during the siege of Madrid, in the Spanish Civil War, when the fascist General Emilio Mola had boasted that he had not four but 'five' columns under his command, as they included a subversive outfit in the city who were waiting to rise up in support of him. The notion of 'fascist fifth columns' would go on to create significant paranoia in the rest of Europe, where the growing fear of the 'enemy within' became the major conspiracy of the time, before finally making it across the Channel to Britain at the height of the 'phoney war'.

At 10.45 a.m. on Thursday 18 January 1940, two huge explosions rocked the mills at the Royal Gunpowder Factory at Waltham Cross, just north of London. The massive blasts killed five workers instantly and three bodies were burned so completely that no trace of them was ever found. The shocking event was seized on immediately and newspapers as far away as Queensland reported that:

'A vast trail of ruin marked the course of the furious blast from two explosions, which roared over the countryside like a hurricane. Steel girders were thrown 500 yards; reverberations were heard at Leamington Spa – 50 miles from London.'[4]

* Essentially any German cruiser with large-calibre guns.

The same paper reported that 'sabotage is suspected' while the British *Daily Telegraph* breathlessly added: '*Scotland Yard warned of Nazi Plot! Works visited this week by detectives.*'[5] In fact, experts rapidly established that the explosions had nothing to do with German agents or saboteurs and were instead the result of a terrible accident – one of dozens of deadly incidents at the site in its 300-year history. But details were mere trifles to a hungry press in need of a good meaty war story and in the 'fifth column scare' the papers had found something to fill column inches so they ran with it. Soon the right-wing *Daily Sketch* and *Sunday Express* were making it their patriotic duty to alert the public to the danger of the 'enemy within', and began spreading spurious tales of Nazi spies, working under the cover of refugee status, carrying out acts of sabotage to hamper the British military war effort. Several times, the London Police Commissioner was directly cited as the source and twice Air Vice Marshal* Sir Philip Game was obliged to deny that it was true.

The *Sunday Dispatch*, with a circulation approaching a million copies a week, went particularly overboard. According to the rag, a fifth column 'made up of Fascists, Communists, peace fanatics and alien refugees in league with Berlin and Moscow' was plotting atrocities and the pacifist Peace Pledge Union was active too, working as an underground cell that sought to endanger 'the very life of the nation'.

As calls mounted for 'something to be done', the politicians busied themselves by asking each other questions in the Houses of Parliament.

'Would it not be far better to intern the lot and then pick out the good ones?' Colonel Henry Burton MP for Sudbury enquired in the Commons on 23 April 1940, in a debate which also featured a discussion as to how much of a fascist Sir Oswald Mosley, leader of the British Union of Fascists, actually was and whether he too should be incarcerated.[6] It might seem remarkable to us, at this distance, that the antisemitic, wannabe British dictator was still at liberty in 1940 but incredibly, the diminished British Union of Fascists (BUF) continued to operate freely

* Game was the last military figure in the role – which from 1953 was held by a career police officer.

until the fall of France that year and Mosley remained at liberty, protected by his fame, his perceived popularity with 'ordinary people', his connections and his immense privilege. Although if the ghastly sixth baronet's story serves any purpose at all it does, I suppose, provide proof that Britain most certainly did have a 'fifth column' in 1940, only it had nothing to do with the Peace Pledge Union and its roots ran deep into the establishment.

Mosley's lavish first wedding to Cynthia Curzon in 1920, when he was still a Conservative* politician, had been attended by King George V and Queen Mary, and he was friends with many other very powerful and influential people. The original 'man of the people' who 'said what everyone was thinking' had a thick wedge of support in the country too and in the 1930s the British Union of Fascists (BUF) had a membership of between 40,000 and 50,000. Two newspapers associated with the party, *Action* and *The Blackshirt* (until 1936) provided a platform for supporters – much as modern Facebook or Telegram accounts might do today – and promulgated the message of hate against Jews, communists, socialists and other 'undesirables' across the country while allowing readers to agree with each other's appalling opinions on the echo chamber that was its 'reserved for readers' letters page. *Action* even advertised merch on its pages and subscribers could buy 'silver and black enamel sleeve links' for three shillings and sixpence or a 'paste diamond flash brooch' for that very special fascist lady in their lives.

Mosley's second wedding to Diana Mitford in October 1936 took place in the drawing room of Nazi propagandist Joseph Goebbels' home in Berlin and was attended by guest of honour Adolf Hitler, but still this dangerous individual got a largely free pass, while his wife was lauded as a great 'society beauty'.

As late as July 1939, just six weeks before the outbreak of war, Mosley held a mass rally at Earls Court, attended by 30,000 – which remains the largest indoor political event ever held in British history. In the early

* Mosley later sat as an independent MP before joining the Labour Party in 1929. Increasingly disillusioned with socialism he formed the New Party in 1931 before establishing the BUF in 1932.

days, the baronet had powerful supporters in the mainstream media too and in the early 1930s, both the *Daily Mirror* and *Daily Mail* were active in their defence and promotion of him. The aptly named Harold Harmsworth, the First Viscount Rothermere from 1919, was initially a massive fan and in 1934 the *Daily Mail* published an infamous piece by him entitled 'Hurrah for the Blackshirts!'. Harmsworth (henceforth Rothermere) subsequently became disillusioned with Mosley after violence broke out at a rally in Olympia that same year but continued to profess admiration for Hitler and Mussolini, believing that Britain should ally with them to fight communism.

Following the 1930 German federal election, when the Nazis won 107 out of 577 seats, Rothermere, writing in the *Daily Mail*, claimed that Hitler's Nazis 'represent the birth of Germany as a nation' and his support remained steadfast right up until the eve of war – when it was no longer tenable.

Rothermere was far from alone in appeasing and supporting Nazi Germany in the 1930s and many among Britain's ruling aristocracy harboured admiration for Hitler. The vicious Duke of Westminster, former boyfriend of Coco Chanel and then the richest man in Britain, was an out-and-out fanboy. The former King Edward VIII, who following his abdication in 1936 became the Duke of Windsor, met the German leader with his wife Wallis in 1937 and in May 1939, made a broadcast from France calling on Britain to come to terms with Germany. Both Windsors were fascist sympathisers and the former king – who was Governor of the Bahamas from 1940 to 1945 – actively plotted to put himself back on the throne while encouraging Hitler to bomb Britain into submission.[7]

Diana Mosley's society sister Unity was an out and out fascist too. Having been a debutante, who was presented to King George V in 1932, antisemitic Unity moved to Germany in 1934 and began stalking Adolf Hitler in Munich before becoming a close friend and possibly even his lover. She shot herself in the head in the English Garden in Munich in September 1939 out of despair at her homeland declaring war on her beloved Nazi Germany and was left brain-damaged although she did not die until 1948. Her sister Diana, who outlived her fascist husband by

23 years, refused to condemn Hitler, who had once dubbed her and Unity his 'angels', to the bitter end – of which more later on.

So yes, Britain did indeed have a fifth column in 1939 and 1940, only it was not the one that the press was going after in early 1940 – but it was instead deeply embedded in the ruling upper classes.

But back in 1940 everyone in the press sought largely to ignore that because, let's face it, immigrants always make a far more appealing target than attractive people, in nice clothes, with fancy hereditary titles.

As the 'Bore War' turned to 'War War', things began to step up a pace and the newspapers did their worst with few more central to the whipping up of fear and loathing of the enemy within than George Ward Price, a celebrity journalist (aka 'special correspondent') at Rothermere's *Daily Mail*. On 24 May, as the British Expeditionary Force retreated towards Dunkirk, he wrote a piece entitled: 'Act! Act! Act! Do it now!' which said:

'All refugees from Austria, Germany and Czechoslovakia, men and women alike, should be drafted without delay to a remote part of the country and kept under strict supervision . . . as the head of a Balkan state said to me last month: "in Britain you fail to realise that every German is an agent. All of them have both the duty and means to communicate information to Berlin."'[8]

Price was as big a hypocrite as he was a fascist. No idle onlooker to events across the previous decade, he had co-founded, with Oswald Mosley, the January Club, a far-right 'debating' society which had been set up explicitly to garner support for the BUF from establishment figures. He was not only a close friend of the British fascist leader but had also interviewed Adolf Hitler several times too. That in and of itself would not have been a problem if his interviews had not gushed with praise for the Nazi dictator.

Three years earlier, in 1934, Price had accompanied Rothermere to Berlin where the two men had been generously entertained by Hitler, Goebbels, Goering and Joachim von Ribbentrop. His fandom secured, in 1937 he penned a memoir *I Know These Dictators*, about his meetings with Mussolini and the German leader, in which he wrote:

'To law-abiding citizens the Nazi Government brought public order, political peace, better living conditions and the promise, some fulfilled, to make Germany once more a great nation.'

Price, in short, was not just a fascist but a long-time influencer for the global fascist cause and yet now – in 1940 – all of that was mysteriously forgotten as this self-promoting popinjay went after the 'Nazi' foreigners in Britain who posed such a threat to the nation.

Beverley Nichols (Oxbridge), another celebrity journalist, writing in the *Sunday Chronicle*, added his own thoughts on the 'fifth column' and what needed to be done:

'I have German friends, but I would very willingly see them all behind bars and I have told them so to their faces. Why should we be blown up as we are walking over a bridge, unless it is strictly necessary?'

Failing to explain why it might ever be 'necessary' to blow someone up while they were crossing a bridge he continued:

'The letters readers send about Germans . . . would make your hair stand on end. Particularly women. There is no dirty trick that Hitler would not do, and there is a very considerable amount of evidence to suggest that some of the women – who are very pretty – are not above offering their charms to any young man who may care to take them, particularly if he works in a munitions factory or the public works.'[9]

Noël Coward, who knew Nichols well and thus thought very little of him, would later waspishly remark that the celebrity journo was someone who had 'observed much and understood little'[10] – but unfortunately, back in 1940, this poor excuse of a man was an influential opinion former, adept at fomenting hysteria and through it, shaping public fears and government policy. You will probably be unsurprised to learn that like Ward Price, Nichols harboured out and out fascist sympathies too and had also spent a full decade cosying up to Mosley and his henchmen. In his 1937 book *News of England*, he wrote that the BUF leader was:

'The only man [. . .] who has in him the qualities of that hero for whom the country has waited so long and waited in vain.'

Nichols was, in short, an appeaser whose admiration for European fascism was obvious right up to the moment that it became unfashionable. So, to say that there was a certain paradox in Rothermere, Nichols, Ward Price and others now ringing alarm bells about the (supposed) fascists in the nation's midst whom they had spent years building up would be the understatement of the century. But do it they did, and apparently without so much as a backward glance, and the British public, displaying a singularly impressive propensity to forget what the very same people had been telling them just a few weeks earlier, lapped it all up.

Side by side with their admiration for the Nazis, the right-wing British press in the 1930s also promoted the depressingly dim-witted and very recognisable trope that Britain was 'full'. Now, with the British Expeditionary Force in retreat on the Continent, they started to add that many if not all of those who had made it here were probably spies hell-bent on sabotage or worse. Between 1932 and 1939, an estimated 250,000 Austrians, Germans, Czechoslovakians, Hungarians* and others had fled their homelands as fascism had engulfed Europe. By war's start, 75,000 had made their way to the UK and while many were freshly arrived, quite a few had already settled down and made lives for themselves here. Most, although by no means all, of them were of Jewish heritage and despite all the post-war lauding of the nation's selflessness in helping them, Britain's record was singularly undistinguished from the start.

Throughout 1938, Lord Beaverbrook's *Daily Express* published articles saying that it was too easy for Jews, and others fleeing persecution, to get into Britain and that the government was operating an open-door policy which simply let 'anyone' in. In language familiar to those of us living in twenty-first-century Britain, the paper particularly questioned the motives of the young men who made it here and who now wanted to work:

'There is no room for the Jews in Britain, where we have 1,800,000

* Hungarians were not interned until 1941 when Hungary formally entered the war.

of our own people out of work . . . there are plenty of uninhabited parts of the world . . . where they may yet find happy homes.'[11]

The US-born Conservative MP Nancy Astor, who – despite being an immigrant herself – hated immigrants, declared that there were 'too many Jews' in England. And the Conservative government itself did everything in its power to show that it was being 'tough on immigration' by creating what nowadays we might call 'a hostile environment' for those who made it. The widespread, postwar assumption that the British state acted magnanimously is thus, I am afraid, a myth. Ordinary people were brainwashed into thinking that migrants were taking advantage of lax laws, that Britain was a 'soft touch', and that many refugees were not 'genuine'; and they believed it, because they read it in the very press that was simultaneously sucking up to Adolf Hitler.

After the horror of Kristallnacht in November 1938, when German state-sanctioned violence against Jewish people saw synagogues and businesses destroyed and hundreds murdered, the mood softened – but only slightly. As a nod to shifting sentiment, the government reluctantly allowed 7,700 German Jewish children in under the kindertransport scheme, but their parents were not included in the offer, which was extended on the strict understanding that the British Jewish Community would fund it all and place no burden on the taxpayer. Most of the parents and older siblings who were left behind would subsequently be murdered in the Holocaust.

In July that year, as the crisis in Europe intensified, Roosevelt's US administration organised a conference at the Spa town of Evian in France and invited delegations from 32 nations to come and discuss the refugee problem. Across the next nine days, representatives from all the world's major powers took turns to stand up and say what a terrible mess it all was, as well as what a tragedy, before adding that they could not possibly do more than the next to nothing that they were doing already. Although not much noticed in the UK at the time, Australia reluctantly agreed to take in 15,000 refugees over the next three years – and that would prove critical as to what happens later in our story.

With the outbreak of war, in September 1939, the British government set up the Aliens Department of the Home Office and established 120 local tribunals across the country to register and examine the case of every single enemy alien over the age of 16 in the land. The vast majority of these were centred on the nation's cities – where most of the refugees lived.

Those interviewed were then classed according to the perceived threat they posed:

A – those deemed to be a security risk, who were then interned immediately.
B – exempt from internment but subject to restrictions by Special Order.
C – exempt from both restrictions and internment.

Some 40 years later, one anonymous interviewee, whom we shall call 'Frank', would explain what happened next to the author Peter Grafton:

'*We were in Newcastle upon Tyne when we came up before a tribunal. The chairman was some Colonel or other . . . very suspicious of Jews but more so of Social Democrats or Communists. My father had always been a devout atheist and liberal Social Democrat but he didn't let on, fortunately, on my advice. I was sent out and they interviewed my parents. My father spoke practically no English. They decided to classify me as "C" because I'd lived in England long enough. With my parents, it was different. First of all, what proof did my father have, short of my word, that he had been in Buchenwald? Though the British were willing to stamp his passport "Refugee from Nazi oppression" he was classified "B" which meant he couldn't move outside 5 miles of his home. He was deeply hurt by this.*'[12]

The machinery of this asylum system moved with remarkable efficiency and by the time of the Waltham Cross explosion in January 1940, some 73,000 people had been interviewed and categorised. The vast majority – some 66,000 people – were classed 'C', while 6,700 were given 'B' and 569 'A' status. Of the approximately 55,000 Jews who had fled tyranny and were now domiciled in the UK most were classed 'C' or 'B'.[13] However, as the press whipped up fear of 'fifth columnists' and as public opinion hardened in the face of rationing and conscription, what limited sympathy there was vanished. As the British Expeditionary Force (BEF) was hounded towards the French coast in May 1940, genuine fears of an imminent Nazi invasion loomed large, as growing panic replaced the former ennui. Neville Chamberlain resigned on 9 May and Winston Churchill became prime minister the following day.

Almost immediately, Churchill began to address the spectre of the enemy within and while it is easy to be critical at a distance of 85 years, we need to remember that the future was unwritten in 1940. While Churchill knew that Hitler was unlikely to attempt an invasion of Britain, the fear among the general population was real and widespread, and despite the myth of 'keep calm and carry on', many people in the UK were genuinely terrified about what would happen next. Some sought to flee the country altogether. My grandmother was one of those who had enough money to do so and taking my 10-year-old Uncle David, she headed west to Bermuda, where they became very comfortable refugees in the home of an old friend. Although of course British people aren't ever allowed to be dubbed that – so we call them and others like them 'evacuees' instead.

They were not alone. By 25 July, some 224,000 applications had been made for the evacuation of British children and the Minister for Information, Duff Cooper, was being criticised in the House of Commons for sending his own son to Canada.

Fear and love can make hypocrites of us all.

Two months earlier, and just a few weeks before Dunkirk, Churchill had given the order for a thick swathe of 'coastal belt' to be declared out of bounds to 'male aliens' and any of them unlucky enough to be dwelling within it and aged 16 to 70 were promptly rounded up and put behind barbed wire. As the weekend commencing 11 May was the Whitsun Bank Holiday, thousands of people had popped down to the coast for a few days by the sea and the foreigners among them now found their sojourns upended as they were put in the backs of trucks and driven off to prison camps.

Across the next four days, around half the 'B's were rounded up too but, in the chaos and general atmosphere of classic British jobs-worthiness, many a completely innocent person was now imprisoned alongside them. Eric Schmidt – a teenage boy who had lived in Britain with his English-born mother since he was one – was among their number and that, despite his older brother serving in the British Army.[14] Schmidt was taken to one of the six transitory camps on the Isle of Man and was later deported to Australia.

Many were reassured that they were not being targeted personally and that it would all be sorted out fairly quickly so that they could then go back to their lives. And later on many of these individuals would insist they were well looked after. Twenty-one-year-old Gunter Altmann, who penned an account of his experience while interned in New South Wales, was one of them:

'In general, we were treated quite decently. We could buy newspapers every day and soldiers could also get us cigarettes, chocolate, fruit etc from the soldiers' canteen. A few times, our Sergeant Major drove to Bournemouth to buy us toiletries and books.'[15]

Unfortunately, many of these campsites were not fit for purpose. They included racecourses, like Lingfield Park in Surrey, where prisoners were housed under the protective awning of the spectator stands – and they lacked heating and basic facilities. But as they lingered there and as the German war machine cast its dark shadow, that was the least of their worries because, ever more, they were becoming the focus for collective hate and there were calls for action to be taken against them. By the time Gunter was transferred to the Huyton camp in Liverpool, he had noticed a singular change in attitude:

'The conduct of the military authorities . . . is very different to how it was . . . Major Wright says at one point: "you are refugees you have no rights whatsoever" and we are treated accordingly.'[16]

The fear and loathing was egged on, once again, by the popular press. As a *Daily Herald* headline screamed 'Secret Swoop on 30,000 Germans!' it was left to a dwindling band of sensible MPs to call for sanity to be restored. Those willing to speak out included the Independent MP Eleanor Rathbone (English Universities), the Conservative Major Victor Cazalet (Chippenham) and the formidable Glaswegian

Labour politician, David Kirkwood. But by the mid-summer of 1940, the number willing to defend the migrants was dwindling as rapidly as the nation's supply of razor blades and bacon.

On 4 June, in his famous 'Fight on the beaches' speech, Churchill talked of the urgent need to intern all those who might 'become a danger or a nuisance':

'Parliament has given us the powers to put down Fifth Column activities with a strong hand,' Churchill said, *'and we shall use those powers, subject to the supervision and correction of the House, without the slightest hesitation until we are satisfied, and more than satisfied, that this malignancy in our midst has been effectively stamped out.'*[17]

It was later claimed that Churchill told his colleagues of his intention to 'collar the lot!', and while I can find no evidence that he ever uttered those words, certainly, the sentiment was there. The Labour leader Clement Attlee, now serving as the Lord Privy Seal, agreed with the prime minister and argued that it was now in the interests of national security to *'transfer overseas a number of the enemy aliens . . . in order to reduce the general dangers which might arise from having large numbers . . . concentrated in a comparative small number of camps.'*[18]

On 10 June, Benito Mussolini declared war on Britain and that meant that 20,000 Italians living in Britain became part of the 'fifth column' too. While some were undoubtedly fans of Il Duce, many of them had lived in Britain for decades and were integrated into their communities, but overnight and in the fevered atmosphere of the times, they became the enemy. Chip shops and ice cream parlours, restaurants, market gardens and other Italian businesses were attacked and about 4,000 men were arrested and carted off to the camps – with many taken across the Irish Sea to the Isle of Man.

Among their number was 31-year-old Carmine Monforte, the director of Strand Milk Bars who later in life as Lord Forte would become one of the UK's best-known businessmen running franchises including Little Chef, Happy Eater, the UK branch of Kentucky Fried Chicken and Travelodge. Another was a Paisley hairdresser, Alfonso Conti, whose son Tom, born in 1941, would go on to become one of Britain's most famous postwar actors.

On 25 June, France capitulated and that same day, the order was given – under Defence Regulation 18b – to round up all the male class 'C's under the age of 70.

'Frank' explains what happened next:

'There was (a) knock on the door at 6:00 a.m. A couple of detectives said "would you please accompany us to the police station?" All three of us, my father, my brother and myself found ourselves in the internment books. Females were not included in that internment order (so my mother was left behind) . . . She never heard from us – for a long time.'[19]

Two weeks later and without fanfare, a requisitioned passenger liner called the SS *Arandora Star* slipped out of Liverpool docks with a cargo of human beings on board including 734 recently interned Italian men, 479 Germans, 86 German PoWs as well as 374 crew and guards. The government had decided to start removing the 'enemy within' by dispersing them to Canada and elsewhere. Several days later (there is some confusion as to when exactly it left) and about 70 miles off the coast of Ireland, the ship was struck by a single torpedo, fired by the German U-boat U-47, and started to sink. While 868 passengers were rescued in a heroic action by the Canadian destroyer HMSC *Laurent*, 805 drowned and the following month, hundreds of dead bodies began to wash up on Ireland's west coast. The next of kin – including those of the crew and military escort who died – received not a penny of compensation, as in 1940 those who abandoned ship or were drowned at sea were subject to the 'ship sinks, pay stops' rule of the merchant navy.

The Minister for Shipping, Mr Ronald Hibberd, later reassured the House:

'I am informed by my right honourable friend the Secretary of State for war (Anthony Eden) that all the Germans on board were Nazi sympathisers and that none came to this country as refugees. None had category B or C certificates or were recognised as friendly aliens.'

It was completely untrue but the lie would remain unchallenged for months.[20]

The *Arandora Star*'s fate had demonstrated, if nothing else, that it was unsafe to send an unescorted ship full of men west across the Atlantic, so instead the British government decided to send them south instead. Just seven days after the ship was sunk and in a demonstration of mind-blowing insensitivity, the survivors were transferred to another transporter at the very same set of docks in Liverpool from which the *Arandora* had departed and were informed, in perfunctory manner, that they were being sent to sea once more.

Their home for the next seven weeks was the HMT *Dunera* and though they did not know it, they were about to embark on a voyage into hell.

* * *

Launched in 1937, the British India Company-owned *Dunera* passenger ship had been leased to the government as a 'Hired Military Transport' (HMT) since the start of hostilities. With a maximum capacity of 1,600 passengers and crew, it was now loaded with 2,542 prisoners plus 309 crew and guards from the 'Pioneer Corps'.

Most of the cargo of prisoners were made up of racial and political refugees aged 16 to 45 who had fled fascism in Germany, Austria, Czechoslovakia and elsewhere. Several older men were also put on board, with the oldest being about 65. In the febrile atmosphere of the times, no distinction was made between these genuine refugees and the PoWs with whom they slept cheek by jowl. These other passengers included 451 'A'-class internees who were all considered dangerous although in fact some of the 'A's were social democrats and communists who had also fled Hitler – only to end up being dubbed Soviet fifth columnists in the UK.

Extraordinary as that might seem now, British officialdom assumed that the 1939 Molotov–Ribbentrop non-aggression pact between the USSR and Nazi Germany had made 'German communists' allies of the National Socialists (Nazis) despite many of them being victims of the tyranny too. The hoary old myth that Hitler's fascists were 'left-leaning' indeed may have partly taken root there and that, despite the Nazi leader repeatedly stressing that he despised communists, claiming in interviews that the term 'socialist' was only in his party's title because he was 'reclaiming' it on behalf of the German people.

In fact, in addition to the systematic murder of six million Jews in the Holocaust as well as millions of 'undesirables' including Romani people, Slavs, homosexuals and even Freemasons, the Nazis also imprisoned and sometimes killed tens of thousands of political opponents, and the first 27,000 concentration camp inmates in 1933–34 were exclusively trade unionists or members of the Communist and Social Democratic Parties.

Such distinctions were now but a detail, in wartime Britain, and everyone was thrown on board together.

Some refugees were tricked into getting on board the *Dunera*. Told that they'd have a better life elsewhere – without the restrictions on their freedom that they faced in the UK – and that the rest of their families would follow, they had eagerly bound up the gangplank. None knew where they were going, or if and when they would come back, but many naively imagined they were being sent to Canada or the USA and thought it could be an opportunity to embark on a better life.

Lording over the embarkation operation from the brig and dressed in a kilt, stockings and military cap was Acting Lieutenant-Colonel William Scott and beside him stood his fellow Scot and deputy, First Lieutenant John O'Neill. On paper, O'Neill was a bona fide hero. As a Sergeant in the 2nd Battalion, Leinster Regiment, during World War I, he had won both a Military Medal and later a Victoria Cross when in October 1918 he had charged and overwhelmed an enemy field battery and two machine gun positions in the course of a week. O'Neill had subsequently had the VC pinned on his chest by King George V himself. On leaving the army, he had then worked as a coal miner but found life on civvy street too dull and so re-enlisted in the RAF, where he briefly served as a Sergeant Armourer alongside a certain John Hume Ross – later exposed as T.E. Lawrence who was living, not very successfully, under an assumed name. Come the start of World War II in 1939, the 42-year-old O'Neill re-enlisted once more – this time in the Pioneer

Corps (AMPC)* as a 2nd lieutenant – where he swiftly proved himself to be an out and out thug.

Each prisoner embarking on the ship was allowed 36.3 kg of luggage, which for most of them amounted to just about everything they owned. The many Jews and dissidents who had already suffered the unimaginable indignities and violence of German concentration camps now faced torment all over again – but this time at the hands of the British troopers – as O'Neill and Scott looked on.

As a report, later submitted by internees to the High Commissioner in Australia, stated:

'Everything carried in the hand or in pockets was taken off the internees. All less-valuable effects . . . were thrown on the ground. Valuables were stuffed into sacks or disappeared openly into the pockets of the searching soldiers. Soon rows of emptied wallets were lying on the deck. Valuable documents, identity and immigration papers, testimonials of all kinds, were taken away, thrown on the ground or even ostentatiously torn up before the eyes of their owners . . . Appeals to the officers standing by were fruitless. Attempts at protests were roughly suppressed . . . All these searches were . . . accompanied by acts of violence and resulted in the loss of an enormous amount of money, valuable articles, toilet necessities, and important documents.'[21]

A Viennese-born prisoner on the ship called Ernst Fröhlich wrote in his diary:

'We were searched by robbers in uniform. They took away not (just) cigarettes and chocolates (but) money, watches, jewels, fountain pens, everything they could get hold of.'[22]

Colonel Scott informed some prisoners that he would personally look after their belongings, only for those items to vanish as well.

Some tried to hide their valuables in their shirts and underwear only to be shaken down. When a refugee called Moritz Chlumetski came on

* The Auxiliary Military Pioneer Corps was a unit of the British Army created to perform light engineering tasks and logistics: building defences, removing rubble, carrying stretchers and moving supplies. They were ill-suited for the role of ship guards and not trained to do the job.

board, clutching his son's valuable violin, it was taken off him by two guards, one of whom then smashed the unfortunate man's foot with the butt of his rifle when he complained. Having had all his precious belongings taken from his person for 'safe keeping', K.J. Koening, a Prague-born lawyer, requested a receipt, only to be told 'you can trust a British officer.'[23]

He never saw his effects again.

Though united in their fate, the men on board inevitably drifted into cliques. There were Sudeten German communists, described by one fellow inmate as a 'rough and intimidating lot' who nonetheless immediately organised a latrine and deck-cleaning rota. Then there was a large group of orthodox Jews, who clung to their Talmuds and Torahs, as well as numbers of German and Austrian secular Jews, political refugees, Italians and 'Nazi Nordics' who were suspected of being U-boat prisoners. Dr Peter Huppert, later to become a celebrated Sydney physician, also noted a clique of 'Oxbridge' types who spoke and acted like refined English gentlemen 'at Henley' and who insisted Monty-Python-like that all of this was perfectly normal and understandable and, more, that it would soon be rectified by the British authorities.[24]

A small but significant number of those on board were intellectuals and artists, and the guards took particular delight in bullying them. The author, Rene von Podbielski, who was carrying the first and only existing draft of a novel he had spent years writing, had it ripped from him and tossed into the sea. Ulrich Alexander Boschwitz, another novelist on the ship, whose book *Der Reisende* ('The Passenger') became a minor publishing sensation when it was rediscovered and reprinted in 2010, suffered the same fate, and the first draft of his book *Das Grosse Fressen* ('The Big Feast') was also thrown overboard.[25] The Orthodox Jews made for an easy target too and throughout the course of the onward journey, many would be forcibly separated from their religious texts, skull caps and prayer shawls, which were then flung into the ocean. Holders of US affidavits were also targeted and had the precious documents – which allowed them onward transit to America – seized from them and torn up in front of their faces.

Several passengers – including an Austrian film actor called Sigurd Lohde – had been put on the ship by mistake. Lohde was destined for the Isle of Man and when he realised that he was heading in the wrong direction, had sought to leave the *Dunera* and board the correct boat only to be ordered to 'Get going'[26] and marched back on board at the point of a bayonet.

Things were about to get a whole lot worse and in the words of the journalist Cyril Pearl, across the next seven weeks the ship turned 'in effect, into a floating concentration camp'.

Two days into the journey, while still in the Irish Sea, a German U-boat fired two torpedoes at the *Dunera*. The first struck its hull with a violent thud but did not explode; the second slid underneath as the ship bounced over a wave in violent seas. The men on board – many of whom had survived the attack on the SS *Arandora Star* – twice held their breath and the ship ploughed on south towards the Atlantic.

Conditions on board were squalid at best. Most of the men were obliged to sleep on the floor as there were barely any hammocks to go round and, having been separated from their luggage and toiletries, the prisoners mostly wore the same clothes for the seven-week voyage. The salt water daily washed over them and took its toll on their already threadbare shirts and trousers and by the time they arrived in Australia, many would be, quite literally, in rags. Issued with one bar of soap between twenty and one towel between ten, they were expected to wash in sea water too and without the means to clean themselves properly, the stench of human sweat and squalor intensified with every passing day. Matters were made far worse by the lack of toilets – just ten among the thousands of prisoners on board – and, within 24 hours of leaving port, a putrid stench was drifting up from the clogged latrines.

Drinking water was severely rationed, even as they passed through the heat of the tropics, and the food soon became inedible. The smoked fish, potatoes and sausages they were supposed to live off swiftly ran out and the men subsisted instead on soup and stale bread, topped off with rancid butter. The artist Fred Schonbach would later recall removing 'the bodies of little white maggots' before tucking into his mug of broth.

By stark contrast, their tormentors ate well and just to rub the prisoners' noses in it, took to ostentatiously throwing their leftovers into the sea in front of the half-starving men.

The sneering 2nd Lieutenant O'Neill VC allowed his men to behave how they wished and throwing food overboard was frankly the least of the Pioneer Corps' sins. The rank and file guards, almost to a fault, were violent and unpredictable goons. On one occasion, early in the voyage, a refugee who tried to go to the toilet in the middle of the night was stabbed with a bayonet and began to bleed profusely. He was taken to the ship's hospital and treated and fortunately, the injury was not life-threatening but it was far from the only incident of extreme violence on board. Another prisoner who complained that a guard had stolen his belongings had his hands handcuffed behind his back and was beaten to a pulp while another soldier smashed his foot with a rifle.

'Now you will be fucking sorry you spoke!' the Sergeant – a thug called Albert Bowles – told him.

Leo Roth – one of the younger internees on board – was awoken early one morning to find a soldier trying to pull the gold signet ring off his finger. Caught red-handed, the infuriated trooper responded by dragging the young man to his feet and marching him to the bathroom, where he set about lathering Leo's hand with soap until he could force the ring off. Roth's finger was nearly broken in the process and he too wound up in the sick bay, where the doctor, Lieutenant Brooks, was so shocked by his account of what had happened that he sought to make an official complaint. Scott ignored him. Another man who reported that some diamond earrings and a brooch had also been stolen was told by a certain Sergeant Helliwell to 'get away with you now' and was threatened with solitary confinement in 'the bunker' if he continued to protest.

The 'bunker' was a three-cell lock-up and the scene of more torment. Very early in the voyage, one young prisoner, who dared to voice objections about the food, was taken there and thrown inside. He remained in solitary for the next 30 days.

One night, the Viennese Bauhaus artist Georg Teltscher – who would later design the 'camp currency' in Australia – had a panic attack.

Rushing upstairs and struggling for breath, he was promptly set upon by members of the AMPC, who beat him to a pulp. When he reported it to the senior officers, no action was taken.

Another prisoner, Dr Hans Fleischer, who saw a corporal steal a platinum watch from a fellow refugee, made a written complaint to Colonel Scott on his behalf, only to be visited by the thuggish Sergeant Helliwell and other NCOs, who menaced him into silence. Later, Scott himself loftily informed Fleischer that to believe him or the complainant would amount to trusting the words of a mere 'enemy alien' over those of a British soldier.

As the resentment stacked up, the ever-more magisterial Scott loftily told the detainees that he did not want to be bombarded with reports of the theft of 'their alleged property'. In a speech to his men shortly afterwards, he actively encouraged the thievery and told them that 'if we were in the position of our guests, after being searched, we would be lucky if we had our belly buttons left'.

In the same speech, he added:

'I close my eyes to any little petty offensive purloining articles. I am an old soldier and I know that the British Tommy looks upon a time like this as an opportunity to help himself to any unattended trifles.'[27]

Psychological bullying was rife. The survivors of the *Arandora Star* were repeatedly told that if this ship went down, they would all die – as every night, the troops deliberately battened down the hatches to stop them getting out in the event of an attack.

Later on, some of those who suffered so badly at the hands of the AMPC men would seek to make sense of it. Koening would point out that as events were playing out in a period of intense uncertainty, the intimidation may have been an outward expression of inner fear and anxiety by men who were ill-equipped to deal with such emotional trauma. Many of these soldiers had been evacuated at Dunkirk and had families back in England who now faced bombing or invasion. On board the *Dunera*, they perhaps saw the opportunity to take revenge on the 'Hun' and offset these inner demons.

Even O'Neill may have had his reasons because it is likely that he was a victim of latent PTSD. Back in October 1918, he had won his VC the day after learning that his much-loved younger brother[28] had been killed in action. The news had apparently sent him into an unbridled fury and his comrades at the time had assumed that his subsequent actions had been driven by primal hatred of the enemy caused by the death of his brother.

Others have made no such apologia and instead have concluded that these men were nothing more than standard-issue thugs for:

'. . . *on occasions when army units were requested to make personnel available for special duties, commanding officers took the opportunity of getting rid of undesirables, and so it happened that the scum of the British Army became the guards of internees on board a ship.*'[29]

In addition to the Pioneer Corps, there were several hundred 'Lascars' on board – some among the thousands of Indian and South East Asian sailors who served on British ships from pre-Napoleonic times until the end of World War II. They kept themselves apart and interacted little with the Europeans on board, although rather typically Scott would later seek to blame them for the thieving and maltreatment of the men in his care.

With the ship so dangerously overcrowded, exercise was limited to a half-hour each per day and the motley band of men and boys would walk barefoot in a circle as machine gunners trained their weapons on them – in case of mutiny. On one occasion, a drunken guard was said to have thrown a broken bottle at them and when it smashed on the deck, they were ordered to run over it barefoot. The onlooking soldiers and Lascars laughed even as several bloody-footed victims were carried off to the sanitorium.

Quite why O'Neill and his men thought they would get away with this shocking behaviour was probably down to the apparent indifference of the man at the top. Colonel Scott had given them licence to behave appallingly and none seem to have paused to consider that some of those on the ship might later complain. After all, among those on board were some very eminent figures indeed, including 39-year-old Hein Heckroth, a Giessen-born artist who had shot to fame in Weimar Germany as a celebrated set designer and costume designer. Hein's wife, Ada, was Jewish and that had informed the couple's decision to move to Britain in 1935 to escape Nazi oppression. In England he had worked as the principal set designer at Glyndebourne Opera's first season, before becoming an art teacher at the 'progressive' school at Dartington Hall where he was arrested in the 'collar the lot' round-up of spring 1940. Following his return to the UK, Heckroth would collaborate with director Michael Powell and his Hungarian co-creative Emeric Pressburger on some of their most famous films of the era including *A Matter of Life and Death* (1946), *Black Narcissus* (1947) as well as costumes and sets on the groundbreaking *The Red Shoes* (1948).

Also on board was Walter Freud, grandson of Sigmund, the famous Austrian neurologist and psychoanalyst who had fled with his extended family from Austria following the *Anschluss* in 1938. Walter would later return to Britain, join the Special Operations Executive and rise to the rank of major before playing a key role in exposing Nazi atrocities and the use of Zyklon B in the murder of millions of Jews.

Other famous and yet to be famous names on the 'passenger' list included Peter Stadlen, the Austrian pianist, composer and musicologist, and Franz Stampfl, who would become the late twentieth century's most famous athletics coach after he trained Roger Bannister to run the first four-minute mile in 1954. Stampfl was one of the survivors of the *Arandora Star* and had trod water in the freezing Atlantic waters for eight hours before being saved.

Hans Kronberger, who would become one of the fathers of the British atom bomb, was also present, as were many distinguished academics, scientists and lawyers who would later make significant contributions to postwar British and Australian society. These were, in short, educated, sophisticated and, in some cases, very well-connected people and all of them were keeping mental notes.

As the miserable journey continued, these and the other men on board took to entertaining and educating each other. Some made music, or wrote poems and song lyrics; others gave lectures on everything from politics, to economics, to natural history. They held debates, delivered English language lessons and even wrote a PoW constitution, penned on a roll of precious toilet paper. Even in the deepest darkness, some find the light, and a group of cheerful, predominantly younger men dubbed 'the Unquenchables' did their best to raise their fellow passengers' spirits while seeking to ingratiate themselves with Scott and his officers – in order to glean information and better rations.

Dark humour abounded. The ship was nicknamed the 'pick-a-pocket battleship' and many popular songs were given new lyrics including the *Dunera*'s very own version of 'My Bonnie Lies Over the Ocean', which now went:

'My luggage went into the ocean,
My luggage went into the sea,
Bring back, bring back,
Oh, bring back my luggage to me!'[30]

They also tried to work out where they were going. Using a school atlas and the stars and sun above their heads, the journey south was plotted by some while others sought to guess what was happening in the world beyond. Scott had imposed a total news embargo on the men – a particular psychological torment at a time when so many loved ones were in Europe facing the full throes of war – and matters only improved slightly when the *Dunera* reached South Africa and a newspaper was smuggled on board. The precious rag was dissembled line by line by the former anti-Nazi and anti-communist 'influencer' Dr Franz Borkenau, who then broadcast what news he had gleaned from his hammock.

None of it was 'good'. The Battle of Britain was raging, Europe was conquered, fascism was winning, hope was in short supply.

Having rounded the Cape of Good Hope, the men now realised they were destined for Australia and still had many miles to travel. As the ship chugged ever more eastward, dysentery and the contagious bacterial skin condition impetigo ran rife. It all became too much for some who began to talk openly about suicide.

On 21 August, Jakob Weiss, an elderly man who had had his visa (in this case to Argentina) ripped up in his face, walked off the side of the ship. One of three men to die on board the ship, his body was never recovered. The other two were Hans Pfeffern – a 53-year-old Austrian judge who had fled the *Anschluss* only to die of a heart attack in the *Dunera* sick bay – and Felix Mann, who officially died of injuries sustained from 'falling down some stairs'. But nobody seriously believed that.

If Colonel Scott, Lieutenant O'Neill, VC, and the men in their command were turning out to be the true villains of the piece, the ship's doctor, Lieutenant A Brooks, was rapidly becoming its hero. Like O'Neill, Brooks was an old soldier who had fought in the Great War. Having escaped a PoW camp he had gone on to qualify as a doctor in Aberdeen in 1925, become a GP in Monmouthshire and then, 14 years later, re-enlisted to serve in World War II. When recruited to serve on the *Dunera,* Brooks was told that he was on a 'secret mission' and believed he was heading to Egypt, but soon found himself caring for beaten-up refugees instead. Brooks, his confidant, the ship's captain Frederick Caffyn and First Officer Smith, increasingly sought to help the men in their charge, but did so in the face of stiff opposition from Scott, O'Neill and their henchmen.

On 26 August, the ship reached Fremantle on the coast of Western Australia and when Customs officials came aboard they were appalled to find hundreds of ragged men in squalor. Complaining about the conditions in the strongest possible terms, when the boat set sail again, on 31 August, Scott was wired by the Australian PoW Information Bureau who demanded to know what was going on. The colonel responded in typically lofty fashion and wired back that apart from the gripes of a few troublemakers, everything was in order.

At the end of his long missive of self-justification, he added a 'personal note' regarding his opinion of those on his ship:

The Nazi PoWs, though 'highly dangerous', were in his own words 'of a fine type, honest and straightforward, and extremely well disciplined . . . their behaviour has been exemplary.' By contrast, the Italians were 'filthy in their habits, without a vestige of discipline, and are cowards to a degree'. But he reserved the lion's share of his contempt for the German and Austrian Jews who were, in his opinion: 'subversive liars, demanding and arrogant . . . they are definitely not to be trusted in word or deed'.[31]

Being at sea for a long period can have a curious effect on the mentality of both crew and passengers. The world beyond can in fact feel suspended altogether but now, as the ship rounded the coast of Australia, it started to encroach on them again. Scott's stolid self-belief, so reinforced by the long absence of land and others in authority, clearly started to crack and three days after that first message, with paranoia and voyage's end both looming, he fired off another telegram. Now it was the South Asian 'Lascar crew' who were to blame for all the thieving and looting on board and it was they who were beneath contempt.

The *Dunera* reached Melbourne on 3 September and Sydney Harbour three days after that, with her arrival making front page news. The (Australian) *Daily Telegraph* reported that 'among the internees were parachutists, other prisoners of war, and hundreds who had been carrying out subversive work in England.'

Australia, so removed from the war in Europe, was hungry for news and the men from the Pioneer Corps, who were veterans of Dunkirk, were greeted like heroes. Scott basked in his new-found celebrity and laid a wreath at the Sydney Cenotaph in Martin Place. Later, he was granted an audience with Australia's Governor-General, Lord Gowrie, VC. That same day, 9 September, Scott paraded his men in the Sydney Showground and thousands turned out to watch. He also addressed a hand-picked audience from Legacy, the Australian organisation for those who had lost loved ones in World War I. Imbued with equal degrees of undeserved self-regard and made up horse shit, the kilted Scott audaciously told them that fifth columnists had posed a real threat to Blighty and that in the early stages of the war: 'British motorists were found guiding German bombers to anti-aircraft guns and searchlight emplacements by headlights, but that had now been dealt with.'

A few days later, 13 internees were put back on board the *Dunera* and quietly repatriated to the UK. They included Franz Borkenau and Walter Freud. Borkenau would go on to write and make German language broadcasts via the BBC. Freud would become a member of the Special Operations Executive and in that guise, was parachuted into fascist Austria on a secret mission in April 1945.

The rest of the prisoners were transported 750 kilometres west to the small, isolated town of Hay deep inside the Australian bush. There, they set about making the best of things by formalising that toilet-roll constitution and publishing an in-camp newspaper *The Boomerang*, whose cheerful tone belied the many horrors they were still facing.

Its opening letter from the editor ended with the moving line:

'Please remember that your mind is not interned, nor is it confined to this camp.'[32]

Meanwhile, the artist Georg Teltscher set about creating a camp currency and eventually there were three denominations of paper notes and metal coins, equivalent to two shillings, one shilling and a sixpence. A local printer eventually stepped in and offered to make the money himself, which the prison authorities then tried and failed to stamp out. Wrapped within the barbed wire on the design for the sixpence note was a further profound hidden message:

'We are here, because we are here, because we are here.'

Soon the camp was witnessing a veritable outbreak of creativity. Internees sketched, painted, made guitars and violins, formed clubs, put on Shakespeare plays and vaudeville entertainments, built a stage and a rudimentary theatre and brought the light in. Peter Stadlen formed a choir and gave piano recitals which were much enjoyed by the inmates, despite the dilapidated state of his instrument. Someone even set up a rudimentary distillery and managed to make knockout hooch.

In marked contrast to the troopers of the Pioneer Corps, the Australian guards turned out to be largely kind and sympathetic. Although Major Grace, nicknamed 'Disgrace' who was the officer in charge of the camp from January 1941 onwards, was viewed as a pompous and arrogant tyrant, the men under his command were another matter. While researching this chapter, I corresponded with the daughter of one internee who remembers her dad, Felix, talking very fondly of these often elderly and fatherly 'diggers' who happily distributed treats and cigarettes to the younger prisoners in their charge and treated them with respect.

Unfortunately, such largesse and generosity of spirit was not evident beyond the camp and soon the same sorts of bigots who had spoken out in the UK were voicing their ugly rhetoric in Australia. One of the most prominent was Archie Galbraith Cameron, the former Postmaster

General and now leader of the right-wing Country Party, who was also a member of the wartime cabinet and a Major at the Directorate of Military Intelligence at Army HQ Melbourne. Cameron began to mutter darkly of the risk posed by the foreigners in the internment camps saying:

'One of the best jobs Adolf Hitler ever did for Germany was when he drove (the Jews) out of the country. Yet we welcome them here. We should not go to a great deal of expense over people who come here to save their own skins.'[33]

Cameron did not have to do much to stir up the hate as Australia had experienced its own anti-migrant hysteria in June and July. At a meeting at Redfern Hall in Sydney on 4 June, the former premier of New South Wales had suggested that Australia's 'fifth column' could well be 'bigger than the Australian army'[34] and within weeks of the *Dunera*'s arrival the perceived threat that the Hay camp internees posed to Australians had grown exponentially.

Fortunately, there were plenty of decent Australians who were willing to step up and help and chief among them were the Society of Friends. The Quakers did their best to clothe, feed and raise awareness of the Hay camp inmates and their cause and the prisoners too set about publicising their plight by writing to the authorities in both Australia and the UK. Collectively, they compiled a 7,000-word report and managed to get their case heard in the UK Parliament. There, Colonel Josiah Wedgwood, the former Liberal and now Labour MP for Newcastle-under-Lyme, highlighted the cause and so too did the *Manchester Guardian* newspaper and by late January 1941, Winston Churchill had apparently forgotten all about his part in the deportations and was calling it all 'a deplorable and regrettable mistake'.

Arriving back in England, on 20 May 1941, Scott faced a general court martial at the Duke of York's barracks in Chelsea and was seemingly unfazed when his 'belly button' speech was read back to him. Scott had not realised that in addition to the doctor and the ship's captain, he had had another 'traitor' on board – a Major Motherwell of the Pioneers, who had ordered a lance corporal and former professional shorthand clerk to take down the Colonel's speech word for word.

During proceedings Scott claimed the major and the corporal had made it up – and the court believed him, striking down the first charge that he had made an 'improper speech' to his men.

On the second charge, of 'failing to hold a proper inquiry' into the violence meted out on an internee, he was found guilty and was sentenced to be 'severely reprimanded' – a fairly light punishment which was basically akin to being 'grounded' for 14 days or slapped on the wrist.

Sergeant Helliwell faced four charges. Two of assaulting prisoners, a third of failing to safeguard a refugee when he was assaulted by his men and a fourth of disobeying orders and failing to provide food, water and blankets to his prisoners. Despite the mountain of evidence, Helliwell was found guilty only on the fourth charge. He too was 'severely reprimanded'.

Acting Regimental Sergeant Major Albert Bowles MM faced 21 charges of theft. Admitting that he had been caught handling other people's valuables, he claimed he had 'found them on the deck'. His commanding officer and the key witness for the defence – a certain Lieutenant Colonel William Scott – stoutly defended his senior NCO and told the court that his 'character was beyond reproach'. Despite that Bowles was made the scapegoat. Found guilty of two charges he was reduced to the ranks and jailed for a year.

Nothing happened to John O'Neill, perceived by many of the men on board to be the main ringleader. Fate caught up with him instead, and he died of a heart attack the following year, aged 45. Twenty years later, on 13 February 1962, his VC and other medals would be stolen from an auction house and have never been recovered. In 2004 the Leinster Regiment made arrangements for a Victoria Cross to be displayed on his headstone at the Hoylake Cemetery in Cheshire. Nowhere in the contemporary local news accounts, or indeed on the Leinster Regiment's webpage, was mention made of his time in the AMPC, or his actions on the HMT *Dunera*.

In the forging of any satisfying mythos of war, a ruthless edit is always required. Which is also why, in the UK at least, almost everyone swiftly forgot that the voyage had ever happened at all.

About half the *Dunera* boys were eventually shipped back to Britain but not all of them made it. On 8 October 1942, while returning via

Cape Town to the UK on the troop ship MV *Abosso*, the author Ulrich Alexander Boschwitz, released from internment at the Hay camp several months previously, was killed when the ship was hit by a torpedo. The 27-year-old was carrying the manuscript of his last novel *Traumtage* with him, and both were lost to the sea.

* * *

Many of the internees who stayed behind volunteered to serve in the 8th Australian Employment Company, which was in effect the Australian equivalent of the Pioneer Corps. Come 1945, 700 of them chose to remain in the country and in time some of these fighting-age 'fifth columnists' rose to become some of the most influential people in the country. They included the famous economist Fred Gruen, Australia's celebrated composer Felix Werder, the physicist Hans Buchdahl, the artist Robert Hofmann and Henry Talbot, who in 1956 set up a studio in Melbourne with friend and fellow internee – Helmut Newton – kickstarting the careers of both men.

Others went on to build new lives and businesses and homes and the close friendships forged in such terrible circumstances lasted many of them for the rest of their lifetimes. The *Dunera* boys would hold reunions and events and their story in time became part of the fabric of postwar Australian history even as it was forgotten back in Britain.

Many of the internees who returned to the UK were only too happy for that to happen, and my correspondent's father Felix rarely if ever talked about it to his family. He was not alone in that.

The tale of the *Dunera* is, after all, a deeply disconcerting one – not least because it runs counter to so many comforting sagas that we in Britain like to tell ourselves about what 'we' did in the war. It in fact upends the satisfying postwar narrative of Britain being the eternal hero of the hour and more pertinently it ruins another, far more modern myth, too. For here, after all, is a stark reminder that brutality and villainy are not unique to other people or other times and that those demonised 'fighting-age men on boats' can in fact turn out to be both the victims and heroes of the narrative.

CHAPTER TEN

ERASED

The Inconvenient Villains

The role of the historical villain is never straightforward. For as we have seen, while some might be wholly deserving of the epithet, others have had it thrust upon them, simply for upsetting some ignoble king or ruining a lovely parable. Many of history's bad guys are undeniably attractive, others repulsive, wicked and despicable; some serve as a litmus test of the mores and morals of their time while others simply become a part of the entertainment landscape. And then there are those who for whatever reason end up on the cutting room floor.

These are the 'Inconvenient Villains' of history and the businessman and lawyer George Remus was just such an example.

Born in Berlin in 1876, Remus was six when his parents, Marie Louise and Carl, left the Old World for the new and having settled in Maryland they moved to Chicago so that Carl could find work. George was a bright child and when his father's search for gainful employment descended instead into alcoholism, the eldest son stepped up and went to work for his uncle, as a pharmacist's assistant, to provide for the family. Diligent, honest and hard-working, the business grew and he grew with it, until eventually he bought his uncle out.

George had greater ambitions than to be a mere peddler of talcum powder and aspirin and was determined to make it big. So, alongside his burgeoning business empire, and having married his sweetheart Lillian, he took a law degree and was called to the Bar in 1900. Subsequently, George was to become one of the brightest and best-known figures on the Chicago legal circuit and swiftly gained a reputation as a 'crusading lawyer' and a master of 'loopholes', who was dubbed 'the man about town with the moonlight smile'[1] by the local press.

George and Lillian had a daughter, the fantastically named Romola Remus, in 1900 and she was very much a chip off the old block. A precocious child, aged just eight she became the first actor to ever play Dorothy Gage in an ambitious multimedia production of L. Frank Baum's *The Wizard of Oz* for Selig Polyscope Pictures and she would go on to make further silent movies alongside fellow Chicagoan luminaries including Harold Lloyd before quitting the business at the top of her game, aged nine, when Selig moved to Hollywood.

By that point, George Remus was not only running one of the most successful legal practices in Chicago but one of its biggest drug store chains too. Adept at switching on the charm, he became ever more popular with the press – even as his marriage fell apart. On 6 March 1915, he filed for divorce from Lillian, leaving her and Romola for a young divorcee – Imogene Holmes. Imogene and her daughter Ruth went to live with him while Lillian began telling anyone who would listen that behind closed doors, George was a wife-beating bastard.

Four years later, in 1919, Prohibition became law and as bootlegging took off, George's work began piling up until a curious thing happened. For as Remus represented moonshine makers, smugglers, hoods and other assorted felons, he came to appreciate that almost all of these criminals were completely out of their depth. Few had a strategy in place beyond getting alcohol and selling it to speakeasies and their rank incompetence gave him an idea. Determined to put the 'organised' back into organised crime, Remus became a bootlegger himself and he went on to make a fortune.

Under the Volstead Act (as you may remember from Capone) the production of alcohol was allowed for 'medicinal purposes' and appreciating that there was a fast ride to a quick buck, Mr Loophole began to exploit it. Realising that 80 per cent of the nation's 'bonded distilleries' – that is, ones that were licensed to still operate – were based in and around Cincinnati, Ohio, he moved his operations there, bought up legal distilleries, started selling his whiskey, completely legitimately, to his own drug companies and then used his own supply chains to distribute it.

George and Imogene grew fabulously rich and built a vast mansion outside Cincinnati, with a huge and ornate indoor swimming pool, a ballroom and a massive dining room where they entertained guests lavishly. Their wild and extravagant parties were the stuff of legend and at their 1921 New Year's Eve bash, gentlemen guests were given diamond-studded stick pins and their partners brand new Pontiac cars as going-home presents. If it all sounds reminiscent of a famous Jazz Age book, well yes; Remus was one among a number of people whom F. Scott Fitzgerald had in mind when he penned *The Great Gatsby* in 1924.

By 1921, George Remus was worth an estimated $40 million ($700 million in 2025 money) but it was all to end in something worse than tears. In 1921 Mabel Walker Willebrandt, recently appointed United States Assistant Attorney General, who later had the bright idea of taking Capone down for non-payment of federal tax, got on his case like a hound on a blood trail. Four years later, in 1925, Mr Loophole came undone and Remus faced the full force of the law. While believing himself to be smarter than the combined forces of the Federal State, he had neglected to realise that he had, in fact, broken the law thousands of times, and having been sentenced to a two-year stretch in Atlanta Federal Penitentiary, he now landed in even more trouble when he made the acquaintance of a fellow inmate called Franklin Dodge. The two men, who shared a cell together, became close confidants, but that was only because the guileless Remus failed to appreciate that the man he was now entrusting with the intimate details of his life story was actually an undercover Prohibition agent.

And now events took a turn so wild and dark that if a novelist were to make it up, they might rightly be accused of stretching credulity.

Instead of using the evidence he had gathered to further indict Remus, Dodge quit his undercover role, resigned from the agency, left the prison, tracked down Imogene, started an affair with her and then set about liquidating all of his erstwhile cellmate's assets. At the same time, he began tipping off former colleagues that Remus had never actually been a US citizen and that he could thus probably be deported as an 'illegal alien' and when that failed, the couple hired a hitman – who, in turn, double-crossed them, by tipping off Remus with regard to their plans.

Fresh out of jail and discovering that he had been stitched up like a German *räucherhering**, on a scorching 7 October evening in the Indian summer of 1927, Remus lost what little cool he had ever had. Having tried to summon his second wife from her hotel to a meeting with him, only to be told she wasn't in, he then saw her exiting the building with 20-year-old Ruth. Mother and daughter climbed into a cab and drove off. Ordering his chauffeur to 'run them down', his limousine then set out in hot pursuit into Eden Park where, having spotted his car, Imogene told her own driver to step on it. A chase ensued and only ended when Remus grabbed the wheel off his driver and smashed his vehicle sideways into the taxi, causing both cars to crash. As Imogene climbed from the wreckage, Remus grabbed her by the wrist, punched her in the face, and yelled: 'You degenerate mass of clay!'

Then he shot her at point-blank range. As shocked bystanders reeled in horror, Remus fled and having hitched a lift from a passing car handed himself in to the cops who told him, to his obvious relief, that his wife had just died.

A sensational trial followed in which George Remus conducted his own defence. Portraying himself as a wronged folk hero, he claimed that he was simply a victim of a bad law and a cheating wife. Worse still he had been double-crossed by a federal agent who had claimed to be his friend and now the system wanted to execute him simply because he had done what any other regular guy would do. Pleading 'temporary insanity', triggered by his wife's infidelity, the jury took just 19 minutes to return a 'not guilty' verdict.

Presiding Judge William Lueders was not convinced however, and declaring Remus 'insane and a dangerous person to be at large' he ordered psychiatric assessments which, inconveniently for all concerned,

* German for 'kipper'.

concluded that he was no psychopath and had probably been in his right mind when he murdered his wife.

Remus took matters to the Supreme Court which upheld the original verdict and in June 1928 he walked free.

He went on to live out the next 22 years of his life in relative anonymity, running a small business in Kentucky and eventually marrying his secretary, Blanche. When he died, in January 1952, the *Cincinatti Enquirer* led with the story on its front page declaring:

'Fabulous George Remus Dies: Made millions as "The Bootleg King"'.[2]

But shortly thereafter, the memory of 'fabulous' George began to drift. At his daughter Romola's passing in 1987 there was no mention of her once infamous father in the obituaries, which instead spoke only of her mother and that first enigmatic performance as Dorothy in *The Wizard of Oz* when she was eight:

'Most recently she had been teaching music on Chicago's North Side, where she lived in an apartment with a cat, a turtle, a parakeet and her clippings.'[3]

While Al Capone has had literally hundreds of biographies, documentaries and films made about him, few have ever bothered to tell the story of George Remus and the reasons for that are themselves enlightening. First of all, George Remus did not fit the part in which he was cast. The grumpy-looking, portly, middle-aged man with a polished bald head and German accent lacked the distinctive 'gangster chic' of contemporary hoodlums and in fact, looked more like a silent-era 'Fatty Arbuckle' type comic than Public Enemy Number Two. Sensibly shunning the violence of his more famous counterparts in Chicago, he also lacked notoriety.

But crucially, the other elements of the Remus story are uncomfortable too. George Remus did not come from the outsider class of Italian Americans or Eastern and Southern Europeans, but was respectable and German and lived in upmarket Cincinnati, the 'Paris of North America'. Though his childhood was tough, he was much more a 'white collar' criminal than an immigrant bootlegger and his downfall was unsatisfying as well, because, having murdered his wife in broad daylight, he didn't face the chair . . . or show remorse . . . or indeed face any consequences – but instead, lived out his life running a small, respectable business in Kentucky. His story – though extraordinary – is thus ultimately unsatisfying as human beings hanker after stories with happy endings and failing that, tales in which the bad guy gets his just desserts.

Despite all the terrible and murderous things he did, it's clear why some remain fascinated with Al Capone. His violent yet glamorous rise and his satisfying fall at the hands of heroic federal agents is the kind of myth that can make the United States feel good about itself. It has an arc. It has a denouement. The tale of George Remus does not, and so he was forgotten.

We think of 'cancel culture' as a modern concept, but nothing is new under this sun and throughout history people have been constantly erased from the narrative. The term *damnatio memoriae* – meaning 'the condemnation of memory' – first coined in Leipzig in 1689 is a useful, albeit contentious, construct to examine the historic phenomenon by which certain figures in antiquity were apparently made to disappear from the historical record and there are plenty of examples.

Hatshepsut, wife and half-sister of the Egyptian Pharaoh Thutmose II, reigned as Queen Regnant of Egypt for about 22 years following his death in 1479 BCE. Assuming all the powers of her sibling, she embarked on a series of ambitious infrastructure projects – but subsequent to her death, her stepson Thutmose III did his utmost to erase her. Whether this was because he did not like her personally, or as a result of political necessity to assert his own masculine authority, cannot be said. Either way, she was struck from the official record of pharaohs and had her name chiselled off monuments.

In the third century CE, the Roman emperor Geta faced a similar fate when his older brother and co-ruler Caracella had him murdered by the Praetorian Guard. Henceforth, Geta's name was struck from frescoes and monuments and it became a capital offence to even speak his name.

Damnatio memoriae has befallen many figures well into the modern era too. In Soviet Russia, Stalin was forever blotting out the faces of former friends and allies from paintings and photographs until his own cult of personality became the subject of damnation following his death in 1953.

Narratives can change too of course and that can lead to once-revered heroes becoming symbols of oppression and hate. Following the fall of communism, Eastern Europe witnessed hundreds of statues to Lenin and other figures being toppled from their pillars. A more recent bout of iconoclasm has led to statues to slave traders like Edward Colston, in Bristol, or Confederate Generals in the southern states of America being brought down too – although this is less about erasing names and figures from history, more about assessing why they are there and whether it is appropriate for them to remain so. We can, of course, still remember who Stalin, Hitler or even Edward Colston were and what they did without having their effigies peering down at us. Indeed, in the case of Colston his name and deeds became more widely known, precisely because his statue was pulled down.

Some people are erased from history through deliberate effort. Others disappear, for no other reason than that they simply do not fit the narrative. And then there are those whom we seek to forget, for no other reason than that they make us feel uncomfortable about ourselves – which is why you have likely never heard of Sergeant Harold Cole.

* * *

In mid-June 1945, with the war in Europe over but its consequences still rumbling on, a British prisoner was taken to the Caserne Mortier disciplinary barracks in eastern Paris and locked in a cell. The inmate had been arrested by MI5 agent Peter Hope at the home of the French military governor in the German city of Saulgau, while posing as a high-ranking British intelligence officer, under the name of Captain Robert Mason; and the French, Americans and most of all the British wanted to question him about his wartime activities.

Locked in the fortified Caserne Mortier, Mason – whose real name was Harold Cole – soon began to ingratiate himself with his Anglo-American guard detail. Insisting that he was in fact a British spy and that his incarceration was the result of a terrible misunderstanding he soon became part of the furniture and when, in the autumn of 1945, he announced that he wanted to write his memoirs, his guards were only happy to lend him a typewriter and procure him a sheaf of paper. Soon, he was typing away merrily in his cell, but the damp conditions were not really conducive to writing such an important work, so he asked if he might be allowed to move to the nice warm guards' room where he could better complete the task. His wardens were only happy to oblige and set him up at a table in the corner of the large room, where like some heroic author in a Hollywood montage, he began to type away furiously once again.

Late on the Sunday night of 18 November 1945, having completed his day's writing he announced that he would now take himself back to his cell but first intended to nip to the toilet. Having bid his guards a hearty goodnight, he gathered up his draft and the typewriter and having nimbly picked up a sergeant's great coat from a chair along his way, strutted straight past the washrooms and out through the gate and down into the Porte des Lilas Metro Station.

Several hours passed before anyone noticed that he had disappeared and when the alarm was finally raised, furious British intelligence agents in London and Paris immediately sprang into action. A mugshot was issued and a memo was circulated. The rogue agent was 'cunning and plausible' and the coat he had stolen contained the ID and papers of a provost sergeant which meant he could move about at whim. The man at large was a 'dangerous traitor' who 'may be armed and will probably resist' and SIS (Secret Intelligence Service) offices and agents as far away as Cairo and Malta were told to keep a watch out for the escapee:

'Born London 24.1.06. Height 5 ft 11 inches. Narrow shoulders. Reddish fair-hair. Blue-grey eyes. Small head, boney [sic] *face, small mouth and false teeth. Long thin legs, prominent Adam's Apple. Has been known to pose as a British Army Officer or German or Frenchman.'*[4]

An MI5 memo, circulated in case he made his way back to the UK, added that: 'He is a very cunning and clever individual and there may be some difficulty in apprehending him.'[5]

Matters were made more complex on account of the 39-year-old Cole having multiple aliases. In just the last decade alone he had been: Captain

Coulson, Paul Delobel, Herbert Hunter, Joseph Deram, P.R.N. Corser, Richard Godfrey, Wing Commander Wain of the RAF and Captain Paul Cole of the Secret Intelligence Service. All that was really known about him was that he was a former Royal Engineers sergeant called Harold Cole and he was now the most wanted British traitor in Europe.

Cole's self-penned biography was never recovered – but given that he was a career liar you can be sure that it would have played hard and fast with the actual truth, which went something like this.

Born on 24 January 1906 at the Charlotte's Lying-in Hospital in Marylebone, young Harold arrived into a world of poverty. His parents Alice and Albert, who had married just a month earlier, lived in Hoxton, nowadays one of the most fashionable areas in East London but then one of the most deprived places in England.

One contemporary, Ted Harrison, would later sum the area up:

'Everyone was poor. You didn't get any money if you were out of work and most jobs didn't provide any sort of pension.'[6]

Most families relied on soup kitchens, the cheapest cuts of meat, charity handouts and found what work opportunities they could. Albert was employed as a barrel maker, longshoreman and bottle washer before enlisting in the 11th Battalion, West Yorkshire Regiment (the Prince of Wales's) at the outbreak of World War I. He died in England two years later as a result of wounds sustained at the Battle of the Somme and was later buried at Chingford Mount Cemetery.[7]

Little is known of Harold's relationship with his family, although a note, written while in prison in 1945, suggests he was eager to hear news of his mother and siblings. A barkeeper whom he befriended in late September 1939 also recalled him being deeply affected by the death of his grandmother, Annie Godfrey. Undoubtedly, the loss of his father would have been life-changing for the 11-year-old boy and it was probably compounded by what happened next, because within a year his mother had remarried a carthorse driver called Thomas Mason* and the family had moved to a slum on Ivy Terrace in Upper Clapton.

* Whose name he later used as an alias.

By 1923, and aged just 17, Harold was in prison. Cole, like Capone, came from the very bottom of the pile and like the New York-born hoodlum, he aspired to be, if not better, then wealthier than those in the world he had left behind. He was quick-witted, articulate, good-looking and charming, and as such made a natural con artist.

His mother's neighbour, Mr Sansom, would later explain:

'To us he was a toff – he didn't speak like us. He was a six-footer, slim built, and always well dressed. The type of person that can walk into clubs – attractive to gullible women.'[8]

Cole had a gift for knowing what buttons to press in people and those who met him tended to either instantly like or actively dislike him.

Jail was an occupational hazard and though he managed to steer clear of the clink for most of the 1930s, by 1939 he was in a cell once more. Now 33, Cole had been calling himself Waid while posing as an RAF Officer in France. There, in 1938, he had sought to fleece a British vice consul out of £50 (*c.*£3,000 in 2025) so that he could fix an imaginary plane and 'fly on to Egypt'. Unfortunately for Cole, the official saw right through him and Harold was arrested on his return to England, where he was convicted and sent to prison for six months. By the declaration of war, in September 1939, he was however free again and immediately presented himself to a recruitment office in Colchester, where he enlisted into the 18th Field Park Company of the Royal Engineers, the logistics and workshop wing of that regiment.

Harold told his comrades that he had been in the colonial King's African Rifles in East Africa and had also served in the Hong Kong Defence Force. Like all good con artists, he was always careful to insert elements of truth into proceedings and there is some anecdotal evidence that he had been to both places. Later that year, he met a fellow sapper who had also been stationed in Hong Kong – and the two men appeared to reminisce in some detail about the colony's nightlife. Later still, in early 1942, Cole had a recurring bout of malaria while in Paris, which he claimed to have first picked up during that Far East posting. So, it may have been true.

Cole's confidence and, on the face of it, winning personality made him broadly popular with the majority of men, while raising the hackles of a small, switched-on, silent minority. He was promoted to lance corporal within a week of signing up and having claimed that he was a seasoned motorcyclist, was appointed company dispatch rider. Harold, as we shall see in a moment, had a bit of a thing about motorised machines and probably wanted to get his hands on a bike – but he swiftly demonstrated that he had absolutely no idea how to ride it. On one occasion, he left a huge hole in a roadside hedge as he disappeared through it, and on another he had to be rescued from under his bike when it toppled on top of him and trapped him like an upturned turtle while he was directing traffic.

In October 1939 the company was sent to France as part of the first wave of the British Expeditionary Force, which by May 1940 would see a total of 390,000 men and women of the Auxiliary Territorial Service (ATS) billeted in northern France, largely around Lille. Cole was stationed at Loison-sous-Lens, a mining town, where he and his men were engaged in digging trenches and building defences in preparation for the anticipated German invasion. Cole hung out at a local railroad bar, where he befriended the married owner and mother of one, Madeleine Deram, whose husband was a prisoner of war. Soon they were having an affair.

By December 1939, Cole had been promoted to lance sergeant* and now had a handful of hardened enemies in the ranks. Around the same time, the unit began experiencing an outbreak of petty theft and when the non-commissioned officers' mess fund was stolen, Harold was put in charge of solving the crime, at which point, a straight-talking Yorkshireman called Martin Moran came forward and said he had seen him breaking in and taking it. The Military Police (MPs) arrested Cole and put the disgraced sergeant in a padlocked stable only for him to escape to Lille. Having been recaptured, Cole was locked up again, only to escape once more. When arrested a third time, several weeks later, he was wearing a stolen officer's uniform and carrying his victim's depleted

* Essentially a corporal being made an 'acting sergeant'.

cheque book – which he had used to wine and dine women across northern France. Cole was now locked in a supposedly inescapable dungeon in the Lille Citadel but soon wriggled out through a toilet window and was on the run in another stolen officer's uniform once more. Over the following week, in typically brazen fashion, he conducted a one-man spot inspection of nearby camps, where he was watered and fed until the MPs caught up with him once again. Imprisoned a further time, the pattern repeated and as Europe plunged towards war, Harold Cole was once more on the loose pretending to be someone he wasn't.

On 10 May 1940, the 'phoney war' ended as the German war machine tore into the neutral Netherlands and neighbouring Belgium and Luxembourg, and made rapid progress into France. The French and British were thrown into disarray and fell back towards the northern coast.

Oblivious to the war that was going on around him, Harold Cole, meanwhile, was back in La Madeleine and having tired of the constant cycle of arrest and recapture, had decided to confront the man whom he blamed for his ongoing predicament. Spotted in the vicinity of his barracks, MPs warned the Yorkshireman, Moran, that his life might be in danger and that Cole may be out for revenge.

Taking the threat seriously, Moran tied up his German shepherd dog Bette at his door and slept with a gun at his bedside only to awake one morning to the sound of his guard dog barking and to find the errant Cockney with the canine at his throat. Cole was arrested once more and sent back to the Citadel at Lille and this time the door was bolted shut behind him. He remained there right up until the moment that tanks of the advancing German army came crashing into the city a few weeks later, at which point his jailer, a man called Sergeant Buck, swung open the prisoner's cell door and said, 'I don't care a bugger what you do – we're off,' before himself heading towards Dunkirk some 40 miles away.[9]

Almost certainly as a result of deliberate choice, Cole melted into the background and as such was to become one of thousands of British soldiers left behind in France.

An estimated 40,000 Allied troops were left behind after the fall of Dunkirk, but in an oft-forgotten chapter in the history of the war, tens of thousands of British and Empire troops were then sent back into France once again – only to get stuck there once more. So when Paris fell to Hitler on 12 June, there were some 100,000 Allied service personnel in the country, and another evacuation was required. Operation Aerial, conducted between 13 and 25 June, saw many of these men evacuated from the southern and western ports of France in 416 Royal Navy, merchant and passenger ships – including the SS *Arandora Star*, which would be sunk two weeks later. In total, about 191,000 British, Polish, Czech, Dutch, Belgian and French personnel and a further 40,000 civilians were evacuated in the operation.

Satisfying monomyths abhor jagged edges and most of us have grown up thinking that Dunkirk was a final retreat, because it makes the bigger saga of Britain standing alone far more satisfying. It is very far from being the only satisfying myth of war that we have continued to believe.

France formally surrendered on 22 June but even then, not everyone was accounted for and thousands of British soldiers remained on the loose in occupied France, trying to evade capture. Some sought to make their own way across the Channel and others headed south over the border into Spain. It was to be over a month until the Germans established anything close to order and it was only then that they started rounding up Allied personnel on the run.

The heroes of the moment were undoubtedly the many ordinary French people who rose to the challenge of helping their British friends. Acts of spontaneous bravery abounded in those early dark chapters of war and thousands of ordinary men and women went out of their way to do their bit. Some gave board and lodging to those still on the loose although unfortunately these selfless acts were not always given the appreciation they warranted. There are stories galore of French citizens holding their heads in their hands as 'Les Rosbifs'* did everything in their power to repay the kindness by blowing their own cover.

On one occasion, French villagers looked on in horror as a drunken Englishman, who had been hidden in a rural farmhouse, played a couple

* Literally – the roast beefs. Broadly affectionate French slang term for the English.

of rounds of darts with a similarly inebriated German soldier in a café. Fortunately, neither seemed to notice that they were hanging out with the enemy. On others the French watched in bewilderment as British servicemen cycled merrily past on the wrong side of the road on stolen bicycles – only to get arrested further down the street. Later on in the war, MI9 (aka Room 900) – the intelligence agency tasked with organising and handling escapes in occupied Europe – would conduct training lectures for aircrews which would include the advice: 'In France you can sleep with a man, you can sleep with his wife, you can sleep with his daughter – but don't pinch his bicycle because if you do, you're off to the knacker's yard.'[10]

MI9 would also train airmen to adopt a philosophy of 'escape mindedness', which included advice on how to avoid 'looking British' and blend into the background. The organisation kept its many secrets close and banned returned personnel from giving interviews to the press on how they had escaped, while actively recruiting successful evaders including, most famously, Airey Neave – the first British PoW to make it out and home from Oflag IV-C (aka Colditz Castle) in 1942.

In May 1940, MI9's chief, Brigadier Norman Crockatt hired the remarkable Clayton Hutton, the real-life inspiration for 'Q' in the James Bond books and films, to run a sub-department that really was called the 'Q Branch'. Their work was every bit as inventive as that of their fictional counterparts and amazing kit was issued to RAF flight crews and PoWs, which included radio receivers hidden in cigar boxes, fake board games, silk maps and 2,358,853 miniature compasses embedded inside buttons and the linings of jackets that could be used to guide the way back home. But back in that summer and autumn of 1940, those trying to make it to Blighty had to rely on their wits and the help of the French public.

Greed, like duplicity, exists in the same abundance everywhere on Earth and some escaping men made easy prey for criminals out to make a quick centime or two. One soldier in Marseille paid 10,000 francs for passage to Casablanca, only to end up in Tunis, some 1,242 miles in the wrong direction.[11] It took him over a year to get home.

All this anarchy and opportunity was just made for Hoxton-born con artist Harold Cole – who now emerged from the shadows like some Orsonic anti-hero and one day, in September 1940, he cycled out of Lille and made his way to Number 1 Rue de Gare in La Madeleine where he knocked at the door. The building was home to François Duprez – a 32-year old city administrator who had kept his job when the Germans took over and who, at considerable risk to himself, was now helping British escapees get back home. Won over instantly by Cole – who was now calling himself Captain Paul Delobel – Duprez lent him a recently vacated house at Number 14 and furnished him with an official ID card. Cole moved in with his French girlfriend, the café owner, Madeleine Deram, and her 13-year-old son before approaching another Monsieur Duprez, unrelated to François, who owned some 16 textile factories locally.

Self-made Henri Duprez was an Anglophile who was now using his wealth and assets to help British servicemen. Cole told him that he was a British agent who had been sent from London to organise an escape line and Henri was immediately taken in.

'Captain Delobel' explained that there were cash flow problems at MI6 and requested that Duprez lend his fledgling organisation money. Convinced that Cole was credible and excited to be part of a real-life spy ring, Henri handed over a wad of cash but just as you might be thinking 'oh, here we go again', Cole defied all expectations and started organising an escape line. Quite why Cole, with his long history of criminality, suddenly went straight remains something of a mystery, but while every move Harold made should be treated with a fair degree of caution, it could equally have had something to do with the stifling social hierarchy of England at the time. Harold Cole had, after all, been born on to the bottom rung of the ladder and at any other period in his life, social mobility could only have been achieved through good luck, hard work or marriage. But in time of war the old structures had gone, along with all the checks and balances and Harold Cole perhaps now saw that he had a chance to become what he had long pretended to be: a hero and a gentleman.

In war, renegades can come into their own and many misfits who found their way into the SOE and MI9 orbit finally found the calling that had eluded them their whole lives. Its ranks bulged with eccentric actors and artists including future *Carry On* star (and Stalag Luft 3 PoW) Peter Butterworth, the future Goon Michael Bentine, the famous pre-war magician Jasper Maskelyne and the antiquarian bookseller Leo Marks – who would later go on to write screenplays including *Peeping Tom* (1960). But it was international and cosmopolitan in flavour too and many who joined or were recruited to its ranks were proto-Eurotrash – whose linguistic skills and knowledge of the continent meant that they could fit in on either side of the Channel.

Cole did not belong to either set and in fact was (on paper, at least) much more akin to Eddie Chapman, the safe-breaker turned Agent ZigZag, who became a key asset to the British, even as he was awarded the Iron Cross by Nazi Germany. Like Chapman, Cole was not only a member of the self-preservation society but armed with Buster Gonadian-sized balls too. So while properly trained agents sought to blend in to their surroundings, Cole deliberately stuck out. Tall, red-headed and partial to wearing pork pie hats and plus fours, he spoke French with a thick Cockney accent and might as well have had a sign pointing at his head saying 'Englishman', but Harold succeeded initially at least, because he had vast reserves of confidence and an ability to bluff his way through.

'He made you want to help him,' Jeannine Voglimacci, a hair salon owner and local businesswoman would later tell the author Brendan Murphy.

Voglimacci's husband was a prisoner of war and at no financial benefit to herself the 36-year-old agreed to help Cole get British servicemen home. Her salon and the apartment above it would become a safe house for escaping personnel over the course of the next few years and there she fed, clothed, mothered and policed 'the boys' before sending them off on their onward journey.

Escapers needed documents, which were at first provided by François Duprez and later by a printer-turned-forger called Jean Chevalier. They also required money and train tickets which were sourced by Henri Duprez and a small army of helpers. Guides too were needed and that was where a teenager called Roland Lepers came in. Lepers dreamed of being a fighter pilot and hoped that by helping Cole he would be able to make it to the UK and join De Gaulle's Free French Forces as a pilot.

On 6 January 1941, the first party set out from La Madeleine. It consisted of eight servicemen who first gathered at Cole's new home on Avenue Bernadette before Lepers and two French friends took them to the station and led them towards Marseille, which lies 621 miles (1,000 kilometres) south on the Mediterranean coast. France was now divided, sliced across its middle by a higgledy-piggledy line, which ran from the Pyrenees in the south inland to a point about 20 miles south of Tours, before heading east towards Switzerland. To the north and west, the Occupied zone was run by the German authorities. To the south and east, Unoccupied France was now a supposedly neutral country, governed from Vichy by Marshal Pétain and his collaborationist administration. The Vichy authorities – in part to seek legitimacy for their decidedly illegitimate regime – took a tough line on rogue British soldiers trying to get into the region, but if they managed to do so, they could get a ship round the coast from Marseille or across the border into neutral Spain and from there hop to Gibraltar and make it home.

An added headache, for those leaving from Lille, was that from late 1940, the city sat within 'the Forbidden Zone' between northern France and the coast and anyone leaving or entering it required an *Ausweis* travel document – of which more in a moment.

The frontier between the Occupied and Unoccupied zones was over 750 miles (1,200 kilometres) long and was relatively porous in places. Lepers had done his homework and found a safe route to Marseille. There, he headed to Le Petit Poucet, a bar on Boulevard Dugommier, where it was known that British agents hung about waiting to assist escapees. Roland soon made the acquaintance of an English army captain called Charles Murchie, who operated under the code name Murphy.

Impressed by the young man, and perhaps seeking to test him, Murchie asked Roland if he would be willing to bring his stranded wife down from Lille. Lepers had wanted to go on to the UK but realising that Murchie would be vital to the La Madeleine network, he dutifully obliged and went back north. Having located Mrs Murchie, he then brought her back down and reunited her with her husband. The grateful captain then introduced him to a fellow British officer called Captain Ian Garrow.

Garrow and Murchie were both technically on the run. Initially, the collaborationist French in Marseille had had a fairly lax attitude to the 'fifth columnists' in their midst and though ostensibly imprisoned at the Fort St Jean, during the daytime they were free to come and go pretty much as they pleased. That changed when on 7 January 1941 most of the inmates were transferred to a new camp at the military school at Saint-Hippolyte-du-Fort, 105 miles (169 kilometres) away; however, during the move some, including Murchie and Garrow, had taken the opportunity to abscond.

Murphy was a middle-aged veteran of World War I who had re-enlisted as an administrative officer in the EFI (NAAFI)* In 1939, he found that he was now the very accidental head of an escape organisation that was smuggling Allied men out of France. Having been reunited with his wife he was hoping to go home and Murchie's number two Garrow was taking over the reins. By May, Garrow was MI9's man on the ground and they would have struggled to have recruited anyone better. Tall and commanding, he inspired confidence in those who met him, even if he did have an unfortunate tendency to put too much trust in those whose paths he crossed. With no direct line of communication to London, Garrow relied on coded messages brought to him by couriers from Gibraltar and Spain and also received cryptic intelligence broadcasts via the French news service of the BBC. Much of his funding came privately from wealthy French benefactors, but it was supplemented by the financially constrained and notoriously tight-fisted MI9 as well.[12]

In the spring of 1941, Lepers told Garrow about Captain Paul Delobel,

* NAAFI – Navy, Army and Air Force Institutes – essentially the armed forces supermarket and canteen.

the British agent who ran the La Madeleine Network and Garrow asked if he could meet him. So, the next time Lepers appeared at Le Petit Poucet, he had 'Monsieur Delobel' by his side. Cole, now sporting a very natty tailor-made suit, immediately came clean and told the Scotsman that he was a sergeant in the RE who had been 'left behind' during the evacuation at Dunkirk. His appropriation of a false identity left Garrow unfazed. It was, after all, a sensible precaution to adopt a pseudonym and many had done the same. Cole told him that he had pretended to be a 'captain' in order to better smooth his credibility with the rank-obsessed French, which would also have made perfect sense.

Garrow was impressed and gave 'Agent Paul' a wad of cash to further his work. Cole was now on the intelligence map and the MI9 payroll, and had in fact become the very thing he had long been pretending to be.

Many historians and even agents within the SIS subsequently questioned why MI9, the SIS and MI5 ran no checks on the man who had now become a key figure in their escape lines. Perhaps they did and perhaps, like Eddie Chapman, they uncovered his record of petty crime and jail-breaking and thought that this made him perfect for the job. If that was the calculation, then they were perhaps right in calling it because everything was to go very right . . . before it went so horribly wrong.

* * *

'Agent Paul's' subsequent exploits soon became the stuff of Resistance folklore.

Early in the operation and probably using Duprez's cash, Cole purchased a stylish Peugeot 302 sedan. While ferrying a group of escaping men to Lille train station one morning, the car broke down and it looked like they were going to miss the connection south. Cole then noticed a group of German soldiers, standing on the opposite side of the road watching them and, hopping out of the car, he marched over and asked them, in perfunctory French, to tow him to the station. Incredibly, they obliged and the escape party made the train and got back to England, where they spoke in awe of Cole's audacity.

Around the same time, a 29-year-old former French Army chaplain in Abbeville called Pierre Carpentier joined the Madeleine line. Abbeville sat right on the border between the Closed zone in north-eastern France and the Occupied zone, and the city's bridge over the River Somme made for an excellent route south. To cross it, you needed an *Ausweis* transit document, blank copies of which could simply be picked up at any post office or tabac. Then all that was required was a photo and an official stamp. Carpentier managed to copy the stamp and, having taken photos of the escaping men, put them on the document. It was brilliantly simple and allowed hundreds of men to simply walk out of the Forbidden zone.

Despite his appalling French, Cole increasingly led the escape parties and enjoyed going via Abbeville as the route gave him the opportunity to spend time in the night spots of Paris on the way to Tours. On one occasion, while accompanying a Welsh sergeant pilot called Taffy Higginson across the River Cher, on the last leg of the trip, in a boat being rowed by a local farmer's wife, they were spotted by a German officer and his sergeant who were drinking in a bar on the southern bank and as they made landfall, the Germans were there to meet them. As the Germans began to question them, Cole spectacularly and performatively lost his temper. Shouting at the men, in the sort of comedic Cockney-ish French that would have made Michael Caine blush, he declared that he was going to report them for drinking in his 'aunt's café' and that they were a disgrace to their uniforms. Unperturbed, the officer persisted and demanded their papers once more.

Higginson, who could speak not a word of French, stayed silent throughout, and when the German tried to question him, Cole explained that he couldn't answer back because he was mad, deaf and mute. At this, the German sergeant openly declared that the man was quite obviously an escaping pilot and the tension rose up a notch. Cole had a pistol in his pocket and Higginson had no doubt at all that he was prepared to use it but, just as things began to look very dicey indeed, fate intervened. Ordered to open his case, Higginson looked on as the Germans peered into it with bewilderment. It was a sweltering hot day and Taffy was carrying a supply of chocolate that had now melted in the heat, rendering the inside of the valise a morass of brown liquid.

Cole could barely conceal his delight. 'Look!' he yelled, 'I told you he was fucking mad – he's shat in his suitcase!'

Clutching a handkerchief to his nose, the German officer ordered Higginson to go on his way and 20 minutes later he was joined further down the road by an exhilarated Cole. The two men laughed all the way to Marseille, where Taffy regaled Garrow with the extraordinary quick-wittedness and bravery of the agent. Garrow sent a report to his superiors, hailing Cole's heroism and a copy landed on the desk of Agent Sunday aka Major Donald Darling of MI9, who was now financing and masterminding the escape routes from neutral Lisbon. Darling – an extremely canny judge of character – read about the escapade with the chocolate and immediately heard alarm bells clanging in his head.

Something about Cole was off:

'He was, according to all reports, the antithesis of the scarlet pimpernel, wearing plus fours and a pork pie hat, speaking rudimentary French with a cockney accent; it seemed incredible that he was not questioned and arrested by the Germans.'

Darling fired off a coded message to Room 900 in London which, in the understated words of his colleague, Airey Neave aka Agent Saturday, was 'unfortunately ignored'.[13]

By early summer 1941, with northern and western France 'raining airmen', the escape lines had never been busier and Cole was doing vital work and doing it well – so no further action was taken. The British wanted to get as many of them back as possible and for a variety of reasons. On a practical level, getting experienced men back saved time, money and effort in training others. It also served the interests of intelligence-gathering and, in addition to being of immense propaganda value, gave those men climbing into their rigs that most important incentive of all – hope that they would return no matter what.

However, as fighter pilots and bomber crews were couriered south in ever greater numbers, the risks rose exponentially as the Germans began infiltrating the networks.

In Lille, the job of disrupting the lines fell to *Hauptsturmführer* Karl Hegener of the Abwehr (German military intelligence) and the six men under his command. They, in turn, relied on collaborators, who were paid well for their treachery and a Dutchman, called Cornelius Verloop, who had served in the French Foreign Legion until the fall of France, was their best man on the ground. Verloop, code-named 'Vindictive', was very good indeed at his work and quite soon everyone in the network was becoming justifiably paranoid. If caught, RAF pilots might expect to be interrogated and then taken to PoW camps. But for those running the lines, capture meant a death sentence. Many hundreds of French women and men would end up tortured, shot or left to rot in concentration camps as a result of their entirely voluntary heroic work.

The fear of infiltration sometimes led to innocent people coming under suspicion. Poles fighting in the RAF were particularly suspect as their lack of English made perfect cover for German agents and on one occasion, an unfortunate Polish pilot aroused the scepticism of the Madeleine line in Lille. Having roughed him up a little, Henri Duprez managed to extract a service number from him and duly went off to check it by radioing London. It turned out that the fighter pilot was telling the truth, but by the time Henri returned, the Polish man – who was supposedly being guarded by Cole – had disappeared and 'Paul' was nowhere to be found. Duprez then discovered that the Pole had wound up in a prison south of Lille but, as Cole had disappeared too, it was unclear what had happened.

This was not the first time that Henri Duprez had had cause to worry about Cole, for while the Madeleine line was ever shorter on funds, 'Agent Paul' appeared to be living the life of an international playboy. Often seen carousing in Parisian nightclubs he drank champagne like it was going out of fashion – and began to do less and less actual hard work. His once-loyal lieutenant, Roland Lepers, had now come to actively dislike him too and confided in his girlfriend and fellow courier, Madeleine Damerment, that Cole's cocksure attitude with the Germans made him suspicious. Unfortunately, the very system itself meant that the alarm could not be raised. The watchword of any escape line, after all, was secrecy. To protect those working in them, the links in the chain were only known to people on either side of each chink and, as such, it was almost impossible to pass messages along the line without exposing the entire network.

'I couldn't go and knock on any door,' Lepers later told the author Brendan Murphy, since 'I didn't know where the doors were.'

Some days after the incident with the Polish pilot, one of the guides, Maurice Van Camelbecke, confided in Henri Duprez that Cole had visited him at his home and had turned up in a black Citroën sedan of the exact type used by the German Abwehr. Camelbecke had the wit to write down the number plate as he departed and a quick check later confirmed that the vehicle did indeed belong to the authorities. When confronted, Cole shrugged it off and reassured Maurice that he had 'the Germans in my pocket' and that he had simply 'borrowed' the vehicle. That worrying turn of phrase was passed on to Duprez, who now began to suspect that Cole was indeed a double agent.

By the late summer of 1941, Garrow had a new deputy. Dr Albert-Marie Guerisse was an astute, 30-year-old former officer medic in the Belgian Army who had fled to Britain during the Dunkirk evacuation. There, he had been recruited into Naval Intelligence and taken the pseudonym and identity of 'Pat O'Leary', a Canadian naval officer whom he had met pre-war. The cover would, it was hoped, explain his rather peculiar non-French, non-British English accent if captured. Seconded to the Special Operations Executive (SOE), Guerisse was involved in the dangerous work of ferrying agents on to the beaches of France until he was captured by the Vichy French in April 1941 and taken to the prison camp at Saint-Hippolyte-du-Fort from where he subsequently escaped.

Guerisse and Garrow immediately hit it off and by July 1941 they had become something of a double act. That same month, Guerisse encountered Cole for the first time and instinctively distrusted him. His lack of faith in the former sergeant only escalated when Cole spun an unlikely tale about evading a German patrol boat and engaging in a gun battle, before seeking to extract money from Garrow for the 'banker' François Duprez. When he had gone, Guerisse told Garrow his feelings and

Garrow confided that he too was beginning to have his doubts but added that Cole's operation got results – so what could he do?

In October, 'Agent Paul' was back in Marseille once again and this time had brought two women 'guides' with him. One of them was a 19-year-old dual British-French national called Suzanne Warenghem, who was now his girlfriend. Cole handed over the airmen and then requested 'expenses' from Garrow, as was his custom, before telling him that he was heading back to Lille immediately to organise the next delivery. The next morning, Guerisse was surprised to see the second woman drinking coffee in a square and when he approached her, she told him that Cole and Warenghem were still very much in Marseille and were planning to go out to a club that night.

Garrow and Guerisse went too and watched from a distance as Cole splashed the cash and danced with the women. When Garrow approached him, a taken-aback Cole immediately blurted out his excuses before adding that he would be back in Lille the following day. With Garrow's concerns now growing, he ordered Guerisse to go north to investigate and having made it to the Forbidden zone, Albert tracked down the town hall clerk, François Duprez, and began asking him where all the money had gone. Duprez was visibly outraged and told the Belgian he had never received a penny from Cole or MI9. But there was more, because Duprez added that some of those whom Cole had set off with from Lille, had never reached Abbeville.

With growing unease, Guerisse returned to Marseille, only to discover that Garrow had been arrested by the Vichy secret police. The Garrow line now became the 'O'Leary line' and with an Australian corporal Bruce Dowding, ('one of the most daring and active members of the organisation') as his second in command, Guerisse took over the operation. The Marseille wing of the line now included some extraordinary characters, including the communist Latvian Jew, Elizabeth Haden-Guest, and the spy and Church of Scotland minister, Donald Caskie, who ran the British Seamen's Mission in Marseille, as well as a local businessman called Louis Nouveau and his friend, a 65-year-old British-born physician Dr Georges Rodocanachi.

All were told to be on their guard when Cole was next in town.

Late in the afternoon of Saturday 1 November 1941, Cole appeared at Rodocanachi's apartment, which was used as a safe house, and was directed to a back room where he was greeted by Guerisse, Dowding and a Greek operative called Praxinos who offered him a glass of whisky. Cole sank into a chair and seemed to be genuinely shocked when told that Garrow had been caught. Soon the conversation turned to the subject of the large sums of money he had been given and Cole explained that it was being put to good use and that the 'Lille banker' François Duprez was in charge of finances and that he knew no more.

At this, Guerisse snapped and rising from his chair he accused the agent of frittering precious funds on expensive clothes, women and champagne. Cole feigned hurt at being accused of such a thing only for the adjoining bathroom door to swing open to reveal François Duprez standing there. In utter fury, Duprez denounced Cole as 'a liar' – which caused the rogue agent to fall to his knees and beg for mercy. Confessing to 'having done something terrible in a moment of weakness' his only reward was a punch in the face, delivered by the Australian Dowding, which left him bleeding and reeling on the floor.

Duprez fired off some choice words before heading back north to warn other members of the network. As he went, Dowding dragged the simpering Cole to the bathroom and, having locked him inside, the three remaining men discussed what they should do next. Dowding stated bluntly that they should kill him and offered to strangle Cole there and then but Guerisse and Praxinos were more cautious. Executing him would mean having to dispose of the body which would have complications of its own and more to the point, as these men were, by turns, Belgian, Greek and Australian they did not believe they had the authority to carry out a death sentence. Cole was, after all, 'British' and his fate should thus be determined by Room 900 in London so they decided to pass him down the line to Gibraltar where SIS could deal with the matter as they saw fit.

Opening the toilet door to inform Cole of his fate, Dowding looked on in horror as the expensive soles of 'Agent Paul's' handmade shoes disappeared through the window. Before he could grab him, Cole was on a ventilator shaft, from which he jumped on to the sill of an adjoining apartment and climbed in. Racing out into the street, Dowding saw Cole pegging it into the back lanes of Marseille and having calculated that any chase might attract the attention of the police, he thought better of going after him and returned inside.

Almost immediately, Dowding and Guerisse packed up and headed north to Amiens where, somewhat incredibly given the circumstances, they took the morning off to go sightseeing. Dowding was a bit of a culture vulture who had a fascination with Gothic architecture, so the two British agents walked about the thirteenth-century cathedral, rubbing shoulders with visiting German soldiers, and admired its stained glass and famous sculptures before parting ways. Dowding then headed into the Forbidden Zone and across the Somme River, into Abbeville where he made contact with the agent-priest Pierre Carpentier and warned him that Cole was a traitor. On hearing the news, Carpentier's panicked stepmother, with whom he lived, began burning every scrap of incriminating evidence she could find, while Pierre muttered darkly that he had put his faith in God who would decide his destiny for him.

A little further north, Cole was having a visit of his own. Although now sleeping with the teenage Suzanne Warenghem, he was still living with Madeleine Deram and her son, and on 6 December, two truckloads of German soldiers arrived at their home and arrested the couple. Whether this was a staged incident, or whether Cole really did only come into the enemy's orbit at this very late stage in proceedings is a moot point, but given that he was almost immediately released, on the balance of probability he was already working for the enemy.

Grim treachery now played out.

On 8 December, Cole arrived at Carpentier's house in Abbeville with a group of escapees, including several British RAF officers and a Polish airman. The Australian, Dowding, was still at the house when they arrived and hid in a back room as, moments later, agents of the German Secret Police (GFP) burst in and took everyone into custody. Dowding managed to escape through a back window and fled to Madeleine Damerment's home where the GFP soon caught up with him. Fortunately, Madeleine was not at home, but her father was taken away.

Corporal Dowding and Carpentier were taken to Berlin, along with other captured members of the O'Leary line, including a coal miner from Lille called Protais Dubois and other loyal lieutenants of Cole – Désiré Didry and Marcel Duhayon – who had all been betrayed by the British agent. In total, some 150 escape-line volunteers were turned over to the Nazis by the RE sergeant and about a third were executed as 'traitors' or 'spies'.[14]

Awaiting execution in his cell, Carpentier managed to smuggle messages out to comrades, family and even his enemy, Cole:

'I have met many Englishmen in my life but you are the first I have known who would sell his country. Thank God I'm not likely to meet another in the short time I have to live.'[15]

On 16 April 1943, Carpentier, Dowding, Didry, Duhayon and Dubois were condemned to death. Two months later, they were beheaded by mechanical guillotine in Dortmund, Germany and buried in unmarked graves. All of them had sacrificed their lives in order to help complete strangers and to defeat the tyranny of fascism. And they were not alone in that fate. In the weeks that followed, Cole's betrayal saw dozens of other people who had once put such faith in the English 'captain' now find themselves in the hands of the Gestapo. A French railway worker who had risked his life to help Cole was imprisoned and so too was the official François Duprez, who was taken into custody at his place of work before being sent to Bochum concentration camp the following year. This brave man – who had helped hundreds of people in the service of a greater cause – died in Sonnenburg concentration camp in 1944.

Cole's apparent indifference to the fate of so many was so chilling that even the amoral Dutch turncoat Verloop was shocked by his treachery. As 'Paul' happily spilled the beans, the 'Abwehr stenographer struggled to keep up' and his 30-page deposition saw just about everyone who had crossed his path wind up in prison, a concentration camp or an unmarked grave. But wily Cole had a habit of never giving too much away and some key individuals, including the beautician, Mrs Voglimacci, remained at liberty. Some later suggested that this demonstrated residual loyalty to his people but more likely, Cole was leaving other suspects alive to cover his own trail. Lepers and his fiancée, Damerment, escaped the purge, but only because they had the good sense to run in time. Having made it to Britain, they broke off their engagement and Madeleine was recruited into the SOE and eventually sent back to France, where, as we shall see in a moment, she crossed paths with Cole one last and fateful time.

Shortly after leaving Lille, 'Agent Paul' was to be found in Paris denouncing everyone he knew – but not his new girlfriend Suzanne Warenghem, who believed him when he told her that he was on the run from the Gestapo and that there was a traitor on the loose. While in Paris, Cole came down with a 'recurring bout of malaria' from that purported spell in Hong Kong years earlier. As Suzanne and her aunt Jeanne nursed him back to health, both women fell under his spell and by the time he was better, all three of them were in love with Harold Cole.

Harold and Suzanne married on 10 April 1942, with her some three months pregnant, and that same week the one-armed MI9 liaison officer Captain James Langley met with Guerisse and Darling in Gibraltar to plot revenge on the turncoat.[16]

Seeking a quieter life, Cole and Warenghem then moved to Lyon in Vichy where in June 1942, Louis Triffe, the head of the Direction de Surveillance du Territoire, quickly had them arrested at the Hotel D'Angleterre for spying. This surprising turn of events shows the complex and often paradoxical loyalties of the time, for though ostensibly an important official in the collaborationist regime, Triffe was very much a French patriot who was also determinedly pro-British. Aware of Cole's treachery, Triffe had moved to protect the Resistance organisations and remaining escape lines that were running through the Unoccupied zone.

Having separated the couple, Triffe then set about trying to convince the heavily pregnant Suzanne that her husband was a traitor responsible for the arrest and murder of scores of people. Somewhat bewildered to find herself being tipped off by an official in one of the very departments that was supposed to be working against her people, Warenghem refused to believe him. But her mind was changed, when some days later, she happened to be present when Cole was punched in the face by a French interrogator and immediately crumbled and confessed everything.[17]

Mr and Mrs Cole were tried by the Vichy authorities on the charge of 'delivering French citizens into the hands of the Germans' and Suzanne was acquitted. Cole was sentenced to death and sent back to his cell. Furious at this betrayal by the man she loved, Suzanne returned to Marseille, made contact with Guerisse and told him everything. Her son was born in October but died in infancy in late January 1943 and further tragedy was to follow. That same month, the O'Leary line was double-crossed by a French traitor named Roger le Neveu, who infiltrated the organisation and then handed the members of the group over to the Gestapo. In early November 1942, the Germans had invaded and occupied the Vichy territory and the days when Triffe could have pro-Nazi agents arrested were now gone.

Guerisse was captured in Toulouse in March 1943 and ended his war as an inmate at the Natzweiler-Struthof concentration camp. Many others, including the 65-year-old physician Dr Georges Rodocanachi, whose safe house had been the stage for Cole's confrontation with fellow agents, were taken to concentration camps too. Rodocanachi died at Buchenwald in February 1944. The O'Leary line was now taken over by its only remaining member: a 62-year-old spinster called Marie-Louise Dissard, who never went anywhere without her cat Mifouf. The authorities were briefly suspicious of her but, having foolishly concluded that she was a batty old woman of no consequence, this 'mad cat lady' was left to her own devices.

She went on to smuggle 250 Allied airmen out of France.

With the German takeover of Vichy France complete, Harold Cole was out of jail and now working openly for the Nazis. He was also hell-bent on revenge and through the winter of 1943 and into early 1944, he set about hunting down the whereabouts of his estranged wife probably with the intention of killing her. Suzanne had in fact been captured by the Germans in September 1943 but had managed to escape the prison in Castres with the help of an SOE agent and fellow inmate called Blanche Charlet. Knowing that Cole was after her, Warenghem adopted the name Aline Le Gale and slept with a revolver under her pillow. Evading the occupation authorities and with her ex-husband hot on their trail, on 14 April 1944 Suzanne and Charlet made it to the coast at Brittany, where they were taken off by the Royal Navy.

Cole was now an employee of the SS and was reporting directly to *Sturmbannführer* Hans Kieffer, head of the SD section in Paris.

Kieffer was heading up an operation called *Funkspiel* – a desperate last throw of the espionage dice, which involved turning captured SOE assets against their handlers. The hope was to lure British agents into their hands, but they were foiled repeatedly because, even under duress, many of the captured operatives made deliberate mistakes in order to signal London to their fate. Under torture or the threat of it, some inevitably buckled however, and when, in February 1944, Kieffer learned of the imminent arrival of a British agent, his SD men were there to greet her. Madeleine Damerment, former fiancée of Roland Lepers, whose father had already been killed by the Gestapo, parachuted straight into their hands and, having been tortured and interrogated, was taken to Dachau concentration camp, where she was murdered in September 1944.

Later that same year, Kieffer was responsible for another war crime when his agents captured 12 SAS men who had been parachuted into the area around Orléans. Kieffer killed five of the prisoners in cold blood – turning him into one of the most wanted men on the Special Operations hit list.

Cole's actual role in *Funkspiel* is a matter of conjecture. Lacking the brains or wit to decipher codes he may have been a sort of 'cultural awareness' adviser, using his knowledge of the home country to explain things that the Germans may otherwise have missed. Either way, he was about to be put out of the first permanent job he'd ever held down as, early on the morning of 6 June 1944, thousands of Allied Airborne soldiers cascaded into drop zones across northern France, heralding the start of Operation Overlord and the liberation of France.

Two months later, on 17 August, with the Allies advancing on the French capital, the Germans fled Paris and among their number was a former Royal Engineers sergeant called Harold Cole who now proudly wore the uniform of a German Gestapo officer.

* * *

By April 1945, Harold Cole was still on the SS payroll and remained in the company of his friend Major Hans Kieffer and his immediate staff. As the Americans and French advanced towards Stuttgart, Cole and Kieffer fled once more and having latched on to a retreating German Army column came under attack by Allied artillery fire near the town of Worndorf. Cole was wounded in the leg and as the net tightened he and Kieffer realised the game was up.

Surrendering under their real identities would have meant inevitable imprisonment, trial and probable execution so the two men came up with a clever plan.

Ditching their uniforms, staff car and documents, they went to meet the Americans. Cole told them that he was Captain Robert Mason, a secret agent working on behalf of the SIS in London and that his two associates were German policemen who had surrendered to him on account of their anti-Nazi sympathies. It was a bold lie but Cole was practised in the art and, with men and women of all nationalities buzzing around the battlefields of Europe, there was little cause for the Americans to disbelieve him. Cole's German companions stuck to their story and Kieffer walked free.

Having changed his identity and moved to the Alpine town of Garmisch, Kieffer took a job as a cleaner in a local hotel where, two years later, his past would catch up with him. Put on trial by the British authorities he was subsequently hanged.

Back in 1945 and on the loose once more, Cole had decided that there was safety in numbers and to that end he was busy establishing his own private army. Having been sent on his way by the Americans, he forged documents that claimed he was on a mission for the US Counterintelligence Corps (CIC) and, having once again stolen an American army uniform, had now recruited two secretaries, Margaret Gaubert and Suzanne Votier, as well as a French confidence trickster called Fernand

Lepage and an itinerant factory worker called Georges Jousset to his gang.

Cole now headed towards Upper Swabia and the town of Saulgau, where he intended to insinuate himself with the French Third Battalion who were based there.

Saulgau was no random dot on the map and he had chosen it deliberately. Realising that it was only a matter of time before his past caught up with him, Cole wanted to get his hands on cash and had learned that a senior local Nazi official Georg Hanft was supposedly sitting on a large sum of it. Armed with his credentials, his American officer's uniform and the Colt pistol and Thompson (Tommy) gun which he carried everywhere, Cole marched into the HQ of the French Army in the city and announced his arrival.

The 'British intelligence officer' commanded immediate respect from Captain Chevauchee, who introduced him to his own intelligence officer, an inexperienced young Frenchman called Lieutenant Dureng. Cole handed them a list of 'most wanted' fugitives in the region, which had Georg Hanft's name at the top and with some delight, Dureng told him that he had, just the previous day, taken the Nazi into custody.

Naive and somewhat in awe of this senior British officer, with his staff and his flash US Army uniform and weapons, Dureng was soon sucked into Cole's gang. Years of close proximity to the SS had now turned Cole into the monster he had always been destined to be and having removed Hanft to a local farm he set about torturing him and other 'suspects'.

The farmer, Anton Kneussle, was no fool and as people were dragged to his farmhouse to be bullied and beaten up, he started taking notes, but all attempts to raise the alarm with the French intelligence officer, Lieutenant Dureng, fell on muffled ears.

As the carnival of savagery played out, Cole introduced two new recruits to the gang. Captain Frank Lillyman and Lieutenant William King were bona fide All-American heroes who had arrived in that first wave of Airborne operations on the night of 6 June 1944. Lillyman in fact claimed to be the first GI to have put his boots on occupied soil and it had already garnered him celebrity back home where he would go on to be something of a GI 'A lister' – posing for magazines and offered free stays in swanky hotels. But brought into Cole's orbit, the gullible and brutish Lillyman displayed no heroic tendencies at all and instead stood by as the thuggish 'Mason' drove around intimidating 'suspects' and stealing their cash.

Lillyman's endorsement only strengthened Cole's credentials – and as the US officer began to boast to American colleagues that he was helping the British spy 'Mason' gather important intelligence from SS suspects, matters took an even darker turn.

On 8 June 1945, Cole got Lillyman, Dureng and a third man to accompany him and the prisoner, Hanft, on a terrifying, booze-fuelled, night-time ride through the French countryside. Having first filled up on food and wine at a local chateau, the drunken Cole then started haranguing the handcuffed Hanft once more and demanded that he be taken to the 'treasure'. As they drove back through the countryside, Hanft insisted for the umpteenth time that no such booty existed and Cole eventually lost his patience and having stopped the car, dragged the man into some woods. Pushing him up against a tree, he then shoved his revolver into Hanft's face and demanded money while his victim begged for mercy. Lillyman then kicked the former Nazi in the groin and when Hanft repeated one last time that he had nothing to give them, 'Mason' lost patience and opened fire with his machine gun.

Dureng and his aide, Camile Allart, then stepped forward and fired into the man's head.[18]

Cole may have thought himself untouchable but, unbeknown to him, he now had a long and growing list of people on his trail that included MI6, MI5, French Intelligence and even Scotland Yard's most famous detective, Reginald Spooner. MI9 were after him too and had been as far back as April 1942, when Donald Darling (Agent Sunday), Albert Guerisse and James Langley had convened in Gibraltar and sworn to avenge the dead. By 1945, that list of victims had swelled to hundreds and Darling, in particular, was on Cole's tail although the task of finding him was easier said than done.

Fellow quislings like William Joyce (aka Lord Haw Haw) and John

Amery,* the Harrow-educated fascist leader of the infamous British Free Corps of the Waffen SS, had both been apprehended quite quickly in large part down to their notoriety, but Cole was not well known and it played in his favour.

Every villain has their Achilles heel however, and just as high-living Al Capone was eventually caught by the taxman, so the womanising Cole was about to fall victim to the friendly fire of Cupid's bow.

In Paris, Darling (Agent Sunday) was in charge of the MI9 bureau that was responsible for compensating the many guides and agents who had acted on the agency's behalf across the previous five years. His office had become something of a meeting point for the disparate survivors of the Comet, O'Leary and Madeleine lines, and one of those who turned up at the door was a Swiss woman called Lotte, who had had an affair with Cole during the war. Lotte did not know of Cole's treachery and Darling made sure that his team kept her ignorant of it. That strategy paid off when one day, the young Swiss woman bounced into the office clutching a postcard from Cole, which she proudly presented to MI9 secretary Sylvia Cooper Smith.

It read:

'Cherie! You see I am safe and well and hope to see you again.

Much love, Sonny Boy.'

Cooper Smith was no mere MI9 staffer and was, in fact, engaged to Albert Guerisse (aka Pat O'Leary), who had recently been liberated from Dachau concentration camp and was now recuperating in her Parisian apartment. Cooper Smith told Lotte that she was sure that Captain Darling would be delighted to see that his old friend was well and took the card into his office. The stamp mark clearly bore the name of the military camp from which it had been sent and a team, led by MI5 agent Peter Hope, were dispatched to Salgau to arrest him. Cole was then taken to the Parisian military prison from which he escaped.

Shortly after his flight, Cole befriended a 42-year-old divorcee called

* Amery, son of Leo Amery, a British Conservative Cabinet minister then serving as Secretary of State for India and Burma, was captured by Italian partisans in April 1945 – and was then surrendered to Captain Alan Whicker who later found fame as a television presenter.

Pauline Herveau who was making preparations to open a brasserie called Billy's Bar, on the Rue de Grenelle, in the 6th Arrondissement. Like other victims before her, Pauline believed everything the army 'physician Monsieur Harry' told her, right up to – and beyond – the moment when the police came knocking on her door.

That moment dawned on 9 January 1946 when two detectives, Edmond Levy and Raymond Cotty, arrived at Billy's Bar having been tipped off by informants who had noticed that something funny was going on in the flat above the premises. The police suspected that Herveau was harbouring either an escaped German PoW or a deserter but the respectable Madame insisted that she ran a respectable joint and that the man in her upstairs spare room was a British army officer who had stopped by that morning to bid her farewell before heading home. Unfortunately, over coffee, he had then come down with a headache and had been obliged to lie on her bed.

Continuing to plead her virtue and innocence, she led the detectives up several flights of stairs to the room calling out 'Cheri, it's the police!' along the way until on the landing at the very top, the little party came face to face with a half-dressed Cole brandishing a gun. Pushing Herveau aside, he opened up on the two French officers who immediately returned fire. Cole had met his match. Cotty was a hardened former Resistance fighter and an expert shot and his bullets tore into Cole, passed through his heart and killed him instantly. The traitor's lifeless body fell backwards through the door and on to Madame Herveau's bed – the long game was over.

Soon SIS typewriters and telexes were spinning into action, relaying the news, in understated fashion, to the offices of military intelligence around the world.

One such memo read:

'With reference to my minute L166/etc of 19.12.45, Harold Cole was liquidated in Paris on January 9th 1946. I would therefore be grateful if you would notify the various D.S.Os to whom you sent copies.

G.T.D Patterson, Major.'[19]

The sensational story was all over the press too.

'British Deserter, Resistance Traitor, Is Killed in Paris' *(Paris Post)*

'Traitor Dies In Gun Battle' *(Continental Daily Mail)*

'Traitor Dies – Trapped in flat after last toast in Champagne' *(Mail)*

Declassified memos at the National Archives in Kew show that the spooks were a gossipy and pedantic lot in 1946 and they not only delighted in Cole's death – but also the many inaccuracies that turned up in the newspaper reports.

The files show that they didn't think much of his accomplices either and they reserved particular scorn for the GI who had latched on to him before going on to cash in on his celebrity. Gathered among the clippings in the security services file is a photograph of Lillyman – taken for *Life* magazine on 3 December 1945 – surrounded by newspapers and a tray of food in a plush hotel. The article, headed 'Soldier Takes his Ease' made no mention of the hero's notorious friend and their drunken, murderous rampage.

* * *

Quite swiftly, the story of Harold Cole faded away from the broader public consciousness. Though mentioned in Airey Neave's memoir *Saturday at MI9* and forensically related in *Turncoat*, Brendan Murphy's brilliant 1987 telling of events, most war historians essentially engaged in *damnatio memoriae* and his name was erased from the liturgy of events. Postwar Britons preferred the bowdlerised narrative of the plucky nation, made up of heroic ordinary people, standing united and alone, like a white knight against the encroaching evil from the East.

Of course there was plenty of room for escaping PoWs whose exploits were rightly celebrated and there was space too for the brave agents of the SOE and the rogue men of SAS and other special forces.

Cheeky Eddie Chapman – aka Agent Zig-Zag – who, having agreed to work for the Nazis, changed sides and worked for the SIS instead, found his place in the narrative too and a film, *Triple Cross* (1966), starring Christopher Plummer, was even based on his extraordinary exploits. Although no mainstream movies were ever made about them, there was space for the Nazi traitors like the upper-class Nazi Amery and William Joyce as well. But that was because, through their example, these ideological traitors served to demonstrate the fate that befell those people who supported Hitler.

Others though largely got away with it and none more so than Sir Oswald Mosley and his Hitler-fawning wife Diana. Released from prison in 1943 they both spent the rest of their lives complaining about the shoddy way in which they had been treated, from exile in France and Ireland, rather than apologising for being antisemitic fascists who had supported Adolf Hitler. Though his postwar efforts to regain power via the ballot box failed, somewhat incredibly, the British Union of Fascists leader remained 'relevant' and a public figure and was even feted in some corners. Despite being a holocaust denier and concentration camp apologist, who sought to discredit or failing that explain away the state orchestrated murder of millions of people, Mosley was even invited on to British television screens in order, for example, to lambast the arrival of Asian-Uganda refugees fleeing the Idi Amin regime in 1972.[20]

Despite having run a party called the 'British Union of Fascists', Mosley even sought to claim that he wasn't right wing and following his death in 1980, many obituarists tried to explain rather than condemn him. The *Telegraph* wrote that he was a 'brilliant man in the Commons . . . compassionate and humane . . . a man of genuine courage and inspiring leadership . . .' There was scant mention anywhere of the fact that this appalling racist had plotted with enemy despots to overthrow the British state.

His widow, Diana Mosley, who remained an enthusiastic fascist to the end of her life, was also afforded a degree of respect that she did not deserve and late in life was celebrated as a great pre-war beauty and icon of her age – even as she spouted Holocaust denial and Hitler fandom on a 1989 edition of the BBC's *Desert Island Discs*. When an unfavourable obituary followed her death, in August 2003, friends lined up to defend her. One letter to the *Telegraph* claimed that while she had once given a Nazi salute during a rendition of 'God Save the King', she was as patriotic as they came. It was all a great big misunderstanding apparently – and all down to her 'upper-class breeding and etiquette' which the little people simply could not understand.

But wherever you stood on the Mosleys – at least they could be explained to some degree and the same could not be said of Harold Cole.

Cole came with no ideological baggage. He was a bad guy without a cause, whose betrayal was forged out of nothing more than greed and cowardice. This vicious, unprincipled murderer, traitor and thief, was in short, the odd piece in the jigsaw of Britain's heroic wartime epic. So, there were no films, no documentaries and just one memorable biography, written some 35 years ago.

Which is unfortunate because, through their example, the likes of Cole demonstrate that out past was complicated and messy and that, for the most part, the people in it were no better or more heroic than those in our present.

We live once again in an era of warfare, warped narratives, disinformation and blurred lines. A moment in time where very bad people would like us to believe that they are the good guys, while the many modern victims of our age are endlessly vilified, downtrodden, bombed and betrayed.

Harold Cole was much more than a traitor. He was worse than that because this con man and thief was able and willing to wreak havoc even as he portrayed himself as the hero of the hour.

And there is no greater warning from history than that.

ACKNOWLEDGEMENTS

My thanks to all who opened up their archives, shared insights, replied to my email inquiries or phone calls and, in some cases, invited me into their homes while writing this book.

Extra special thanks to the following:

Patrick and Anne Casement
Chipping Campden Historical Society
Carol Jackson
Steve Davis (San Francisco)
Chuck Stucker (San Francisco)
Veronica White
Matthew Stadlen
Lorraine Newman and St Dunstan's, Hunsdon
Alistair King
Peter David Smyrna Baptist Chapel, Penyfai, Bridgend
Theo Loizou
Ian Clark (Oundle School)

Many thanks too to the large team of people who helped make the book happen including:

Yvonne Jacob, Raiyah Butt and everyone at Headline
Oliver Holden-Rea
Doug Young and the team at Pew

And then there are the invaluable others:

My *Byline Times* team and particularly Hardeep Matharu, Peter Jukes, Stephen Colegrave for their enduring support, inspiration and friendship

My first critic and wife Helen

My son, research companion and secret weapon James

My daughter and sounding board Sophia

My allies and sometime travel companions Per Laleng and Toby Thompson

My cousins Tessa Fantoni and Gemma Utting

Plus: Charlotte Mullins, Paul Ayres, Philip Trafford, Charles Jones, Andrew Chappell, Sam Sandercock, Paul Hurley, Simon White, Guy Parker and Matthew Tombs who have all in some way helped me along the path while writing this book.

And finally, my late parents Hannah and Peter Scott whose encouragement and love sustains me long after they are gone.

ENDNOTES

Chapter One: Scapegoats

1. A few hundred metres.
2. Lang's very enjoyable account of the Campden Wonder is included in his 1904 collection, *Historical Mysteries*.
3. *The Campden Wonder* (1676) by Thomas Overbury.
4. *The Campden Wonder*, p13.
5. Notes by Lord Maugham, *The Campden Wonder* by Sir George Clark, 1958.
6. *The Campden Wonder*, p16.
7. *Mr Harrison is Missing* by Jill Wilson, Campden and District Historical and Archaeological Society, p17.
8. Physic, in its broader seventeenth-century Aristotelian context, is a study of all science, nature and even philosophy. Molière's bourgeois gentilhomme (1667) asks his philosophical tutor what physics is and receives in reply, '[the science] that explains the principles of natural things, and the properties of bodies; that discourses about the nature of the elements, metals, minerals, stones, plants and animals; and [that] teaches us the cause of all the meteors'.
9. *The Campden Wonder*, p19.
10. *Truth Brought to Light: Broadside Ballad* – author unknown, Bodleian Collection.
11. As quoted by Andrew Lang, *Historical Mysteries* (1904).

Chapter Two: The Traitors

1. 'Why I hate my uncle.' *Look* magazine, 4 July 1939.
2. Interview with Mikal Gilmore, *Rolling Stone* magazine, 27 September 2012.
3. The Bible, New International Version, John 12 verse 6.
4. *Hampshire Chronicle*, Winchester, Saturday 31 August 1782.

5. *Account of Sir Roger Casement Reinternment*, Deidre McMahon, Irish Archives, Spring 1996.
6. 'Mystery of Casement bones solved, 87 years on,' *Guardian*, 6 December 2003.
7. 'Kossuth's Irish Courier,' by Roger Casement but written anonymously, *United Irishman*, 25 February 1905.
8. *16 Lives: Roger Casement* by Angus Mitchell, p24.
9. From *African Drums* by Fred Puleston (1930). Quoted by Brian Inglis in *Roger Casement* (1973), p27.
10. *Some Poems of Roger Casement* (1918), The Talbot Press. Introduction via Project Gutenberg.
11. *Roger Casement* (1973) by Brian Inglis, Hodder & Stoughton, p67.
12. 'Conrad and Roger Casement' by Jeffrey Meyers, *Conradiana Journal*, Vol 5, number 3 (1973) p69.
13. New York Public Library, Quinn Papers collection, 24 May 2016, letter from Joseph Conrad.
14. *King Leopold's Ghost* by Adam Hochschild, p35.
15. *King Leopold's Ghost*, p39.
16. *Casement the Flawed Hero* (1984) by Roger Sawyer, p24.
17. *King Leopold's Ghost*, p161.
18. *King Leopold's Ghost*, p228.
19. *Presbyterian Pioneers in the Congo* (1917) by William Henry Sheppard.
20. Hansard Foreign Office and Diplomatic Service debate, 23 March 1891. https://hansard.parliament.uk/Commons/1891-03-23/debates/58cf2712-db5a-4a35-9ab2-9e1caf7391e9/ForeignOfficeAndDiplomaticService
21. *The Story of the Congo Free State* (1905) by Henry Wellington Wack, p367.
22. *Roger Casement* (1973) by Brian Inglis, p107.
23. *King Leopold's Ghost*, p264.
24. *Roger Casement's Diaries: 1910: The Black and the White*, edited by Roger Sawyer, Pimlico, p63.
25. *Roger Casement,* by Brian Inglis, p83.
26. *16 Lives: Roger Casement*, by Angus Mitchell, p227.
27. *Roger Casement* by Brian Inglis, p302.
28. *Roger Casement* by Brian Inglis, p332.
29. *Daily Mail*, 28 June 1916.
30. *Ireland, Empire and British Foreign Policy: Roger Casement and the First World War*, by Margaret O'Callaghan (Queen's, Belfast).
31. *Roger Casement*, p83.
32. *Roger Casement*, p332.
33. *Casement the Flawed Hero* (1984) by Roger Sawyer, p127.
34. *Daily Mail*, 28 June 1916.
35. Bad Gay podcast, Season 3 Episode 7, Roger Casement.

36. Joesph Conrad: The Three Lives (1979) by Federick Robert Karl, Farrar Straus & Giroux, p799.
37. Roger Casement letter to Elizabeth Bannister, Irish National Archives, 25 July 1916.

Chapter Three: Peasants

1. 'Pilot Describes Ceausescu's Futile Attempt to Escape', *New York Times*, 1 January 1990.
2. *Kiss The Hand You Cannot Bite* by Edward Behr, p171.
3. 'Half a Million Kids survived Romania's Slaughterhouses of the Souls', *The World*, Vlad Odobescu, 2015.
4. Behr, p171.
5. Behr, p22.
6. *The Crowd: A Study of the Popular Mind* (1895) by Gustave Le Bon.
7. Ibid.
8. 'London Riots: I don't want kids today to go down the same path', BBC 7, August 2021.
9. *Froissart's Chronicles Book II Chapter 73*, translated by Geoffrey Brereton, Penguin.
10. *The Peasants Revolt* (2004) by Alastair Dunn, Tempus Press.
11. Size of shoes fact from *Summer of Blood* by Dan Jones, p16.
12. Fact about being put to death from *Fashion Rules of the 14th Century,* St John's College Cambridge.
13. *Summer of Blood.*
14. *Anonimalle Chronicle.*
15. Dunn, p101.
16. Ibid.
17. Ibid.
18. National Archives London Reville, No. 13, p199–200 as cited on People of 1381 database.

Chapter Four: Bloody Mary

1. Quoted in Catholic.com encyclopaedia. *Mon. Germ. Hist. Scr.*, xxii, pp379–475.
2. *Syntagma juris universi* (1582) Pierre Gregoire libr. 15, cap. 3, num. 23.
3. John Wycliffe's English Bible, Genesis Chapter 2 verse 23, modern spelling edition, Terence P. Noble publisher.

4. Letter patent from King Edward VI, May 1553, quoted in *Mary Tudor: England's First Queen* (2009) by Anna Whitelock, Bloomsbury.
5. Anna Whitelock, p165.
6. *History of England (1850–1870)*, by James Anthony Froude, Chapter 30: Queen Jane and Queen Mary, source Gutenberg Project.
7. Letter to Mary from Privy Council, National Archives, Tuesday 11 July 1553.
8. Greg Wilkinson, 'Juana La Loca', *British Journal of Psychiatry* published online by Cambridge University Press, 27 July 2020.
9. Anna Whitelock, p173.
10. *The Myth of Bloody Mary* (2007) by Linda Porter, Portrait Books, p36.
11. Ibid.
12. Linda Porter, p90.
13. Linda Porter, p100.
14. Anna Whitelock, p208.

Chapter Five: Gangsters

1. *Al Capone: The Biography of a Self-Made Man* (1930) by F.D. Pasley, Faber, p60.
2. Ibid.
3. *Two Gun Hart: Lawman, Cowboy and Long Lost Brother of Al Capone* (2015) by Jeff McArthur, Bandwagon Books, Kindle edition.
4. Ibid.
5. 'How the Italian-American Dream became a racial nightmare', by Isabel Robertson, *Interzine,* 16 September 2020.
6. *Are Italians White?* (2003), Jennifer Guglielmo (Editor), Routledge.
7. *Capone: His Life, Legacy and Legend* (2016) by Deirdre Bair, First Anchor Books, p10.
8. Bair, p15.
9. *Little Caesar* (1931) Warner Bros, directed by Mervyn LeRoy, screenplay by Francis Edward Faragoh, Robert N. Lee and others.
10. Bair, p20.
11. Al Capone interviewed by Cornelius Vanderbilt Jr, *Liberty* magazine, 17 October 1931, reprinted in Penguin Book of Interviews, edited by Christopher Silvester, Penguin, 1994.
12. Otto English correspondence with film-maker Steve Davis, friend and associate of Chuck Stucker who grew up on Alcatraz. Note: the line it references should say 'soft almost feminine voice'.
13. *The Use and Need of the Life of Carry Nation*, by Carry Nation, revised Edition 1905, Project Gutenberg.
14. Carry Nation, chap IX.

15. 'Changes in suicide and homicide rates during Prohibition in the United States from 1900 to 1950', Statista.com.
16. Bair, p37.
17. Al Capone interview, *Liberty* magazine, 17 October 1931.
18. *Al Capone* by F.D. Pasley, p4.
19. Ibid.
20. *Bismarck Tribune*, 21 November 1930, p3.
21. *Louis Armstrong: An Extravagant Life, an Extraordinary Life* (1998) Harper-Collins, New Edition.
22. *Al Capone*, by F.D. Pasley, p9.
23. *Inventing the Public Enemy: The Gangster in American Culture, 1918–1934* (1996) by David E. Ruth, University of Chicago Press, p58.
24. Al Capone, *Liberty* magazine, interview, 1931.
25. Bair, p78.
26. Sinclair, p4.
27. Mayor William Hale Thompson Inaugural Address, 18 April 1927, Chicago PublicLibrary.https://www.chipublib.org/mayor-william-hale-thompson-inaugural-address-1927/
28. Bair, p183.
29. Bair, p241.
30. 'God Awful Silence', *Time* magazine, 26 August 1935, *Time* magazine archive.

Chapter Six: The Illuminati

1. *Proofs of a Conspiracy Against All the Religions and Governments of Europe* (1798) by John Robison MA, Third Edition, Chapter II. Source: Gutenberg Press.
2. *The Rosicrucian Philosophy in Questions and Answers*, from 'Mysteries' (2022) by Max Heindel, Legare Street Press.
3. Papal Bull of Clement XII, 28 April 1738.
4. *Die Korrespondenz des Illuminatenordens. Band I: 1776–1781.* Edited by Reinhard Markner, Monika Neugebauer-Wölk and Hermann Schüttler. Tübingen: Max Niemeyer Verlag, 2005, pp4–5, 8–11. Translation: Bill C. Ray.
5. EAU15: The Spanish angle: Urological problems of Charles II (1661–1700) EAUpublicationhttps://uroweb.org/news/eau15-the-spanish-angle-urological-problems-of-charles-ii-1661-1700
6. *An Answer to the Question – What is Enlightenment* (1784) by Immanuel Kant, New York Public Library, translated by Ted Humphrey (1992) Hackett Publishing.
7. *The Growth in Literacy in Western Europe 1500–1800* by Dr Robert A. Houston, University of St Andrews research paper, 18 February 2018.

8. Encyclopaedia Britannica online https://www.britannica.com/science/siren-noisemaking-device
9. Correspondence between George Washington and G.W. Snyder, August 1798, US National Archives Washington.
10. Ibid.
11. Thomas Jefferson to Bishop James Madison (letter), US National Archives, 31 January 1800.
12. *The Phantom Terror* (2014) by Adam Zamoyski, HarperCollins, p350.
13. *Behind World Revolution – The Strange Career of Nesta H Webster* (1982), Insight Books, p26.
14. *Secret Societies and Subversive Movements* (1924) by Nesta Webster, Christian Book Club of America. Via Gutenberg Press online.
15. Source 'Famous Freemasons', United Grand Lodge of England online.
16. 'Zionism versus Bolshevism – A struggle for the soul of the Jewish people', by the Right Honourable Winston Churchill, *Illustrated Sunday Herald*, 8 February 1920, p5.
17. *Behind the World Revolution*, p4.
18. *At Birch Society Headquarters* by Tim Sullivan, Associated Press, 21 January 2024.
19. *The Harvard Crimson*, 29 October 1962. https://www.thecrimson.com/article/1962/10/29/robert-welch-defends-birchers-as-large/
20. Lyrics to Bob Dylan's 'Talkin' John Birch Paranoid Blues'.
21. *Washington Post*, https://www.washingtonpost.com/history/2021/01/15/john-birch-society-qanon-reagan-republicans-goldwater/
22. *The Harvard Crimson*, 29 October 1962. https://www.thecrimson.com/article/1962/10/29/robert-welch-defends-birchers-as-large/
23. Infowars Broadcast, 10 January 2017.
24. *Illuminati: The Cult that Hijacked the World* by Henry Makow PhD, Silas Green Publishing, p1.

Chapter Seven: Monsters

1. *The Strange Case of Doctor Jekyll and Mr Hyde* (2003) by Robert Louis Stevenson, Penguin Classics, p40.
2. *Michel Beheim, German Meistergesang and Dracula* by David B. Dickens and Elizabeth Miller, International Conference of the Fantastic in the Arts (2003) research paper, p5.
3. *Michel Beheim, German Meistergesang*, p5.

4. *Vlad the Impaler – In Search of the Real Dracula* (2003) by M.J. Throw, Sutton, p92.
5. *Vlad the Impaler*, p95.
6. Ibid.
7. 'The Translations of John Tiptoft', by H.B. Lathrop (ed), *Modern Language Notes*, Vol. 41, No. 8 (December 1926).
8. *Vlad the Impaler*, p154.
9. *Dracula, Prince of Many Faces: His Life and Times* (1990) by Radu Florescu, Little, Brown.
10. *Vlad the Impaler*, p166.
11. *The Histories Book 10* by L. Chalkokondyles.
12. Ibid.
13. 'The Death of Sir Henry Irving', *Guardian*, archive, 14 October 1905.
14. 'Two Sharp Teeth' by Philip Ball, *London Review of Books*, 25 October 2018.
15. *An Account of the Principalities of Wallachia and Moldavia* (1820) by William Wilkinson, Longman, Chapter One. Source: Gutenberg Project.
16. 'A Wilde Desire Took Me: The Homoerotic History of Dracula by Talia Schaffer', Johns Hopkins University, *ELH*, Vol 61, Number 2 (Summer 1994).
17. *Experiences of the Cholera in Ireland* (1873) by Charlotte Stoker.
18. Ibid.
19. *Vlad the Impaler*, ch 3.
20. Copyright Registration form for Bram Stoker's *Dracula*, UK National Archives, 19 May 1897.

Chapter Eight: The Diseased

1. 'Lawrence leads Arabs into Damascus', *Manchester Guardian*, 1 October 1918 (*Guardian* archive).
2. *The Seven Pillars of Wisdom* (1926) by T.E. Lawrence, Doubleday, Doran and Co, New York, p647.
3. *The Secret Lives of Lawrence of Arabia* (1971) by Phillip Knightley and Colin Simpson, Thomas Nelson and Sons, p106.
4. *The Seven Pillars of Wisdom*, p656.
5. *Pale Rider* (2017) by Laura Spinney, Penguin Random House, p47.
6. 'Impact of 1918 Influenza Pandemic on Greater Syria', by Kjell Jostein Langfeldt Lind, SOAS MA.
7. 'Skipper's War: The story of Oxford Prep School and its old boys in WWI', 2 April 1921 – online website.
8. 'Impact of 1918 Influenza Pandemic on Greater Syria', by Kjell Jostein Langfeldt Lind, SOAS MA.
9. Ibid.

10. White House Press Conference, CNBC broadcast, 18 March 2020.
11. 'A Very British Dictatorship: The Defence of the Realm Act in Britain 1914–1920,' by Andre Keil, Taylor & Francis online.
12. *The Great Influenza* (2005) by John M. Barry, Penguin, p171.
13. Ibid.
14. *The Thief in the Night* by Mark Honigsbaum, British Online Archives, April 2024.
15. *ABC* newspaper, Madrid, 22 May 1918, archive.
16. *Newspapers from the Pandemic: Reporting on the Spanish Flu* by Rose Staveley-Wadham, British Newspaper Archive blog, 14 January 2021.
17. Ibid.
18. *Pale Rider*, p65.
19. *Pale Rider*, p95.
20. *Pale Rider*, p161.
21. 'The 1918 flu pandemic left Spain a more unequal country', by Sergi Basco, Jordi Domenech, Joan Roses, LSE blog 12 March 2021.
22. *Pale Rider*, p161.
23. PBS Placing Blame – Influenza 1918.
24. *Fake News and the Flu* by Hannah Mawdsley, Wellcome Collection blog, 18 September 2019
25. *The Great Influenza*, p181.
26. Ibid.
27. *Going Viral: Covid Conspiracies in Historical Perspective* by Cameron Givens, Ohio State University, July 2020.
28. *Immigration, Ethnicity and the Pandemic* by Alan M Kraut, Association of Schools of Public Health, National Library of Medicine, Bethesda.
29. Ibid.
30. *The Great Influenza*, p98.
31. 'Mask Resistance During a Pandemic Isn't New,' by J. Alexander Navarro, *Michigan Medicine*, 29 October 2020.
32. *Oregon Daily Journal*, 16 January 1919 – front page story.
33. *Pale Rider*, p105.
34. *Buffalo News* archive, 4 November 1918.
35. *And We Were Young: Oundle School and the Great War* (2017) by Colin Pendrill, Helion and Company Ltd, pp298–301.
36. 'The Waste Land' (1922) by T.S. Eliot, Part V: What the Thunder Said.

Chapter Nine: Illegal Immigrants

1. 'Migration Event: when did the first humans arrive in Britain?' by Josie Mills, UCL research, 24 February 2019.

2. *The Beaker People: A New Population for Ancient Britain* by James McNish, Natural History Museum, 22 February 2018.
3. 'So, I'm related to William the Conqueror and David Cameron', by John Crace, *Guardian*, 2 February 2018.
4. *The Townsville Daily Bulletin* (Australia), 20 January 1940 archive.
5. 'Sabotage Suspected in Arms Explosion', *Daily Telegraph*, 19 January 1940 archive.
6. *Aliens debate Hansard*, 23 April 1940, vol 360, pp32–33.
7. *Traitor King* (2021) by Andrew Lownie, Blink, pp231–36.
8. *The Dunera Scandal* (1983) by Cyril Pearl, Angus and Robertson, p7.
9. *The Dunera Scandal*, p8.
10. *The Noel Coward Diaries* (2022) (eds) Graham Payn and Sheridan Morley, Weidenfeld & Nicolson.
11. *The Dunera Scandal*, pp1–2.
12. *You, You and You* (1981) by Peter Grafton, Pluto Press, pp18–19.
13. *Collar the Lot – Britain's Policy of Internment* WW2 by Roger Kershaw, July 2015, National Archives (article).
14. Hansard debate, Wednesday 29 January 1941.
15. *Stories from the Dunera and Queen Mary: Gunter Altmann Internment in England and Australia part 1*, translated by Kate Garrett, Monash University, Melbourne Australia (online resource).
16. Ibid.
17. War Situation debate, Tuesday 4 June 1940, Hansard Vol 361.
18. *The Dunera Scandal*, p9.
19. *You, You and You*, p20.
20. Loss of Arandora Star debate, House of Commons, Tuesday 6 August 1940, Hansard.
21. *The Dunera Boys: Seventy Years On*. Transcriptions National Library of Australia.
22. Ibid.
23. *You, You and You*, p22.
24. *The Dunera Scandal*, p40.
25. 'A Life Striving to Stay One Step Ahead of the Nazis', by Charlie Connelly, *New European*, 5 April 2021.
26. *The Dunera Scandal*, p22.
27. *The Dunera Boys: A Quaker Response to the Treatment of WW2 Enemies* by Roy Wilcock, Australian Quaker Tapestry Project.
28. Professor Hugo Wolfson, National Archives of Australia. https://kitchener-camp.co.uk/research/hmt-dunera/
29. 'VC sergeant's bravery is recognised at last', North Wales Live, 1 November 2002.
30. *The Dunera Boys: A Quaker Response*, p12.

31. *Dunera News*, Issue 115, June 2023.
32. *Hay Internment Camp Records (1940–1941),* Manuscripts Collection, MS 5392.
33. *The Dunera Scandal*, p117.
34. *The Fifth Column in WW2* (2015) by Robert Loeffel, Palgrave Macmillan, Ch 3, p59.

Chapter Ten: Erased

1. 'The Rise and Fall of the Bootleg King Bob Batchelor', *American Heritage*, Vol 67, Issue 1, Autumn 2022.
2. *The Cincinatti Enquirer,* Monday 21 January 1952, p1, archive.
3. 'Romola Remus Dies' – obituary, *Los Angeles Times,* 21 February 1987, archive.
4. G.T.D. Patterson Memo, 19 November 1946, Harold Cole aliases file KV/2417, National Archives Kew.
5. Memo to Brigadier H. Shapcott, 19 November 1945, KV 2/417 National Archives Kew.
6. 'My Childhood in Hoxton from 1902–1918', by Ted Harrison, taken from *When We Were Kids on the Corner of the Street*, Hoxton Hall and Hackney Adult Education Institute, 1983.
7. Commonwealth War Graves Commission.
8. *Turncoat: The Strange Case of Traitor Sergeant Harold Cole* (1988) by Brendan Murphy, Macdonald Press, p26.
9. *Turncoat*, p41.
10. *Home Run: Escape from Nazi Europe* (2008) by John Nichol and Tony Rennell, Penguin, p81.
11. *Home Run*, p39.
12. *Saturday at MI9 by Airey Neave*, First Published 1969, reprinted by Pen and Sword Military 2010, pp78–79.
13. *Saturday at MI9*, p82.
14. *Turncoat*, p82.
15. *Saturday at MI9*, p84.
16. *Home Run*, p156.
17. Ibid.
18. *Saturday at MI9*, p82.
19. *Saturday at MI9*, p309.
20. *Turncoat*, p236.

INDEX